# Differential Europe

# Governance in Europe
Gary Marks, Series Editor

# Differential Europe

*The European Union Impact
on National Policymaking*

Adrienne Héritier, Dieter Kerwer,
Christoph Knill, Dirk Lehmkuhl, Michael
Teutsch, and Anne-Cécile Douillet

ROWMAN & LITTLEFIELD PUBLISHERS, INC.
*Lanham • Boulder • New York • Oxford*

ROWMAN & LITTLEFIELD PUBLISHERS, INC.

Published in the United States of America
by Rowman & Littlefield Publishers, Inc.
4720 Boston Way, Lanham, Maryland 20706
www.rowmanlittlefield.com

12 Hid's Copse Road
Cumnor Hill, Oxford OX2 9JJ, England

British Library Cataloguing in Publication Information Available

**Library of Congress Cataloging-in-Publication Data**

Differential Europe : the European Union impact on national
policymaking / Adrienne Héritier ... [et al.].
        p. cm. — (Governance in Europe)
    Includes bibliographical references and index.
    ISBN 0-7425-1103-0 (cloth) — ISBN 0-7425-1104-9 (paper)
      1.  Transportation and state—European Economic Community countries. 2.
Europe—Economic integration. 3. Europe—Economic conditions—1945- I.
Windhoff-Héritier, Adrienne, 1944- II. Series

HE242.A2 D53 2001
388.94—dc21

                                                        2001019010

Printed in the United States of America

⊖™ The paper used in this publication meets the minimum requirements of American
National Standard for Information Sciences—Permanence of Paper for Printed Library
Materials, ANSI/NISO Z39.48–1992.

# Contents

# Tables and Figures

# Preface and Acknowledgments

This book was written in the context of a research project that we started at the Faculty of Sociology/Research Area Political Science at the University of Bielefeld, continued at the European University Institute in Florence, and completed at the Max Planck Project Group "Common Goods: Law, Politics and Economics" at Bonn. It was funded by the German Science Foundation with means granted in the context of the Leibniz prize bestowed to Adrienne Héritier (jointly with Helmut Willke). The European University Institute generously offered its facilities for the research work to be carried on. We would like to thank President Patrick Masterson and the Department of Social and Political Sciences as well as Andreas Frijdal, head of Academic Services, for their generous support. For Dirk Lehmkuhl, Dieter Kerwer, and Michael Teutsch, it was of particular importance to be accepted as researchers in the doctoral program of the European University Institute.

The ongoing research has been presented and discussed at various conferences and workshops where we received useful comments, such as by Renate Mayntz and Fritz W. Scharpf at a workshop organized in November 1995 at the Max Planck Institute for the Study of Societies at Cologne and by Helmut Willke and his collaborators at two workshops organized in Florence and in Munich. Florence Rudolph has given important substantive insights on France. Filippo Strati, director of Studio Ricerche Sociali in Florence, introduced us to transport policy issues in Italy.

We are particularly indebted to our respondents in Britain, France, Germany, Italy, and the Netherlands, who so patiently gave us information and fruitful inspiration. Finally, we would like to thank Clare Tame, our native speaker, for the scrupulous checking and unwearying correction of the texts, and Maria Byström,

Maria Elena, and Francesca Manfredini for their support as research assistants. We are grateful to Maureen Lechleitner, Viola Stark-Woldring, and Gabi Scherer for important logistical and technical support.

Adrienne Héritier, Dieter Kerwer,
Christoph Knill, Dirk Lehmkuhl,
Michael Teutsch, and Anne-Cécile Douillet

Bonn, September 2000

# Glossary

| | |
|---|---|
| ANITA | Associazione nazionale imprese trasporti automobilistici |
| ASLEF | Associated Society of Locomotive Engineeers and Firemen |
| ATOC | Association of Train Operating Companies |
| BAG | Bundesanstalt für den Güterfernverkehr |
| BR | British Rail |
| BRB | British Railways Board |
| CBI | Confederation of  British Industry |
| CCNL | National Labor Contract |
| CEC | Commission of the European Communities |
| CER | Community of European Railways |
| CGE | Compagnie Générale des Eaux |
| CGEA | Compagnie Générale d'Enterprises Automobiles |
| CIPET | Commissione interministerial per la pianificazione dei trasporti |
| CIT | Chartered Institute of Transport |
| CNEL | Consiglio nazionale di economia e del lavoro |
| COMU | Coordinamento dei macchinisti uniti |

| | |
|---|---|
| Confcooperative | Confederazione cooperative italiane |
| Confetra | Confederazione generale italiana del traffico e dei trasporti |
| Confindustria | Confederazione generale dell'industria italiana |
| CPC | Certificate of Professional Competence |
| CPRE | Council for the Protection of Rural England |
| CRP | Common Railway Policy |
| CTP | Common Transport Policy |
| DETR | Department of the Environment, Transport, and the Regions |
| DoE | Department of the Environment |
| DoT | Department of Trade; Department of Transport |
| EC | European Community |
| ECJ | European Court of Justice |
| EFL | External Finance Limit |
| ENEL | Ente nazionale per l'energia elettrica |
| ENI | Ente nazionale di idrocarburi |
| EP | European Parliament |
| EPIC | Etablissement public industriel et commercial |
| EPS | European Passenger Services |
| EU | European Union |
| EVO | Algemene Verladers en Eigen Vervoer Organisatie |
| FAI | Federazione Autotrasportatori Italiani |
| FEDERSPEDI | Federazione Nazionale Spedizionieri |
| FIAP | Federazione Italiana Trasportatori Professionali |
| FIAT | Federazione Italiana Trasporti |
| FISAFS | Federazione Italiana Sindacati Autonomi Ferrovieri di Stato |
| FITA | Federazione Italiana Trasportatori Artigiani |
| F&L | European Freight and Logistics Leaders Club |

| | |
|---|---|
| FNTR | Fédération nationale des transporteurs routiers |
| FoE | Friends of the Earth |
| FS | Ferrovie dello stato |
| FTA | Freight Transport Association |
| HSE | Health and Safety Executive |
| IRI | Istituto per la ricostruzione industriale |
| IRU | International Road Union |
| LOTI | Law on Inland Transport |
| NDL | Stichting Nederland Distributieland |
| NIWO | Stichting Nationale en Internationale Wegvervoer Organisatie |
| NPM | New Public Management |
| NS | Nederlandse Spoorwegen |
| OPRAF | Office of Passenger Rail Franchising |
| ORR | Office of the Rail Regulator |
| PSO | Public Service Obligation Grant |
| RCEP | Royal Commission on Environmental Pollution |
| RFF | Réseau ferré de France |
| RHA | Road Haulage Association |
| RMT | National Union of Rail, Maritime and Transport Workers |
| ROSCOs | Rolling Stock Leasing Companies |
| RPI | Retail Price Index |
| RPR | Rossemblement pour la Republique |
| RVI | Rijksverkeerinspectie |
| SACTRA | Standing Advisory Committee on Trunk Road Assessment |
| SMP | Single Market Program |
| SNA/CASA | Sindacato nazionale autotrasportatori confederazione di artigianato |

| | |
|---|---|
| SNCF | Société Nationale des Chemins de Fer |
| TLN | Transport en Logistick Nederland |
| TOCs | Train Operating Companies |
| TSSA | Transport Salaried Staffs Association |
| UNATAV | Unione autotrasportatori toscani alta velocità |
| Unice | Confederation of European Industries |
| UNITAI | Unione imprese e trasporti automobilistici italiana |
| UNOSTRA | Union nationale des organisations syndicales de transporteurs routiers automobiles |
| VAT | Value added tax |
| WAG | Wet Autovervoer Goederen |
| Wgw | Wet goederenvervoer over de weg |

# 1

# Differential Europe: The European Union Impact on National Policymaking

*Adrienne Héritier*

The European Community (EC) affects the policy fabric of all member states, but that impact is differential. In some instances, new policy goals have been added to national agendas and fresh policy instruments are applied, while old ones become less important or are openly challenged. In other instances, when European and national policy objectives are concurrent, national practices may be reinforced, or even redirected, by EC policies. In all instances, however, a reconsideration of national policy practices occurs wherever the EC extends its activities and, more often than not, a process of transformation is sparked off by European legislation. This transformation not only involves policy aspects *strictu sensu*, such as the general problem-solving approach and policy instruments used, but also the administrative structures and patterns of interest intermediation in which the implementation of these policies is embedded. For example, the European liberalization of transborder road transport drove Germany to abolish policy instruments, such as the regulation of tariffs and quotas in road haulage, and to give the corporate bodies formerly responsible for controlling national tariffs new tasks. In environmental policy, too, new self-regulatory practices for industrial operators and eco-auditing procedures were incorporated into policy implementation and are now used alongside other "classical" state licensing procedures.

The German experience is by no means unique. Britain had to accept the environmental principle of precautionary action and the setting of legal pollution standards, putting an end to the "cozy" bargaining processes between environmental inspectors and industrialists, which gave place to more formal procedures. In road transport, however, Britain found itself in full accordance with Eu-

1

ropean deregulation goals and practices. Similarly, in the Netherlands we find a
striking congruence between the lines of domestic and European road and rail
policies. By contrast, Italian road policy "drifted away" from European policy
goals, and it reinforced its protectionist practices in the face of EC liberalization
until recently.

As this illustrating evidence shows, the process patterns and policy outcomes
of Europeanization have not been uniform across the member states and do not
reflect either the well-defined will of a "unified supranational actor," or a pervasive problem-solving rationality that imposes itself "automatically" so as to increase the overall efficiency of European policy decisions in the context of a
transnational interdependence of policy problems. Instead, the political reality of
European policymaking is "messy" insofar as it is uneven across policy areas and
member states, institutionally cumbersome, and subject to the dynamics of domestic politics, each with its own particular logic. As a consequence, the outcomes of European policymaking tend to be much more diverse than one would
expect and preclude any simplistic explanation of Europe-induced changes.

With regard to the process generating this diversity, one must bear in mind first
and foremost that the transformation sparked off by Europe is an interactive
process and not a one-way street in which European institutions impose their policy decisions upon member states. Instead, member-state actors exert influence in
the shaping of policies at the European level by which they themselves are subsequently transformed (Héritier, Knill, and Mingers 1996). Furthermore, we can
detect a parallelism between European and national policy developments that, although they evolve independently of one another, also intersect and have a
reciprocally reinforcing, counteracting, or neutralizing impact. That is, endogenous national policy developments and Europe-generated processes of transformation merge and influence each other. Additionally, Europeanization leads to diverse outcomes because EC legislation is, in its initial phase, often loosely
phrased so as to leave room for differential solutions at the member-state level.
This is caused by the explicit will of member states to defend their policymaking
power, backed up by the principle of subsidiarity. Another related reason is that
member states, subject to a need of consensus, are frequently unable to agree on
precise policy solutions at the Council level and therefore settle for framework
solutions.

In short, national policy repertoires and policy patterns have indeed been
subject to change in the course of Europeanization, but in a way that is both
complex and differentiated. They have been enlarged, modified, reversed, but
also confirmed through EC policymaking. It is hardly surprising that an ambitious undertaking in joint policymaking such as the EC is likely to generate
manifold policy changes at the national level. What is perplexing, however, is
that so much remains to be empirically investigated and conceptualized regarding the way in which policies and structures are affected in different policy fields in the member states. What is clear is that the interlinking of Euro-

pean and national policy processes are relatively inconspicuous and politically invisible, constituting the exact opposite of the politically salient, spectacular and controversial "history-making" decisions, such as treaty revisions (Moravcsik 1998). Such "everyday decisions" consist of a large number of small, incremental issues that, besides lacking visibility, are frequently complicated matters that are not easily accessible to the layman and thus generate little public interest. But it is the repeated and continuous nature of these issues, together with their low visibility, that unobtrusively brings about changes in national policy patterns, policy outcomes, administrative structures, and patterns of interest intermediation. These incremental processes require close empirical examination.

The research presented in this book is a contribution to the current debate on "Europeanization." Europeanization is defined as the process of influence deriving from European decisions and impacting member states' policies and political and administrative structures. It comprises the following elements: the European decisions, the processes triggered by these decisions as well as the impacts of these processes on national policies, decision processes and institutional structures. Beyond its purely formal aspects, Europeanization is also used in terms of a qualitative change caused by European decisions in the policies, polities, and politics and administration of member states. Indeed, the substantive change engendered by the process of Europeanization has been described as having substituted the old, individual, national "logics" of policymaking and politics with a new, supranational European "logic" (Ladrech 1994; Radaelli 2000). This assertion is too limiting in terms of the current research; rather Europeanization may be said to extend from a subtle and incremental reorientation of national policymaking (Ruggie 1998; Kohler-Koch 1996c), to substantial changes where European policies "crowd out" their national counterparts and modify patterns of political and administrative behavior.

In the last decade, research on the input of European decisions having an impact on national policies and politics has undergone a rapid transformation in terms of both conceptual sophistication and empirical richness. Various theoretical approaches provide distinct heuristics of the process of Europeanization, which in turn imply different sets of variables and causal patterns in accounting for the modus operandi and impact of Europe on different dimensions of member-state activity. These different research approaches may be grouped along two dimensions in terms of their theoretical foundations and focus of analysis (see also Radaelli 2000). The theoretical approaches used may be categorized as follows: an actor-based (rational choice) institutionalist approach, an institution-based (historical, sociological, and constructivist) approach, and an ecological organization theoretical approach.

Taken in turn, the actor-based institutionalist approach seeks to account for the impact of Europe on member states in terms of the rational strategic action of corporate actors with specific preferences in distinct institutional contexts that limit and/or facilitate the pursuit of these strategies and establishes a systematic connection between domestic political conditions and incentives to comply with European policy demands (Martin and Simmons 1998; Héritier, Knill, and Mingers 1996). The institution-based (sociological/historical/constructivist) approach accounts for changes brought about through Europeanization in terms of a gradual adaptation to changing institutional rules and norms by applying a "rule of appropriateness" (March and Olsen 1989; Olsen 1996; Knill and Lenschow 2000a); the variant that focuses on the cognitive dimension of institutions that provide particular interpretations of the world and convey ideas and belief systems stresses that change occurs through discourse (V. Schmidt 1997), deliberation, and identification (Caporaso, Cowles, and Risse 2000). Finally, organizational ecology (diMaggio and Powell 1991) highlights the mechanisms of coercion, mimetism, and normative pressure in the spread of European influence (Radaelli 1997a, 1997b). The two last approaches have some elements in common, such as the normative influence.[1]

These theoretical approaches help us understand "how" change occurs, while the second perspective, that of the focus of analysis, raises the question of precisely "what" is subject to Europeanization. The focus may be member-state policies (problem-solving approaches and instruments), political institutions and political processes, or administrative structures and processes.[2]

A brief discussion of the individual elements of research cited in table 1.1 gives a rough overview of the current state of research. Looking first at policies, the actor-based institutionalist studies argue that a mismatch between European policy demands and national policies generates a pressure to adjust on the part of member states. Variations in domestic structures (defined in terms of veto points) lead to distinct national responses to the same external pressure of defined Euro-

**Table 1.1.    Strands of Research Europeanization**

| Focus/ Explanatory Approach | Process Mechanism | Outcomes: -Policies -Polity -Adm. structures |
|---|---|---|
| Actor-centered (institutional) approach | Goal-oriented strategic interaction in specific institutional context | -Convergence or continuing diversity -Loss/gain of competences |
| Institution-based (historical, sociological, constructivist) approach | -Path-dependence -Deliberation/discourse -Resonance of norms and ideas | -Convergence or continuing diversity |
| Organization ecological approach | Emulation, diffusion | Convergence |

pean policy expectations. Thus, the process of change triggered by European demands and its outcomes is conceived of as a process of overcoming an institutionally defined number of formal and factual veto points. Given a need to adjust, a large number of veto points—as in a politically decentralized political system with elements of associational self-regulation—will make policy adjustment more difficult to introduce, and inversely, a low number of veto points will facilitate policy adjustment. As a result, the policy effects of Europeanization in member states are expected to vary according to the relative institutional ease with which European policy demands can be accommodated with existing national policies (Héritier 2000; Haverland 2000; Knill and Lehmkuhl 1999). Depending on whether or not this is the case, convergence with respect to European policy requirements or continuing diversity may ensue.[3]

The institution-based (sociological/historical/constructivist) explanation follows a different line of argument, claiming that a change at the domestic level follows the "logic of appropriateness" with respect to existing institutional rules. That is, new policy requirements are accommodated if they can be incorporated into existing policy principles. Hence, if European policies follow similar principles and ideas, and there is mutual resonance, adjustment is relatively simple, and if this is not the case, adjustment is difficult. However, the argument runs, in the case of a divergence of policy ideas, a mutual rapprochement is still possible (V. Schmidt 2000) where there is a defined forum for a common policy discourse in which over time mutual learning and a diffusion of ideas occur among policymakers and, eventually, policy preferences are transformed (Jachtenfuchs, Dietz, and Sung 1999; Radaelli 1997a, 1997b; Knill and Lenschow 2000a; Caporaso, Green Cowles and Risse 2001). Two outcomes are conceivable. Where there is resonance and similarity between European policy exigencies and member-state practices, we can anticipate convergence. Where there is dissimilarity and a lack of resonance, continuing differences are likely to occur, unless common policy views emerge due to a joint policy discourse.

Finally, organizational ecology theory singles out "coercion" (imposition), "mimesis," and "normative influence" as the processes by which organizations (the member states) assume the behavioral patterns and policy solutions of other organizations (the member states and/or Europe) that are successful in problem solving. In other words, the European Union imposes solutions upon member states, or there is a strong normative pressure exerted by European bodies, or member states emulate each other in applying policy practices, and the European arena acts as the promoter of such processes of mimetic learning (diMaggio and Powell 1991; Harcourt and Radaelli 1999; Thatcher 1995; Harcourt 2000). In any of the three above cases we can expect a convergence in policy contents.

Regarding the types of policies analyzed, Europeanization research has covered a variety of areas. Our own research has investigated the impact of Europe on national environmental policy (Héritier, Knill, and Mingers 1996; Héritier et al. 1994; Knill and Lenschow 1998), while at the same time examining the typical patterns of "exerting influence" on the Commission's legislative policy drafting. Hooghe, Marks, and Keating have analyzed regional and structural funds policy for their distributional effects and structural impact on the administrative structures of the member states (Hooghe 1996; Marks 1996; Hooghe and Keating 1994). Similarly, the impact of European social policymaking and rulings by the European Court of Justice on national social policy (Leibfried and Pierson 1995; Rhodes 1995) and labor relations (Streeck 1995a) have been studied. Another focus of research examines the extent to which the politics of market integration have sparked off a "race to the bottom" in national regulatory policymaking (Scharpf 1997a, 1999) as, for example, in transport policy (Héritier 1997a; Kerwer 2000).

Turning to the second focus of analysis, that is, the impact of Europeanization on political institutions, we can detect various subfocuses. One of these investigates the impact of Europeanization on formal political institutions, that is, the formal governmental structures of member states, such as national and subnational parliaments and executives, while another focuses on informal political institutions such as political parties, associations, and social movements. With respect to formal political institutions, much research has centered on whether national institutions have gained or lost competences and power. In the actor-centered/institutionalist literature, in the shape of liberal intergovernmentalism (Moravcsik 1993, 1998; Putnam 1988), a change is seen to be brought about through the strategic action of governmental actors exploiting institutional rules. It is claimed that national governmental actors can increase their power by playing a multilevel game (Putnam 1988) and mediating between European policy demands and domestic policy pressure to their own institutional advantage ("cutting slack"; see Moravcsik 1993, 1998).[4]

By contrast, a related branch of institutionalist research differentiating between various types of national governmental institutions indicates a loss of competences incurred by national parliaments. Precisely because national executives negotiate legislation at the European level, the national parliaments subsequently are not free to reject the compromises that have been forged in protracted negotiations at the supranational level (Anderson and Burns 1996). The question of gain and loss of formal competences has been scrutinized with respect to the subnational formal political actors as well, an issue that is particularly acute in federalist systems (Goetz 1995; Benz 1998; Börzel 1999). Here the argument is similar to that used with respect to national parliaments. The policy commitments made at the European level in the negotiations between national governmental actors and European actors erode the competences of subnational actors in shaping such policies. In some countries, however, subnational bodies regained these formal competences in the European decisional process itself (as, for example, in Germany; see Börzel 1999). Moreover, in particular policy areas, European policies have been shaped in such a way as to introduce new formal competences for subregional actors, such as under the "partnership principle" in regional/structural funds policy.

Sociological institutionalist theories do not offer specific answers as to whether individual formal actors at the national level gain or lose power and competences as a result of the process of Europeanization. By contrast, one may infer from organizational ecological theory that, some (European) organizations being able to impose their solutions upon others (coercion), this has the consequence that both national and subnational formal actors cede competences to formal actors at the European level. Organizational ecology theory would also lead one to suspect that specific organizational solutions, such as the independent regulatory agency, proposed at the European level in order to perform legislative, monitoring, and conflict-solving tasks, are emulated in the regulatory policies of member states (mimesis).

A substantial body of research focuses on the implications of Europeanization on informal political actors, particularly associations and, albeit to a lesser extent, political parties. Most of the literature dealing with the impact of Europe on associations is based on a rational–strategic action or institutionalist approach and focuses on the relative gain or loss of influence on policymaking typical for particular types of associations and the specific new modes of seeking access to European bodies (see, for example, Streeck and Schmitter 1985; Kohler-Koch 1996a; van Schendelen 1984; Knill and Lehmkuhl 1999; Lehmkuhl 1999; Aspinwall 1999; Coen 1998). The central argument is that, with increasing importance of European decisions for economic activities at the national level, particularly with the Single Market Program, national associations seek access to European bodies, in particular, to the European Commission that drafts legislation. To facilitate access they either form European associations—in which case national associations lose part of their influence to their European counterparts—or establish their own bureaus of representation in Brussels (Kohler-Koch 1996a; Mazey and Richardson 1993; Aspinwall 1999; Green Cowles 2001; Coen 1998). These changing functions have implications for the patterns of state–association relationships in member states (Lehmkuhl 1999). Another body of research reveals that the European Commission actively promotes the influence of associations at the national level in shaping policies. A typical example is regional funds policy with the introduction of the "partnership principle" (Hooghe 1996; Marks 1996; Hooghe and Keating 1994).

There is much less research on the impact of European policymaking on the structure and functioning of national political parties against the background of the changing nature of political boundaries (Bartolini 1997). But it was found that Europeanization did not affect national political parties to the same extent as associations (Mair 2000).

Furthermore, there is a strand of Europeanization research focusing on the question as to how Europe affects administrative structures and practices in member states (Héritier 2000; Knill 1999; Knill and Lenschow 2000a; Toonen 1987; Bauer 2000). Here again, all three theoretical approaches are pertinent when accounting for the effect of Europeanization on administrative structures in terms of convergence or continuing differences (Page and Wouters 1995), and the relative loss and/or gain of administrative decision-making power. The actor-centered/institutionalist approach argues that administrative actors affected by European policies with particular administrative implications will defend their institutional interests as best they can when implementing European policies (Héritier et al. 1994; Héritier 2000). The impact of a process of Europeanization of administrative structures, thus understood, would predict the persistence of different administrative structures across member states and—depending on the strategic success of one actor group over another—a gain or loss of competences (Page and Wouters 1995). By contrast, the "fusion theory" (Rometsch and Wessels 1996) reasons that there is no zero-sum game with respect to administrative decision making and that there is instead an increase of joint decision making on the part of both actor groups.

The historical institutionalist approach[5] emphasizes both the prevalence of the logic of appropriateness, that is, that existing structures determine the extent to which European adjustment demands are accommodated, as well as the influence of new administrative ideas and belief systems conveyed with the content of European policies. New administrative ideas and administrative experiences with European policies are exchanged in the meetings of administrators from different member states. This should in turn enhance the process of convergence of administrative structures and processes (Knill and Lenschow 2000a).

Organizational ecology theory arrives at a similar conclusion on the basis of a mimetic process of learning (Harcourt 2000; Radaelli 1997a) with a diffusion of administrative practices that have proved successful in one member state (Page and Wouters 1995).

Finally, there are Europeanization studies that take a more holistic perspective and focus on the impact of Europeanization on the structure and process of national decision making per se, rather than analyzing a single policy or political/administrative aspect. Rational-institutionalists emphasize the transformation from the welfare state to the regulatory state (Majone 1996). Other studies focus on the impact on nation-state sovereignty (Kassim and Menon 1996). Still others claim that the overall nature of policymaking structures is changing from traditional forms of government to a mode of governance by functional networks (Kohler-Koch 1996c). Another holistic perspective is taken by raising the question as to the changes in the entire policymaking cycle (Mény, Muller, and Quermonne 1996). Finally, another approach highlights the impact of Europeanization on the political economy of a member state (particularly with the Single Market Program see; Schmidt 1997).

How is our research to be situated in the context of this rich body of literature on Europeanization? We started out with identifying an empirical "puzzle," the puzzle that Europe matters in different countries in different ways and that we don't know why. Hence we need an explanatory program accounting for these differences rather than convergence. The brief overview over the existing theories on

Europeanization and its specific focuses leads us to a combination of two approaches. Our analysis is predominantly based on an actor-centered/institutionalist approach; but—by including existing problem-solving approaches/policy belief systems as one explanatory variable—the first approach is linked with elements of sociological institutionalism.

## CONCEPTUALIZING AND EXPLAINING THE DIFFERENTIAL IMPACTS

While the impact of European policymaking on member states has often been described as a process of deepening integration, harmonization, and convergence, we argue the contrary. As our *first proposition* we claim that a European policy has different impacts in different member states so that, far from being uniform, member-state responses to European policy requirements present a diverse picture of variegated processes of change, both great and small. How, and to what extent, "Europe matters" varies, depending first on the member-states' preexisting policies, and second on the political process in which these policies are embedded.

The need for policy adjustment is high if existing national policies differ from clearly defined European policy demands. By contrast, if there is a high degree of conqruence between EC policy requirements and national legislation, or where EC legislation is phrased in vague terms, only a modest, if any, need for change ensues, and European policies merely invite change rather than insisting on it. This view of the impact of EC legislation policies on member-state policies has been termed the "match or mismatch" (Héritier, Knill, and Mingers 1996; Héritier 1997a) or "fit or misfit" perspective (Börzel 1999; Caporaso, Green Cowles, and Risse 2001). Accordingly, we may formulate a *second proposition* that, where national policies differ from well-specified European policies, the member state is under pressure to adjust to the latter. Nevertheless, gauging the impact of European policies so schematically by analogy tends to miss the complex dynamics of political processes induced by European policy inputs at the national level. It is only through such a domestic political process—and this is the second aspect—that the domestic policy outcomes of European legislation are determined (Héritier 1997a; Knill and Lehmkuhl 1999). Hence, beyond a rough assessment of the similarity of European policy demands and existing national policies, the analysis has to include this domestic process in order to understand the impact of European policies on national legislation, and to assess whether and how Europe "matters." But how can such complex domestic political processes be made accessible to general claims? We argue that, given a difference between European policy demands and preexisting national policies, and given that the preferences of key actors are similar to European goals, it depends on the reform capacity of a country whether or not a policy, in the sense of Europe, is realized.

Reform capacity is defined in terms of integrated political leadership, based on formal competences or factual consensus capacity. Accordingly, our *third proposition* is that, given a need to adjust, and given that the prevailing preferences of key political actors are in accordance with the goals defined by the EC, adjustment depends on the reform capacity of the member state. In cases where there are few formal and factual veto positions, the probability of adjustment is high. In cases where there are many formal and factual veto positions and there is no corresponding consensual capacity to build a supportive coalition, the probability of adjustment is low. In cases where there are few formal, but many factual, veto positions, the probability of adjustment is high.

However, even this further analytical step does not fully grasp the complexity of domestic political processes sparked off by European policy inputs. What is needed is a more dynamic view of domestic policies. To this end, it helps to think of European and national policymaking as two separate, but parallel, policy streams, which intermittently interlink. While actors at the two levels relate to each other, both processes also have an endogenous dynamic of their own. This becomes clear if we start from the assumption that there is a policy similarity between European and domestic policy goals, and consequently no pressure to adjust. There may, however, still be an endogenous policy development at the national level, which causes a new response by national actors to European policy demands. This response cannot be judged in terms of a simple congruence or noncongruence with European policies, nor can it be grasped by simply assessing the reform capacity as defined above. Instead, this specific interlinking of the European and national policy streams has to be conceived of differently. In particular, the dimension of time has to be incorporated into the analysis of the impact of European policy requirements on national policies.

For example, French road haulage policy had already been deregulated before being faced with European demands for liberalization. When European policy demands were presented, France was already in line with EC legislation. Not only that, but the national debate had already moved on to reregulating the impact of liberalization in order to safeguard those public-interest goals that constitute such an important element of the sectoral ideology dominant in France. Hence, the European policy input in France, despite the initial congruence between EC legislation and national policies, triggered a movement against European policies and strengthened those domestic actors most critical of liberalization, namely the unions. This shows that, in spite of the initial congruence, there is a "second order" divergence between the two levels that derives from the uneven evolution of policies over time at the European and domestic level. The opposite process has been sparked off in German road haulage policy, which was at the pre-liberalization stage when faced with European demands for reform, and where the pro-liberalization political actors enjoyed a "tailwind" as a consequence so that the European policy input helped tip the balance of political forces in favor of reform.

**Table 1.2.   Uneven Policy Stages and Domestic Political Process**

|  | Pre-reform | Reform | Post-reform |
|---|---|---|---|
| EU |  | X |  |
| France |  |  | X |
|  |  |  | Opposition to EU supports reform of reform |
| Germany | X |  |  |
|  | EU supports pro-reform |  |  |

How could this more complex view be conceptualized in an attempt to systematically explain the impact of Europe on domestic policies? Two perspectives should be brought to bear in the analysis. First, the notion of policy stage (pre-reform, reform, post-reform) introduces the time dimension and focuses on the unevenness of policy developments in member states and Europe over time (see table 1.2). The different stages are characterized by different policy goals and concomitantly different dominant actors' preferences and beliefs. Second, the notion of reform capacity needs to be reconceptualized in a more dynamic sense so as to take account of an alteration in the factual veto positions and dominant coalitions due to European policy inputs. This analytical perspective allows us to view European policies as an input in a domestic political process, moving through stages—pre-reform, reform, post-reform—which may be exploited by national actors in order to enhance their chances of realizing desired policy goals in the domestic arena. In order to understand to what end, we must identify the specific stage, with its prevailing policy preferences and belief systems, in which the national policymaking process is located, in relation to the stage in which European policy, with its respective preferences and beliefs, is positioned. Given that the formal aspects of the capacity to reform—for example, the number of formal veto positions and formally integrated political leadership—are relatively constant, the European policy input is exploited to change factual veto positions and to build new supportive coalitions. Thereby, EC legislation may alter the existing "opportunity structure" for domestic actors (Knill and Lehmkuhl 1999). They offer new "access points," such as the European Commission, the European Parliament, and the European Court of Justice, where national actors may press to take influence on national policies by giving relevant inputs that become parameters in national politics and that the actors in question may exploit to achieve their policy goals. Moreover, new coalitions partners may be "available" within the context of European multilevel policymaking, such as other national associations with similar policy goals whose support is sought in order to realize a policy objective at the supranational level that in turn reinforces one's own position at the domestic level.

Against the backdrop of this more complex attempt to explain the impact of European policies on member-state policies, we come to the *fourth proposition* as an answer to the question of Europe's impact on domestic policies. That is, if national policies are congruent with European policies and, additionally, have moved on beyond the European requirements to a subsequent policy stage, then EC legislation may strengthen the forces supporting this new policy.

## THE EXPLANATORY APPROACH

In explaining the impact of European legislation on member-state policies in terms of an initial policy difference with European policy demands and the reform capacity as defined by institutional structures (formal veto positions) and contending political forces (factual veto positions and supportive coalitions), we conceive of the policy process as the interaction of goal-oriented actors in a given institutional context that may restrict, but also facilitate, the deployment of goal-oriented strategies. The specific aspects of the policy issue, understood in terms of the underlying interest constellations, also have an impact on the policy process. We furthermore presume that the interaction is influenced by the predominance of specific ideas and problem-solving approaches or belief systems relating to a policy problem. The latter delimit the range within which the purposeful strategic action of the actors involved is accepted as legitimate.

In assuming that actors conduct their exchange and negotiations in the context of a specific institutional setting that at the same time restricts, facilitates, or offers incentives for interaction, we contend that institutions matter in shaping policy outcomes. Institutions comprise formal and sanctioned rules, such as laws and court rulings and organizational statutes, but also softer normative rules, such as generally respected social norms (Knight 1992) that can be socially sanctioned when transgressed (Mayntz and Scharpf 1995). The institutional orientation of an actor renders his or her actions calculable because they offer generalized and reliable information as to their intentions (Scharpf 1997a; Knight 1992; Burns and Flam 1986). In this sense, institutions provide a stable background against which actors can make intelligent or satisfying choices and thereby help limit transaction costs (Tsebelis 1995; Williamson 1975). Institutions, however, are not only instrumental insofar as they reduce uncertainty about the behavior of other actors, but also have a weight of their own and over time influence the preference formation of actors, their ways of devising strategies, and their behavior in general. Nevertheless, institutions do not determine actions (Windhoff-Héritier 1991), but often only vaguely prescribe them, or delimit repertoires of possible courses of action (Lehmbruch 1991) "which still leave scope for the strategic and tactical choices of purposeful actors" (Mayntz and Scharpf 1995). Moreover, they may be contradictory with respect to the behavioral expectations they create. In this way an explanation that relies exclusively on institutions does not suffice, but additional factors, such as actors' preferences and beliefs, have to be introduced in order to account for a policy outcome.

Focusing on actors operating in a particular institutional context, we assume that public and private, individual and corporate actors with specific preferences and normative and cognitive views (Scharpf 1997a) have a stake in a particular policy area and seek to influence the process according to their goals within the limits imposed by institutional prescriptions. Actors in a given policy area depend on their mutual resources (Emerson 1962) in order to "produce" the policy; they constitute a policy network (Héritier 1993; Richardson 1996) and engage in a process of exchange of distinctive resources and negotiations with other "consequential actors" (Laumann et al. 1978). These resources range from financial means, legal competences, information, expertise, networking capacity, and access to the media. The relative power of an actor depends upon the nature and quantity of his or her resources. In other words, the power of an actor is defined by his or her available fallback options in the event that an agreement cannot be reached; the greater the number of fallback options, the more powerful the actor in question.

Beyond actors, guided by specific preferences and beliefs, acting in a specific institutional context, aspects of a policy area offer clues to understanding the policymaking process. However, it is not the descriptive details of a policy area that matter in an attempt at generalized explanation so much as the systematic overall aspects of a policy area. We argue that the substance of policy problems gives rise to specific strategic interactive constellations among policy actors: redistributive problems tend to create conflict since the benefit of one actor implies a loss to another, whereas coordination problems should not generate conflict, because all actors stand to win. However, these substantive problem types do not translate directly into interest configurations and political cleavages because—once more the institutionalist argument comes to bear— they are also filtered through the institutional interests and roles of political and administrative key actors (Scharpf 1997a).

The goal-oriented actions of actors in a specific institutional context do not only entail material goals, but also imply ideas and belief systems about what constitutes a policy problem and the basic mode for dealing with it. Ideas, while not independent of interests, cannot be reduced to them. Rather, ideas tend to filter the perception of interests (Singer 1993). Problem-solving approaches constitute the ideological background of a policy field, a framework of ideas that qualifies both the goals of a policy and the instruments that can be used to achieve them (Hall 1992). Policy ideas often are buttressed by scientific knowledge that is shared by "epistemic communities" (Haas 1992) or "advocacy coalitions" with their relatively stable "deep core belief systems" (Sabatier 1993).

In our explanatory model, the four explanatory elements—institutions, actors, policy, and beliefs—are linked and hierarchized. We try to account for as much as possible by looking at the institutional preconditions of the reform capacity of a country in which the relevant domestic actors seek to pursue their goals, as determined by their preferences and beliefs. The lines of conflict of the pertinent policy area are determined by the specific problem at hand and interest constellations linked to it.

Analyzing policymaking processes in the European context implies a perspective of multilevel government. Multilevel government, that is, "making politics" across multiple levels of government and national boundaries, is seen as an opportunity for strategic action by domestic political elites. The ability to form coalitions across levels and national boundaries, and the access to new authoritative actors at the supranational level, such as the European Commission, the European Parliament, and the European Court of Justice, may offer the chance of making a shift to the European arena when domestic politics have reached a gridlock (Tsebelis 1995). In negotiating at the supranational level, national governmental actors may point to domestic restrictions in order to gain a better negotiating position at the international level. Inversely, external pressure is invoked in the domestic political arena to achieve specific policy goals (Putnam 1988; Moravcsik 1993, 1998). In short, playing on various levels and in multiple arenas enlarges the number of strategic opportunities for change that may be used by national governmental actors to influence the mode of adjustment to European policy goals.

Multilevel governance in policy networks—in contrast to multilevel government—includes private actors in the analysis of policy shaping. European policy networks consist of interlinked national policy networks. This is not to say that in a specific policy area all nationally relevant actors also play a role in European policymaking and are informed as to the goals and strategies of all other national and European network actors, but that key players are aware of each other's interests and will take them into account (Schneider, Dang-Nguyen, and Werle 1994). European policy networks are less stable than their national equivalents and are relatively fluid. Because the institutional structure of Europe is fragmented, and the EC comprises fifteen national policy networks often with diverse, albeit frequently competing, problem perspectives and regulatory styles, there is a lack of cohesion, which has specific consequences for policy processes. There is more room for policy improvisation, policy entrepreneurship, and opportunities for first movers to influence policymaking in collaboration with important European actors, often in the European Commission. Inversely, the highly pluralist pattern of European policy networks is a consequence not only of the attempts by numerous actors to exert influence in the European political process, but also of a deliberate networking strategy employed by the European Commission (Kassim 1994).

## THE EXPLANANDUM: CHANGING POLICIES, ADMINISTRATIVE STRUCTURES, AND PATTERNS OF INTEREST INTERMEDIATION

The explanandum consists of the changing policies, administrative structures, and patterns of interest intermediation caused by European policymaking. Two different dimensions of change are scrutinized here: changes in policies and changes in structures. The policy dimension comprises two aspects, the overall problem-solving approach in dealing with the policy problem at hand, and, more specifically, the instruments applied in this context to solve the problem. Second, we focus on changes in administrative structures induced by Europeanization and changes in patterns of interest intermediation.

The dominant problem-solving approach in a policy area is defined as a relatively consistent system of ideas supported by scientific knowledge, as to how a problem should be solved, and comprising a set of value priorities and causal assumptions for the realization of the solution (Sabatier 1993, 1998). They describe a course of action to be followed, what activities are possible and desirable, and what consequences will follow from the pursuit of particular policies (Hall 1986). The central elements, or core values, of such belief systems are changed less easily than the more secondary aspects of instruments regarding their realization (Sabatier 1993). Policy instruments give a more precise definition of how to realize specific policy goals by specific actions. That is to say, they indicate how actors are induced to perform, and what they are expected to do, in light of defined policy goals. The range of instruments extends from public monopolies, command-and-control linked with negative sanctions in the case of noncompliance, to vague prescriptions and incentives to induce actions, such as tax abatements, and mere persuasion to perform some action or meet some commitment, or information about desirable actions and the impacts of a specific course of action. In this way, a liberal problem-solving approach calling for the deregulation of markets will, by definition, employ the price mechanism as the main instrument, while a protectionist regulatory practice will resort to command-and-control instruments with regard to market access and prices.

The second type of transformation to be accounted for is the changes in administrative structures and interest intermediation patterns. These are closely linked with the dominating problem-solving approach and related instruments. Thus, as an instrument, command-and-control presupposes hierarchically organized administrative structures controlling the behavior of regulatees and allows, in the case of noncompliance, the imposition of sanctions. Transformation may occur due to instrumental change and be reflected in the distribution of administrative competences at the horizontal and vertical level. Entire administrative functions may become obsolescent as a result of a shift from command-and-control to market instruments. Alternatively, new tasks may be created, such as the regulation and supervision of the newly created markets, that require the creation of new regulatory bodies. These changes also imply changes in patterns of administrative interest intermediation. Since policymaking in complex societies is never solely dependent on state activities, but relies heavily on the input of resources of private actors (Mayntz 1993), the nature of this interaction is vitally important.

Patterns of administrative interest intermediation vary considerably across member states. While the French bureaucracy traditionally maintains a claim of relative autonomy (Suleiman 1974), the German administration has always relied on the cooperation among public and private actors in various sectors such as social policy, health and safety, and, indeed, transport in formulating and implementing secondary legislation (Windhoff-Héritier 1989). Against the variety of empirical forms of administrative interest intermediation a whole range of typical patterns and formal structures may be discerned that vary with respect to the number of associations involved (bipartisan, tripartisan, multipartisan), the extent of state involvement, or the degree of latitude of association vis-à-vis the administration, the discretion of the bureaucracy to involve associations (Lehmbruch 1991), and the degree of sectoral segmentation in integrating associations into policymaking. In some countries, it is the sectoral associations that are generally involved in "private interest government" (Streeck and Schmitter 1991)—a form that is mostly found in the implementation phase—whereas in other countries, it is the central peak organizations of large producer groups that are regularly involved in the preparatory process of legislation (Lehmbruch 1991). Changes in these patterns of administrative interest intermediation, such as a strengthening of private actors through European liberalization policies, may be induced by the adoption of European policies.

## CHOICE OF POLICY AREA AND COUNTRIES

In answering the question, How do different member states respond to European legislation?, we carry out an empirical investigation of market-making policy, namely road haulage and rail transport policy. Transport as a market-making policy is in contrast to market-correcting policy dealing with the negative external effects of market processes already studied in previous research on environmental policy under a similar analytical question (Héritier, Knill, and Mingers 1996). European intervention must be viewed against the background of these different policy types. Assuming a continuum of intensive state intervention at the one pole and markets and societal self-regulation at the other, European influence in some instances implies accepting state activities as such, but changing the modes and goals of intervention. Market-making policy implies the exact opposite, that is, the abolition of state regulation so as to allow societal or market mechanisms to deal with a problem. In the first instance of market-correcting policies, a variety of national regulatory styles clashes in the European arena. Outright competition may ensue in which member-state actors seek to impose their regulatory tradition upon the European level in order to protect their domestic industry and to save on the costs of institutional and ideological adjustment. One specific mode of intervention may emerge from the European decisional process as *the* European approach to problem solving; alternatively, a compromise may be reached where national implementers may choose from among a combination of various instruments; or framework legislation is enacted that offers national implementation latitude in the choice of instruments with which to realize general European objectives (Héritier, Knill, and Mingers 1996). If market-making European policies are designed to dismantle state activities in order to enhance societal self-regulation or market processes, the outcome observed may only be that of a minimally regulated market. As an intermediate response, however, activities of reregulation at the national level may be identified that, again, try to cope with the negative external effects of the liberalization process. European transport policy is directed at liberalizing and deregulating highly regulated road haulage markets and privatizing state monopolies in rail transport. It represents a case where the frontiers of the state are rolled back. Regarding conflict structures, by the abolition of trade barriers, all actors theoretically stand to gain from the efficiency obtained in a larger integrated market. However, conflicts over the distribution of the achieved gains, between large and small hauliers and among member states, may arise.

Within the area of transport we concentrate on road haulage and rail transport, in themselves quite distinctive areas, but which have in the past been closely linked in policymaking. Road haulage was characterized by a high degree of state intervention, whereas rail transport, as a public monopoly, was part of the state. Because it requires little capital and relatively modest professional skills to enter the market in road haulage, this market tended to produce ruinous competition. In order to protect small and medium-sized businesses from such competition, but also to protect the railways from competition from road transport, access to the market has been limited by state intervention. Rail transport, by contrast, is characterized by high start-up costs, and in general by high fixed or sunk costs in relation to total costs, and by periods of sustained and recurrent excess capacity (Baumol, Panzar, and Willig 1982). It is on these grounds that the public ownership and regulation of the nationally integrated railways systems has been legitimized. Furthermore, the railways have traditionally played an important role in national defense and indeed the building of a nation-state, and they represent one of the most determined examples of state monopoly and control. Railways have been dominated by technicians (mostly engineers) with little interest in marketing. Finally, railways are among the most inward-looking of European transport industries. Their operations have been overwhelmingly domestic, and their managements have little experience of international markets (Staniland 1993). For these reasons, rail transport, in contrast to road transport, has been institutionally deeply entrenched. It encompasses broad-based organizations, a complex network structure, and a long-standing tradition. As a public-sector enterprise, the railways have always been subject to a high level of state intervention and political overview, and consequently they provide a good test case of the EC's ability to liberalize public-sector utilities. We can expect liberalization and deregulation to meet with more sizable institutional opposition in the rail sector, from the established institutions of interest representation, than in the road haulage sector, which is frequently dominated by small and medium-sized hauliers. However, as mentioned above, road transport has to some extent been drawn into state regulation precisely in order to protect the railways from too much competition. As a consequence, this subsector has, over time, developed an elaborate system of associational self-regulation that constituted an important source of political resistance to deregulation during the reform process.

Against the background of this choice of policy area, the guiding propositions presented above can be specified.

- European transport regulation has a differential impact on member states; if national transport regulation is in a stage of pre-liberalization and differs from well-specified European liberalization requirements, this member state is under pressure to adjust; for example, by changing its protectionist instruments or by dismantling public monopolies.
- Given a need to adjust, and given that the prevailing preferences of key political actors favor liberalization, adjustment depends on the reform capacity of the member state.
- If there are few formal and factual veto positions, adjustment is highly likely.
- If there are many formal and factual veto positions that need to be overcome, that is, where formal governmental structures are fragmented and there is no corresponding consensual capacity to build a supportive coalition, adjustment is unlikely.
- If national transport regulation is congruent with European liberalization policies, no adjustment is required.
- If national transport regulation is not congruent with European liberalization policies, but additionally has moved on to reregulation, then the EC liberalization policy may strengthen the forces opposing pure liberalization.

Given that our main explanatory factors are the stage of policy development, prevailing belief systems, and reform capacity as defined by the number of veto positions and integrated political leadership, our choice of countries has followed the systematic variation of these independent variables. Assuming that the contextual variables—state of development of the economy, democratic political systems, and exposure to international market pressure—are the same in all countries under study, we selected countries with a variation of stage of liberalization, reform capacity, and dominant ideologies. In road haulage, Britain, France, and the Netherlands had already liberalized their road haulage industry when confronted with European liberalization requirements, whereas Italy and Germany were still in a stage of pre-liberalization. In the rail sector, all countries were in the process of liberalizing when faced with the European rail reform, but varied with respect to dominating sectoral belief systems: France, Italy, and, to a certain extent, Germany adhere to a public-service philosophy of the railways, while

Britain, laying claim to consumer friendliness, openly professes market-liberal-ism, and the Netherlands seek to reconcile both goals. Regarding road haulage, until recently Italy and Germany stuck to a protectionist ideology, whereas the Netherlands and Britain proclaimed market principles, and the Netherlands again reconciled the latter with sectoral industrial policy, while France, having adopted measures of market liberalization, questioned the reform in view of its tradition of service to public goals. With respect to reform capacity, we find a marked variation between Britain, which has a high reform capacity due to strong integrated political leadership, and Italy, where it is weak due to fragmented and short-lived political leadership. The reform capacity of France, the Netherlands, and Germany is medium range. In the case of France, we find a strong formally integrated political leadership with many veto positions but subject to adversarial politics. The Netherlands is faced with many factual veto positions and is reliant on consensual policymaking. And in Germany reform capacity is hampered by formally weak integrated political leadership and multiple factual veto positions that make it difficult to muster the political forces necessary to pass reforms.

## METHOD AND PLAN OF THE BOOK

The data needed to reveal the conditions for, and the forms of, changes in policies and structural aspects were collected by means of in-depth case studies using intensive interviews and document analysis. In order to cover all relevant actors of policymaking at the national and European level, interviews were conducted with twenty-eight actors in Britain, twenty-three in France, thirty in Germany, thirty-eight in Italy, and twenty-three in the Netherlands. The interviews took place over four years from January 1994 to December 1997 with members of government departments, national parliaments, regulatory agencies, public monopolies, implementing administrative authorities, expert bodies, sectoral trade associations, employers' associations, and trade unions (see the appendix). With few exceptions, all interviews were tape-recorded and subsequently subjected to a qualitative interpretation in relation to the questions and propositions outlined above.

In this chapter, Adrienne Héritier has formulated the research questions and the propositions and presented the analytical approach. Dieter Kerwer and Michael Teutsch analyze the dynamics of the European Common Transport Policy and show how the European Commission, after several failed attempts to realize a European reform policy in both sectors, eventually managed to bring about a European Council decision under the impact of the integrated market program and a seminal verdict by the European Court of Justice. The authors conclude that the outcomes of the European decisional process reflect the high demand for consensus typical of European Council decisions. For this reason, both in road haulage and in the railways, European policies do not impose far-reaching and precise prescriptions on the member states to which these have to conform. Instead, considerable latitude is given to them regarding the implementation of European policies. In the chapters that follow, the road haulage and rail policies of the individual countries are presented and explained in terms of the scheme outlined above. In the chapter dealing with Britain, Christoph Knill examines fundamental reforms, based on a high formal reform capacity, which took place independently of the European influence and led to a radical liberalization both of the road haulage and rail sector. Concerning France, Anne-Cécile Douillet and Dirk Lehmkuhl find a split development, where the already liberalized road haulage sector is subject to reregulation when European policy demands are faced, hence triggering a countermovement against EC liberalization demands. In the rail sector the reform is modest due to a prevailing strong interventionist and service public tradition of regulation. In the case of Germany, Michael Teutsch examines how, in a country long characterized by state interventionism, transport policy has undergone significant changes in recent years, giving more weight to market mechanisms. Europe played an important role, particularly in road haulage, in overcoming the multiple factual veto positions and in building the consensus of diverse interests needed to bring a reform about. Italy is largely characterized by policy inertia in spite of the European influence. Until recently, decision making has stuck to the traditional path, with Italian transport policy only "going through the motions" with old routines still dominating despite widespread dissatisfaction with the results. This outcome is due to the strong tradition of state interventionism and the resistance of particularistic private interests in the transport sector, which render attempts of public actors to bring changes about unlikely. Examining the Netherlands, Dirk Lehmkuhl finds that a substantial reform in both sectors is brought about that is congruent with European policy goals. Europe is used to build support for the reform coalition at the domestic level. In the final chapter, Adrienne Héritier and Christoph Knill draw comparative conclusions and show that European impact on countries differs highly across countries depending on the nature of the policy demands, the specific policy stage in which a country finds itself, and the domestic institutional and political constellations.

## NOTES

1. However, the mechanism of diffusion, that is, imitation of successful problem solutions, is peculiar to organizational ecology.

2. A special strand of literature (Stone Sweet 2000; Conant 2001) focuses on the Europeanization of the national legal systems. Since this is not part of the research question of our book, this literature is not summarized here.

3. Convergence is defined as a decrease of the variation in specific indicators of policy practices and political and administrative institutional structures (Martin and Simmons 1998) between member states (horizontal level) or between European policy demands and national policies (vertical level).

4. See also Grande 1996 ("paradox of weakness").

5. Points to the weight of preexisting institutional structures into which, according to the logic of appropriateness, new institutional demands have to be fitted if they are to be taken on board.

# 2

# Transport Policy in the European Union

*Dieter Kerwer and Michael Teutsch*

Anyone observing the process of European integration is likely to be puzzled by the development of the Common Transport Policy (CTP). Although the Treaty of Rome (1957) assigned a high priority to the issue of transport, a common policy only gained momentum in the mid-1980s. This is not to say that decisions regarding transport were not taken at the European Community (EC) level, but that until recently European transport policy did not essentially change the way in which transport issues had traditionally been dealt with in Europe: that is, as a strictly national issue or by means of bilateral agreements among member states. This peculiar pattern of policy development in the CTP had been a major disappointment to both academic observers (e.g., Lindberg and Scheingold 1970) and commentating practitioners alike (e.g., Hallstein 1974; degli Abbati 1987; Erdmenger 1991), and this chapter tries to explain the pattern by posing two questions. First, why was European transport policy condemned to insignificance for such a long time? And second, what are the reasons for the increasing dynamics and relevance of this area of decision making? In answering these questions we will reveal why it was possible for the dissenters to veto any progress in the past and why this has no longer been possible in more recent times.

These questions are of course highly relevant in the well-known debate between neofunctionalist and intergovernmental explanations of European Union (EU) integration (see, e.g., Lindberg and Scheingold 1970; Stone Sweet and Sandholtz 1998; Moravcsik 1998). Important elements that the advocates of these competing theories typically include in their rival explanation of success and failure in European integration processes, such as the transnational activity of eco-

23

nomic actors, the politics of autonomous supranational organizations, and, alternatively, member-state preferences, are also crucial factors in the development of EU transport policy. However, these rival explanations are in fact two sides of the same coin. Supranational and intergovernmental elements are both fundamental characteristics of the EU setting rather than competing explanations for European integration processes (Schmidt 1998). Our case studies thus concentrate on institutional and policy specific explanations for EU policymaking. We will show that conflicting member-state preferences and autonomous supranational organizations are constant factors in EU policymaking, and that varying outputs may therefore be explained much better by the opportunities offered by the institutional structures in which these decision-making processes are embedded and by the availability of credible solutions for the policy problems under discussion.

The chapter ends with an observation about the character of the policy output. The EU institutional setting provides specific incentives for the realization of particular policy types (Majone 1996; Scharpf 1996; Streeck 1995), and we can trace these effects also in our case studies. The common European policies developed for both road and rail reflect the high demand of consensus as a basis for European decisions. In both cases, policies do not impose broad and precise prescriptions on the member states to which these have to conform, if they do not want to violate EC law. Instead, the EU pushes for realization of a common market, but within that framework considerable leeway is given to the member states as to how to implement the European policies and how to react to new competitive situations. This finding is interesting in two different ways. On the one hand, it reveals specific characteristics of supranational integration processes and specifically certain limitations to the solution of particular policy problems (Scharpf 1999). On the other hand, it is significant with respect to the European influence on the member states, which is analyzed in subsequent chapters. Given the ambiguous and flexible character of the EU policy output, Europeanization processes in the member states promise to be a complex process of adaptation following diverse patterns rather than a simple and uniform process of implementation.

## ROAD HAULAGE

Since the late 1980s, road haulage regulation has undergone a dual process of Europeanization and liberalization. The framework of the EC has gained increasing importance for setting the rules under which European hauliers operate, and the transfer of tangible decision-making competences to the EC came together with a change of character of transport-related policies in Europe. Transport was traditionally a policy field characterized by strong state intervention, whereas EC integration has been accompanied by a process of liberalization at both the supranational and domestic levels.

European road transport had traditionally been characterized by separate national markets and interstate agreements on aspects of international transportation. Today the EC provides for a uniform regime for cross-border road transport and sets the rules for the access of nonresident hauliers to the domestic markets of other countries, known as "cabotage." But while the process of market creation has proceeded successfully, the development of rules for standard setting and to avoid negative externalities, that is, market-correction, has lagged behind. Recent EC policies succeeded in reducing state intervention in cross-border haulage, but where the EC tried to set new rules concerning market correction, the actors involved often found it difficult to reach agreement. Moreover, as the opening of markets tends to make it more difficult for national legislators to maintain policies that create costs for national industries or interfere with their freedom to act, road transport is a good example of the imbalance between the processes of positive and negative integration in the EC (cf. Scharpf 1999). The reasons for this development can be found in the evolution of the institutional setting of the EC and in the dominant constellations of interests, which together made particular strategies to act by the European Commission and the member states possible at specific points in time.

## Why Deadlock?

The development of the CTP was hampered from the outset by the contrasting regulatory approaches and conflicting economic interests of the member states. Although "the Six" had agreed in principle to develop a common transport policy, the difficulty of reaching agreement on specific policy measures witnessed during the negotiations on the treaty was not resolved by leaving the respective title relatively vague (degli Abbati 1987: 34; Weinstock 1980: 201). Instead, ongoing conflict during decision making over concrete policies thwarted the Europeanization of this policy field.

Of the six founding members of the European Economic Community (EEC), France, Germany, and Italy, with national policy regimes characterized by a high degree of state intervention in transport markets, were traditionally skeptical of a liberal transport regime at the European level. These large countries historically placed special emphasis on the development of their national railway systems with consequent restrictions on road haulage concerning price setting and licenses. Furthermore, they also tried to use transport policy as a means to accomplish regional, industrial, and social policy goals. With respect to the CTP, the main interest of these countries could be defined as defending their particular domestic approach of regulation.

In contrast, the Dutch have been the most pronounced supporters of a liberal approach to European transport policy. As a relatively small country, road haulage has been the dominant mode of transport on domestic markets. Rail-related policy goals have not interfered with the regulation of road haulage, and Dutch hauliers have always held an important market share of international road transport markets. The Dutch, having a large and highly competitive transport sector with its potential for expansion, saw themselves as the future hauliers of Europe. Consequently, they were the main supporters of the lifting of existing restrictions to market access in cross-border road transport within the EC and the introduction of cabotage allowing nonresident hauliers to operate on foreign domestic markets (degli Abbati 1987: 32; Erdmenger 1983: 5–8).[1]

Supranational decision making in the road transport sector has always been a battle for opening of markets on the one hand, and the harmonization of competitive conditions between hauliers from different countries and among different modes of transport on the other. The questions discussed in the latter context were tariffs, taxation, the charging of infrastructure costs, and social and technical regulations. But while the principle of fair conditions for competition was agreed upon by all actors, the same actors handled the issue in very different ways. Whereas some treated these issues within the primary framework of market creation without attaching further tasks to them, those member states that pursued interventionist policies in their national transport policies advocated the establishment of a similar regime on a European scale and demanded the harmonization of competitive conditions on a very high level. Moreover, as Germany, France, and Italy had no specific interest in opening their markets, they regarded harmonization as a precondition for market creation. In contrast, the remaining countries argued that less-than-perfect solutions regarding harmonization would suffice for the creation of a common market, and that questions of liberalization and harmonization should be handled separately, so that complications in one field would not impede progress in the other.

The contrasting approaches made it very difficult to reach agreement on transport matters in the EEC, especially after the introduction of unanimity voting in the European Council following the Luxembourg compromise in 1966. Even though Article 75 of the treaty (now Article 71) foresaw qualified majority voting after the end of the transition period in 1969, any single state could veto advances in the CTP if it considered it in its interest to do so. As a result, the CTP developed only very slowly with respect to both market creation and market correction during this era (degli Abbati 1987; Schmitt 1988; Kiriazidis 1994).

Nevertheless, diverging interests and the need to reach unanimous agreement cannot alone explain the rather poor record of the EC's policy output in the road transport sector before the 1980s. Under certain conditions, decisions may be reached in negotiation systems even when the participating actors hold diverging interests, for example, by the creation of package deals (cf. Scharpf 1997b). In EC road haulage policy, the use of this strategy failed for a long time, first, because the proposals being discussed were often too complex for the involved actors to assess. Second, it failed because, in addition to diverging interests, noncooperative orientations were particularly diffuse among the member states at that time. Finally, noncooperative orientations in European policymaking did not have any severe economic impact on international transport markets because of the existence of a fallback solution in cases of nonagreement, that is, bilateral treaties.

From the outset, the EC's institutional setting provides some precautions to ease finding common solutions. For example, the European Commission is designed as an actor with an institutionalized interest in developing a common European policy and can therefore be expected to do all in its power to propose policies acceptable to the member states. The European Commission did indeed develop a detailed transport policy program already during the 1960s (Erdmenger 1983; degli Abbati 1987). However, the European Commission's policy was acceptable neither to the traditionally high-regulating member states, because they opposed the European Commission's emphasis on the liberalization of services (Erdmenger 1983, 12), nor to those advocating a liberal approach, because the concrete proposals for harmonization did not always take the preexisting situation sufficiently into account and were too often inspired by the coordinative aspirations of the large member states. Moreover, according to some observers, the European Commission also made strategic mistakes. Instead of trying to find common denominators for first steps toward a common policy, it initially formulated a concept for the substitution of national policies by a fully-fledged European regime. This included a host of complicated questions such as the fair charging of infrastructure costs and the steering of transport markets through pricing policies, which proved overambitious and too complicated to be agreed on (Weinstock 1980: 206–7; Schmitt 1993: 306).

Other commentators considered that it was a mistake not to tackle the problem of railways properly: the lack of an EC rail policy had inhibited the development of a common road transport policy, as the large countries in particular feared that the liberalization of road transport would have worsened the position of the railways on transport markets (Erdmenger 1983: 56–57). However, supranational policymaking proved difficult enough when initiatives for liberalization were accompanied by efforts to ensure fair competition between hauliers from different countries. Linking decisions in the field of road haulage to rail policy would have complicated the situation, as the latter proved to be one of the most thorny issues for EC action during that period.[2] That is, any effort to pursue a multimodal policy approach was legitimate against the background of market interdependencies between the different subsectors and, specifically, the coordinatory efforts of some member states. Such an approach, however, carried the risk of overloading the EC's decision-making capacity, which was a prime reason for the EEC's initially poor policy output in the sector.

As a consequence of these experiences, the European Commission switched to a more pragmatic approach in the early 1970s (Weinstock 1980; Erdmenger 1983). After the failure to introduce an ambitious European transport regime, the many transport-related issues were now pursued separately, in order to find solutions in specific areas and, in consequence, to make incremental progress with the CTP. However, the European Commission could not stop some member states from maintaining the political linkage between liberalization and a high level of harmonization. The problem inherent in this strategy was that instead of using the high number of issues up for decision constructively, so as to create package deals and trade-offs, some member states instead employed it to increase the number of veto points. They were accused of presenting demands known to be unacceptable to other countries or to be highly complicated, because failure to agree with harmonization could be cited in order to refuse any further steps toward the liberalization of transport markets. Thus, whereas the harmonization of competitive positions undoubtedly was—and is—an important issue, the insistence of these countries on wide-ranging solutions to the problems of harmonization was often inspired by the desire to impede the opening of markets, to defend their interventionist domestic policy approach, and to protect their highly regulated industries from foreign competitors. Despite the treaty obligation, there was widespread disinterest on the part of some member states in proceeding with a CTP, and the general dissatisfaction with the pursuit of European integration, especially in the 1970s, made national representatives even less inclined to make substantive concessions on certain issues or to make consistent efforts to promote EC legislation (degli Abbati 1987: 47; Schmitt 1993: 305–6).

To explain the slow development of the CTP, a further point must be taken in consideration. Neofunctional analysts of the integration process explained the initial failure to introduce a CTP, and the prevalence of diverging national interests rather than an EC perspective, by the absence of national actors able to define and promote an EC-wide vision for transport policy (Lindberg and Scheingold 1970: 169–70). But the overall institutional arrangement beyond the EC structure itself also played an important role. The pressure to develop an EC transport policy was also weakened by the existence of alternatives. Member states could still use bilateral or multilateral agreements to adapt the rules for international transport to their respective needs. Moreover, some international regimes for transport already existed, such as the European Conference of Transport Ministers and the Mannheim Convention on Navigation on the Rhine. Therefore, in contrast to the view of the EC's founding fathers, the development of a common policy was not always regarded as an absolute necessity for the European integration project when faced with the practical problems arising from the implementation of the treaty provisions. Although the EC's inaction in this field might have meant foregoing some advantages and extra profits generated by a swifter development of a CTP, the common market for goods did not suffer as a direct effect (Weinstock 1980: 205). Hence, the alternative regime of bilateral agreement constituted a sufficient second-best solution, making the need to proceed with an integration of national transport policies within the framework of the EC less urgent.

To conclude, the failure to introduce a CTP within a reasonable period of time was a consequence of the inability to reconcile the opposing interests and regulatory approaches of the member states under the condition of unanimity voting in the European Council. In addition, the complexity of the problems under discussion and specific actor strategies increased the difficulties to find a consensus even further. Finally, the existence of alternative ways of regulating international transport weakened the pressure for a common policy within the EC framework. Hence, a combination of a particular institutional structure and specific interest constellations was the main factor responsible for the initially sluggish development of the CTP.

## Why Did It Take Off?

The year 1985 is often regarded as a watershed for supranational transport policy. EC transport policy has gained an increased dynamic since the mid-1980s, which subsequently also led to considerable progress in concrete policy outputs. Three factors helped unblock the situation and contributed to the subsequent acceleration of the EC's decision-making process: the "inactivity verdict" of the European Court of Justice;[3] the political dynamics set off by the European Commission's white paper on the Completion of the Single Market;[4] and the announcement by the Council of Transport Ministers that in the course of the implementation of the SMP all quantitative restrictions in the field of transport would be abolished.[5] Today there is a fully developed European regime for road freight transport. Given the difficulty of establishing a CTP in the preceding period this development requires some explanation. The evolution of the CTP is interpreted here as a consequence of a change in ideology by some member states, and of institutional developments systematically supporting the acceleration of the policymaking process. But because preferences were distributed very differently in the fields of market creation and market correction, and since the institutional structure created divergent conditions to take action in the two fields, the liberalization process could be completed, whereas legislative advances in the field of harmonization, although existent, proceeded more slowly.

### Policy Development

In the last ten years the process of market creation has made huge steps forward with respect to cross-border transport and access of foreign hauliers to foreign domestic markets (cabotage). In 1988 the European Council decided to abolish all quantitative restrictions to cross-border road haulage as of January 1993.[6] From this time, cross-border transport in Europe has been governed by EC rules that established a liberal regime, making bilateral or multilateral agreements between member states obsolete, and abolishing numerical restrictions to licenses for international transport inside the EC, now issued on the basis of qualitative criteria.[7] Concerning cabotage, the treaty stipulates that rules concerning the access of foreign hauliers to the domestic markets of other countries were to be issued by the end of the transition period, that is, before 1970 (ex-Article 75 [2]). Nevertheless, a provisional regulation that introduced a limited number of licenses was not endorsed before 1989.[8] The definitive system was agreed upon in 1993. Between 1993 and 1998 the number of available licenses increased from year to year, and as of July 1998 access to foreign markets was entirely open for nonresident hauliers.[9] In sum, the liberalization process has been completed in the road haulage sector, making the single European transport market a reality.

The same cannot be said of the *harmonization* process. Questions related to technical and social regulation are today dealt with in a routine fashion, whereas price regulation has been completely abandoned.[10] Consequently, all hauliers are now subject to the same, liberal pricing regime on international transport markets in the EC. Harmonization could not be attained within the old interventionist policy approach, which was highly demanding with respect to decision-making capacity, and was only achieved in conjunction with the complete abolition of the old rules.[11]

Fiscal questions proved to be the most difficult to reach agreement about harmonization in the road transport sector, although some steps forward were taken in the early 1990s. In 1992 the EC issued a directive setting minimum levels for fuel taxes.[12] A year later, the European Council agreed on minimum levels for vehicle taxes and allowed those member states who did not use tolls to introduce annual charges for the use of road infrastructure up to certain maximum levels.[13] Although it would seem that the former difficulties in this field were overcome, the content of these decisions is further evidence of the EC's ongoing difficulties in accomplishing harmonization and reaching agreement on effective rules for market operation. To start with fuel taxes, according to a European Commission report the minimum levels on fuel excise duty did not have a marked impact. The European Commission noted that all member states have increased their national rates of duty on motor fuels without the pressure of increased minimum rates.

> Indeed [ . . . ] an increase of 20 per cent in the minimum rate for unleaded petrol would be necessary, simply to keep pace with national rates for this product. On the other hand, as all Member States have increased their rates, very little rate approximation has occurred. Rather than simply proposing an increase of the minimum rates at this stage, the Commission believes that the issue needs to be examined to see whether other, complementary measures might be needed to assist the approximation process.
>
> (COM (95) 285 final, § 6.3.6)

With vehicle taxes and infrastructure charging, the result is slightly different. The European Commission noted that

> [f]ollowing the entry into force of Directive 93/89/EEC an adjustment towards the minimum levels set in the Directive has been realized. Currently the majority of the Member States apply vehicle tax rates above the minimum levels (which in the case

of France, Greece and Italy, Portugal and Spain are 50 per cent lower until 31 December 1997). The UK and to a lesser extent Germany and Ireland apply considerably higher rates.

(COM (96) 331 final, § 2.2.1.1)

Thus, some harmonization has occurred in this field, in particular, the introduction of a common charging system for the use of primary roads in Denmark, the Benelux countries, Germany, and later Sweden ("Eurovignette"), based on the 1993 directive. However, this instrument only affects some member states, whereas the EC as a whole is characterized by the continuing existence of different charging systems. Moreover, there are still significant variations in vehicle taxes across countries.[14] Thus, the result of the approximation process concerning vehicle taxes and infrastructure charges is still unsatisfactory. More important, the 700 European Currency Unit (ECU) minimum level for annual vehicle taxes (plus a derogation for some countries) and the maximum level set at 1,250 ECU for the Eurovignette in the 1993 directive reveal that the approximation of hauliers' financial duties occurred at a relatively low level. This is not only true with respect to countries such as Germany—which had tried unilaterally, but unsuccessfully, to introduce annual road user charges of about 4,500 ECU on its territory in 1990 and which advocated a tripling of the rate in a revised directive— but is also valid when the European Commission's calculations of the high external costs in road transport are taken into account (CEC 1995b), which can only be read as an implicit appeal to increase the fiscal burden on certain kinds of road transport. Therefore, some harmonization did occur in the field of taxation, but it did not lead to much leveling out of the fiscal burden for transport operators. Moreover, the low level at which harmonization occurred may jeopardize other political goals, such as the internalization of the external costs of transport. This judgment also holds true after the modification of the directive in 1999.[15] If one takes into account that the 1993 directive on vehicle taxes and road user charges, with its circumscribed practical effects, was taken in conjunction with the decision on the final introduction of cabotage that ultimately completed the process of market creation, the bias of the EC's recent transport policy in favor of liberalization becomes even more evident.

Summing up, today European road transport markets are to a large degree subject to EC legislation. The provisions of the Treaty of Rome have finally been put into practice through a market-oriented policy regime, comprising social, technical, and fiscal regulations. But whereas the liberalization process has been completed, the scope of the harmonization process is still limited. The following sections attempt to explain this development, concentrating on the reasons why the policy development could be accelerated by the second half of the 1980s, and on how the EC's output, and specifically its leaning toward liberalization with respect to other policies, was shaped by specific interest constellations and an institutional context that favored certain strategies and solutions over others.

*Interest Constellations*

The easiest way to explain the take-off and the unbalanced development of the EC's transport policy would be changed policy preferences. That is, the member states finally agreed to pursue a CTP—and specifically to complete the liberalization process even without going very far towards harmonization— because in contrast to earlier periods they now considered market creation important that they were unwilling to delay it until the most difficult harmonization problems were solved. Our country studies do indeed provide evidence of a broader acceptance of a liberal approach to transport policy in most member states (see also Button and Pitfield 1991; Kiriazidis 1994: 11), because the old market-protecting instruments had not achieved their goals: the black market thrived in dealing with licenses, ruinous competition persisted, and the railways continued to lose market shares. Moreover, after the publication of the 1985 white paper "Completing the Internal Market" and the subsequent launch of the "1992" project, market creation topped the EC agenda in the second half of the 1980s. The Milan European Council had welcomed the European Commission white paper and asked for the establishment of an internal market that would among other things also include a "free market in the transport sector."[16] Eventually, the transport ministers endorsed this strategy. At their council meeting in November 1985 they declared that they would create a common transport market *without quantitative restrictions* by 1992 at the latest.[17] This was a political decision going beyond what was legally required by the EC treaty and the European Court of Justice's (ECJ's) "inactivity verdict" of May 1985. In that ruling the ECJ had demanded action, but not a complete liberalization of market access. Thus, it would have been sufficient to introduce EC licenses for cabotage as for cross-border transport abolishing all discrimination based on the nationality of the operator. It would not have constituted a legal problem *per se* to keep certain quantitative restrictions, provided they were nondiscriminatory (Erdmenger 1991: 1,211). Consequently, we can conclude that the liberalization of transport markets gained wider acceptance in the Council—precisely the institution whose internal conflicts of interest had for so long deadlocked the EC's decision-making process and prevented progress in the CTP—on the back of the general decision to create a single European market for goods, capital, services, and labor.

The same cannot be said of harmonization. Specifically, regarding taxation, there was no convergence of interests. Therefore the most important conflicts remained. Harmonization was much easier to achieve in areas such as social and technical regulation, because such regulatory policies do not entail major redistributive conflicts for the negotiating states, the cost is very low for public actors and difficult to calculate in advance for the affected private parties (Majone 1994, 1996), and because their effective implementation can always be delayed. But insofar as harmonization is linked to fiscal questions, the decision-making process

becomes more problematic, because the issue is connected to ambitious, unc
and frequently contested goals, because the institutional variety of membe
states' domestic charging systems must be taken into account, and because it
raises redistributive conflicts between different member states and their respective transport industries.

Concerning the first point, the member states used taxes and road user fees to
pursue a variety of goals. Their primary objective was to raise revenue for transport specific expenditure, above all for financing infrastructure building and
maintenance. But in addition, these taxes were also used by some governments to
raise funds for the general budget and to pursue political goals such as favoring
freight over passenger transport, environmentally friendly vehicles over more
damaging vehicles, or rail over road transport. However, some countries rejected
the political goals that others used as a justification for maintaining a comparatively high level of fiscal duties. Thus, the fact that not all member states shared
the same goals with transport charging is a first reason for the difficulty of reaching agreement as to the use of specific instruments and levels of taxation in the
EC framework.

Furthermore, EC legislation on taxes had to take into account variations in
the kind of instruments traditionally used by member states to charge transport
users and to finance infrastructure building and maintenance. Each country
charged road users through a particular mix of annual vehicle taxes, fuel excise
duties, and road user charges or tolls. Some member states used tolls, while access to the road network was free in other states. Consequently, the level of fuel
taxes and vehicle taxes varied considerably across countries. Given such diverse national charging systems, harmonization on the supranational level was
difficult to achieve even when considered desirable in principle. As long as
transport took place predominantly nationally, all infrastructure users were subject to the same fiscal duties imposed by the national legislator. The particular
mix of instruments had specific advantages and disadvantages, but in the last
instance, all infrastructure users contributed in a similar way to the infrastructure costs indirectly created by them. However, the opening of commodity and
service markets within the EC was expected to lead to a further increase of the
number of nonresident hauliers using transport infrastructures. As a consequence, the variance in the national charging system creates deviations from the
"user pays" principle and competitive distortions between different infrastructure users, especially in cases where duties are not directly levied where the infrastructure is actually used.

In short, the liberalization of market access created most problems for those
countries using high vehicle and fuel taxes rather than a toll system, and whose
infrastructure was used by many foreign vehicles.[18] This is the situation in
which Germany found itself and explains why Germany continued to insist on a
parallel solution being found for the liberalization of cabotage alongside fiscal
harmonization in the 1980s and early 1990s. As in earlier conflicts concerning

liberalization and harmonization, it made its consent on the former issue dependent on an agreement on the latter, and was thus largely responsible for the delay of the final decision on the introduction of cabotage until 1993. As far as the taxation is concerned, Britain and the Benelux countries used similar instruments to those of Germany, but without suffering the same acute consequences. Britain, due to its geographical location, does not attract as much international traffic as the more centrally located member states. In the Benelux countries, the much lower vehicle taxes placed national operators in a competitive position, the use of their infrastructure by nonresident operators was considerably smaller than that of their own hauliers abroad (Mückenhausen 1994: 520), and harmonization was only a subsidiary issue, because in particular the Dutch saw their main interest in obtaining access to foreign markets. Finally, Italy and France were not affected by this problem, because their domestic toll systems ensure that all infrastructure users, irrespective of nationality, pay for usage.

As the harmonization of vehicle taxes at the high German level was impossible to achieve, Germany advocated the introduction of annual road user charges for its primary road network and a parallel reduction of its national vehicle taxes. Whereas vehicle taxes were levied on the basis of the principle of nationality, that is, where the vehicle was registered, the new charges were based on the principle of territoriality, that is, where transport operations took place. In practice, this meant that Germany tried to extend its national vehicle taxes to nonresident hauliers using the German road network.

This generated a conflict over redistribution, making it extremely difficult to reach agreement in the Council. The change of the German charging system would not have changed much for German hauliers, but it would have implied that the haulage industry in countries with lower taxes and vast activities abroad, such as the Dutch, lost their previous fiscal advantage with respect to German operators. It is not surprising that these countries condemned the introduction of road user charges as an attempt to increase the revenue of the German state at the expense of foreign road users and vetoed any such efforts for a long time. Incessant conflicts of interests made it extremely difficult to reach agreement on fiscal matters in the Council.

We can conclude that there was indeed convergence toward the acceptance of liberal transport regimes on the one hand, and persisting conflict over fiscal harmonization on the other. The Germans in particular defended a position—in appearance very similar to their former stance—arguing that the liberalization process be accompanied by a high level of harmonization, and making their agreement on cabotage conditional on a solution being found for taxation. However, given the low level of fiscal harmonization achieved in the 1993 package deal—which also included the final introduction of cabotage—Germany was only partly successful in pursuing this strategy. To explain this outcome, we should note that new institutional developments on the EC level made it more difficult to pursue a strategy of issue linkage in the Council.

*Institutional Changes*

Changes in the EC's institutional setting made a decisive contribution to the higher legislative output of the CTP from the 1980s onward, to overcoming the preceding deadlock, and, in the last instance, to the bias inherent in the policy output. In particular, the establishment of new procedural rules in the shape of qualified majority voting in some areas, the potential application of the principle of "direct effect," and the legal closure of certain exit options, all helped change the conditions under which decisions could be taken, as the consequences of failed agreements, which eventually also changed the incentives to the negotiation parties to pursue certain strategies and to agree to specific outputs.

*The ECJ 'Inactivity Verdict' and the Threat of 'Direct Effect.'* In May 1985, the ECJ published its "inactivity verdict"[19] when it ruled that the Council had violated the treaty by not establishing rules on the freedom to provide services in international transport, and specifically cabotage, within an adequate period of time, as demanded by the treaty. Never before had the Parliament, and subsequently the ECJ, made use of Article 175 (now Article 232) and stated that an EC institution had violated the treaty by inactivity. This ostensibly increased the commitment of the involved actors to move forward with the CTP and to find solutions for pending problems.[20] As the ECJ ruling obliged the Council to become active, it constituted a political resource for those in favor of pushing ahead with a CTP. However, the treaty's more specific formulation on the freedom to provide services in international transport and cabotage on the one hand, and the rather general provisions on accompanying measures on the other, led to a structural bias toward liberalization. The ECJ confirmed the Council's obligation to liberalize transport services, but left it up to the Council to decide on further action (Erdmenger 1983). Consequently, the countries that benefited most from the ruling were those pushing for the liberalization of transport services, whereas the actors who emphasized the importance of harmonization—including some of the initiators of the European Parliament lawsuit—remained dissatisfied with the content of the ruling despite their formal success.[21]

The second, and arguably more important, point linked to this decision was that if the Council continued to be inactive following this verdict, it would have run the risk of a second lawsuit and the application of the principle of direct effect, that is, the implementation of specific treaty provisions without any further legislative decision, to the liberalization of international transport services and cabotage (Erdmenger 1991: 1,211; Gronemeyer 1994: 267). Consequently, the Council had to become active if it wanted to retain some control of the policy development. The application of the principle of direct effect was dependent on the existence of specific obligations indicated in the treaty, that is, to the provisions concerning liberalization. In other words, in the absence of agreement in the Council, the liberalization of EC transport markets could have been pushed through by ECJ rulings, whereas harmonization would still have relied on reaching difficult agreements in the Council. The "default condition" would no longer lead to complete deadlock of the CTP, but to liberalization pushed through by the European Commission and the ECJ without any measures concerning harmonization. Thus, in the difficult search for consensus in the Council vis-à-vis harmonization, it had become more difficult for the "harmonizers" to find a package deal that would combine liberalization and high levels of harmonization, which explains why they finally agreed to a compromise whose scope remained rather limited with respect to fiscal harmonization.

*Exit Options.* The situation in which the negotiation parties found themselves was also influenced by the fact that some specific institutional arrangements in the decisional process closed certain options for member states dissatisfied with the EC policy output on fiscal harmonization. Above all, member states that did not already have a toll system were not in a position to introduce a national infrastructure charging system to change the distribution of costs between foreign and domestic enterprises on their national markets unilaterally. The technical infrastructure, that the countries which apply tolls had included into their road construction plans from the outset, could not be installed on very dense highway networks without creating ridiculously high costs. Moreover, technical—and cheaper—alternatives such as electronic charging were not yet available. Finally, the introduction of a general toll system would most probably encounter strong political resistance also at the domestic level.

Moreover, the EC legal framework prevented the unilateral use of instruments, such as the introduction of annual road user charges for heavy vehicles. Germany, which had done so, was halted by an ECJ ruling on the basis of Article 76 (now Article 72) of the treaty. By themselves, the road user charges were nondiscriminatory, but together with a reduction of the German vehicle taxes the package discriminated against foreign hauliers.[22] In this way, Germany, due to its embeddedness in the EC framework, had in practice lost control of the regulation of its national market.

*Voting Rules.* The "harmonizers" were also disadvantaged by the institutional framework as a result of changes in the voting rules. Ex-Article 75 stated that decisions concerning the CTP were to be taken by a qualified majority after the end of the transition period in 1969; and after the launch of the Single Market Program and the enforcement of the Single European Act, the European Council started to make more regular use of qualified majority voting (Teasdale 1993). But this did not apply in all fields of transport-related policymaking. Legislation on fiscal harmonization was not only based on the treaty's transport specific provisions, but also on Article 99 (now Article 93) regarding the harmonization of indirect taxes, which requires unanimity voting in the European Council,[23] making it much more difficult to reach an agreement in the field of taxation.

What is more, the existence of a qualified majority in favor of the introduction of cabotage in the European Council deprived the German government of its strategic option to block its introduction if no parallel decision on the tax issue was taken. For a while, the German veto positions with respect to the liberalization of cabotage could be upheld with the help of France, Italy, and even Spain.[24] However, the latter gradually changed their attitudes toward transport liberalization in the light of domestic learning processes or did not attach the same importance to cabotage as the Germans. Hence the prospect of the German government being outvoted on the issue of liberalization without obtaining any political compensation in the field of fiscal harmonization became a realistic option, which meant that it had to show a more compromising attitude if it did not want to lose its allies.

### The Biased Output

The outcome was a package deal that included the issues of cabotage and fiscal harmonization. This shows that other member states had accepted some of the German assertions regarding fair conditions for competition. In practice, however, the concrete measures contained in the package completed the liberalization process, whereas progress on fiscal harmonization and the promotion of the "user pays" principle was limited. The German delegation was happy to obtain any form of compensation, considering that the EC had made a first step toward tax harmonization and confirmed the territoriality principle as a rule for the future development of infrastructure charging on the supranational and domestic level.[25] For other member states, the package deal made liberalization and access to attractive foreign markets possible. Moreover, for this group it was also important that the European Council kept control over the development of national charges even in the future, as it established both the maximum level for road user charges and the principles according to which tolls may be raised, that is, excluding national solutions that do not conform to agreed EC standards.[26]

## Interests, Institutions, and Biased Integration

Responsibility for the long-term difficulty of achieving policy output in a CTP may be laid at the door of the member states with their conflicting interests, just as the success of more recent efforts may be explained with their convergence around a liberal mode of regulation. However, the case study has also shown that the policy field was prone with conflict even in more recent times. Hence, changes in the institutional structure made a decisive contribution to the policy development we have witnessed.

Generally speaking, the EC institutional structure requires a high level of decisional consensus. Under these conditions, central characteristics of the policy area under consideration here, that is, the interdependence of various issues and the deliberate creation of political links between them, increased not only the complexity of the decision-making process, but also the number of veto positions, making progress in any of the areas under consideration arduous. In other words, crossed veto positions between the member states were the main factor responsible for the prolonged deadlock of the CTP.

Some of these parameters have gradually changed over time, while others have remained unchanged. With respect to the distribution of interests, the issues linked to a liberalization of transport markets have gained wider acceptance among the member states. Thus, today one finds a more homogenous distribution of preferences with regard to market integration. In contrast, the conflicts of interests over fiscal harmonization remain significant. Whereas some actors continued to try to link the two areas, a majority of member states are no longer willing to delay the liberalization process until the time when all other transport-related conflicts are resolved. At this point, it is important that the institutional setting has become favorable to negative integration: first, because decisions on market creation may be taken by a qualified majority in the Council (unanimity still valid for tax harmonization); and second, because the potential application of the principle of direct effect to transport liberalization ensures that even in the absence of agreement in the European Council, there are other, that is, legal instruments to go ahead with market creation. In contrast, in the case of the harmonization of competitive conditions, failure to reach agreement in the Council would have resulted in the absence of any regulation. There were no alternative ways to issue rules in this area, on either the supranational or national level. This institutional setting had important consequences for the strategic options open to actors, making the political strategy to construct a linkage between different questions more difficult to pursue. The threat that different questions could be dealt with and decided separately and independent of their reciprocal effects increased the pressure on those hoping for simultaneous solutions in different areas to agree to certain solutions, even when these did not entirely correspond to their distinct interests. In this sense, the new institutional setting of the late 1980s and 1990s avoided an overload of the EC's decision-making process and its deadlock, but was at the same time largely responsible for its biased output.

## NEW RAILWAY POLICY OF THE EUROPEAN UNION: FULL STEAM AHEAD?

In the early 1980s the feeling that the European railways had entered into a profound crisis was widespread with the steady decline of the railways' share in the market of passenger and freight transport. In 1985 the European Conference of Ministers of Transport, which represents nineteen European states, called for urgent measures to improve international rail transport service because "European railways are at present in a particularly difficult competitive situation which could become almost desperate unless vigorous action is taken immediately" (ECMT 1985: 8).

One of the perceived reasons for this development was the unfavorable situation of railways in intermodal competition, especially with respect to road haulage. It was believed that government interference, with the consequent imposition of public-service obligations and low management autonomy, and the fact that railways had to bear infrastructure construction and maintenance costs, were responsible for the poor economic performance of the railways. However, what may have contributed even more to the widespread diagnosis of crisis was the fact that there were internal structural impediments that prevented the railways from adapting sufficiently to the new demand for transport services that places greater value on the quality of service, such as flexibility and reliability, and less on quantity. These structural impediments can be attributed to railways as a technical system, which is inevitably a relatively inflexible mode of transport better adapted to low-quality, high-quantity transport. A further disadvantage of railways is the low level of international integration of railway systems that were developed in a national framework (ECMT 1985: 48f). A low degree of technical compatibility such as power supply and signaling systems increases costs of transborder freight transport. The quality is further reduced by administrative differences that prevent the development of single tariffs and door-to-door services. The international fragmentation of the railways is a major obstacle to their success in intermodal competition, because they enjoy a competitive advantage over long distances. According to the European Commission, the crisis of the European railways contributes to a general crisis of mobility, because the loss of shares in the transport markets to road haulage increases accidents and reduces the environmental sustainability in Europe (CEC 1996b: 5).

## Policy Development

Despite these symptoms of crisis the railway policy of the EC shared the fate of the CTP in general.[27] Until the mid-1980s it never surpassed its very modest initial stage, and when attempts were finally made to shape an integrated CTP, they included all transport modes with the exception of rail (Ross 1994: 193). Rail policy had not been entirely neglected by the EC, but it was simply not integrated with other policy measures.[28] The main aim of the early railway policy was to reduce disadvantages for railways in intermodal competition due to state intervention and to increase the transparency of the financial relationship between the individual member states and their respective national railway systems (Erdmenger 1981: 88). This approach was not very successful. Ten years later public-service obligations had not been reduced and state aids to railways had increased. Only the transparency of the financial relationship between states and their railway systems increased (Erdmenger 1981: 89). Until the mid-1980s this situation remained unchanged (Whitelegg 1988: 58). The CTP conceived of the railways as a financial problem that did not take into consideration any broader context, and did not offer any constructive proposals but only "financial imperatives dressed up as transport policies" (Whitelegg 1988: 56).

In the second half of the 1980s the EC tried to relaunch a Common Railway Policy (the CRP). One could have expected the policy to seek a possible solution to the poor economic performance of the railways by scaling down their activities to those that were economically successful (Befahy 1995: 15). These measures could have reduced significantly the financial burdens of the member states, most of which have to subsidize their railways heavily. In its action programs and legislative proposals the European Commission pursued quite a different strategy, however. In particular, the various national projects for high-speed trains (HSTs) permitted the EC to design its strategy as a *growth strategy* with the advantage of an increased political viability of the EC's railways.[29] This may be why the EC's "rediscovery" of rail policy since the mid-1980s has been led by a European Commission "newly intent on assuming a much more activist and multifaceted role in HST planning, development and funding" (Ross 1994: 193).

Since Directive 91/440 EEC, the CRP has been extended to all major areas of railway policy and, despite of the rhetoric of subsidiarity, no significant area of railway policy has remained in the exclusive competence of the member states.[30] A recent European Commission white paper offers a comprehensive outline of a "strategy for revitalizing the Community's railways' (CEC 1996b). The policy problem that has to be addressed by the EC is expanded. Whereas the earlier policy identified the financial crisis of the railways as the main problem, this is now seen only as a symptom of decline of this mode of transport caused by the rise of other modes, especially road transport (CEC 1996b: 7–9). According to the European Commission, however, the decline of the railways is not taken as evidence of the fact that this mode of transport is outdated and should be abandoned. Railways could compete with other modes of transport if its disadvantages in intermodal competition such as public-service obligations or higher infrastructure costs were removed,[31] and, even more important, if railways were to offer services closer to the demand of the users (CEC 1996b: 10). It is the firm belief of the European Commission that the establishment of a market will be an important means for creating new transport services by attracting new operators and increasing the efficiency of the former monopolies. The strategy of revitalizing the railways in the medium-term is therefore aimed at creating a single market for rail services for both passenger and freight transport by means of two connected measures. Under the precondition that both road and rail have to bear the internal and external costs of the usage of their respective infrastructures, it is hoped that the services offered by rail can compete with road transport.[32]

The core idea of the European CRP is to reverse the decline of European railways by introducing competition among different railway companies, so that intermodal competition, especially with road transport, will be supplemented by *intramodal competition* on a *European scale*. This implies that any European company may provide any service throughout the European Union. This is a radical idea that challenges the widely accepted policy belief that for technical and economic reasons railways are "natural monopolies" and must be protected from intermodal competition.

There are several reasons to assume that intramodal competition is the core of the CRP. First, this goal is in line with the Single Market Program in general and especially with the policy pursued in other network utilities such as telecommunications and electricity, where the principle of competition of different suppliers on the same infrastructure has also been applied. Furthermore, as detailed below, most of the recent decisions and the obligations that have arisen until now have been concerned with the introduction of intramodal competition.[33] The programmatic declarations of the European Commission propose to move ahead on this track. Finally, the other goals associated with the CRP, especially achieving technical compatibility between the different national railway systems ("interoperability") and increasing the environmental sustainability of transport, may be subsumed under the market building project. "Interoperability" is a precondition for competition on a European scale, and environmental sustainability is increased with the "revitalization of the European railways," because a growth of the sector will be able to divert traffic away from road transport, which involves higher environmental costs.

The ambition of the CRP to introduce intramodal competition has given rise to some important questions within the policymaking community. The problems identified questioned the shape of future policy development and outcomes. First, the separation of infrastructure and the provision of services gave rise to problems of coordination between the two domains that may reduce flexibility and scope and thus the quality of services offered (Befahy 1995: 28). Second, it is not yet clear how competition between different companies operating on the same track could be introduced. New competitors are at a disadvantage in relation to the established national monopolies. How are they going to obtain access to rolling stock, specific management knowledge, and trained staff without prohibitive costs (Nash and Preston 1993: 98)? Third, new challenges for the management of infrastructure arise with the advent of on-the-track competition (Dodgson 1993: 51). The technical characteristics of the railway network call for a common timetable that does not discriminate among operators. Furthermore, a prerequisite for the functioning of the market is a system of infrastructure charging (Baumgartner 1993: 43–45). This is difficult to develop because the infrastructure capacity of a railway network is not fixed but depends on a number of interacting variables,[34] making it far more difficult to convert capacity of the railway infrastructure into time slots and sell them, as is done, for example, in the case of airport landing strips. Infrastructure usage costs are even more elusive when external costs are to be included in the calculation.

In addition to the two sets of problems regarding the domestic feasibility of the EC's reform project, there are also external problems to market creation. To date, national railways have been developed as national systems. In order to make railways more attractive, international traffic must be developed, because the railways can only develop their competitive advantage over competing modes of transport over long distances, especially in freight transport. This requires efforts of *technical standardization* between different national railways so as to ensure "interoperability" (CEC 1996b: 23ff.). Some of these problems, such as different power supply systems, can be resolved by interface standardization, but others require the harmonization of technical standards, a challenging task within the EC framework.[35] The most important case in point is the different signaling systems that will have to be redesigned on a European level and implemented in all the member states (Ebeling 1994).

A final, and paradoxical, effect of introducing competition in the provision of transport services has been that private investment in infrastructure financing has been jeopardized. State-owned enterprises guarantee a certain usage of infrastructure over a long period of time, whereas private companies do not. Railway monopolies reduce, whereas open markets increase, the investment risks for private investors in the infrastructure, creating a trade-off between the market for transport services and the market for private infrastructure capital.

In presenting the list of problems, we are not arguing that the European railway reform is technically unfeasible, as there is always the chance that technical problems have been exaggerated to prevent undesired change,[36] but that the problems indicate clear and formidable *uncertainties* in the course and the consequences of the CRP. The Community of European Railways therefore advocates slow but steady progress, because "the proposal of the Commission on liberalizing the railway market will be touching mainly unknown territory" (CER 1996: 6).

To date, the European railway reform has concentrated on four different aspects of railway administration.[37] First, new principles about *railway management* have been adopted. According to the CRP, the current practice of perpetual interference by the administration should be abolished and be replaced by a management along private-enterprise principles. Railways would be free to determine their investment and business plans, to establish international consortia with other railway companies, to make decisions on staffing and public procurement, to expand their market share, and to establish activities in fields associated with railway businesses. Eventually, tariffs could be abolished to allow railways themselves to determine the price for their services offered.

Second, *financial regulations of railways* covering aspects internal to the railways as well as aspects of the financial relationship between states and railways were adopted. Until the end of 1992, railways were exempt from the EC rules on state aids. From 1993 onward, these rules are introduced, but member states are obliged to create conditions to make the application of these rules viable: member states are obliged to reduce debts so as to make financial management according to economic criteria possible and to improve railway finances.[38] Any state aid granted to reduce these debts or to cover operation losses has to be authorized by the European Commission. An authorization as a necessary precondition usually involves state aids being linked to a restructuring program designed to increase competitiveness. The rules on state aids do not cover compensation for public-service obligations, and for exceptional social costs such as early retirement schemes. Furthermore, infrastructure investments are not legitimate, provided there is no distortion of competition, even for the purpose of regional development.

Another aim is to establish *the rules for a future market of transport services* that will stipulate the conditions for market access and market processes. The following obligations have resulted from EC legislation. First, since January 1993 access rights for railway enterprises are granted, albeit in a very limited way, that is, only for specific enterprises and specific market segments.[39] Furthermore, the conditions of access rights such as licensing, the allocation of infrastructure capacity, and charging for infrastructure have been specified, but only entered into force in June 1997.[40] To date, cooperation agreements between railways to exploit the new access rights in international passenger transport and combined transport have been exempted by the European Commission from European competition rules.

Closely connected with the previous measures is the *separation of management of rail infrastructure and operation*. Here, only the separation of accounts is compulsory, and cross-subsidies between the two areas are prohibited. Organizational separation (the creation of a subdivision for infrastructure within the organization) or institutional separation (the creation of a different company for infrastructure management) is optional. This provision is a necessary precondition for an increase in financial transparency and for the establishment of competition, since the financial separation of the network from its operation is a prerequisite to allow the calculation of the costs of infrastructure usage, which in turn is a precondition for the access of other railway companies on the railway infrastructure.

The four main goals of the CRP may be summarized in two different dimensions of organizational reform and regulatory reform. Organizational reform consists of the application of new management principles to make the former state railway companies more autonomous, and the reform of financial regulation in the form of contracts regulating the financial relation between the administration and the railways. Regulatory reform consists of the separation of activities related to rail infrastructure and the provision and operation of transport services and the introduction of rules for market access and operation.

The analysis of the European policy development shows that the new CRP is an ambitious policy designed to bring about a radical change in the organization of railway systems in Europe. However, it is important to note that to date this policy has only resulted in rather *modest binding obligations*. This observation is not only based on the fact that the CRP is largely implemented by directives, which according to the EC treaty only specify goals and grant member states leeway to implement these. In particular, little progress had been made with the regulatory reform. The liberalization of market access is restricted to "groupings of railway enterprises operating international services between the Member States" (CEC 1996b: 15) and where the constituent enterprises are established and have a right to offer international combined transport to operate throughout the EC, and only became binding in June 1997 (CEC 1997: 5). The European Commission proposal to extend these access rights to all freight transport and to international passenger transport[41] was still undecided two years later.[42] In the meantime, the European Commission decided to liberalize access rights on a voluntary basis by proposing "trans-European rail freeways for freight" (CEC 1997: 7f).[43] The underlying idea is that member states would agree on certain rail corridors on which all operators could access and where the use of the infrastructure would be simplified, for example, by simplifying access or by a transparent charging system. Consistent with the principle of keeping binding legal requirements to a minimum, it was decided that "the definition of a freeway and their subsequent implementation by Member State railways must respect Community law. Nevertheless, freeways will, *on a voluntary basis*, take a number of issues further than the requirements of Community law" (CEC 1997: 9, italics added).

Furthermore, the separation of infrastructure and operation has been limited to accounting but has not been extended yet to organizational separation. The European Commission now believes that in order to safeguard the access to rail networks, the management of infrastructure and the provisions of services should be carried out by two different business units (CEC 1996b: 19). However, this has not been included in the amendment proposal of Directive 91/440/EEC.[44]

The noncompulsory nature of CRP is illustrated by the fact that the single member states apply the rules in quite different ways and to different degrees without infringing EC law, depending on the national context.

## The New European Rail Policy: Finally Taking Off?

The new European railway policy may be considered innovative insofar as it entailed a major increase in the scope of the decision-making activity at this level. The comparative ease with which the new CRP has taken off is remarkable, especially when compared to road haulage.[45] Less than two years elapsed between the communication of the Commission's liberalization proposal and its adoption by the Council (Schmuck 1992: 42). This is below the average decision-making time concerning transport issues of "often several years" (Erdmenger 1996: 45). What is more, regarding railway policy, it is certainly not justified to speak of a deadlock as in the case of road haulage policy.[46] Given the problems of expanding the scope of European policymaking in general and more specifically in the transport sector, the question is why the new European railway policy took off much more easily than road haulage. In fact, the decision by the Transport Council in June 1991 to liberalize European railways was taken not only swiftly, but also unanimously by all the representatives of the member states (*Agence Europe* 1991c: 5).[47] The explanation offered here rests on two main factors. The basic principles of the new railway policy were much less controversial than in the case of road haulage. This in turn was largely due to the limited legal obligations and the ambiguity of the directive inaugurating the new railway policy. The general momentum of the Single Market Program has contributed less to the decision-making dynamics.

## The Bottleneck in the Decision-Making Process: The Council of Ministers

According to the EU Treaty, the decision-making process in the CTP involves the European Commission as the initiator of new policies and the Council of Ministers as the final decision maker. Although the role of the Parliament has become more important over time (Erdmenger 1996: 44f.), it is the Council of Ministers that is the crucial obstacle for the decision-making process. Its principle of unanimous decision making allows any member state opposing progress to veto new policy proposals. Although this rule has been changed to the principle of qualified majority voting by the Single European Act, for transport the principle of unanimity is still in force whenever unfavorable consequences for regional development and the operation of transport systems are given. Although this does not imply a right to veto, member states continue to have a possibility to insist on unanimity (Erdmenger 1996: 46f.). This procedural possibility to reintroduce formal unanimity may also account for the fact that a consensus was aimed for in any case in the railway reform. In the past, the different actors performed the following roles. On the one hand, the European Commission supported by the Parliament and the ECJ promoted the creation of a Single European Market in transport. On the other hand, the Council of Ministers built up an impressive record of resistance to policy initiatives. In the case of railway policy, the Parliament deviated somewhat from its earlier record when it adopted the view of the Community of European Railways (CER) that the infrastructure manager did not necessarily have to be institutionally separate from national railway companies,[48] but overall it did conform by condemning the Council of Ministers for its attempts to hamper efforts to liberalize the access of new railway enterprises (*Agence Europe* 1995: 13). The following section shows that in the case of the CRP of Ministers the Council of Ministers, conformed to its tradition as well: it opposed liberalization.

## Coalitions in the Council of Ministers

The fact that the decision by the Council of Ministers to adopt a new railway policy was taken unanimously does not imply that interests did not diverge over the new policy. Rather, two broad coalitions may be distinguished.[49] The first coalition consisted of Britain and the Netherlands. This group may be seen as unconditional supporters of liberalization. During the negotiations both countries already planned railway reforms going beyond the requirements discussed. They had no specific interest in exporting their reform plans to other European countries. Apparently, Britain did not need the support of a European reform to overcome national resistance, and the Dutch, until recently, have not assigned a major priority to railway policy (see Lehmkuhl in this volume). The second coalition comprised conditional supporters of the new railway policy. These countries identified different problems with the proposed liberalization, especially technical compatibility and operational security (*Agence Europe* 1991a: 7). The position of Germany, France, and Italy, the three remaining countries under study in this volume, are representative of the second coalition and may be described as follows: the German representatives in the Council of Ministers were generally in favor of the new railway policy but had difficulties in developing clear preferences, because the domestic German railway reform had not produced any conclusive results (see Teutsch in this volume). The Italian representatives did not develop any clear preferences at all. In fact, there does not seem to be a continual dialogue between the Commission which initiated the reform and Italian representatives. France has been most skeptical about railway liberalization in Europe (see Douillet and Lehmkuhl in this volume).[50] It opposed both elements of liberalization, the division between infrastructure and operation, and the free access to the national railway network by other than the national enterprises. This has been true until recently when France opposed the creation of European freight freeways. The basic principle was to slow down liberalization as much as possible. Presently the French position is not merely defensive. It tries to promote a different reform vision by stressing cooperation between different (national) railway enterprises. Technical compatibility between different national networks becomes a major concern in this perspective. Furthermore, France tries to reassert the definition of railways as a public service as opposed to the European market view. France seems always on the verge of leaving this coalition and resort to outright opposition toward the EC policy trend.

The position of the national governments in the Council of Ministers is roughly equal to the position of the national railways within the Community of European Railways (CER), the main lobbying association at the EC level. This association cautiously welcomes the liberalization policy and tries to solve the new problems and to moderate the pace of the reform (CER 1996). Within the CER, the French railways are the only railways that fundamentally oppose liberalization. They therefore continually seem to risk isolation.[51]

## Decision-Making Strategies

The brief overview of the preferences of the major players in the decision-making process indicates the considerable potential for resistance to the liberalization of railway policy. The majority of member states belonged to the coalition of conditional supporters, and France was on the brink of outright opposition. Why, then, was a decision about a fundamental change of the CRP reached in a comparatively short period of time? The general momentum of the Common Market Program may have played a role.[52] However, the two major factors that explain the surprising consensus were the following. First, the directive was successful in changing the preferences of the decision makers. The new perspective on rail described above in terms of an expanding market of railway enterprises that replaced the former concept of infrastructure was attractive because it offered a reform perspective. It was successful in revising the terms of the debate about the railway reform.

> If the directive was a success, it was not so much a success with what it did directly, but what it did indirectly, and that is to create a new thought process to be applied to the railways, to think again about what railways were supposed to be doing, how they were supposed to be run.
>
> (interview commission, 20 March 1997)

The second reason for the rapid advent of the new CRP is its high degree of *ambiguity*, that is, the same policy may be interpreted differently by different actors, thus becoming more acceptable to all (Baier, March, and Saetren 1988: 158–61). Several aspects of the CRP are responsible for this.

- The technical uncertainties with respect to intramodal competition implied that the development of the EC would be an open process.
- The CRP linked aspects of the traditional European railways policy, such as increasing management autonomy, and the solution of financial problems (i.e. those concerned with organizational reform), to the more controversial and innovative market regulation.[53]
- Ambiguity was enhanced by the incremental way in which the CRP was introduced; as mentioned, it contains only very limited, legally binding steps toward liberalization.

All three aspects allowed the proponents and opponents to endorse the CRP in its present stage. Reform skeptics point out the formidable technical obstacles involved, the modest legal obligations, and the traditional elements of the policy, in order to play down its significance. Reform enthusiasts, on the other hand, believe that technical obstacles will be resolved in time, that liberalization constitutes the core of the new policy, and that further incremental steps will follow to foster the implementation of the program. This compromise allowed actors to arrive at a decision without having to resort to majority voting in order to override vital national interests.

In sum, two factors are responsible for the fact that the rail reform started off much more rapidly than road haulage policy, although they both have to meet the high consensus requirements of EC decision making. First, the interests of the actors converged insofar as they all believed that a reform would be necessary. Second, the ambiguity of the railway policy allowed actors to arrive at a generally acceptable compromise.

## SIMILARITIES AND DIFFERENCES: A GENERAL EXPLANATION FOR THE DEVELOPMENT OF EUROPEAN TRANSPORT POLICY

In comparative perspective, some differences between the decision-making dynamics in the area of road haulage and railway become apparent. Even though the formal institutional decision-making framework, especially the voting rules within the Council of Ministers, is the same for both areas, it has different consequences for the two subsectors. In road haulage, voting rules led to a protracted stalemate due to "crossed veto positions" that were a consequence of a fundamental divergence of interest between the member states about how a common market should be created, whereas in the case of railways they seem to be somewhat less important for an explanation of a late advent. Here, a further obstacle for fundamental reform has been the lack of ideas on how to develop an effective CRP, able to overcome the deeply entrenched interests of the national railway monopolies.[54] In the language of the "garbage can model" (Kingdon 1984) one has to distinguish between two slightly different reasons why a policy window did not open in the EC context. In the case of road transport, it was mainly *differing interest* together with a specific *institutional setting* that were responsible for the long delays, whereas in the case of rail the policy window remained closed for so long, also because of the *absence of viable solutions* to a given problem. The general problem of introducing competition in the public utilities relying on networks such as electricity, gas, and water also applied to the railways. Consequently, solutions to this problem developed late in Europe.[55]

The differences between the development patterns of road and rail are only variations to a common pattern. In more general terms the late take-off of the CTP may be explained by a different notion of the transport sector in different countries. In fact, in Europe two different paradigms of transport policymaking exist, a "Continental approach" and an "Anglo-Saxon approach" (Button 1991). According to the first, transport is not an economic sector but part of the infrastructure of the economy and even part of the welfare state by providing public service to its citizens. In this perspective, the strategy of liberalization without careful harmonization to create a common market runs in the face of the tradition of state intervention built up to secure its performance. On the other hand, the Anglo-Saxon tradition cannot accept any wide-ranging interference with what it perceives as market processes. Transport policy paradigms are institutionally embedded and thus relatively stable. Modern nation states developed their first experience of economic policy with managing railways (Dobbin 1994), and railways were also intimately linked to the process of nation building. Railway policy was tightly linked to the "continental approach," whereas its problems were until recently not thought about in detail within the Anglo-Saxon approach. This explains why, in contrast to road transport, there were no competing coalitions regarding rail policy within the EC, and why it was so difficult for innovative proposals to emerge in this subsector.

In spite of the different reasons for the common development of road and rail policy, however, the explanation for the long period of stagnation in transport policy in terms of diverging policy paradigms and the lack of solutions to specific problems also gives us a clue as to the common partial explanation for policy take-off. As has often been observed, since the mid-1980s Europe experienced a "neoliberal turn" (Jobert 1994), a general shift away from interventionist policies associated with the Keynesian welfare state and to regulatory polices favoring market mechanisms (Majone 1994). This general trend called state interventionism in public utilities in general into question. Subsequently, the continental transport policy paradigm has also come under pressure. In the field of road haulage this shift favored the view of "liberalizers" with respect to the "hamonizers," whereas in the field of rail it meant that a conceivable solution for the economic difficulties of this mode of transport became available after many years of policy stagnation. A good example that shows how difficult it has become to argue against the introduction of market principles is the French attempt to prevent liberalization of transport by referring to notions of public service (Bauby 1997). This example also shows that the continental paradigm has not been entirely replaced by the Anglo-Saxon one. However, there can be no doubt that it has become increasingly challenged. Among the followers of the continental approach, the view that liberalization may not contradict it as much as was thought in the past is beginning to gain ground.

The idea that this change in the general distribution of preferences could be reflected in concrete policy development in the transport sector was reinforced by certain institutional changes. The increasing challenge of the continental paradigm does not imply that the neoliberal turn led to general consensus on the approach of the CTP. It was precisely because the policymakers advocating the Single Market Program on the general level anticipated that their liberalization policy would meet the resistance of specialized interests in the different sectors, that they facilitated the decision-making mechanism in the Council of Ministers, that is, made qualified majority voting the rule when it came to decide on these questions. Thus, even though this institutional reform cannot be seen as completely separate from the "neoliberal" turn, from the perspective of the specialized policymakers in a sector such as, for instance, transport, the institutional change, however, became a major factor influencing the chances with which different policies could be pursued. It was shown how resistance to policy proposals designed to promote a common market in transport became more difficult, especially in the field of road haulage, because new voting rules and the potential application of the principle of direct effect changed the strategic options available to the negotiating parties as well as the consequences of nonagreement. The same institutional rules were in theory valid for railway policy, but their potential for facilitating decision making was much more circumscribed because a great number of veto points could be upheld, in fact, even if the new institutional rules were designed to abolish them. That is, the ECJ's inactivity verdict could indeed be interpreted as a duty to develop also a CRP, and a country opposing a specific railway policy could be outvoted under the new rules, but this was hardly consequential for the strategic options that were in fact available to the different actors. The mechanism of negative integration was much less powerful in the railway sector. As a technical system, the railways are highly integrated, that is, they are characterized by a close interconnectedness between infrastructure and operation. Therefore, even if markets were legally opened by the hierarchical power of EU law or a majority decision in the Council of Ministers, in contrast to road transport no single train could run on the network of a third country provided there is no decision on the harmonization of certain technical and organizational parameters. In other words, it is de facto impossible to impose majority decisions on dissenting actors regarding rail policy, because their collaboration is definitely needed during the implementation phase. This, in turn, practically invalidates the shift from unanimity to qualified majority voting at the stage of policy formulation.

To conclude, the take-off of a CTP can be explained by two factors that weakened the position of the harmonizers and allowed the EC to choose a liberal approach. First, the neoliberal turn questioned the continental approach to transport policy, making it more difficult to argue against liberalization. This is the trend toward *delegitimizing* the continental transport policy paradigm. Second, with regard to certain questions, the inactivity verdict and the changed voting rules reduced the power of the harmonizers to resist even in the face of decreased legitimation. This is the trend toward *disempowering* the coalition subscribing to the continental transport policy paradigm.

## CONCLUSION: THE PROSPECTS FOR EUROPEANIZATION

European decision making is based on subterfuge (Héritier 1999). Given the high demand for consensus and the perpetually diverging interests of the member states, it is essential that strategies be found to circumvent potential policy deadlocks. Subterfuge, however, comes at a price, and has at least two systematic effects. First, European decision making leads to a considerable amount of *non-decision*. Policies building markets are favored over policies correcting market failures (Scharpf 1999). Second, European decision making favors policies that have limited legal obligations over policies that severely constrain member states. European social policy is the best example for this tendency toward *voluntarism* (Streeck 1995). Thus, the high costs involved in reaching decisions systematically affect the policy outcome and subsequently also the way Europe influences the member state level.

The CTP also bears the traces of the institutional conditions of European decision making. The commission's policy program today focuses on achieving economic as well as social and environmental policy goals connected to the transport sector. Its activities range from economic regulation and infrastructure policy to research and development and social and technical regulation (CEC 1992). Yet, liberalization is the priority. In road haulage, market-building went ahead without parallel action to tackle the problem of congestion or pollution aggravated by market liberalization. Furthermore, national remedies to these problems may no longer be possible. Europe vetoed the German road pricing scheme for lorries and the Austrian curb on Alpine transit, exporting its nondecisions to the national level as well.

The CTP also shows signs of the second type of influence of European decision making: Albeit in different ways, the precondition for achieving policy compromises in both road and rail policy was the limited scope of binding obligations that resulted from it, or to phrase it positively, a strong element of *voluntarism* in the final policy result.[56] In the case of *road haulage*, the voluntaristic character of the policy depends on the *limited scope of liberalization*. The EC's liberalization measures are restricted to hauliers operating on foreign territory and do not prevent member states from restricting market access (for national hauliers) or impose a compulsory tariff system on their territory (for national and foreign hauliers).[57] Therefore, and given that harmonization is not very far reaching, the member states are formally left a wide margin for adaptation to EC policies. However, apart from the legal rules, this margin will be heavily conditioned by the concrete effects of liberalization on the specific economy under consideration. While some member states will feel under strong economic pressure to adapt their national rules to the new situation created by the opening of markets, others may be less affected by negative integration. The latter may therefore enjoy a wider margin for decisions and indeed opt for policies whose costs are retained prohibitively among the former group of countries. Thus, the EC leaves the member states leeway for making decisions on the condition that no major economic interests are affected by the opening up of markets provided by EC legislation.[58]

*Railway policy*, too, is characterized by voluntarism. As opposed to the case of road haulage, however, this is not due to a liberalization bias. Although it is true that railway policy proceeds in a similar fashion to road by giving priority to removing barriers for market access in 1991 and only specifying the rules needed to implement this in 1995, there is a difference between road and rail. Because of problems of 'interoperability' of different railway systems, liberalization and harmonization cannot be decoupled as easily in the road haulage case. In rail policy, liberalization was only introduced for a very limited market segment. Thus, the *scope of liberalization* was restricted much more than in the case of the road haulage policy to ensure approval of the European policy. A second technique to circumvent a potential policy deadlock was to enhance the *ambiguity* of the new European railway policy. This included elements of traditional railway policy, such as improving the financial situation of the railway enterprises or increasing the autonomy of the railway management, and as regards the demanded separation of infrastructure and operation three different models of divergent scope were offered in the European directive itself. Therefore, very different responses at the national level may be justified with reference to the European rail policy.

If the observation that the CTP today is not so much about designing and implementing a comprehensive regime of rules for transport services, as about small incremental steps towards establishing a different but more compatible system of national rules that leave considerable freedom of action for the member states, is correct, then we are faced with an analytical challenge: the contention is that the specific policy bias of EU transport policy also has consequences for processes of Europeanization, and that Europe does not only influence its member states by the more trivial process of implementation. We would instead expect this implementation process to give rise to a complex process of competition among rules and mutual adjustment among member states, and it is these different patterns that we seek to map and explain in the following national case studies.

## NOTES

1. The first enlargement of the EC in 1973 with the accession of the United Kingdom, Ireland, and Denmark strengthened the liberal camp. Apart from their liberal domestic regulatory regimes, it has been particularly important for these countries to have access to the central and economically most developed regions. As far as international transport is concerned, the same basic interest holds true for Greece, Spain, and Portugal, which joined the EC in 1981 and 1986, respectively (Erdmenger 1983, 7–8).

2. Interview ex-DG VII, 22 May 1996.

3. Case 13/83 (*European Parliament* v. *Council*), [1985] ECR 1513.

4. COM (85) 310 final.

5. EC Bull. 11-1985, 2.1.161.

6. Regulation 1841/88, OJ L 163 of 30 June 1988, p. 1.

7. Regulation 881/92/EEC, OJ L 95, 9 April 1992, p. 10; Directive 96/26/EC, OJ L 277, 14 October 1988, p. 17.

8. Regulation 4059/89/EEC, OJ L 390, 30 December 1989, p. 3.

9. Regulation 3118/93/EEC, OJ L 279, 12 November 1993, p. 1.

10. Regulation 4058/89/EEC, OJ L 390, 30 December 1989, p. 1. The EEC system of price regulation of 1968 had already been modified and essentially liberalized by the substitution of bracket tariffs with nonbinding reference tariffs in 1977 (Regulation 2831/77/EEC, OJ L 334, 24 December 1977, p. 22).

11. An explicit EC pricing policy, however, only exists for international transport markets. National tariff systems are not subject to EC norms. The ECJ has repeatedly ruled that national transport tariffs do not conflict with European competition rules: Case C–185/91 (*Bundesanstalt für den Güterfernverkehr* v. *Gebr. Reiff GmbH & Co.KG*), [1993] ECR I–5801; Case C–153/93 (*Federal Republic of Germany* v. *Delta Schiffahrts-und Speditionsgesellschaft mbH*), [1994] ECR I–2517, p. 25; Case C–96/94 (*Centro Servizi Spediporto Srl* v. *Spedizioni Marittima del Golfo Srl*).

12. Directive 92/82/EEC, OJ L 316, 31 October 1992, p. 19.

13. Directive 93/89/EEC, OJ L 279, 12 November 1993, p. 32.

14. In the mid-1990s, vehicle taxes for a 38-ton truck ranged from 4,100 European Currency Unit (ECU) annually in the UK and 2,676 ECU in Germany, to 1,038 ECU in the Netherlands, 787 ECU in France, 711 ECU in Italy, and 307 ECU in Greece (Committee of Enquiry 1994, 37).

15. The 2191st Council meeting, Transport, Luxembourg, 17 June 1999, Press Release C/99/134.

16. EC Bull. 6–1985, 1.2.5.

17. EC Bull. 11–1985, 2.1.161.

18. In the common market, tolls have a considerabale advantage over vehicle taxes in implementing the "user pays" principle. Tolls apply equally to all hauliers irrespective of their nationality. They are therefore better adapted to an increasing share of foreign hauliers than vehicle taxes, which are restricted to domestic firms only.

19. Case 13/83 (*European Parliament* v. *Council*), [1985] ECR 1513.

20. In the words of an eyewitness, "I remember the Council meeting after May 1985 [when the ECJ decision was published] very well. By chance, the German Minister of Transport, Mr. Dollinger, was sitting next to me and I witnessed his fiery plea. I remember his words literally: 'Such a condemnation must never happen again to us, my colleagues.' The condemnation of the Community's legislative body for Treaty violation by inactivity indeed was a unique event. It truly made an impression" (interview ex-DG VII, 22 May 1996).

21. Interview ex-DG VII, 22 May 1996.

22. Case C–195/90 (*Commission* v. *Federal Republic of Germany*) [1992] ECR I–3141.

23. Directive 93/89/EEC, OJ L 279, 12 November 1993, p. 32.

24. Interview MP/CSU, 31 January 1996.

25. The German minister of transport has frequently pointed out that besides the introduction of road user charges, Directive 93/89 EEC also allows those member states unable to introduce tolls to institute electronic user charges in the future, thus restoring a degree of autonomy in the field of road user charging (Wissmann 1997).

26. For example, it was established that all charges must be related to infrastructure building and maintenance costs (Directive 93/89/EEC, OJ L 279, 12 November 1993, p. 32, Art. 7h), which would, at least for the time being, exclude calculations designed to internalize (disputed) external costs and politically motivated use of fiscal instruments to discourage the use of road transport with respect to other transport modes. On the basis of this disposition, Austria was contested by both the other member states and the European Commission because it raised its tolls for Alpine transit in 1997.

27. Compared to other modes of transport, the railways are tightly coupled systems requiring a high degree of vertical coordination among infrastructure, traffic control, and services and between different services (Baumgartner 1993: 36–38). This is why railway policy cannot distinguish easily between passenger and freight transport. The following discussion of rail freight therefore includes aspects of passenger transport as well.

28. The EC's early railway policy may be summarized by three regulations concerning railways that date back to 1969 and 1970. Regulation 1191/69/EEC had the objective of reducing public-service obligations of railways to improve the situation of the railways in intermodal competition. Regulation 1192/69/EEC was an attempt to render the financial relations of the state to the railways more transparent by making compensation payments for social-service obligations imposed by the state mandatory and by prohibiting other types of financial aids that would distort intermodal competition. The circumstances under which state aids may be granted is specified in Regulation 1107/70/EEC. Other regulations

regarding intermodal competition were more programmatic in character (Schmuck 1992: 41).

29. The political viability of the new railway policy is enhanced in two ways: national railways will find expanding more attractive than downsizing, and resistance on environmental grounds is much more difficult, because rail is environmentally friendlier than road transport.

30. This does not mean that member-state discretion in implementation is negligible; on the contrary, Directive 91/440/EEC explicitly calls upon the member states to adopt the legislation that in their opinion is needed to implement the directive (OJ L 237, 24 August 1991, p. 28).

31. In principle, the commission's policy is to expose rather than protect railways from intermodal competition. In a proposal to the Council the commission proposed to abolish the possibility for member states to deny access for international bus transport of passengers on the grounds that it would seriously affect a comparable rail service (CEC 1996b: 15, n. 7)

32. At the present stage of research it is an open question as to whether the railways would be able to survive on a level playing field in intermodal competition. First of all, infrastructure pricing is a problem. External costs are difficult to calculate objectively for both rail and road, and for railways even internal costs seem to be a hard task for transport economists (Baumgartner 1993: 43f.). But even if the presumptions of the pricing models are not contested and the prices for services could be estimated, uncertainty about the determinants of the choice of transport users would prevent any prediction of the possible future share of rail in the transport market.

33. Cf. Directives 91/440/EEC, 95/18/EC, and 95/19/EC.

34. The capacity of an infrastructure depends on, for example, the technical characteristics of the track and the trains using them, the mix of faster passenger and slower freight trains, the free intervals needed for maintenance, and the capacity of the train stations.

35. A list of all obstacles to a complete integration of national railway systems in terms of interoperability is provided by Baumgartner (1993: 38ff.).

36. See, for example, Hylen (1997: 121) for the view that the problems of the European railway reform are often exaggerated.

37. The most important legal provision is Directive 91/440/EEC.

38. The exemption from state aids of the railways granted by Regulation 1107/70/EEC has been abolished, and the obligation of financial normalization has been introduced by Directive 91/440/EEC.

39. Directive 91/440/EEC "has created the right of access for *groupings* of railway enterprises to operate *international* services between the Member states *where the constituent enterprises are established* and the right of enterprises offering *international combined transport* to operate throughout the Community" (CEC 1996b: 14, italics added).

40. Directives 95/18/EC and 95/19/EC.

41. Cf. COM (95) 337 final.

42. Cf. COM (97) 34 final.

43. Cf. COM (97) 242 final.

44. Cf. COM (95) 337 final, pp. 21–23.

45. The following description of the decision-making history that led to Directive 91/440/EEC and thus to the start of the new railway policy is based on Schmuck (1992: 41f.).

46. Admittedly, a 1984 commission proposal already contained a provision about the separation of infrastructure and operation (Schmuck 1992). However, it seems fair to set the start of the decision process at the beginning of 1990, because the 1984 proposal did not yet include the idea of a liberalization of access rights to create intramodal competition. Therefore, the 1984 proposal may still be seen as part of the traditional EC approach to the railways. This is also the view of the commission railway policymakers (interview commission, 20 March 1997).

47. Moreover, in the view of the commission officials responsible for railway policy, the decision-making process is characterized by a low level of conflict (interview commission, 20 March 1997).

48. Interview Community of European Railways, April 1996.

49. See Kiriazidis 1994; interview commission, 20 March 1997; *Agence Europe* 1991a, 7.

50. Interview commission, 24 March 1997; interview European Freight and Logistics Leaders Club, 18 March 1997.

51. The risk of isolation may be illustrated by the fact that the positive opinion of the CER about the latest railway policy initiatives of the commission is only opposed by France. This is more remarkable in light of the fact that the CER usually does not launch an initiative if there is disagreement among its members (interview CER, 17 April 1996).

52. Since 1988, the commission justified its liberalization directive with Article 90 of the EC Treaty, thus implying that certain public monopolies infringe the EC treaty. A few months before the Council of Ministers' decision to adopt the railway reform, the ECJ confirmed the commission strategy (Taylor 1994: 322–26). The threat of Article 90 liberalization, however, did not play a role in the decision to adopt the new railway policy, the reason being that the support of the member states on which the effective use of this instrument depends was minimal (S. Schmidt 1998).

53. In a letter to the commission the French railways, for example, expressed their disagreement only with the liberalization aspect of Directive 91/440/EEC (*Agence Europe* 1991a, 10).

54. The first far-reaching commission proposal only dates back to the end of the 1980s (interview commission, 20 March 1997, Rees; interview commission, 29 March 1997, Wilson), before which time rail policy had been very modest indeed. This is unlike the case of road haulage, where the way to a CTP that was finally successful in the beginning of the 1990s had been promoted by the commission since the beginning of the 1970s.

55. The earliest attempts to introduce competition in the railway sector date back only to 1988 in the case of Sweden (Hylen 1997: 98–100) and 1994 in the case of Britain (Nash 1997: 58–62).

56. The term *voluntarism* echoes the analysis of the European social policy by Streeck (1995). According to this analysis the new type of social policy developing within the EU heavily relies on nonbinding proposals as opposed to the traditional compulsory social policy of the European nation states. The usage of the term *voluntarism* is less radical here, since we do not want to characterize the whole transport policy as "neovoluntarist." Obviously this would not be correct, since in this area legally binding decisions make up the bulk of the decision making. In transport, the distinction between compulsory and volun-

tarist policy is less clear cut. There is a voluntaristic *tendency*, since the scope of the binding obligations is limited.

57. This has been stressed forcefully by three ECJ decisions that confirmed the compatibility of national tariff systems with the EC rules.

58. This is not to say that the pressure to adapt national legislation can be derived directly from the actual development of the markets as measured by price levels, number of national and foreign operators, and so on. The way economic developments will gain political salience is of course influenced by a great variety of other factors as well. However, for the argument made here to be valid it is not necessary that economic pressures are measured exactly; it suffices that they are interpreted by some actors as being important, which usually presupposes that at least some pressure is actually felt or is a realistic possibility.

# 3

# Reforming Transport Policy in Britain: Concurrence with Europe but Separate Development

*Christoph Knill*

After a long period of stagnation, the early 1990s mark a watershed for the future of a common European transport policy in the subsectors of road haulage and railways, with the enactment of directives to promote a more liberal regulatory regime. In both sectors the requirements for institutional adaptation of existing national regulations appear limited, but the impact of supranational activities should not be underestimated. On the one hand, such activities indicate key steps that will be followed by institutionally more demanding measures. On the other hand, both the economic perception of, and ideological reaction to, European activities at the national level seem to have significantly changed the broader regulatory context in some member states, leading to national reforms going partly beyond legal European requirements (as demonstrated in the cases of the Netherlands and Germany), or provoking reactions of rejection (as was the case in Italian road haulage policy). In other words, transport policy in most of the member states under study can no longer be explained without any reference to European developments.

This statement, however, does not apply to the particular case of Britain, where national and European developments appear to be relatively unconnected and independent of one another. In both road haulage and rail, fundamental reforms took place that, although concurrent with European policies, were the result of separate, purely national developments. This lack of connection is not surprising, given the time lapse between British (1968) and European (1993) road haulage liberalization. Much more striking, however, is the case of the railways, where British reforms occurred even *after* corresponding European activities.

How can we explain the emergence of concurrent, but separate, regulatory forms in British and European transport policy? Two aspects are of particular relevance in this respect: the liberal Anglo-Saxon approach dominant in British transport policy is in line with the regulatory philosophy that became dominant in European Union (EU) transport policy during the 1980s; and the high reform capacity within the British political system that allows for the comparatively fast and far-reaching adaptation of regulatory strategies in light of past experiences. The high reform capacity can mainly be traced to the low number of institutional veto points in the British political system. In this way, opposing actors have limited opportunities to block or reduce the scope and scale of governmental reform proposals. Hence, regulatory reforms in both cases under study were basically shaped by learning from national experience. That is, past strategies were revised in light of their success or failure at achieving an efficient provision of services, rather than reflecting the result of political compromises and package solutions.

The combination of these two explanatory factors in British road haulage and railway policy implied that the reforms originated in, and were shaped by, purely national developments. Although these developments—as a result of the liberal regulatory approach—were concurrent with EU policies, they were not linked to or influenced by European provisions and went beyond the latter. This does not mean, however, that the developments in both cases followed the same rationale, allowing for the definition of an overall logic or trajectory in British transport policy. Such a conclusion would be misleading, since both cases, although belonging to the same policy field, are not interlinked by a coherent policy-specific concept, but reflect completely separate and independent areas.

Moreover, it should be emphasized that the missing connectedness of British and European policy developments may change when the focus of European policy is directed toward aspects that are in potential conflict with the traditional British approach, as, for example, in the recent striving toward a more integrated approach to transport policy at the European level. As will be shown in the case of road haulage, this led to a parallelism of European and national developments with respect to infrastructure provision and finance. A further impetus for mutual enforcement of national and European policies may be expected from the change of government in Britain, since the Labour Party, which has been in office since May 1997, is strongly committed to a more integrated approach to transport policy.

## ROAD HAULAGE POLICY IN BRITAIN: CONFIRMATION BY EUROPE AND PARALLEL AGENDAS

The EU legislation to liberalize road transport introduced in 1993 was not new for the British. Long before the catchwords *liberalization* and *deregulation* had entered the political discourse, British policy was oriented toward free markets in order to realize an efficient transport system. Given the experience of previous regulatory approaches and the high national reform capacity, steps to liberalize the British transport market had already been taken at the end of the 1960s. Interestingly, the reform was enacted by a Labour government, an aspect which—in stark contrast to the case of the railways—underlines that regulatory change did not occur in the context of a dominant-party political ideology, but was an attempt to overcome regulatory deficits emerging from previous approaches.

Hence, for many member states European liberalization implied substantive pressure to adapt, whereas for the British it meant a *confirmation* of their long-established policy. It comes, then, as no surprise that the dominant problem-solving philosophy, the related instruments, and established patterns and structures of interest intermediation found in Britain have not been significantly challenged by EU activities.

Although EU transport policy in Britain mainly contributed to institutional continuity rather than institutional reform, this does not mean that the effects of European developments remain invisible in British road haulage policy. Most of these effects, however, are incremental adaptations to the setting of policy instruments without changing their basic characteristics, that is, so-called first-order changes (Hall 1993). There is, however, one exception to the general picture that may involve changes in policy instruments: the current discussion on the introduction of road pricing, which is closely linked to the debate on infrastructure policy and the external costs of transport. Interestingly, in this context we can observe a *parallelism* of national and European influences.

How can we explain the distinctive effects of EU policy on the British regulatory approach? This question is answered in two steps. First, we examine British policy to regulate the haulage market in more detail. Second, on the basis of these findings we attempt to understand continuity and change in national road haulage policy in the European context.

## The National Regulatory Context

The regulatory approach pursued in British road haulage policy reflects the liberal Anglo-Saxon tradition—the achievement of policy goals is left to market forces with state intervention playing a minor role (Button 1993b). This philosophy is apparent with respect to both policy instruments and administrative interest intermediation.

### The Regulatory Philosophy

The dominant regulatory philosophy in British road haulage policy—that is, "the overwhelming framework of ideas and perceptions related to particular policy problems" (Hall 1993)—places the main emphasis of state activity on the generation and maintenance of the regulatory framework for free and unhindered market competition. Priority is placed on maximizing the internal efficiency of the transport system via the market rather than by the state. "In the UK, public policy is driven by the notion that the market and economic activity are exogenous to, and prior to, the state" (Dobbin 1993: 7). The British concept is therefore more "radical" than the approach currently pursued in, for example, the Netherlands, where market liberalization and parallel state activities to enhance international competitiveness are not perceived as contradictory philosophies (see Lehmkuhl in this volume). This may be because, in the British view, transport is conceived of as a pure service "for which the primary objective of policy is simply to meet demand at the lowest possible cost" (Button 1993: 154). By contrast, the macro-economic effects of the transport system—that is, regional, social or environmental objectives—are considered less important than microeconomic efficiency (Gwilliam 1979).

However, the regulatory philosophy dominant in British transport policy shows far-reaching variations over time. A glance at developments since the 1930s reveals regulatory variations of every conceivable nature, ranging from extreme versions of nationalization and complete liberalization, to mixtures of state and market coordination.

In 1933, the Road and Rail Traffic Act introduced far-reaching regulatory restrictions to market access for hire-and-reward hauliers. On the one hand, quantitative restrictions were designed to protect the railways from losing further market shares in freight transport. On the other hand, they were intended to resolve the problem of ruinous competition within the road haulage sector (Button and Pearman 1982: 18). The Labour government's ambitious plans for the creation of an integrated and coordinated transport system brought about a further increase of state intervention, and in 1947 the major part of the transport sector—railways, road haulage, public transport, and waterways (including docks and ports)—were nationalized (Christopher 1976: 192). When the Conservatives came to power in 1953 this led once more to changes in British transport policy. The Conservatives felt that the state coordination of the transport market was inflexible and inefficient and argued that the only possible solution to this problem was via "co-ordination through the interplay of market forces" (Christopher 1976). In reprivatizing the road haulage sector, the Conservatives fell back upon the regulatory concept in place before the 1947 nationalization. The new approach, however, was more liberal compared with the old practice, as it made the question of market access more dependent on the interests of the freight forwarders, and not—as in the 1933 act—on the consent of hauliers operating in the market. The Transport Act of 1968, often referred to as a "watershed in British transport history" (Button 1974: 26), finally instituted an almost complete liberalization of the road haulage market. "The 1968 Act was liberal in the sense that it introduced a framework of legislation and licensing to provide a basis for 'fair' competition, leaving the actual co-ordination of modes . . . to market forces." (Button 1974: 27; see also Cooper 1991: 86). Since that time, quantitative restrictions have been abolished and access to the British road haulage market has been solely dependent upon individual qualitative conditions.

It is interesting to note that the 1968 liberalization was then perceived less as *deregulation* than as another form of *regulation*. The policy change, introduced by a Labour government following the proposals of a Parliamentary Commission (Geddes Committee),[1] was based on experience with previous approaches that had in many respects brought about unwanted results (Button and Chow 1983: 242). In this way, a regulatory change in road haulage policy, largely consistent with the ideological ideas of the Conservative Party in government since 1979, was put in place and set the stage for future liberalizations in transport policy. The Transport Act of 1985 introduced the privatization and deregulation of public transport (White 1995: 200). The most recent example is the privatization of British Rail. A rolling back of the state, however, is visible not only with respect to the regulation of different transport modes, but also in the field of infrastructure policy (Jones 1993; Burnham, Glaister, and Travers 1994).

*Regulatory Instruments*

The liberal British approach is expressed in the choice of policy instruments, which make access to markets solely dependent on individual qualitative conditions. With respect to market operations, government's influence on transport prices is indirect via the imposition and fixing of taxes.

Referring to the regulation of *market access*, the Transport Act of 1968 introduced two significant innovations to the previous licensing system. First, the system of quantitative restrictions was abandoned in favor of a qualitative licensing procedure. Second, the licensing conditions for own-account and public-account operations were broadly adjusted. This adjustment, however, was modified by European legislation in 1974 (further amended in 1989 and 1997),[2] which redefined qualitative licensing conditions for private hauliers. Therefore, two license types can be distinguished in Britain: the restricted operator's license for own-account operations, and the standard operator's license for private haulage.[3] Generally, an applicant for a standard license must satisfy three conditions. He or she must have proof of professional competence, that is, the applicant or one of his or her employees must hold a certificate of professional competence (CPC); be of good repute, in that the applicant cannot be accused of any serious legal offenses; and have sufficient financial standing to maintain an operational center and run a business, which means that the applicants must deposit a certain amount of money depending on the number and maximum weight of their vehicles (Bayliss 1987: 10). The decision on whether or not an applicant meets the qualitative criteria lies with the regional licensing authority, the Traffic Commissioner.[4] Several actors are legally entitled to object to the granting of a license, but the Traffic Commissioner decides independently after having considered all arguments raised by objectors.[5]

With respect to *market operation*, British hauliers are subject to a vehicle excise duty and a fuel duty. Since 1994, the fuel duty is annually increased by 5 percent.[6] As explained below, the taxation of road transport is currently subject to reform discussions in the context of the potential introduction of road pricing schemes.

## Interest Intermediation

Both the dominant liberal philosophy and the related policy instruments have implications for the patterns of interest intermediation. These implications can be observed in all aspects related to the interaction of public and private actors: the structure and organization of the state, the structure and organization of interest associations, and typical patterns of interaction between public and private actors with respect to policy formulation and implementation.

*State Structure and Organization.* The overall responsibility for the formulation and implementation of British transport policy lies with the Department of the Environment, Transport, and the Regions (DETR), established by the Labour Party after its takeover in 1997 by merging the formerly separated Departments of Transport (DoT) and the Environment (DoE).[7] Another important actor in transport policy is the Treasury, which is responsible for setting tax rates and charges. Thus, the DoT has no direct influence over the rates of vehicle excise and fuel duties. This structuring can largely be traced to the general absence of direct earmarking of public revenues in Britain, that is, "the allocation of tax received from one group of taxpayers to expenditure benefiting the same group" (Truelove 1992: 5).

The licensing authorities, the Traffic Commissioners, enjoy independent status as separate statutory bodies appointed by the secretary of state. They carry out their tasks independently of the DoT, bear sole responsibility for their decisions, and do not act on behalf of the department.[8] This particular institutional arrangement must be understood against the background of the general regulatory approach. State intervention in market coordination is limited to controlling qualitative aspects of licensing, hence there is no need for a huge and powerful implementation authority. Instead, it makes sense to leave this task to an independent tribunal-like body that can base its decisions on information provided by the different statutory bodies and representors.

*Key Societal Actors and Their Interest Positions.* The dominant problem-solving philosophy and related policy instruments have an important impact on the structure and interest positions of relevant societal actors. Thus, the fact that the state is reluctant to intervene in the transport market avoids organizational fragmentation of the relevant interest associations. Since the market is the dominant mode of coordination and the state only defines the broad regulatory framework to guarantee unhindered competition, there is no particular need for a fragmented, specialized organization of private interests to demand specific forms of state regulation advantageous to them. By contrast, detailed state intervention via price controls, as in Italy, favors a fragmented structure of interest associations, because pure market competition, as pursued in Britain, is transposed into an "influencing-the-bureaucracy" competition, implying specialization and fragmentation of transport interests with respect to differing market positions.

Two organizations appear to play a key role in the regulation of the road haulage market: the Road Haulage Association (RHA) and the Freight Transport Association (FTA). Although the Confederation of British Industry (CBI) should also be taken into account in this context, it generally remains in the background and only intervenes more actively when key issues concerning industry as a whole are at stake. Environmental organizations have only had sporadic success in exerting influence over haulage market regulation, namely when the issues at stake allow them to mobilize broad public support. This holds, for example, for the question of increasing maximum weights for heavy goods vehicles. In relation to infrastructure provision, however, these groups have been relatively successful in gaining access to the political–administrative system.[9]

The two transport associations, the FTA and RHA, differ in their resources and membership. While the RHA represents private hauliers, FTA members are mainly own-account operators and shippers, although some bigger private haulage companies have joined the FTA in recent years.[10] The FTA therefore encompasses a broader industrial spectrum (ranging from chemical industries to supermarkets) and represents both the supply and demand sides of transport services. Moreover, in contrast to the RHA, it sees itself as a "multimode organization," with interests in both road and rail transport. Nevertheless, the FTA concentrates its activities on road transport as the dominant mode. Most of its resources are generated by the provision of services for its members, including training in management or the transport of dangerous goods, legal assistance, engineering, and vehicle inspection. These selective incentives (Olson 1965) have enabled the FTA to achieve significant increases in membership and resources with about 350 employees and an office in Brussels.[11] In addition to its membership in international and European associations,[12] the FTA increasingly seeks to influence European policies on its own.[13] In contrast, the RHA, mainly representing the smaller haulage companies, has more limited resources and primarily focuses its activities on the national level.

Although the RHA and FTA represent different memberships, their interests coincide to a large extent with respect to European and British transport policy. This correspondence, however, is not based on identical "rationalities." With its broad membership structure, the FTA more or less represents the interests of British industry as a whole. The FTA's main concern, therefore, is to promote the international competitiveness of the industry by reducing transport costs. It is this broad industrial perspective that makes the objectives of the FTA and the CBI almost congruent.[14] The RHA, on the other hand, is largely concerned with the position of private hauliers in relation to international and intermodal competition.

Against this background, the two associations share similar interests when it comes to issues of market operation, including such aspects as the improvement of road infrastructure, the reduction of tax rates, or the raising of maximum vehicle weights.[15] However, RHA and FTA hold different positions when it comes to the question of market access. Given its heterogeneous membership, the FTA pushes for a further relaxation of financial licensing conditions in order to enhance the competitiveness in the haulage market and to reduce transport costs.[16] In contrast, the RHA is generally concerned with maintaining the status quo, that is, by making market access for new hauliers more difficult by stricter criteria on financial standing.[17]

*Patterns of Interaction between Public and Private Actors.* The patterns of interaction between public and private actors in British road haulage policy are characterized by relatively consensual and pragmatic relationships. These patterns cannot be understood in light of the British state tradition alone, but must also be interpreted in the context of sector-specific factors. Thus, the British understanding of the state—whereby public activity occurs not as a result of intentional government action, but emerges from competition among social groups bringing their interests to bear on the political process—implies the participation of private actors in the formulation and implementation of policy (Dyson 1980: 43; Badie and Birnbaum 1983: 121). Although detailed operating procedures vary by problem, there is an overall preference for consultative and negotiatory practices (Jordan and Richardson 1982).

The practices in road haulage not only reflect this general picture, but are favored by the dominant sectoral regulatory philosophy and policy instruments. The fact that the state only regulates the qualitative criteria for market access means that informal and pragmatic relationships between administrative and societal actors carry no particular risk of regulatory capture, since existing regulations present few targets for private actors to address in order to obtain more favorable market conditions.

Consensual interactions between administrative and societal actors are apparent both in the close formal and informal links between the DoT and the transport associations, and in the interactions between these and the licensing authorities. Although the licensing authorities carry out a role independent of state or societal influences, this independence does not exclude cooperative and consensual relations with the transport associations. A far-reaching exchange of information takes place on both formal and informal levels.[18] This pattern of interaction by no means implies that the transport associations always get what they want. Their objections to transport licenses are often rejected by the Traffic Commissioner, who generally sticks to his independent role as broker between different private and public interests and therefore sets great store by not getting into a "cozy" or "chummy" relationship with one of the parties.[19] An important factor in ensuring the independent role of the licensing authorities is the relative transparency and openness of the licensing procedure. All license applications must be published in the local press, and the public participates in the licensing process directly, by belonging to a group of representers, or indirectly via the participation of local councils.

To sum up, the British approach to the regulation of the haulage market reflects a liberal philosophy conceiving of transport as a pure service that can be provided most efficiently by the market. Accordingly, policy instruments are characterized by a low degree of state intervention. Market access is controlled solely with respect to individual qualitative criteria, and only market processes are influenced indirectly by fuel and vehicle excise duties. In line with the market approach, licensing is in the hands of an independent statutory body rather than a hierarchical state authority. Furthermore, there is a consensual relationship between relevant public and private actors, which is facilitated by the integrated structure of British transport associations.

It is interesting to note that, although starting in the early 1930s with nearly the same regulatory approach as all other countries under investigation, the British development was characterized by several far-reaching reforms, while policies in the other four countries developed along distinctive institutional paths. At least three institutional factors may explain these differences.

First, the Westminster model allows for a greater capacity to change policies than do other democratic systems. This is mainly due to the strong party governments and the consequent concentration of power in the executive (Dunleavy 1993: 3). It is therefore, *ceteres paribus*, easier to draw lessons from experience, that is, to reverse past policies that failed (Olsen and Peters 1994: 16). On the other hand, one could argue that this dominance of the center restricts learning capacities, since the channels for other perceptions and expert knowledge are more limited than in, for example, federal systems with a multitude of political arenas (see Czada 1993: 93). To some extent, this aspect has its functional equivalent in the important role of royal commissions and parliamentary committees which enjoy an influential role in British policymaking (Knill 1995: 300). These commissions reflect a broad spectrum of different experts and representatives of society and constitute important filters and channels for the generation of policy ideas (Sabatier 1993; Hall 1993). Second, the fact that British civil servants change their area of responsibility every three years reduces the problem of regulatory capture by a specific clientele (van Waarden 1995: 357). The opportunities for interest associations to influence the bureaucracy in order to prevent policy changes are therefore more limited than in administrative systems where civil servants remain in the same position throughout their careers. Third, one must remember that the British approach to the regulation of the haulage market was—apart from the short period of nationalization—less interventionist than its Italian or German counterparts. Thus, Britain introduced quantitative restrictions for *market access*, whereas the other countries additionally intervened in the *market process* by defining minimum or maximum prices. Such an approach implied a much more detailed regulatory framework (i.e., different prices for the transport of different goods, decisions on price adaptations, and so on) and therefore led to a stronger institutional entrenchment that made reforms more difficult to achieve (see Krasner 1988: 74). On the basis of these findings we can now turn to investigating British transport policy within the European context.

## British Road Haulage Policy within the European Context

It was only in the 1980s that the project to establish a liberal transport market throughout the European Community (EC) made significant progress, culminating in the 1993 directive on the liberalization of cabotage, which abolished quantitative limits for access to national markets from 1998 onward. The 1993 compromise implies both liberalization and the harmonization of market regulations. Thus, minimum rates for fuel and vehicle excise duties are established, and member states are free to impose road charges according to the principle of territoriality. Other measures to harmonize market conditions enacted at the EU level were related to qualitative licensing conditions and technical and social regulations.

Whereas the main focus of EC activities was on the creation of a liberal haulage market, with the harmonization of market conditions as a secondary objective, other problems related to transport (i.e., external effects and infrastructure provision) fell outside the EC approach to transport policy. Recently, however, this orientation has changed somewhat. This is particularly illustrated by the commission's green paper on the external costs of transport initiated by the transport commissioner, Neil Kinnock (CEC 1996a).

If one bears in mind the characteristics of the British regulatory approach outlined above, EU legislation appears to be in line with the British concept. It is not surprising, therefore, that Britain clearly supported European liberalization policy since joining the EU in 1973, because EU legislation more or less confirmed the British concept while requiring only incremental changes with respect to the setting of policy instruments. More far-reaching changes may only emerge where parallel developments on a national and supranational level can be observed.

### The British Role at the European Level: Supporting Market Liberalization

Since joining the EU in 1973, Britain has supported the liberalization of the European haulage market. First, given Britain's specific experience with different forms of market regulation, the evaluation of the more interventionist style of regulation pursued prior to 1968 showed that quantitative licensing restrictions had neither succeeded in protecting the railways nor in achieving satisfactory results with respect to road safety. To date, experience with the liberal approach has not led to the significant market distortions anticipated by some economists, while at the same time it has managed to produce better results for road safety, as applicants must now demonstrate their qualitative ability to run a business (Bayliss 1987: 9ff.). Second, British support for European liberalization was strengthened on ideological grounds when the Conservative Party came to power in 1979 and the consequent "rolling back of the state," with privatization, deregulation, and liberalization became the cornerstones of public policy. Liberalization of the European transport market was therefore pursued, not only in the light of economic competitiveness and policy experience, but also as an ideological goal in itself.

We should note, however, that Britain is more a supporter than a proponent or initiator of liberalization of the EU haulage market, mainly because European liberalization may be expected to produce relatively minor effects on the British market. Due to its geographical position as an island, the British's involvement in international traffic is much lower than for typical transit countries such as Germany. With about 7 percent of the European market share, the proportion of British hauliers operating on the international market is comparatively small, and there is a relatively minor presence of foreign hauliers operating in Britain (CEC 1994). The economic interests linked to EU market liberalization in Britain have therefore not been perceived as being as essential, for instance, in the Netherlands, where road hauliers have traditionally been oriented toward the European market.[20]

### The Effects of European Liberalization: Confirming the British Approach

Against the background of a liberalized British haulage market in place long before European liberalization was introduced in this sector in 1993, it is no surprise that the changes occurring at the EC level generally confirmed the regulatory approach followed in Britain, while supranational activities to harmonize market conditions only brought about minor changes to British regulations. A look at the different dimensions of state activity under study indicates the obvious nature of this statement.

The existing regulatory philosophy in Britain, with its emphasis on the internal efficiency of the transport system, was not forced by any adaptive pressures stemming from European regulatory activities. The same holds true for policy instruments. The qualitative licensing criteria introduced in Britain in 1968 were by and large confirmed by subsequent EU legislation, which only required minor adaptations concerning the setting of policy instruments.

The first area where minor adaptations were necessary relates to the regulation of market access, namely qualitative licensing criteria. In this area, EU legislation enacted in 1997 requires a certain strengthening of the British arrangements concerning financial standing, good repute, and professional competence of license applicants. Hence, EU legislation implies a slightly more restrictive regulation of market access. Moreover, it allows member states to test the professional competence of those national hauliers who acquired their license in another country. This specific arrangement was basically advocated by the Dutch, who complained that many Dutch hauliers had avoided the strict national competence examinations by acquiring the—presumably, easier to obtain—British Certificate of

Professional Competence (CPC) license.[21] Initially, the British government was not in favor of the directive, arguing that restricting market access would lead to a reduction in competition. Given the limited implications for the British, however, it finally accepted the proposal.[22]

Second, EU legislation brought about changes with respect to maximum vehicle weights. As a result of European legislation, maximum weights for trucks should be increased from 38 to 40 tonnes in 1999. This weight already applied in all other member states since 1993, but Britain had put through an exceptional ruling in the Council of Ministers negotiations, claiming that more time was needed to carry out improvements to bridges in order to carry higher lorry weights prior to implementation. A more important reason, however, lies in the fact that the government gave way to strong environmental pressure against a background of high costs for the necessary improvements to the road network.[23]

A third area where changes have not yet occurred, but are heavily demanded by the British transport associations, concerns reductions in vehicle and fuel excise duties. The demands of the hauliers stem from the harmonization provisions of the 1993 directive on the liberalization of cabotage. On the basis of these provisions, Germany and the Netherlands have introduced road charging (together with Belgium, Denmark, and Luxembourg), at the same time significantly reducing tax rates for national hauliers in order to compensate them for the additional costs caused by road charging. Since the German tax reductions, and given that Britain has so far refrained from introducing road charging, Britain now has the highest tax rates in the EU. Furthermore, British hauliers, in the same way as their continental counterparts, are now faced with territorial road charging in most continental countries, but are excluded from compensating tax reductions and therefore complain about the competitive disadvantages caused by these developments.[24] The fact that the British government has so far refused to grant national hauliers comparable tax reductions may be traced to the relatively small number of haulage companies operating internationally.[25] Furthermore, the problem may prove to be short-term given the current debate over the introduction of road pricing schemes comparable to the "Eurovignette."[26]

With no important changes in the existing regulatory approach, one cannot expect significant departures from the patterns of interest intermediation at work so far. While the consensual relationships between transport associations and public administration thus remained unaffected, we can observe two other developments brought about by EC activities in road haulage regulation: a remarkably strong orientation of the transport associations toward European policymaking; and a slightly increasing conflict of interests between the two transport associations.

In particular, the FTA, the larger and more influential of the British transport associations, has striven in recent years to influence the formulation of EU transport policy.[27] Besides its high financial and personnel resources, an important factor facilitating the FTA's active role at the European level is its particular membership structure, which encompasses both shippers and hauliers. This allows for an effective coordination of different industrial interests and for a more effective lobbying activity in Brussels. As shown below, the parallel policy developments at the national and European levels with respect to the external costs of transport and infrastructure provision constitute a further factor explaining the active role of the FTA in supranational policymaking.

Second, European liberalization has to some extent emphasized the different interest positions of the two associations. Thus, the FTA mainly perceives the liberalized European market as an opportunity to reduce transport costs by increased competitiveness. On the other hand, although generally supporting market liberalization, the RHA, representing the smaller private haulage companies, is mainly interested in conserving the status quo by the imposition of stricter licensing criteria. Hence, the RHA strongly supported the corresponding European legislation, whereas the FTA saw it as a restriction of market competition. One should not, however, exaggerate the relevance of this minor polarization, since there is, in sharp contrast to the Italian case, still a broad spectrum of congruent interests.

## *The Parallelism of National and European Developments*

While European legislation to liberalize the road haulage market confirmed the British approach and the harmonization of market conditions only meant incremental changes to the British approach, we can also identify a parallelism of national and supranational policy developments that may lead to more far-reaching changes. Thus, both at the national and the European level we can observe a growing concern for the external costs of transport and infrastructure provision.

At the national level, policy changes were initiated by the Conservative government during the early 1990s. Besides significantly cutting back the road-building program from 1994 onward and increasing efforts to provide infrastructure by private investment, the government announced the introduction of a 5 percent annual increase in fuel taxes and launched extensive studies on the introduction of road-pricing schemes (Jones 1993; CIT 1994).

These national developments may be understood in terms of a "holy alliance" of the Conservative government, environmental organizations, and expert commissions. On the one hand, the political influence of actors demanding a reorientation of British transport policy increased during the 1990s. Thus, environmental associations were increasingly able to rely on broad public support for cutting down heavy vehicle traffic and road-building projects.[28] Furthermore, many of the demands made by environmental associations concerning road building, a modal shift from road to rail, and the integration of external costs of transport were confirmed by reports from prestigious and influential scientific committees (Owens 1995). Most important in this respect are the reports by the Royal Commission on Environmental Pollution (RCEP)[29] and the Standing Advisory Committee on Trunk Road Assessment (SACTRA),[30] which were both published in 1994. In stating that the government has failed "to provide this country with an effective and environmentally sound transport policy" (RCEP 1994: 223), the RCEP in some respects proposed a radical departure from the policy followed to date in Britain. It argued for a 50 percent reduction in the road construction infrastructure program and the investment of the financial savings thus produced in rail infrastructure improvements to achieve a significant increase of freight transport by rail. Furthermore, the commission demanded a doubling of fuel prices by the year 2000 in order to cover the external costs of road transport (RCEP 1994: 246ff.). The report published by SACTRA significantly questioned the previous "predict-and-provide" strategy in national road-building programs, concluding that the building of new roads might actually generate new traffic rather than resolve existing problems of congestion (SACTRA 1994), a particularly salient criticism when one considers that SACTRA has historically been seen as closely allied with road interests (Page and Robinson 1995: 13).

The demands of these actors were partly in line with the objectives of the Conservative government to reduce public spending and to increase private-sector involvement in the provision of infrastructure. In this way, the Conservatives were able to use environmental demands and scientific knowledge as a resource to help legitimize a further rolling back of the state and a reduction of the budgetary deficit. However, the government made no attempt to realize the substantive demands made by these actors in terms of a modal shift from road to rail and the internalization of the external costs of transport. Instead, its objectives were basically to improve the budgetary situation by reducing public spending while simultaneously raising revenues through annual increases in fuel taxation.[31]

This situation, however, changed to some extent with the takeover by the Labour Party in May 1997. The Labour government is explicitly committed to an integrated transport policy directed at a better coordination of different transport services and the integration of other policies, such as environmental and regional policies. Besides the merging of the DoE and DoT to improve coordination between the transport and the environmental field, however, so far no substantive changes were announced. Moreover, there seem to be no significant changes concerning the Conservatives' policy on private financing of infrastructure (what is now referred to as "private–public partnerships") and the introduction of road pricing schemes in the near future.[32]

The initiatives of the Conservative and Labour governments have so far provoked strong opposition from industry. Thus, industrial associations are critical of the budget cuts for road construction and demand long-term planning for the extension of the road infrastructure. The quality and density of the British road network, in the view of industry, is no longer in line with the growing demands created by traffic. The outcome, according to industry, is increasing competitive disadvantages with industries in other EU countries.[33] While clearly opposing the cuts in road investment, the industry would agree to the introduction of road pricing provided that the revenues gained were used exclusively to improve the road network.[34]

However, this objective runs counter to the fiscal interests of the Treasury, which refuses to accept any budgetary restrictions by this kind of ring fencing.[35] Industry therefore fears that the road pricing plans of government, such as an increase in fuel taxes, will only make transport services more expensive and thus lead to economic disadvantages, while offering no improvements with respect to transport efficiency and infrastructure.[36]

Against this background, the active role played by British transport associations with respect to European policymaking becomes more understandable. The discussion on the external costs of transport launched by the commission was seen as a chance to bypass—from the view of industry—the negative developments at the national level. Thus, the FTA in particular tried to influence the preparation of the green paper on external costs initiated by the transport commissioner, Neil Kinnock, at a very early stage. Here, the FTA had already built up close informal links with members of Kinnock's cabinet before their official appointment.[37] Interestingly, some crucial statements made in the green paper are in line with the demands made by British industry, that is, the purpose "not to increase the costs of transport" but to make transport more efficient, or the perception of infrastructure charging as being "crucial for mobilizing private capital for infrastructure construction" (CEC 1996a, i–iii).[38] To date, the FTA has been quite successful in using the new institutional opportunities emerging from the Europeanization of national policies to pursue its own interests. The influential role of the FTA at the supranational level was favored by the comparatively high level of resources it could invest in developing new policy solutions. Furthermore, the parallel developments taking place at the national level at an early stage directed the FTA's attention to problems of external costs and infrastructure provision. In a sense, the FTA therefore succeeded in playing a "trendsetter" role (Kohler-Koch 1996a: 218) at the European level.

Although no concrete policies or policy proposals have yet emerged from supranational activities, it seems likely that the parallel developments on the national and European levels in the near future will lead to the introduction of road pricing schemes in Britain. There is no way of knowing, however, whether the new instrument will be applied in a way that fits the demands of both industry and environmental organizations.

## Summary

As liberal market regulation was already in place in Britain long before supranational transport policy took shape, European liberalization was primarily a confirmation of the British approach. It is therefore not surprising that Britain, since joining the EU in 1973, has supported supranational initiatives in this respect.

This general picture does not mean, however, that apart from incremental changes no further reforms will occur in British road haulage policy. As we have seen, it is likely that instrumental changes in market regulation will occur in the near future, with the introduction of road pricing schemes. Interestingly, the discussions with respect to this instrument are shaped by parallel developments at the national and supranational levels that have emerged in the general context of infrastructure provision and the external costs generated by transport systems.

## THE PRIVATIZATION OF BRITISH RAIL: A NATIONAL REFORM WITHOUT EUROPE

The Railways Act of 1993 without a doubt marks a watershed in the history of British railways. It implies fundamental changes to the, until 1994, publicly owned industry. The reform of British Rail (BR) not only implies the transformation of a public-sector monopoly into private ownership (as was the case in many earlier privatizations of public utilities),[39] but also the introduction of different forms of competition, and the establishment of formal contractual regimes between the different actors involved (Gibb, Lowndes, and Charlton 1996: 36). Along with these different patterns of restructuring, a substantial organizational fragmentation of the formerly corporate body in both vertical and horizontal dimensions can be observed. Accordingly, the existing relationship between the state and nationalized industry was replaced by a regulatory framework, allowing for the control and supervision of private activities at arm's length by government.

Given that these changes appear to be in line with the European policy objectives defined in Directive 91/440, which contains the first, modest, steps toward a liberalization of the railway sector, one would assume that the British railway reform was significantly influenced and shaped by European requirements. A closer look at the factors responsible for the British reforms, however, reveals that the privatization of BR was a result of purely national developments and that European policy had no significant influence with respect to the origin and outcome of the British reform.

Railway reform in Britain may instead be understood in terms of the striving to apply a given national solution to a specific policy problem perceived. This process requires the analytical distinction of two explanatory steps. First, we must investigate the factors that shaped the reform. Thus, at the heart of the neoliberal philosophy of the Conservative government there was a standard solution to public-sector industries, namely, privatization.

Although the privatization of BR was always "whirling around" in Conservative heads, the specific problem of the railways, as a loss-making industry, inhibited the application of the standard Conservative solution. Privatization only became a feasible option when the concept was refined by learning from experience with other utility privatizations, public-sector reforms, and railway reorganizations.

Second, we have to explain the strategies providing the opportunities for government to carry out the reform despite significant opposition and a high degree of economic uncertainty. Before starting any explanation, however, the basic changes have to be assessed and described in more detail.

## Reforming the Railways: A Mixture of Different Recipes

The far-reaching reforms introduced with the Railways Act of 1993 can be illustrated along three dimensions: the organizational structure, the regulatory framework, and the patterns of finance and investment.

### Organizational Fragmentation and Privatization

The former structure of the publicly owned railway system was based on a single organizational entity. Under the British Railways Board (BRB), different tasks and functions extending from the provision and maintenance of infrastructure and rolling stock to freight and passenger operations were integrated into a single, hierarchically structured organization. Although internal reorganizations of BR implemented in 1992 established a virtual organizational separation into central services and five business sectors (InterCity, Network SouthEast, Regional Railways, Freight, and Parcels),[40] the different businesses remained integrated in a single corporation.[41]

The new system put in place a far-reaching vertical and horizontal fragmentation of the formerly integrated structure. With respect to the vertical dimension, the institutional separation of train and infrastructure operations was established. Thus, the whole infrastructure of BR was transferred to Railtrack. Railtrack is responsible for infrastructure provision and maintenance, the supply of access to tracks and stations, and the management of time-tabling, train planning, and signaling (Railtrack 1996).

There were several developments in horizontal separation. First, BR's train operating businesses were split into more than thirty different units. The three passenger businesses were broken up into twenty-five train operating companies (TOCs), and the freight and parcels businesses were separated into seven companies.[42] Second, European Passenger Services (EPS), which operates the Eurostar services through the Channel Tunnel in conjunction with the French and Belgian national railways, and Union Railways, which is planning the high-speed rail link to the Channel Tunnel, are now both independent companies separate from BR (Birginshaw 1994: 13). Third, passenger rolling stock was separated from the TOCs and divided up into three rolling stock leasing companies (ROSCOs). The ROSCOs took over all domestic passenger trains of BR and lease this stock to the TOCs. Fourth, a broad range of service companies was set up, including infrastructure and maintenance services, rolling stock heavy maintenance depots, marketing services, technical services, and training activities and establishments. (See figure 3.1.)

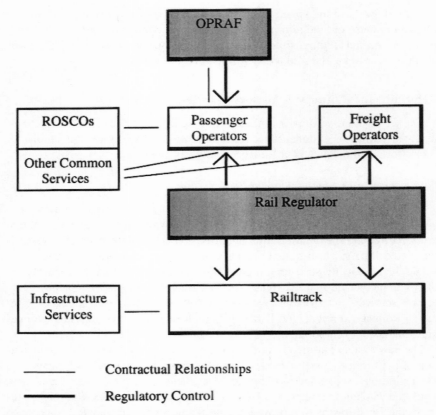

Contractual Relationships

Regulatory Control

**Figure 3.1.   The New Structure of Railways in Britian**

The organizational break-up of BR into separate businesses was followed by the transformation of these services into private-sector operations, completed in April 1997. Most of the business units (EPS, Union Railways, rolling stock, freight, service units) were sold off to private companies or management buyouts. The twenty-five passenger services were franchised to private companies. Railtrack, the only business not subject to horizontal separation, was privatized by stock-market flotation in May 1996. The residual BR that remained in the public sector no longer pursues any trading activities, and its functions are limited to the administration of property not subject to privatization and remaining tasks related to the documentation and processing of business sales.[43]

While previously different business units were linked by means of formal and informal intra-organizational coordination, the new structure implies a contractual matrix of horizontally and vertically separated companies, that is, intra-organizational coordination is replaced by formal contractual relationships between different units of the railway industry.[44] Train operators, for example, have to contract with Railtrack in order to obtain access to track. Contractual relations also exist between the TOCs and ROSCOs with respect to the leasing of rolling stock. Furthermore, both Railtrack and the ROSCOs contract out a great deal of maintenance and management services to the different service companies. Contractual relationships are also in place between the TOCs and the Office of Passenger Rail Franchising (OPRAF) with respect to the franchising of passenger operations. In order to encourage parties to enter into contracts, the contractual framework has taken on board the idea of so-called performance regimes, so that the contracts contain economic incentives for all actors involved, reinforced by a system of bonus and fine payments depending on the extent to which the contracts are honored.[45]

## The Regulatory Framework

Privatization does not imply that railways are operated without any further involvement on the part of the public authorities. As in earlier denationalizations, privatization is accompanied by the establishment of a regulatory framework that controls and oversees the operations of private actors. The role of the state is reduced to the regulation of private market activities and the subsidizing of unprofitable passenger services. This contrasts with the former characteristics of the state–railway relationship. As was the case for all nationalized industries, the interactions between the sponsoring department and the management board were based on a statutory framework that only vaguely defined the rights and responsibilities of the parties involved. Thus, the BRB, whose members were appointed by the (then) DoT, was subject to general guidance by the secretary of state but had an autonomous position with respect to day-to-day management. Despite this formal autonomy, however, BR management was faced with permanent government intervention. This was especially true for aspects of finance and investment and had significant consequences for BR's capability of long-term planning (Gwilliam 1979: 13; Pryke 1981; Kay and Thompson 1991: 25). The following section therefore takes a closer look at regulatory structures and instruments and the arrangements with respect to finance and investment governing the operations of the privatized railways.

*Regulatory Structure.* In most other British privatizations only one regulator was established, but in the case of the railways, regulatory functions are carried out by two regulatory bodies whose main duties and responsibilities are defined in the Railways Act: the Office of the Rail Regulator (ORR) and OPRAF. ORR mainly deals with aspects of competition and monopoly control, that is, the classical regulatory functions to control privatized industries. The establishment of OPRAF, on the other hand, may be traced to the franchising provisions. These reflect a peculiar characteristic of the railway privatization, that is, that not all TOCs are economically profitable, and some may therefore be subsidized, and OPRAF is responsible for allocating these subsidies. Both organizations have the status of so-called nonministerial government departments, but differ with respect to their degree of independence from government. Since OPRAF is allocating public money provided by the DoT, it is generally subject to guidance from the secretary of state. These instructions, however, allow ample room for maneuver in the day-to-day management of OPRAF. ORR, on the other hand, has operated completely independent of governmental control since 1997.[46]

OPRAF's principal responsibilities include negotiating and awarding passenger rail franchises on the basis of competitive tendering, and monitoring their performance. The primary objective of OPRAF is to obtain "value for money," that is, good quality of service at lowest possible cost (in the case of unprofitable services), and highest possible profit (in the case of profitable services).[47] ORR's main tasks are to consider the applications for operating licenses, to approve track access agreements and prices, and to protect consumer interests. While OPRAF's overriding objective is the reduction of subsidy payments, the regulator is primarily concerned with the promotion of competition.[48]

In addition to OPRAF and ORR, another body, the Association of Train Operating Companies (ATOC) was created to carry out the functions generated by the breakup of passenger services. Its tasks cover the regulation of through-ticketing, revenue sharing between different companies, and the provision of an over-all system of information. ATOC was already in place before the TOCs were franchised to private operators. It is interesting to note that on completion of the franchising process ATOC became a private association. It is therefore feasible that in the future, ATOC, in addition to its regulatory activities, will act as an interest association on behalf of its members.[49] In addition to these regulatory bodies, Her Majesty's Railway Inspectorate, part of the Health and Safety Executive (HSE), continues to supervise and regulate rail safety (DoT 1994).

*Regulatory Instruments.* The transformation of the railways in Britain introduced different degrees of competition for different business units. Infrastructure was transferred to a private monopoly, and competitive frameworks were established for train operations. Freight operations are characterized by competition *within the market*, whereas the passenger sector applies more limited forms of competition *for the market* and competition *by comparison*, so that the ways in which these businesses are subject to regulatory oversight differ to some extent.

Generally speaking, market access for both passenger and freight services requires operators to hold an operating license. Both granting and enforcement of licenses fall within competence of the ORR. For freight train operators the license requirement is the only restriction to market access (Birginshaw 1994: 14). However, despite the formal preconditions allowing for competition *within* the market, there are some practical restrictions to market access. First, in contrast to the passenger sector, rolling stock in the freight sector has not been transferred to the ROSCOs but has instead been allocated to the operating businesses. Market access therefore implies significant rolling stock investment for new entrants, which may potentially reduce competition between operators.[50] Second, although the government initially intended to avoid market concentration in the freight sector, it became obvious that, due to the competitive situation between road haulage and rail freight, the sell-off of different businesses to different bidders proved unrealistic. Hence, apart from Freightliner, all freight businesses were sold to the same company,[51] so as to enable rail operators to compete with road haulage.[52]

Turning to passenger operations, market access is handled more restrictively. Instead of competition within the market, passenger operators face competition *for the market* (Domberger 1989: 274).[53] Market access is restricted by a competitive bidding process for franchises, which grants the successful bidder a regional monopoly for a limited period.[54] Both the annual subsidy payments and the detailed service obligations to be met by the franchisee are specified in formal contracts, or "franchise agreements." Furthermore, the franchising process is characterized by another competitive element: competition *by comparison*. In dealing with different franchisees, OPRAF gains an understanding of the level of services generally achievable under given circumstances. Hence, OPRAF was able to significantly reduce its subsidy payments it agreed to in subsequent franchise agreements.[55]

The regulatory control of the privatized railways, however, is not limited to market access, but also deals with market operations. Thus, OPRAF monitors the performance of the franchisees in light of the franchise agreements. Furthermore, all market activities are subject to regulatory oversight by ORR. The main instrument of the regulator is the approval of access agreements between train operators and Railtrack. In this context the control of Railtrack's monopoly power is particularly important. Thus, the "span" within which Railtrack and train operators may negotiate on charges for track access is determined by the regulator in the light of the market developments and Railtrack's investment and performance. However, given that the "negotiation span" is reviewed every five years,[56] the regulator has limited opportunities for additional intervention in Railtrack's activities.[57]

*Finance and Investment.* In analyzing the changes in the railways' finances and investments we must distinguish between public subsidies for unprofitable passenger services, and investment in infrastructure and rolling stock. The need for public subsidies may be traced to the political decision that the railways should provide passenger services even on lines and in areas where demand is either insufficient or unprofitable. Despite recommendations contained in Committee reports (including the Beeching Report in 1963 and the Serpell Report in 1983) to trim down BR's passenger operations, the government rejected the option of passenger line closures (Button 1974: 41–42; Gwilliam and Mackie 1980: 46–47), a basic decision thar remained unchanged during the privatization process. In order to operate unprofitable passenger services, BR received a public service obligation grant (PSO) from the DoT, which was paid as a block grant, that is, a lump sum payment that did not specify the specific loss-making services to be financed (Gritten 1988: 8).

In order to finance investment in rolling stock and infrastructure, BR was allowed to borrow from the National Loans Fund up to a specified level defined by the overall external finance limit (EFL), which was set by government for every nationalized industry (Gwilliam 1979: 14). Since the EFL was negotiated on a year-by-year basis, BR faced high uncertainty and low flexibility with respect to long-term investment planning. This problem was aggravated by the existence of a so-called investment notification system, which required BR to ask for the DoT's approval of every single investment, although the money had already been allocated to BR in the annual budget.[58] Moreover, BR was not allowed to borrow from other sources, which again reduced its financial flexibility (Harman et al. 1995: 8). Finally, since public accounting requirements inhibited the consideration of long-term commercial merits generated by large-scale investment, BR's ability to legitimize higher investment rates was restricted (Gritten 1988: 8; Nash and Preston 1991).

The 1994 reform of BR ushered in significant changes with respect to finances and investments. Given the high degree of economic uncertainty involved, and the relatively recent implementation of the reform, any assessment of potential reform effects is difficult to make, but we can identify both positive and negative expectations for the future of the railways in Britain.

With respect to the franchising of passenger services, the objective of the Conservative government was to significantly reduce public subsidies in the long run. The assumption is that the competitive tendering for twenty-five separate units brings about a more efficient allocation of subsidies than the block grant system applied since 1974. Furthermore, the subsidy reduction over the franchising period is designed to provide significant incentives for cost reductions of the franchisees.[59] Some observers have voiced doubts as to the likelihood that the system will work in the way intended by government and presume that franchisees will strive for cost savings by reducing services. Given that the franchisees may influence only 20 percent of their costs whereas the other 80 percent are determined by charges for rolling stock and track access, there may be limited room for efficiency gains.[60]

The government is no longer involved in the financing of infrastructure and rolling stock investment. Capital is now provided by the private sector. In the reformer's view both the economic self-interest of the actors involved and the performance regime provide sufficient incentives for private investment. Thus, since Railtrack's income is more or less fixed by the charging provisions defined by ORR, the only way to raise income is to cut costs and to sell more pathways. The more and the better the tracks, the higher Railtrack's income.[61] Similarly, franchisees are expected to invest in rolling stock in order to improve service quality and thus increase income by attracting more passengers. The validity of these assumptions has, however, been questioned by opponents of the reform.

The first problem is the absence of legal provisions on the handover of assets by franchisees after the franchise period. It is assumed that no incentive exists for franchisees to maintain and refurbish their rolling stock.[62] Second, critics suggest that the average pricing of Railtrack is likely to lead to underinvestment. Thus, there is no incentive for operators to increase volume, since their is no reduction of marginal access charges for every additional unit transported. Instead, marginal cost reduction is legally prohibited to Railtrack, because charges would sink below Railtrack's "negotiation span" as defined by ORR.[63] Third, it is argued that there are important "economies of scope" stemming from a vertically integrated structure that would facilitate investment. These advantages are dismissed within a fragmented industry structure. The separation of infrastructure, operation, and rolling stock increases the transaction costs of coordination with respect to new investment, given the close technical interdependence between railway infrastructure and rolling stock (Preston 1996: 6; Gibb, Lowndes, and Charlton 1996: 49). Important transaction costs originate from the allocation of economic risks related to infrastructure investment between the actors involved. Thus, in every single case it must be clear exactly who pays for track upgrading, that is, Railtrack or the operator who wants new tracks to be built.[64]

## *The British Railway Reform: A Unique Experience*

In sum, the reform of BR is shaped by a unique mixture of elements, consisting of far-reaching vertical and horizontal fragmentation, the sell-off or franchising of the separated businesses to the private sector (including infrastructure), the introduction of different forms of competition, the establishment of a system of formal contractual relationships and incentive regimes, and the introduction of a complex regulatory framework including two regulatory bodies. The scale and scope of the reforms set in place with the Railways Act of 1993 go beyond any other privatization of nationalized industries in Britain, but also beyond any other railway reform in Europe. We need to emphasize not only the uniqueness of the reform, insofar as it was characterized by far-reaching institutional transformations, but also its experimental character, in that it was marked by a significant degree of uncertainty, that is, just how far the new structure would be able to provide sufficient incentives for investment and proper implementation of the franchise agreements. Given the unique and experimental character of the railway reform in Britain, several questions arise: What were the reasons for the reform, that is, where did the reform originate? How can we explain its specific content? And which factors allowed the government to put through such significant changes and to carry out this kind of experiment? The following sections address these questions in more detail.

## Explaining Britain's Railway Reform, or How to Apply a Given Solution to a Specific Problem

In pursuit of an answer to the questions raised above, the basic argument developed in this section is that the railway reform in Britain may be understood in terms of learning from experience how to apply a given solution to a specific problem. Both the perception of the problem and standard solutions were mainly defined within the neoliberal philosophy of the Conservative government, expressed both in the government's approach to industrial policy in general and transport policy in particular. Therefore, the question as to why BR was privatized appears easy to answer: BR was perceived as an inefficient, loss-making, and heavily subsidized public-sector industry, and privatization, as the standard solution to these problems, was at the core of the dominating neoliberal problem-solving philosophy.

Given the peculiarities of the railways, however, the coupling of solution and problem turned out to be relatively difficult. The privatization of BR only became a feasible option when the concept could be refined by learning from experience. The shaping of the reform therefore may be explained against the background of earlier railway reforms, other public utility privatizations, and administrative reform policies. A full explanation of British railway privatization furthermore requires an investigation of the factors affecting the government's learning capacity, that is, its ability to revise its policies in light of past experience. As detailed below, the British railway reform may be explained by purely national factors with supranational developments playing a relatively peripheral role.

## Coupling Problem and Solution

The dominant problem-solving philosophy in a policy sector may be conceived as a "framework of ideas and standards that specifies not only the goals of policy and the kind of instruments that may be used to attain them, but also the very nature of the problems that are meant to be addressing" (Hall 1993: 279). This definition implies that the dominant philosophy influences both the perceived problem and the conceived solutions (Dobbin 1994: 20–21). In the case of BR, however, the linkage of conceivable solution and perceived problem proved rather difficult. The difficulty was not to change a stable "belief system" (Sabatier 1993: 122–23) of how to tackle problems in industrial policy in general and transport policy in particular, but how to apply the generally available solutions to the particular case of the railways. It was only after a shift in the policy objectives linked to the problem-solving philosophy that the privatization of BR became feasible.

*The Regulatory Philosophy.* After World War II, a Keynesian economic policy developed in Britain, implying the nationalization of many industrial sectors (including the railways), a development that to some extent contradicts the British tradition of a liberal state characterized by the supremacy of the market over the state (Badie and Birnbaum 1983: 124; Dobbin 1993: 7). However, state intervention remained less pronounced than in other European countries. This is apparent in the transport sector where policy has always been characterized by an approach emphasizing the internal efficiency of service provision rather than macroeconomic effects of transport system (Button 1993: 154; Gwilliam 1979: 12). Due to this philosophy, the problems perceived with respect to the railways were related to their financial situation and efficiency rather than taking into account potential welfare benefits (e.g., with respect to regional, industrial, and environmental, policy) and promoting its development by public funding (Dobbin 1993).

The dominant approach to transport policy experienced a significant acceleration and amplification with the Conservative takeover in 1979. The neoliberal philosophy favored by the Conservatives marked a paradigm shift in the general approach to economic policy (Hall 1993). The neoliberal approach is directed at "rolling back the state" by reducing public-sector involvement and the promotion of a free-market economy driven by enhanced competition (Gibb, Lowndes, and Charlton 1996: 36; Reynolds and Coates 1996: 246ff.).

With respect to the public-sector industries, a standard solution emerged within the liberal approach: privatization. Since British transport policy was characterized by a liberal approach, the transport industry was seen as an ideal candidate for privatization (Gibb, Lowndes, and Charlton 1996: 36). In 1981 provisions were made to sell off BR's ancillary services such as Sealink, BR Hovercraft, BR Hotels, and the nonoperational property of BR. The National Freight Corporation was privatized in 1982. The Transport Act of 1985 signaled the final breakup of the nationalized bus industry and its sell-off to private-sector interests (White 1995: 193ff.; Dodgson 1994: 235).

*The Railway Problem in the Context of a Liberal Philosophy.* At first glance it is surprising that the privatization solution was only applied to BR in the early 1990s. But in contrast to other public-sector industries, the railways faced a particular problem that made privatization more difficult. In contrast to former public utilities on the government's selling list, BR was a loss-making undertaking and dependent on public funding. On the other hand, "trimming down" BR by closing unprofitable lines due to the particular fondness of the British public for their railways was never considered as politically feasible (Dodgson 1994: 232; Gibb, Lowndes, and Charlton 1996: 35).[65]

Seen against this backdrop, the problem of privatizing BR is particularly apparent when considering the basic objectives government attached to privatization during the 1980s. Thus, during the initial stage of privatization, revenue raising and reducing public spending were most important (Gamble 1988: 114). After 1985, as government finances improved, public borrowing was no longer perceived as a threatening problem. Privatization came to be seen mainly as a means of spreading entrepreneurialism by promoting a society of shareholders. This development went along with the privatization of the large public monopolies such as gas, water, telecommunications, and electricity (Suleiman 1990: 116). During this stage, privatization was considered as being more important than liberalization, that is, it was often a case of public monopolies simply being transformed into private monopolies with competition being less important than liberalization. Moreover, by the selling off of monopolies as a whole, investors were prepared to pay a higher price for shares (Massey 1992: 493).

Since BR was a loss-making industry, privatization was not a feasible option during the initial stage when the main goals of government policy were revenue raising and the reduction of public-sector borrowing. In order to attract private investors, public funding for unprofitable services would either have to be continued or line closures would become unavoidable. Both options were rejected by government, the first alternative providing no significant relief for public finance, and the latter being politically unattractive. The only options available to achieve the objectives of raising revenue and reducing public borrowing were to sell off BR's ancillary services and to continuously reduce BR's external financial limit (Zahariadis 1996: 410–11). For similar reasons, the privatization of BR was not considered during the mid-1980s when the promotion of individual shareholders became more important and an outright sale to individual investors would not have attracted interest because of the poor state of BR's finances. On the other hand, a company break-up or a sale to institutional investors would have diminished proceeds and contrasted with the Conservatives' objective to promote popular capitalism (Zahariadis 1996: 414).

In the early 1990s, however, the hierarchy of privatization objectives changed again. In light of experience, which is analyzed below, the main rationale for privatization is no longer share-selling to individuals, but the promotion of competition both by liberalization and commercialization (involving activities such as contracting out, competitive tendering, and performance regimes) (Zahariadis 1996: 415). Due to this shift, a successful coupling of a given solution (privatization) and the specific problem of the railways became possible.

First, the new priorities linked to privatization no longer inhibited a breakup of BR into profitable and unprofitable operations, and selling off the profitable parts to institutional investors became feasible. Second, the shift in objectives no longer conflicted with the privatization of a loss-making industry. Instead, the promotion of competition was conceived of as fitting the particular case of the railways. Thus, competition was introduced both by liberalizing market access for rolling stock, freight operations, and service units and by commercializing the remaining businesses and in establishing franchising contracts and contracting out obligations. Furthermore, the trend toward commercialization is apparent with respect to the contractual framework affecting the various business units and the performance regimes.

To conclude, the reform of BR originated in the striving to apply a standard solution, namely privatization, to a nationalized industry that was perceived as loss-making and inefficient in the context of a neoliberal problem-solving approach. Thus, the question was not "To sell or not to sell?" but "How to sell?". It was only when a shift in the government's objectives linked to privatization took place that the given solution could be applied to the perceived problem. The following section takes a closer look at how this shift in privatization objectives was brought about and how it influenced the concrete outcome of the railway reform.

*Shaping the Solution: Learning from Experience*

Why did the British select this fragmented form of privatization with its mixture of franchising, contracting out, liberalizing, and private monopoly? This is surprising, given the range of other, economically less uncertain, models discussed, such as the "regional option" dividing BR up into a number of vertically integrated geographically based regions (Gritten 1988); the "sector option" with companies based on BR's existing business sectors and a principal operator on each line bearing responsibility for infrastructure (e.g., InterCity); the "track authority option" implying a separate track authority owning the infrastructure and charging private operators for track access (Irvine 1987); or the "British Rail option" proposing to privatize BR as a whole.

The concrete shaping of the railway reform may be interpreted in terms of learning within "core beliefs," that is, "to refine existing paradigms, technologies and competencies rather than to fundamentally re-examine them" (Olsen and Peters 1994: 8). The process of learning related to instruments or 'secondary aspects' (Sabatier 1993) is based on past experience: actors repeat behavior associated with success and avoid behavior associated with failure (Olsen 1995: 30). The "refining" of the privatization concept applied to BR was based on three sources of experience: former privatizations, public-sector reform models, and railway reorganization.

*Former Privatizations.* Both the separation of infrastructure and operations and the introduction of competition before privatization may be traced to experience of former privatization of nationalized utilities, in particular, telecoms, gas, water, and electricity. Both telecommunications and gas had been privatized as a whole, that is, public monopolies were transformed into private monopolies, with competition only being introduced gradually after privatization.[66] In both cases it became apparent that not separating infrastructure from operations would create problems for the introduction of competition in the operations sector (Suleiman 1990: 118; Vickers and Yarrow 1989: 239). Moreover, it turned out that—apart from the anticompetitive behavior of the former utilities—establishing competition in the wake of privatization was more difficult to achieve than introducing competition prior to, or alongside, privatization. Due to the significant market power of the privatized monopolies, competition developed more slowly than in sectors where the public monopoly had been divided up before privatization, as was the case in the electricity generating industry (Suleiman 1990: 119; Zahariadis 1996: 417). In light of this experience the belief grew within government that in order to achieve competition and efficiency, BR should be divided up before privatization and that the ownership of the network should be separated from the provision of services (Bradshaw 1995: 17).[67]

Another aspect of the privatization of utilities was the strong position of utilities' management when it came to influencing the style of privatization. Since the utilities were privatized as a whole, the full cooperation of management was essential for government in order to secure successful flotation. The utilities thus had significant bargaining power when negotiating the specific market arrangements with government (Vickers and Yarrow 1989: 239; Bradshaw 1995: 16). Against this background government favored a breakup of BR, since privatization as a whole would have increased BR's bargaining power with respect to public subsidies for unprofitable services.[68]

The lessons learned from the privatization and deregulation of public bus services may also have facilitated the introduction of franchising. Although in this case access to the market is open, there is a system of competitive tendering for the operation of unprofitable local bus services subsidized by local government (White 1995: 198). The system appears to have been very successful. Costs were reduced, and there were relatively few complaints by bidders and local authorities as to the practicability of the system (Dodgson 1994: 247).

*Public-Sector Reform.* The British railway reform is not only characterized by the experience of earlier privatizations, but also by concepts applied to reform Britain's public administration. These reforms, commonly referred to as "the new public management" (NPM), are designed to promote incentive structures (such as market competition and commercialization) to the public sector. They stress three main instruments: agencies, contracts, and charters. The disaggregation or fragmentation of the bureaucracy by agencification was introduced with "The Next Steps" initiative (Efficiency Unit 1988). At the core of this initiative is the creation of semiautonomous agencies responsible for operational management by separating management functions from policymaking functions, which remain with the relevant departments. Each agency has a contract-like framework document that sets out its objectives and performance targets (Dowding 1993: 187–88). Contracts furthermore play an important role in the government's promotion of market testing. Market testing involves identifying specific blocks of tasks or functions in agencies to be contracted out by competitive tendering. The Citizen's Charter introduced in 1991 contains key objectives to improve the quality of public services, such as publishing explicit performance standards, complete information about running services, and effective remedies (Rhodes 1996: 9–10; see Hood 1991; Pollitt 1993).

Evidently, public-sector experience with new management concepts such as contracting out, the introduction of performance regimes, and the organizational separation of functions (the purchaser/provider split) had important consequences for the design of the railway reform. Thus, classical privatization concepts such as "sell off" to private investors and creating an appropriate regulatory framework were combined with reform ideas applied in the public sector. This appears to be particularly relevant with respect to the introduction of performance indicators, the contractual framework, and the organizational fragmentation of the railway industry. The privatization of BR therefore reflects a confluence of strategies applied to privatize nationalized industries on the one hand and to reform public administration on the other.

*Previous Railway Reforms.* During the 1980s and early 1990s significant re-organizations have taken place within BR. Prior to 1982, BR was organized along a four-tiered structure of board headquarters, region, division, and area. The linchpins of this rather extensive hierarchical structuring were the five regions (Gourvish 1990: 114). In 1982 a major reform was introduced that replaced the regional organizations by sectoral management. Five market-based business sectors were created: InterCity, Provincial (later Regional Railways), Network SouthEast, Freight, and Parcels. Each sector was given bottom-line responsibility for its services. An internal market was created insofar as business sectors charged others for the use of their assets (Reid 1990: 16). In 1991, a further important change was introduced when the business sectors took over responsibility for production, and virtually all human resources were allocated to them. Moreover, each of the sectors was divided up into several self-accounting profit centers.[69] Alongside internal reorganization, a cultural change took place making BR a commercial and business-led rather than a technical or production-led industry (Gourvish 1990: 118). These reforms, which were directed at making BR's operations more efficient, led to significant financial improvements. By 1989, BR's financial deficit had been halved compared to 1982, and InterCity and Freight had turned the corner into profit. Only the two other passenger businesses still required financial support (Reid 1990: 16). Thus, by the time privatization was announced, BR was among the most efficient and productive railways in Europe (Gibb, Lowndes, and Charlton 1996: 41).

BR's internal reforms may mainly be understood as an attempt to secure its institutional persistence by adapting to environmental pressure stemming from the radical neoliberal reform policies pushed forward by the Conservative government.[70] This pressure was exerted in several ways. First, the government's commitment to privatize became manifest with respect to both the sell-off of BR's ancillary services and the accelerating sale of other nationalized industries. Second, starting in 1983 the government introduced a program of significant PSO reductions on BR and imposed profit and cost reduction targets for each of BR's main railways activities (Pendleton 1993: 49–50). Third, during the 1980s several proposals on railway privatization had been published by right-wing think tanks (Adam Smith Institute 1993; Beesley and Littlechild 1983; Irvine 1987; Gritten 1988).

BR tried to strengthen its legitimacy by embracing forms and practices that were widely valued by Conservative ideology. The demand for isomorphism, that is, the similarity with the broader environment, became the driving force behind organizational change (DiMaggio and Powell 1991). Thus, promoting organizational change in line with efficiency, cost reduction, commercialization, and competition became crucial in the process of internal restructuring. At about the time when the government published its administrative reform proposals in a white paper on *Competing for Quality*, BR announced its reform policy using a strikingly similar slogan, *Organising for Quality*.

Paradoxically, BR's strategies to defend its institutional identity had the unintended consequence of facilitating privatization and fragmentation instead of inhibiting them. First, the improved financial performance achieved by internal reforms facilitated privatization by making BR more attractive for private investors. Second, government could draw on the positive experience made by BR in introducing the profit center concept when deciding on privatization. Thus, the existing profit centers in the freight and passenger businesses were turned into privatized or franchised business units with only slight modifications.[71] A third lesson learned from BR's internal reforms is related to the power of the railway unions. The three unions involved, the Associated Society of Locomotive Engineers and Firemen (ASLEF), the National Union of Rail, Maritime and Transport Workers (RMT), and the Transport Salaried Staffs Association (TSSA), had clearly objected to BR's internal restructuring (Pendleton 1993: 47; Dodgson 1994: 240) and inhibited further reform such as the introduction of contracting out regimes. Thus, the division of BR into separate units, which allowed for a reduction of the unions' power to organize national railway strikes, played an important role in the government's privatization decision.[72]

In sum, the specific way in which BR was privatized may be understood in terms of learning from experience stemming from three main sources: former privatizations, public-sector reforms, and prior railway reorganization. Evidence from the privatization of other public-sector industries indicates that in order to introduce competition, liberalization should be introduced prior to, or parallel with, privatization, and ownership of infrastructure and network should be separated. Moreover, with respect to franchising, government could draw on lessons learned from bus deregulation and privatization. Railway reform was also inspired by the recent wave of administrative reforms. This is particularly obvious with respect to the introduction of performance regimes, contractual frameworks, and the organizational fragmentation. In deciding on the specific form of organizational fragmentation, government could build on structures already set in place by internal railway reforms. The resistance of the railway unions and their national strike power, which became particularly obvious with respect to BR's internal reforms, provided a further impetus for the government to split up BR in several units. Paradoxically, BR's adaptation to external pressure, which was intended to secure institutional persistence, had the unintended consequence of facilitating the breakup of BR.

## Paving the Way for Privatization: The Capacity for Change

So far, we have analyzed the reasons underlying the privatization of the railways and the factors influencing the concrete way in which it was shaped, but we have not examined which factors enabled the government to put through such a fundamental reform in the face of strong opposition. In what follows we examine how several institutional and process-related factors provided government with the opportunity to change its strategies in light of past experience.

*Institutional Background.* In the case of railway privatization three institutional factors were of particular relevance: strong executive leadership; the institutional position of BR; and the membership structure of the railway unions. The first aspect, strong executive leadership, may be traced to specific aspects of the British political system that allow for the concentration of the power in the executive. Apart from democratic control by general elections, there are limited institutional constraints impeding the government once it has decided to put a change through Parliament (Dunleavy 1993; Rhodes 1996). Hence, the British political system is characterized by a high capacity for exploring new possibilities and learning from experience (Olsen and Peters 1994: 16). Due to its strong position the government put through its reform proposals with only slight modifications (Nash 1993), although there was a broad range of opposing actors (including the Labour Party, the railway unions, and interest associations such as Transport 2000, Save our Railways,[73] and the Railway Development Society) that could rely on broad public support.[74] "Rail privatization has been driven through much such as the poll tax, to which it has often been compared, with virtually no supporters outside the government and many well-informed objectors" (*The Independent* 1995).

Second, the institutional position of BR provided relatively limited opportunities for defending its institutional identity. Although the legal and administrative framework guiding the relationships between the DoT and the BRB allowed the railways a certain degree of autonomy in their day-to-day management, BR had no formal decisional rights with respect to strategic decisions and was obliged to implement these decisions along the lines stated by the DoT.[75]

Moreover, the institutional position of the railway unions in order to successfully influence the political decision-making process was rather weak. This may be traced to two factors. On the one hand, due to their differing membership the three unions (ASLEF, RMT, and TSSA) had different interests related to privatization.[76] RMT represents grades of staff whose job skills are relatively general, such as platform and rail staff. Since these jobs are quite easy to replace, RMT was strongly opposed to privatization. TSSA (representing clerical and management staff) and ASLEF (representing train drivers) have membership whose job-knowledge and skills are more industry-specific. Privatization for these unions was not necessarily perceived as a threat, but as an opportunity to improve the working conditions of their members (Pendleton 1993: 65). This divergence of the unions' interest positions inhibited coordinated action in order to significantly influence the outcomes of the political decision-making process.[77] On the other hand, coordination within RMT, the largest and most influential of the railway unions, was weak and ineffective due to the contrasting political positions within RMT's management.[78]

*The Privatization Process.* The institutional background, however, does not fully explain how and why the Conservative government succeeded in putting through its plans for railway privatization against a broad-based opposition.

Instead we have to take into account the particular strategies pursued by the main actors involved, given the opportunities and restrictions defined by the institutional constellation. In this context, the interactions between BR and government and government and opposition require particular attention.

BR's main objective was not to avoid privatization, but the organizational breakup of its vertically integrated structure (Gibb, Lowndes, and Charlton 1996: 40). In much the same way as the contracting-out frameworks in the public sector, BR's aim was to function as a private-sector service purchaser contracting out the provision of service operations.[79] Given its weak institutional position, BR tried to achieve its objectives by continuing internal management reforms along the trajectory followed from 1982 onward. As mentioned earlier, however, internal reforms had the unintended consequence of facilitating privatization. Hence, internal reform paradoxically weakened rather than strengthened BR's position in the decision-making process. Moreover, the resistance of the railway unions with respect to BR's internal reforms helped convince the government of the need to split up BR into independent units in order to weaken the influence of the unions.

In addition to BR's organizational breakup, the government excluded the latter from participating in the franchise bidding process. The restrictive behavior of government may be traced to the fact that BR, on account of its expertise, would have an advantage in the bidding process, and by winning the franchises it would make a nonsense of privatization (*The Independent* 1993).[80]

With respect to the interaction between the Conservative government and the Labour opposition the election timetable had a significant impact on the strategies pursued by both (corporate) actors. From the perspective of the Conservative government, rail privatization had to be a success, and one of the main conditions for that success was the interest of private investors and franchise bidders. Private investors, on the other hand, could only be attracted when there was sufficient political and economic certainty with respect to the stability and workability of the privatized system. By contrast, the Labour Party's main objective was to inhibit successful privatization by increasing the degree of uncertainty for potential private investors by committing itself, when privatization was announced, to the renationalization of the railways in case of its electoral victory in 1997.

The success of this strategy, however, was dependent on the progress of the sales process. The more of BR that was sold and franchised, the more difficult it would be for Labour to stick to its declaration of renationalization, due to the high levels of public spending this would imply. The government's strategy therefore was to increase certainty for investors. The objective was to complete the sales and franchising process as swiftly as possible so as to make renationalization an ever less realistic option, given the high amount of public spending involved.[81]

The government realized its objectives of completing the privatization of process on the eve of the general elections in May 1997. This was facilitated by two factors. First, changes in the privatization timetable significantly accelerated the, hitherto rather sluggish, privatization process. In this context it was important to encourage the flotation of Railtrack that took place in May 1996 and proved to be a watershed for privatization insofar as "people suddenly realized that it really was going to happen" (interview DoT, Feb. 1997). The flotation of Railtrack was an important step in increasing certainty in the expectations of private investors, since it prevented a future Labour government from carrying out its threat to restore a publicly owned railway. Second, the striking impact of the floatation of Railtrack on rail privatization was reinforced by the fact that Stagecoach, a national bus company, decided to bid for franchises and in April 1996 started to run its first passenger service (*The Independent* 1995). Stagecoach enjoys a good reputation in the city, and its involvement strengthened the belief within the financial markets that rail privatization would occur and be a success. The positive attitude of the city with respect to rail privatization, on the other hand, increased certainty for private investors.[82]

Labour therefore had to adjust its policy position with respect to the railways. Instead of renationalization, it announced a less radical program, including the creation of a strategic rail authority (based on the residual BR) to reintegrate the fragmented framework and to promote investment by organizing public–private partnerships and strengthening the powers of the regulator in order to promote investment.[83]

Given its modified policy program, Labour's election victory in May 1997 has had limited consequences for the railways industry. While the regulatory framework established by the Conservative government remained basically unchanged, only minor adaptations were enacted, including changes in governmental guidance for the operations of OPRAF (obliging OPRAF to actively encourage the use of the railways and to supervise the operations of Railtrack). Moreover, the new government launched a broad consultation process concerning the establishment of a strategic railways authority (based on OPRAF and the relevant divisions within the DoT) and increased the regulatory powers of ORR in order to control the operations of Railtrack and the ROSCOs.[84] These reforms were ratified in 1999, including the removal of safety control competences from Railtrack to the strategic railways authority. As a consequence of the government change, Railtrack had already voluntarily agreed on a stricter investment program. Under the shadow of potential regulatory changes introduced by the Labour government, Railtrack—initially heavily criticized for its underinvestment—accepted stricter requirements of the regulator, although the latter could not rely on corresponding legal powers to intervene into Railtrack's operations.[85]

This chapter has so far explained the privatization of BR with reference to purely national factors. Both the origin and outcome of the reform were traced to national factors of influence: the neoliberal philosophy; learning from experience with former privatizations, public-sector reforms, and railway reorganization; and both institutional and process factors providing the opportunity to put through and enforce privatization. In light of these purely national explanatory factors, the question arises as to what extent supranational policies have affected the reform process.

## The Influence of EU Policy: Peripheral to National Reform

Starting with the most important point, EU policy did not have a significant impact on either the shape or origin of the British railway reform, although the British reforms and the European policy activities point in the same direction.[86] This may be traced to the fact the British policy went far beyond the European provisions. Thus, Directive 91/440, the main European measure enacted to date to promote railway liberalization, only requires member states to introduce a division of infrastructure and operation on the basis of accounting. Moreover, third-party track access in freight transport is limited to the small group of international joint ventures. Railway reform in Britain goes beyond these provisions in dividing operation and infrastructure institutionally and in establishing open access in the freight market. In much the same way, the proposals of the commission's 1996 white paper, *A Strategy for Revitalizing the Community's Railways* (CEC 1996b), sets out objectives that Britain has already achieved: the abolition of state monopolies and the creation of a market for railway services.[87]

The only aspect that required detailed coordination between the British government and the EU Commission was related to questions of state aid. Thus, the subsidy arrangements for the unprofitable franchises had to be harmonized with the provisions of EU competition policy, and this process of coordination required intensive consultations with the commission. There was, however, no substantial problem to bring the franchise agreements into line with EU competition policy, since national and European provisions point in the same direction in this respect.[88]

Although EU policy did not play a key role in shaping the outcome of the British railway reform, Britain supported Directive 91/440[89]—first, because Britain is generally in favor of market liberalization in order to complete the single European market, and second, because the British government could to some extent use the directive as a resource to support its own domestic privatization plans: "The directive was preparing the way for what we would like to do anyway" (interview DoT, Feb. 1997). This was especially the case with respect to the government's intention to separate infrastructure from operation. However, since the national reforms went beyond the provisions of the directive, legitimating national policy by EU legislation was only important—albeit limited—in the initial stages of the national debate on reform.[90]

It is likely that Britain's interest in the directive was mainly due to its legitimatory function for national reform rather than to the British preference for market liberalization. This may be derived from Britain's indifferent stance on the commission's 1996 white paper, although the content is in line with both the British liberalization policy in general and its railway reform in particular: "We didn't have any input into the White Paper at all. We looked at it and thought, the deal is done as far as we are concerned. The only question is whether the rest of Europe is prepared to follow it" (interview DoT, Nov. 1996).

To sum up, European policy only exerted a peripheral influence on the British railway reform. The concrete outcome of the national changes was only slightly affected by the provisions of EU competition policy. This required intensive coordination between the British government and the commission, but no substantial problems or contradictions had to be resolved. There is some evidence that the supporting role of the British with respect to the formulation of Directive 91/440 may be traced to the government's intention to legitimate national reform by reference to the directive. This statement, however, should not be overestimated, since the British reform went far beyond the provisions of the directive.

## Summary

A mixture of several recipes was applied in reforming British railways that brought about fundamental transformations for which there is no precedent either at the European or at the national level. The different concepts combined include privatization, organizational fragmentation, the introduction of different competitive frameworks, formal contractual relationships, and the establishment of a unique regulatory structure consisting of two regulatory bodies that carry out complementary functions. These changes in many respects go far beyond the railway reforms in other European countries and supranational policy initiatives. Thus, in Britain an institutional separation of infrastructure and operation was set in place. Furthermore, market access in the freight sector is completely liberalized. In the passenger sector, on the other hand, a franchising regime was introduced implying competitive tendering from private bidders for the operation of services. In sharp contrast to other European countries, all businesses created out of BR are owned and operated by private actors.

Although the British reforms and supranational policy point in the same direction, Europe did not count, insofar as EU policy was peripheral to national reforms. It was only with respect to questions of state aid where a certain coordination between the British government and the commission took place. Furthermore, the government was able to justify its reform proposals during the initial stages of the national debate by referring to EU policy. Against this background Britain supported the relevant Directive 91/440.

The privatization of BR was basically a national solution to a national problem. In this context a standard type of solution, privatization, was provided by the neoliberal philosophy promoted by the Conservatives since their takeover in 1979. The privatization of the railways, however, turned out to be difficult throughout the 1980s, since BR was a loss-making industry. The situation only changed after experience allowed for a refining of the privatization solution and thus its link to the case of the railways. Learning was based on experience from three sources: former privatizations, reforms in the public sector, and railway reorganizations.

The implementation of the refined solution, despite significant opposition and high economic uncertainty, should be understood in light of the particular institutional context and the strategies pursued by the main actors involved.

# CONCLUSION

This analysis of British road haulage and rail policy points to three general conclusions. First, we found that in both areas national reforms were concurrent with European developments, but originated from, and were shaped by, purely national factors. That is to say, national reforms were not linked to, or influenced by, European developments. This result may be traced to two basic conditions affecting the making of British transport policy: the liberal ideology (generally concurrent with the EU approach), and the high reform capacity inherent in the British political system, allowing for the revision of regulatory strategies in light of past experience.

Second, although this general picture of the relationship between national and European policy holds true for both cases under study, there are fundamental differences with respect to the logic guiding political change in road haulage and railway regulation, indicating that both cases reflect separate and independent areas. This becomes obvious when considering the impact of the explanatory factors in more detail. To begin with the regulatory approach, we may identify a twofold regulatory separation in British transport policy. On the one hand, transport policy is *sectorally* separated from other policy areas, such as environmental, regional, or social policy. This missing linkage of transport policy with other policy areas is a consequence of the dominant liberal philosophy that regards transport as pure service and focuses on the microeconomic efficiency of service provision. On the other hand, British transport policy is also shaped by *sub-sectoral* regulatory separation. In other words, within the overall objective of efficient service provision, different modes of transport are taken as separate cases following distinctive logics. Accordingly, there is no integration or coordination between different subsectors, such as railfreight and road haulage.

As a consequence, problems and solutions perceived with respect to the railways were basically linked to their status as a *public utility* rather than their function as a means of transport. The proximity of the railways to the public sector had a significant impact on the concrete perception of problems and solutions within the broad concept of a liberal regulatory approach. This separated view of transport helps us understand not only the long-term lag between road haulage reform and railway privatization, but also the fact that both cases were characterized by differing versions of the liberal regulatory approach. Thus, road haulage reform occurred long before catchwords such as "deregulation" or "liberalization" had entered the political discourse. The establishment of a liberal regime therefore was perceived as another form of regulation and to a lesser extent as deregulation. Railway reform, by contrast, took place in the context of a strong ideological commitment of the Conservative government toward a "rolling back of the state" and increasing the efficiency of the public sector.

According to these differences, regulatory reform in both areas followed distinctive logics, which may be summarized as "problem-oriented learning" in the case of road haulage versus "ideology-oriented learning" in the case of the railways. Regulatory reform of road haulage was characterized by the search for solutions to problems of regulatory failure of past strategies applied. Although regulatory reform took place within the context of a liberal approach, the question was not to liberalize road haulage at any cost but to design market regulation in such a way that service provision meets the objective of microeconomic efficiency. In the case of the railways, the situation was the other way around. Learning was related to the question of how to apply a standard solution defined within the neoliberal philosophy of the Conservative government, namely privatization, to the specific problems perceived with a particular public utility, the railways.

In addition to these differences, regulatory reform was also affected by varying degrees of proximity to the public sector. Thus, as a result of the close linkage between the railways and the public sector, reform strategies were shaped not only by past experience with railway regulation, but also by more general experiences drawn from other privatizations and reforms in the public sector in general. By contrast, the reform of road haulage regulation could not rely on experience drawn from similar areas, but was shaped by lessons drawn from earlier attempts to regulate the sector.

Finally, the case of road haulage shows that the separate and unconnected development of national and European policies may be restricted to cases where European policies are basically reflecting or confirming the traditional British approach rather than requiring the introduction of new elements. As the parallelism of national and European policy developments with respect to infrastructure provision indicates, however, a closer linkage between both levels does not necessarily exclude the potential for concurrent developments. This holds especially true with respect to the present Labour government, which is committed to a more integrated approach to transport policy, an objective that resounds with recent activities by the commission in this area.

# NOTES

1. The Geddes Committee reported that the policy objectives relating to road safety, avoidance of congestion, the environment, efficiency of the transport system, and the protection of the railways could not be achieved by a system of quantitative licensing (Bayliss 1987: 10).

2. Council Directive 74/561 was amended in 1989 and 1997 to establish qualitative criteria for operational access to the market in the absence of quantitative restrictions to market access.

3. Interviews DoT, Nov. 1995; Traffic Commissioner, Jan. 1996. See Bayliss 1987: 10.

4. In Britain, there are eight regional traffic areas.

5. Two groups of actors legally entitled to object can be distinguished: statutory bodies and representors. The statutory bodies include the police, local authorities, trade unions, and the transport associations. Representors are owners or occupiers of land in the vicinity of an operating center (Cooper 1990). Objecting groups have the right of appeal to the Transport Tribunals, which can reverse the decision of the licensing authority. Tribunals are composed of professional and lay judges (interview DoT, Nov. 1995).

6. RCEP 1994: 114; interview DoT, Nov. 1997.

7. Since this analysis is basically related to developments that took place before this organizational change, throughout the text reference is made to the previous organizational structure, unless indicated explicitly. Moreover, for the sake of clarity, only the organizational structure for England will be described. Although responsibility for some tasks lies with the particular ministries for Scotland (Scottish Office), Wales (Welsh Office), and Northern Ireland, no substantial differences arise from this division of labor. For a more detailed overview see Burnham, Glaister, and Travers (1994: 3ff.).

8. Interviews DoT, Nov. 1995; Traffic Commissioner, Jan. 1996.

9. Interview DoT, Nov. 1995.

10. Interviews FTA, Nov. 1995, April 1996; RHA, Nov. 1995. In this respect the RHA and FTA have overlapping memberships (interview FTA, April 1996).

11. Interview FTA, Nov. 1995.

12. Both the RHA and the FTA are members of the International Road Union (IRU). In addition, the FTA represents the political interests of the CBI on transport issues within the relevant UNICE committees (interview FTA, Nov. 1995).

13. Interviews FTA, Nov. 1995; RHA, Nov. 1995.

14. Interview FTA, Nov. 1995.

15. Interviews RHA, Nov. 1995; FTA, Nov. 1995.

16. Interview FTA, Nov. 1995.

17. Interview Traffic Commissioner, Jan. 1996.

18. Interviews RHA, Nov. 1995; FTA, Nov. 1995; Traffic Commissioner, Jan. 1996.

19. Interview Traffic Commissioner, Jan. 1996; interview CIT, Jan. 1996.

20. Interview CIT, Jan. 1996.

21. Interview DoT, Nov. 1997.

22. Interview DoT, Nov. 1997.

23. Interview DoT, Nov. 1995.

24. Interviews FTA, Nov. 1995; RHA, Nov. 1995.

25. Interviews DoT, Nov. 1995; CIT, Jan. 1996.

26. Interview DoT, Nov. 1997.

27. Interviews FTA, Nov. 1995; April 1996.

28. Interviews BRF, May 1995; DoT, Jan. 1996. In the transport sector, Transport 2000, financed by Friends of the Earth (FoE) and the Council for the Protection of Rural England (CPRE), plays an especially important role in the political debate. The influence of environmental organizations, however, is largely restricted to the field of infrastructure policy— with respect to market regulation in the road haulage sector, environmental groups did not constitute an important actor disposing of important resources (interview DoT, Jan. 1996).

29. The RCEP is an independent standing body established in 1970 to advise the queen, Parliament, and the public on environmental protection matters. RCEP policy recommen-

dations have generally, although sometimes with long time lags, a significant influence on the policymaking process in Britain (see Knill 1995).

30. SACTRA is a committee of experts that advises the DoT on matters of road infrastructure.

31. Interviews RCEP, Nov. 1994; DoT, Nov. 1995; FTA, April 1996.

32. Interview DoT, Nov. 1997.

33. Interview CBI, Nov. 1994; CBI, 1995.

34. Interview FTA, April 1996.

35. Interviews DoT, Nov. 1995; Nov. 1997.

36. Interviews FTA, Nov. 1995; April 1996.

37. Interviews FTA, Nov. 1995; April 1996.

38. Interview CEC, DG XII, April 1996.

39. Nationalized industry means that the railways were owned by the state. BR, however, never was a state agency or part of public administration. Accordingly, the term *privatization* in the British sense means *material* privatization, as opposed to the concept of *formal* privatization, implying no change in ownership but only in the industry's legal basis.

40. For details on the internal reorganization of BR see below.

41. Interviews BRB, Feb. 1997; DoT, Feb. 1997.

42. Interviews DoT, Nov. 1996; Freightliner Ltd., Nov. 1996. Three regional companies were established dealing with the transportation of heavy and bulky goods so far carried by Trainload Freight. Freightliner is moving containers from deep-sea ports inland and vice versa. The Channel Tunnel railfreight business is left to Railfreight Distribution. Furthermore, Rail Express Systems responsible for carrying letters for the Post Office and Red Star, BR's express parcel business, were set up as independent companies.

43. Due to this fundamental restructuring, BR staff decreased from 120,000 before privatization to 35 in April 1997 (interview BRB, Feb. 1997).

44. Interview DoT, Nov. 1996.

45. Interviews Railtrack, Nov. 1996; OPRAF, Nov. 1996.

46. Interviews OPRAF, Nov. 1996; ORR, Nov. 1996.

47. OPRAF 1996: 37; interview OPRAF, Nov. 1996.

48. Interview ORR, Nov. 1996.

49. Interviews DoT, Nov. 1996. Against the background of ATOC's regulatory activities, ATOC membership is compulsory for passenger train operators (interview RIA, Feb. 1997).

50. Interview Freightliner Ltd., Nov. 1996. Market access seems to be only realistic for larger companies such as British Steel or National Power, which already under British Rail owned their own freight wagons. So far, however, only National Power has decided to operate its own freight services (interview British Steel, Feb. 1997).

51. The company is English, Welsh and Scottish Railways (EWS), which is owned by the American consortium Wisconsin.

52. Interviews BRB, Feb. 1997; CIT, Jan. 1996; DoT, Nov. 1996.

53. Interview DoT, Feb. 1997. The Railways Act contains, however, provisions for the strengthening of competition in the passenger sector. Both in March 1999 and March 2002 the regulator is empowered to review the market and to decide upon the gradual introduction of open access regimes (interview DoT, Feb. 1997; OPRAF 1996: 65).

54. Generally, these contracts last for seven years; if the franchisee intends to invest in rolling stock, longer periods up to fifteen years are offered in order to allow for capital amortization (interviews CIT, Jan. 1996; OPRAF, Nov. 1996).

55. Interviews OPRAF, Nov. 1996; DoT, Feb. 1997.

56. The British approach to regulating private utilities provides for a five-year regulatory lag, that is, within each five-year period the regulated price ceiling is adjusted in light of general price level changes (retail price index, RPI) (Kay and Thompson 1991: 27).

57. Interview DoT, Feb. 1997.

58. Interview DoT, Feb. 1997.

59. Interview OPRAF, Nov. 1996.

60. Interview Save our Railways, Feb. 1997; Preston 1996: 11. Available evidence so far reveals rather mixed results. On the one hand, there is a certain inclination that private operators pursue a policy of far-reaching staff cuts in order to work profitably. In some cases, this policy led to significant problems with respect to service delivery, which became most obvious in the case of South West Trains in February 1997. Moreover, some companies tried to increase efficiency by reducing the number of coaches, leading to overcrowded trains. On the other hand, recent developments show an improving performance of the franchisees, which to some extent can be traced to the rather rigid intervention of OPRAF in the former two cases, where the firms faced significant fines (interviews OPRAF; DoT; ORR, Nov. 1997).

61. Interviews Railtrack, Nov. 1996; DoT, Nov. 1996.

62. Interview BRB, Feb. 1997; Save our Railways, Feb. 1997.

63. Interview British Steel, Feb. 1997; Save our Railways, Feb. 1997. In order to cope with this problem, EWS and Railtrack agreed on reduced access charges for new freight traffic carried by EWS. EWS in turn pays Railtrack a lump-sum payment over a certain period of time (interviews British Steel, Feb. 1997; Railtrack, Nov. 1997).

64. Interviews DoT, Nov. 1996; Railtrack, Nov. 1996. Again, evidence reveals a mixed picture. On the one hand, rolling stock investment seems to be no particular problem, although the operators initially were quite reluctant to invest into new rolling stock (interviews RIA, Feb. 1997; OPRAF, ORR, Nov. 1997). By contrast, despite high profits, Railtrack's investment plans remained far below the levels expected by the Rail Regulator. After the Labour take-over in May 1997, however, Railtrack accepted more ambitious investment objectives (see below).

65. Interview BRB, Feb. 1997.

66. Besides the primary objective of spreading popular capitalism, the fact that successful flotation was heavily dependent on the cooperation of the utilities' management crucially influenced the style of these privatization's. The full cooperation of the management was essential for a speedy flotation. In order to secure this cooperation, government had to make provisions with respect to the market position of the privatized utilities (Vickers and Yarrow 1989).

67. One could certainly argue that the separation of service operation and infrastructure provision emerged as a result of a diffusion of corresponding policy ideas promoted at the European level. Since the factual effects of policy diffusion are problematic to assess, it is rather difficult to reject or confirm such an argument. Given the direct and more pronounced experience drawn from national policy, however, it seems to be rather unlikely that European policy ideas had a significant impact in this context.

68. Interview DoT, Feb. 1997; interview CIT, Jan. 1996.

69. Interviews BRB, Feb. 1997; DoT, Feb. 1997; Pendleton 1993: 50–51.

70. This strategy becomes apparent in the statement of the then chairman of BR, Rob Reid: "Our strategy was shaped by government directives" (Reid 1990: 15).

71. Interviews BRB, Feb. 1997; DoT, Nov. 1996. Thus, the nineteen former passenger profit centers were transformed into twenty-five TOCs (interview BRB, Feb. 1997).

72. Interview BRB, Feb. 1997. A series of major railways strikes in 1989 further contributed to the government's striving to weaken the unions (interview ORR, Nov. 1996). The objective to restrict union power, however, is not only related to the particular case of rail privatization, but has always played an important role on the agenda of the Conservative government (Gamble 1988).

73. Save our Railways is an umbrella organization set up by Transport 2000, the Railway Development Society, the railway unions, and a large number of individual members. The association was particularly established in order to stop rail privatization (interview Save our Railways, Feb. 1997).

74. Interviews Save our Railways, Feb. 1997; DoT, Feb. 1997.

75. Interview DoT, Feb. 1997.

76. The interests of the unions differed not only with respect to privatization, but also at a more general level. Thus, Pendleton (1993: 64) points out that ASLEF and RMT have a history of difficult and sometimes acrimonious relations.

77. Interview BRB, Feb. 1997.

78. Interview BRB, Feb. 1997.

79. Interviews DoT, Feb. 1997; BRB, Feb. 1997.

80. According to the Railways Act government had to approve BR's participation in the bidding process for every single franchise. Since corresponding applications of BR for the first eight franchises were rejected, however, BR decided to refrain from further applications (interview BRB, Feb. 1997).

81. Interviews DoT, Nov. 1996; OPRAF, Nov. 1996.

82. Interview DoT, Nov. 1996.

83. Labour Party 1996: 21ff.; interview Labour Party, Nov. 1995.

84. These proposals are currently discussed in the broader context of an integrated transport policy. A corresponding white paper was announced to be published by mid-1998.

85. Interviews ORR; OPRAF; DoT; Railtrack, Nov. 1997.

86. Interviews DoT, Feb. 1997; CIT, Jan. 1996.

87. Interview DoT, Nov. 1996.

88. Interview DoT, Feb. 1997.

89. Interview DoT, Feb. 1997.

90. Interview CIT, Jan. 1996.

# 4

# Strengthening the Opposition and Pushing Change: The Paradoxical Impact of Europe on the Reform of French Transport

*Anne-Cécile Douillet and Dirk Lehmkuhl*

The contradiction in the way in which European integration affected governance structure and policies in France poses an analytical challenge. To cope with this challenge we refer to the dynamics of the two-level game. Using the concept as a heuristic device allows us to account not only for the institutional and policy impact of European integration at the national level, but also to relate this impact to the domestic politics: hence, both the French role in the process of policymaking at the European level and the implementation of European policies at the national level depend on domestic politics (Evans 1993; Young 2000).

A first aspect refers to the finding that the influence of European Community (EC) legislation is not univocal. On the one hand, EC legislation gives new arguments to those national actors who principally support liberalization and now can refer to the "European constraint." On the other hand, European policies can strengthen the position of those national actors supporting reregulation or opposing liberalization; the latter is presented as a new challenge requiring protection for national industries and their workforce. Given this ambiguous influence we could observe a liberal domestic reform and a reform of the reform. A second aspect shows that this seemingly incoherent development is even more obscured by the finding that the domestic "liberal-reform and reform-of-the-reform" process is linked with a strong opposition of French officials against the European liberalization policies. A division of labor between the government and the administration forms the background of this finding. Forced by the logic of party politics, governments of all colors were obliged to account for the resistance of potential voters. The administration in contrast, being immersed in the European logic, was solicitous to cautiously incorporate competitive elements in the regulatory framework. The overall objective of these behavioral strategies was to slow down the process of liberalization at the European level while making the reform acceptable at the domestic level.

The examples of road haulage and railways show that the specific influence of EC legislation depends on the respective sectoral and national configuration of political actors, which, in turn, varies according to a country's respective policy stage between liberalization, deregulation, and reregulation, and to the prevailing problem-solving approach. In the case of road haulage, there was no pressure to adapt French regulations to the liberalization and deregulation of European transport markets of the late 1990s. Instead, the deregulation of French road transport, fueled by domestic policy developments, had already occurred in the mid-1980s. Thus, in the 1990s, the European influence did not strengthen the position of actors in favor of liberalization. On the contrary, the liberalization of transport markets in the European Union (EU) contributed to a reregulation in terms of a reinforcement of social legislation at the domestic level. This reregulation was largely due to the pressure exercised by societal actors, such as hauliers' associations and trade unions, which had stressed social issues in the wake of the domestic reform, and whose position in the domestic arena has been significantly strengthened by referring to the potential negative consequences of European deregulation policies.

With regard to the railways, France was formerly already largely in line with the modest European requirements when it reformed the nationalized railways in 1997. The origin of the reform can be attributed to the domestic level, provoked in particular by the disastrous financial situation of the (SNCF), but the nature of the reform of the governance structures of the railways was also influenced by European policies. These changes, however, are only very cautious steps in the direction of a liberalization of the railway markets because of the resistance of key societal actors, who legitimized their position largely by referring to the potentially negative impact of a Europe-induced process of liberalization. The resistance of French policymakers to European policies of liberalization thus takes the form of a two-level game played with divided roles: while French civil servants try to promote European policy proposals, politicians explicitly opposed them in the political arena. They do so because the realization of domestic reforms is easier when presented in opposition to European policies.

In brief, our findings point to the importance of the specific domestic configuration of political forces that "reverberates with" European influences. It is these distinctive configurations in the national policymaking arenas that help explain how domestic and European patterns of policymaking are linked, and how the process of European integration influences structures and actors in the member states. In order to trace this influence we concentrate on three factors: a *policy-related factor*, focusing on whether or not European policies exert pressure to adjust domestic policies and regulations in a specific stage of liberalization; an *ideological factor* favoring a specific problem-solving philosophy that makes certain solutions more likely than others; and the country's *institutional structure* granting *de jure* or *de facto* veto positions to specific actors or groups of actors.

Our two subsector studies illustrate the impact of European integration on national patterns of policymaking, either by restructuring them or by providing new opportunities for domestic actors. The analysis summarizes the main developments in the regulation of road haulage and rail and goes on to present the analytical framework in which we interpret the findings.

## FRENCH TRANSPORT POLICY: BETWEEN LIBERALIZATION, DEREGULATION AND REREGULATION

### Road Haulage

Two dates epitomize the changes that have taken place in French road haulage policy over the last twenty years: the period of 1986 to 1989 when the main regulative constraints were suppressed; and 1994, when a "contrat de progrès," concentrating on social issues and constituting a search for a new kind of regulation, was signed. With respect to the first, the failure of the regulatory framework[1] undermined the legitimacy of government policy in this sector and stimulated the process of liberalization between 1986 and 1989. Under the former framework, the restriction of market access had occurred through licensing procedures in order to limit the number of vehicles allowed to operate in the sector. After partial reforms initiated in the 1960s, these licenses were abolished in 1986.[2] The number of authorizations still grew following the 1986 decree, but more slowly. Quantitative restrictions came to an end in the early 1990s, and the number of authorizations increased rapidly, from 60,724 in 1990 to 86,708 in 1994 (Bernadet 1997: 97). They were eventually abolished in 1998 with the full liberalization of cabotage within the EU.[3] On the other hand, the system of compulsory prices (*tarification routière obligatoire*, TRO) was relaxed by the end of the 1970s and abolished, first for bulky and heavy goods in 1987, and subsequently for all products in 1989, when tariffs were substituted by indicative rates.[4]

Thus, after a process of liberalization culminating in the years 1986 to 1989, the French road haulage market was much more market-oriented than in the 1970s, and there was no substantial contradiction between French road haulage policy and European principles. Instead, liberalization was carried out before similar decisions were taken at the European level and there was therefore no real need for adjustment. Furthermore, since the early 1990s measures have been adopted to regulate the road haulage market, leading to a reinforcement of social legislation. The liberal framework has been maintained, but access to, and the functioning of, the market are subject to public intervention.

The reform measures ushered in a new kind of regulation, based on qualitative rather than quantitative criteria. The 1990 law[5] and the 1992 decree[6] introduced "professional requirements," prescribed specific capital requirements,[7] and introduced the notion of *"respectabilité,"* or the reputation of an applicant. In 1998 a law on road haulage stepped up professional training requirements. Another series of provisions imposed limits on the time spent on duty, or *"temps du service."* In principle, driving and resting hours are defined at the European level,[8] but the European provisions do not define the notion of "working time." In the wake of the 1992 strikes, the Ministry of Transport fostered negotiations between employers and workers, and in 1994 an agreement was signed by the hauliers' associations and two trade unions for long-distance haulage, imposing full payment for the entire time spent on duty rather than just driving hours. This social agreement, which is not only about working time but designed to effect a general modernization of the profession, also introduced market-correcting regulations. It established a new type of relations between government and the hauliers, with agreements replacing decrees, and the state fostering negotiations between trade unions and professional organizations. However, the social agreement of 1994 was not signed by all the members of the profession, and those who did sign it were reluctant to respect it, as shown by the 1996 strikes, when truck drivers demanded the reduction of working time and the payment of all hours spent on duty. As a consequence of the strike, two decrees were passed at the end of 1996, extending the notion of *temps du service* to all enterprises and establishing a maximum of three unpaid hours in total service time.[9] After an attempt to regulate the sector through agreements between societal actors, decrees were once again resorted to.

The new price legislation reintroduces a kind of market regulation, even if such measures are a far cry from the TRO since they do not establish a system of mandatory tariffs. New legislative measures have been adopted to combat low tariffs and the consequences of cutthroat competition. A 1992 law[10] imposes fines for principals paying subcontractors below cost prices, and another law established in 1995 imposes penalties on hauliers offering transport services for too low prices.

The impact of this regulatory trend, together with the adoption of measures to restructure the profession,[11] has nevertheless been limited due to ineffective implementation and control (Bernadet 1997: 302–3). Social legislation in particular is difficult to enforce, since its application is often seen as a constraint on competitiveness, as shown by the reaction of the professional associations to the 1996 decree,[12] making the French transport market more deregulated in practice than it is in theory (Button and Pitfield 1991: 2).

## Railway Regulation

The history of the French railways, the Société Nationale des Chemins de Fer (SNCF), has been characterized by a relatively high level of state intervention designed to protect both freight and passenger rail transport from intermodal competition using the policy instruments of regulation and nationalization. The goal of such protection was the fulfillment of public-service obligations and the state control of developments in the rail sector. Nevertheless, over the last thirty years various reforms have relaxed state control and clarified the responsibilities of the state and the national rail company. The first wave of reforms took place in the 1970s with the introduction of the principle of compensation for public-service obligations and the development of contractual relations between government and the SNCF. This led in 1983 to the transformation of the SNCF into an autonomous public entity (Etablissement public industriel et commercial, EPIC), responsible for railway infrastructure and transport operation. The most incisive reform, however, was the creation of a new structure responsible for rail infrastructure, the *Réseau ferré de France* (RFF), in 1997. Although French rail policy has been in line with EC Regulations 69/1191 and 1893/91, calling for the compensation for public-service obligations, and in accordance with Directive 91/440 and its daughter directives, designed to increase transparency and to enable railway enterprises to behave more commercially; yet, the way in which French policymakers adjusted the regulatory framework to European requirements reveals the peculiar links between French domestic processes and European decisions. To delineate this linkage we refer to the four pillars of Directive 91/440: the improvement of the financial situation; managerial autonomy; the separation of infrastructure management and transport operations; and the extension of access rights to rail infrastructure.

Concerning the improvement of the financial situation, the policy led in France has been in accordance with the European orientations. Specific measures, such as contractual relations between government and the SNCF, have been adopted from the 1970s to reduce the national rail company's deficits. The budget was balanced in 1989 but with a financial injection of 138 million FFr. made by government. In 1989, when the new contract was discussed, the government took on a part of the SNCF debt (38 billion FFr.) through the creation of a defeasance structure in January 1991. The debt is still formally part of the SNCF's liabilities but comes under a separate accounting system and is almost totally taken on by the government. Since that date, however, the SNCF has been free to borrow on the world's capital markets and has built up heavy debts, amounting to more than 200 billion FFr. in 1996. The objective of the 1997 reform was to reduce this SNCF debt by transferring it to the entity responsible for rail infrastructure: around 70 percent of the indebtedness has been transferred to the RFF to allow the SNCF to balance its budget. Moreover, the government was to take over an additional 28.3 billion FFr. transferred to the defeasance created in 1991. Since 1991, the French government has therefore tried to improve the financial standing of the SNCF as recommended by the European Commission and in line with the provisions of Directive 91/440. The mechanism set up in 1991 is in fact very similar to the solution suggested by Article 9 of the directive when it stipulates that "Member States may take the necessary measures requiring a separate debt amortization unit to be set up within the accounting departments of such enterprises."

Second, French rail policy reveals a general trend to extend a greater degree of autonomy to the SNCF. However, the domestic policy differs from its EU equivalent in terms of a hierarchy of goals. In France the improvement of the financial standing of the SNCF is a goal in itself, and commercial autonomy is an instrument, whereas for the commission financial viability is a precondition for the introduction of market forces in the rail sector (CEC 1996: 33). Indeed, financial problems often fueled reform attempts in French rail policy, and many solutions were tried before the European provisions. As the SNCF's difficulties have usually been attributed to its public-service obligations, the reforms in 1969 that gave more commercial autonomy to the railway enterprises, supported by the relatively strong movement in favor of a more market-oriented organization of transport,[13] were intended to improve the financial state of the SNCF.

Third, as a result, the SNCF now has more autonomy in terms of both public-service obligations and the appointment of directors, but in the eyes of the European Commission this autonomy is still limited. Public-service obligations, such as the obligation to exploit the entire network and to transport all passengers and freight, were relaxed in the early 1970s: the principle of compensation for all public-service obligations was introduced, and to meet its obligation to transport the SNCF was allowed to resort to road haulage, through private services or the creation of its own services. For most lines, a ministerial refusal to effect closure meant that the costs incurred by the continued use of the line must be compensated. Finally, several reforms also gave the SNCF more autonomy in the matter of rate fixing and tariffs. The 1982/83 measures also gave more institutional autonomy to the national enterprise. The number of government representatives on the board of directors was reduced.[14] The president is still nominated by the government, but proposed by the board. There has thus been a movement toward more management autonomy: the respective tasks of both the government and the SNCF have been defined more precisely, public-service obligations have been relaxed, and freight tariffs are freely fixed. The European Commission accordingly considers that France has complied with Directive 91/440 (Articles 4-5), but notes that the government still determines long-term objectives and has to approve all key decisions (CEC 1998: 8). Indeed, even if the 1983 reform relaxed the state's direct influence within the board of administrators, as a public entity the SNCF is still under state supervision. There is a government commissioner with an advisory capacity on the board who presents the government's position, and there is also a supervisory body, under the aegis of the Ministry of Economics, with an advisory capacity, mainly for proposals with financial consequences for the SNCF. Moreover, public authorities still define the general quality and coverage of rail transport services. Governmental supervision also extends to wages and the employment policy of the SNCF, as in 1982 and 1997 when left-wing governments asked the SNCF to employ more people.

Finally, the goals of financial soundness and managerial autonomy set by the European Commission are part of a larger project to introduce market forces into the rail sector. The core element of the commission's strategy is to open access to rail infrastructure (CEC 1996, 1998). In this respect, the French railway reform, which mainly consists of the creation of a new public entity responsible for rail infrastructure (RFF), is very limited in comparison with those undertaken in Britain, the Netherlands, or Germany. The 1997 reform, which introduced an institutional separation of infrastructure management and transport operations, also reinforced the role of regional authorities in rail transport, but the impact of both has been rather limited.

Under the 1997 law,[15] the RFF is responsible for developing and planning the rail network. It also owns the rail infrastructure, which formerly belonged to the state, and receives infrastructure charges from the companies operating on the French network. The SNCF is thus only responsible for running the national railways. This institutional separation goes further than the current EC requirements, namely separate accounting, and is in line with the 1996 white paper, which recommends the separation of infrastructure management and transport operations into distinct units, with separate management and accounting.

Despite this, the reform is in fact rather limited. The SNCF is still responsible for all transport operations (Article 149), which effectively maintains the national monopoly for rail transport operations granted to SNCF in 1937. The only limitation is the implementation of European provisions on access rights—groupings offering international transport services, railway enterprises operating international combined transport goods and services, and international groupings with one French enterprise are granted transit or access rights to the French rail network.[16] Hence, as far as access rights are concerned, although France applies the letter of Directive 91/440, such provisions have little impact since no railway enterprise has yet demanded access rights for combined transport services. As for international groupings, the agreements such as Eurostar and Thalys are not very different from the cooperation agreements signed by the SNCF.[17] The SNCF's monopoly is therefore once again well protected. The law also hampers the development of competition on French railway network and limits the scope of the institutional separation insofar as the SNCF is responsible for infrastructure management of RFF. In other words, the SNCF deals with traffic management and the functioning and maintenance of technical and security equipment. The 42,000 railway employees responsible for infrastructure maintenance are still employed by the SNCF.

A final aspect of the reform passed in February 1997 is the regionalization of local transport services offered by the SNCF, albeit on an experimental basis. In accordance with the 1995 law on national and regional development (Article 67, Law 95-115), regions are now responsible for regional passenger rail transport, and seven, out of a total of twenty-two, regions have signed a convention in return for state subsidies. The SNCF's monopoly is maintained for both local and national rail services since public transport is not open for competitive bidding, but the regional conventions should provide new incentives through penalties and controls. This is not in contradiction with the European legislation, as Article 10 of Directive 91/440 (access rights to railway infrastructure) only refers to international services. As far as the separation of infrastructure management, transport operations, and access rights are concerned, France is in line with European rules, but fails to encourage the competition recommended by the commission (CEC 1998).

## Summary

This description clearly shows that the regulation of French transport markets has undergone significant changes in recent years. In road haulage France seems to confirm Majone's statement that "what is observed in practice is never total deregulation but a combination of deregulation and reregulation" (Majone 1990: 3).[18] After the 1986 to 1989 reforms introducing a liberal framework, there has been a move toward reregulation. The question is, why the "early" deregulation in road haulage was followed by reregulation at the very time when the policies pursued at the European level were pushing in the direction of deregulation. In finding an answer to this question we must look for factors that help explain the reform of the railways. When compared to its British, Dutch, or German counterparts, the French reform has indeed been limited. The SNCF's monopoly has been preserved for all rail transport services, and the separation between infrastructure and transport operations is incomplete, since the SNCF still manages and maintains infrastructure on behalf of the RFF. Does the relatively low degree of convergence between the French and European reforms indicate that French reforms have been driven by domestic processes, or is there a link between domestic and European policies? In other words, both subsector reforms present a similar puzzle. Endogenous factors appear to be responsible for stimulating the alteration of respective regulations and may also help explain the outcome of the reform processes. Were this to be the case, there would be no link between domestic and European structures of policy processes. This is, however, hardly plausible given that policymaking and implementation in Europe take place in complex patterns of the multilevel structure of an "ever closer Union." Hence, the question arises as to the nature of European influence on domestic processes. This linkage is not to be understood as a stimulation of converging developments across the member states. Nor can we conceive European regulations and policies as exerting pressure to which national patterns of policymaking and national regulations simply must adapt.

In order to detect how European requirements have "reverberated" in specific sociopolitical settings, we focus on the configuration in the domestic arena with its institutional framework and politics. First of all, we observe that French policies were either in substance (as in road haulage) or formally (as in the case of the railways) in line with European requirements of liberalization and deregulation. Hence, we propose that the impact of Europe is not directly related to the need to adapt national policies to European requirements. Instead, we must look at how

European policies affect the opportunity structure for domestic actors, defined as access points to the arenas of policymaking and new coalition possibilities in a specific stage of liberalization. By differentially empowering national actors, European policies not only tend to alter the strategic opportunities and constraints for action at the domestic level, but also change the domestic political climate in order to stimulate support for European reform objectives (Knill and Lehmkuhl 1999). In other words, it is within the specific sociopolitical setting with its institutional features and its predilection toward a specific problem-solving approach where European influences are processed in one way or another.

## ACCOUNTING FOR REFORM: A SHIFTING BALANCE BETWEEN TWO ADVOCACY COALITIONS

To develop our argument, we will address the road and rail case according to the explanatory scheme outlined in the introductory chapter, beginning with a look at the policy starting point, that is, the policy stage of liberalization, deregulation, or reregulation, then focusing on the specific problem-solving approach, and finally turning to the question of how European influences are processed against the background of the French institutional structure and political context in terms of a shifting balance between two advocacy coalitions.

### Early Liberalization and Internal Reforms: No Need to Change Policies

The empirical findings in both cases indicate that there was basically no need to adapt French transport policies to European requirements. In the case of road haulage, decisions taken at the European level do not appear to have much direct impact on national policy developments, either through legal constraints or through economic pressure. Indeed, market access and price legislation were liberalized in France before the introduction of cabotage, while there were no European requirements for the reregulation that occurred in France.

As far as taxes are concerned, European directives did not affect the French system, which consists of vehicle excise duties, fuel taxes, and road user charges. Regarding vehicle excise duties, Directive 93/89 introduced a minimum rate for vehicles of more than 12 tons, but France was authorized to set rates 50 percent below this minimum until 1997. It was only in December 1998 that the French *taxe à l'essieu* was modified to comply with this directive. There is no European constraint on fuel taxes, which are 50 percent higher in France than the European minima. Finally, since France already had a toll system, the Eurovignette did not affect the French tax structure. Nor did the CTP indirectly put economic pressure on the road haulage sector through cabotage, that is, competition with foreign hauliers making state aid or the suppression of regulatory constraint necessary to offset European competition. As it turned out, cabotage amounts to only 0.1 percent of internal traffic, while France ranks third, after the

Netherlands and Belgium, for ton-kilometres (tkm) of cabotage. As a consequence cabotage is not perceived as a real threat in the road haulage sector.[19]

These findings are very strong arguments against any interpretation relating a European impact only to an adaptation of national to European policies. The same holds for the reregulation that has taken place since the early 1990s. On the contrary, the French government made various attempts to harmonize social norms at the European level.[20] For example, in 1996 and 1997 it unsuccessfully presented proposals for a "social memorandum" to the European Council of Ministers demanding social activities of the European Union. Hence, reregulation was not triggered by Europe.

In the case of the railways, the relationship between domestic reforms and European requirements must be assessed in light of a high degree of conformity between French rail policy and the European model, and until the mid-1990s, the reforms appear to have been unrelated to the developments at the European level. On the other hand, European rail policies may have influenced the 1997 reform to some extent, although this reform was not a direct implementation of EU requirements.

As described above, it was mainly the disastrous financial situation of the French railways that has spurred several reform steps, progressively modifying the principles of rail policy and reducing the level of state intervention. Since the late 1960s, efforts have been made to improve the financial standing of the SNCF, to strengthen its management independence, and to grant more institutional autonomy to the national enterprise. Hence, since the early 1990s, French rail policy has been in line with most European requirements: public-service obligations have been compensated, the management autonomy of the SNCF has been increased, and there has been a massive debt release. There was thus no misfit between national policies and the European legislation and therefore no adaptation pressure.

What complicates the assessment, however, is the 1997 reform. The establishment of the RFF as a new structure administering rail infrastructure while the SNCF is in principle responsible for operations is the most important of all reforms, which may be explained in two ways. First, one can interpret the 1997 reform as a reaction of the French government to the requirements stipulated in Directive 91/440 and its daughter directives. The institutional separation of infrastructure management and transport operations even goes beyond European requirements, which only demand separate accounting.

Second, one can interpret the reform as being mainly driven by national factors, of which the financial situation of the railways was the most dramatic. The SNCF has always suffered financial problems, but the difficulties grew rapidly in the years preceding the reform. [21] It is this specific context in which the creation of the RFF occurred. In 1995 there was already talk of creating a defeasance structure to take on part of the SNCF's liabilities and assets (*Le Monde* 1995a; Grassart and Recoura 1996),[22] but the question was not seriously debated before the 1995 strikes. During these strikes, the railway employees protested against the planned contract for the period of 1996 to 2000, and against the proposed reform of their pension scheme. The three-week strike was also an opportunity to air many of the problems facing the rail sector. In response, the government set up committees, comparable to the road haulage roundtables organized by government after the 1992 roadblocks, to examine the question of the railways. In both cases the government responded to the strike not only by providing immediate solutions, but by placing the problems of the sector on the governmental agenda. In 1995 and 1996, two reports made by working parties of civil servants were submitted to the minister of transport (Stoffaës, Bertold, and Feve 1995; Martinand 1996). Debates were then organized within the economic and social committee, in the CNT (Conseil National des Transports) and at the regional level. These reports and the debate that followed helped generate the idea of creating a separate entity. The government eventually announced a reform in June 1996.

Thus, we find a parallelism of domestic factors and European influences. What is apparent, however, is that there is no direct link between national and European level in the sense that a gap between domestic and European policies generated pressure to adapt, to which the French government subsequently reacted. Since the reform is basically homemade, what is needed is a detailed examination of the domestic processes. In both cases the social dimension was at the heart of public interventions, leading either to reregulation or stimulating social unrest. Consequently, it is worthwhile addressing those factors that influence the problem-solving approach in France in general, and in the transport sector in particular.

## A "Continental Philosophy" and the Notion of "Service Public"

In contrast to an Anglo-Saxon approach where public intervention is subject to strict efficiency criteria, French transport policy has an underlying "continental philosophy" that considers transport "as an instrument in a wider, social framework and focuses on the role transport can play in achieving larger, usually distributional objectives" (Button 1994: 53). Although this typology tends to conceal the changes that French transport policy has undergone, it indicates the importance of ideological factors in shaping transport policymaking in France. The overall impression is that the general coordinates for public policymaking have a marked bias toward intervention, often revolving around the notion of "service public." Indeed, we can trace the existence of this approach in both subsectors.

This approach treats transport as an input in a wider social production function involving broader industrial issues, regional policy, and social equity and justifies state intervention to regulate the sector to reduce market failures. It is reflected in Article 1 of the *Loi d'Orientation sur les Transports Intérieurs*, the 1982 Law on Inland Transport (LOTI). Although this law marked a turning point in public regulation by introducing liberal principles to reduce the level of state intervention, it still used expressions such as "the internal transport system . . . contributes to the national unity and solidarity and to the country's economic and social development." Measures to regulate road haulage were first established in the 1930s to protect the sector from inter-modal competition and economic crisis. A 1934 decree thus established a committee to "coordinate" modes of transport by defining the principles for local agreements between rail and road transport companies and banned the expansion of road haulage. The objective was to reduce overcapacity and consequent ruinous competition in the road haulage sector,[23] but also to protect the railways. Following World War II, the general coordinatory principles of 1934 were restated with the official objective of using the least costly means of transport for the nation.

One justification for state intervention in road haulage was the goal of protecting the railways. In France, rail transport for freight, but also for passengers, has indeed long been considered a "public service," and this justified the protection of the railways and the state intervention in their functioning. Built in the nineteenth century, based on a combination of private initiative and state intervention, much political consensus has subsequently developed around the notion of service public. The railway monopoly, however, was always more effective in France than in the rest of Europe for geographical reasons, because the quality of the waterways and the dispersion of the population impeded the development of other modes of transport, and because this well-established nation-state did not suffer from regional divisions (Jones 1984). The growing state intervention from the beginning of the century did not improve the rail companies' precarious financial situation. Therefore the various rail companies were consolidated in the SNCF in 1937, a joint-stock company in which the state was a majority shareholder. After World War II, the relations between the SNCF and the state were defined in a convention that stipulated that the state had key rights to monitor the company's activities and upheld the notion of public service. Over the years, this notion became partially synonymous for a large number of functions and tasks related to the modern welfare state, including equal access, universal services, and the obligation to exploit unprofitable lines. The historically entrenched notion of service public continues to be of importance in French transport policymaking. It is precisely those public interventions in markets based on the idea of public service that have come under substantial pressure from the European policies of liberalization and the deregulation of international markets (Héritier and Schmidt 1999). If we want to know how European policies impact on domestic structures, we must examine the politics in the domestic policymaking arena of both sectors in more detail.

## Domestic Constraints and Opportunities

It was argued and empirically demonstrated that there was little pressure to adapt, as previous endogenous national reforms had brought both sectors largely into line with European stipulations. Why, then, did the French government oppose liberalization policies at the European level, given this accordance with European demands, and how are the opposing policy developments at the national level to be accounted for? The existence of two opposing advocacy coalitions (Sabatier 1998) in the domestic arena offers an answer to these questions. These coalitions involve administrative officials and state economists in favor of policies of liberalization and deregulation on the one hand, and societal actors opposing liberalization and demanding reregulation on the other. The existence of these two opposing coalitions and, in particular, the shifting balance between them, helps explain Europe's impact on domestic processes, and the linkage between the European and domestic levels of policymaking.

### Road Haulage: European Liberalization Pushing Domestic Reregulation

In the case of road haulage, the development of the regulatory framework, after a phase of substantial liberalization and deregulation, experienced a social reregulation, which makes the existence of two opposing advocacy coalitions particularly obvious. To trace the causes for these changes in the mid-1980s and early 1990s, we refer to the interests and strategic position of the actors at stake, that is, to these coalitions, the administration, politicians, and societal actors.

What are the factors that led to the 1986 "watershed" liberalization, bringing an end to licensing procedures and compulsory tariffs? Senior civil servants and state economists were the promoters of the reform, with political actors slowing down or accelerating reforms. Before the 1986 elections, the conservative Rassemblement pour la Republique (RPR), which went on to form the next government, published a document on transport policy that was critical of state intervention and called for the application of liberal market principles in the transport sector (RPR 1986), so that although limited state intervention was allowable for passenger transport for "public-service" reasons, market forces could be left completely free for freight transport. Legislation and taxes therefore had to be reduced. The RPR thus promoted liberal views during the electoral campaign, in this area as in many others. It was indeed under the newly formed RPR-UDF government that the 1986 decree put an end to the licensing system and that rate controls were subsequently abolished.

This may give the impression of political change as the decisive factor in road haulage reform, but the change was not so sudden. The decree abolishing the licenses system was established only a few days after the formation of the new government, because it had been prepared beforehand, and the 1982 Law on Inland Transport (LOTI), adopted under a socialist government, had already introduced liberal principles to reduce the level of state intervention.[24] Indeed the LOTI provided for the substitution of licenses with authorizations. In 1985, the minister of transport announced the end of the licensing system, and in 1986, when the new government came to power, the draft legislation was already prepared. The pause in the liberal reform, initiated in the 1970s, after 1981 may thus be explained by political change, but this change did not mean a return to a previous regime but a pursuit of new liberal trends. The same phenomenon occurred in 1986 when the political change may have accelerated reform, but the process had already been initiated under the previous government. When the socialists returned to power in 1988, the reforms of 1986 to 1988 were not questioned. Consequently, political change cannot fully explain developments in road haulage policy.

What we see is a progressive change of "policy paradigm" (Hall 1993),[25] not directly linked to the election of a new majority, even if the debate on policy paradigms became the object of electoral competition.[26] This affected not only road haulage but occurred in the context of a change in the "global" policy paradigm or *référentiel* (Muller 1990),[27] or "neoliberal turn" (Jobert 1994). For instance, the abolition of the system of compulsory pricing (TRO) occurred in the context of the suppression of state control on prices under the December 1986 legislation. Indeed, whereas Keynesianism was well established in the French administration after World War II and justified state intervention in many sectors (Rosanvallon 1989), in the 1970s many state economists were convinced by neoliberalism. Jobert and Théret (1994) show that the change of policy paradigm in the French administration derives from the spread of new economic theories, mainly from the United States, stressing the limits of state intervention. These new economic theories were defended mainly by government economists, as opposed to other civil servants and university economists.

The Guillaumat Report (1978) reflects that liberal ideas had indeed become widespread after a period of marked state control insofar as it advised the abolition of rate controls and the relaxation of regulations, leaving market forces free to operate. Moreover, the composition of the committee that produced the report is indicative of the influence of state economists: three civil servants out of four were from the Ministry of Economics, and the representative from the Ministry of Transport could attend the meetings but was not a member of the committee. In any case, in the early 1980s Ministry of Transport officials were heavily critical of economic regulation and appeared to prefer liberal solutions.[28] The spread of new notions within the administration is a key element of the liberalization process, as civil servants were able to promote a new model that inspired partial reforms in response to "anomalies" and that eventually became a political program implemented by a newly elected government. With the diffusion of liberal solutions within the administration, government reports (Guillaumat 1978; Commissariat Général du Plan 1983) concluded that state regulation had failed and proposed reforms to relax state intervention that were introduced in the 1970s and 1980s, irrespective of the political color of the government in power. The reforms that took place from 1986 to 1988 may thus be explained as the result of a change in the general opinion prevailing within the administration, based on the development of new theories and policy failures.[29] The transport administration's proposed liberal solutions were not opposed by hauliers in 1986, and the absence of opposition facilitated the liberalization of prices and market access.

By contrast, developments of the 1990s reveal the important role played by societal actors in French road haulage policymaking although, the French political system does not provide them with an institutionalized veto position. This important role derives from specific features of these associational actors and their interaction with governmental actors. With a membership of 15,000 out of a total of 36,000 road haulage enterprises, the FNTR (Fédération nationale des transporteurs routiers) is the most important of the haulier associations. UNOSTRA (Union nationale des organisations syndicales de transporteurs routiers automobiles) also wields some power and organizes small enterprises.[30] Furthermore, the impact of trade unions, in particular the CFDT (Confédération française démocratique du travail) and the FO (Force ouvrière), on developments in French road haulage policy should not be underrated, as they negotiate agreements with the professional organizations. Both hauliers' associations and trade unions were represented in a number of institutionalized forms of public–private interactions.

Since 1947, hauliers have been represented by the Conseil supérieur des transports (CST),[31] consisting of hauliers' representatives, ministerial representatives, experts, members of Parliament and trade unionists, hauliers, transport users, and local authorities. Its role is advisory and, according to trade unions and civil servants, it is of little use,[32] rarely proposes new solutions to problems, and is only an arena where the administration has contacts with hauliers' representatives and trade unions. The other body responsible for transport matters—previously price setting and now monitoring prices and costs—is the CNR (Comité national routier). Until the 1980s, the groupements professionnels routiers were responsible for monitoring rules at the local level, and the bureaux régionaux de fret kept hauliers informed and shared the available goods among them.

The regulation of the transport market thus created links between the administrative structures and the profession. The CNR, where the FNTR representatives have an overwhelming majority, is a way for the two organizations to impose their views on the administration, through, for instance, the reports published by the CNR (Ocqueteau 1997). In addition to these institutionalized contacts, there are direct contacts between the administration and the professional organizations,[33] which allow the latter to influence national policymaking. Yet, a major complaint of civil servants is that the professional associations are lacking any sense of long-term perspective,[34] a complaint largely due to the ambiguous positions of the main haulier associations. Until the mid-1980s, the FNTR and UNOSTRA rejected dirigisme by opposing tax increases, controls, social legislation on working time, and the creation of freight platforms (Commissiariat Général du Plan 1983) while simultaneously demanding state protection. That is, they defended the idea of a less regulated market while insisting on the need for an only incremental change (UNOSTRA, *Les Echos* 1979a: FNTR, *Les Echos* 1979b). Then in the 1980s, the question of liberalization divided the very diverse members of the FNTR: the smallest enterprises favored price control as a form of protection and the abolition of licenses as a chance to regain market shares from their larger counterparts (Ocqueteau and Thoenig 1997),[35] whereas the bigger undertakings simply put priority on price liberalization.

Thus, for a long time both rivalries between the FNTR and UNOSTRA and the heterogeneity of the FNTR's membership stimulated an ambiguity in the position of hauliers with a twofold impact. On the one hand, while already provided with a strong position in the centralist French polity, the administration was even further strengthened by the absence of opposition. This constellation facilitated the implementation of the policies of liberalization and deregulation in the 1980s. On the other hand, the lack of strategic capacity on the private side devaluated the institutionalized patterns of interest intermediation. In French politics, the patterns of public–private interaction in the transport sector are generally a far cry from corporatist and consensus oriented. Realistically speaking, the influence of hauliers, organizations, in particular the FNTR, is linked to their capacity to carry out industrial action, as in 1984 and 1992, and the minister's concern to avoid such conflict in the short term (Cohen 1992; Ocqueteau 1997: 16, n. 9).[36]

The reliance of interest organizations on industrial action rather than on institutionalized patterns of interest intermediation became particularly apparent in the aftermath of the liberalization of the 1980s. After the "passive" support of liberalization and in light of the difficulties faced by the profession,[37] the FNTR and UNOSTRA complained of a lopsided liberalism characterized by free prices and cutthroat tariffs accompanied by high levels of taxation, social constraints, and state controls, and demanded lower fuel taxes and the regulation of a "foolish market" (FNTR 1996: 2). They called for the banning of excessively low prices, the establishment of a professional structure to enforce prices, and the support of stricter qualitative criteria for access to the profession and the stepping up of controls on subcontracting.[38] In a period of high unemployment, the relatively high rate of job creation in the road haulage sector lent weight to the hauliers' claims.[39] Their common interest in such state intervention induced a rapprochement between UNOSTRA and the FNTR.[40] Both organizations, eager to "regulate liberalization" and willing to participate in the negotiations that followed the 1992 industrial action by hauliers, signed the *contrat de progrès* and supported some forms of market regulation, thus constituting a factor favoring developments in French road haulage policy.

The July 1992 roadblocks functioned as a "triggering device," that is to say an "unforeseen event" that "helps shape issues . . . defined by the initiators" (Cobb and Elder 1983: 84), which started a new reform process. Initially, this movement mainly concerned independent workers, protesting against a new system of sanctions linked to driving licenses, the *permis à points*. Nevertheless, it was an opportunity for employers to highlight sectoral problems and for drivers to draw attention to their working conditions. As a response to such claims, the government set up the Dobias Commission, consisting of economists, civil servants, trade unions, and hauliers' associations. The commission found that the former policy did not produce satisfactory results and that new rules had to be defined in the framework of the 1986 liberalization (Commissariat Général du Plan 1993). In this context, the first law on subcontracting was voted in 1992 and, after the publication of another report by the commission in March 1994 (Commissariat Général du Plan 1994), a social agreement was signed the following November. This commission had a direct impact, insofar as it put problems on the agenda and fostered the emergence of new solutions, and an indirect impact, in that it favored the growth of trade unions,[41] previously weak in this sector. In the negotiations, the unions championed, among other things, the notion of working time, and membership subsequently rose from 3 percent in 1992 to 7 percent in 1997 (*Le Monde Emploi* 1997: II), whereas the general trend in France at the time was one of dropping union membership (Labbé and Croizat 1992). This rise in membership produced an increased level of influence: whereas during the 1992 roadblocks, workers' organizations did not play a significant role, in 1996 and 1997, the unions led the strikes with a clear distinction being made between employers and workers.

To sum up, the measures adopted in the 1990s to regulate road haulage do not have the same scope as those of the mid-1980s and late 1980s and cannot be defined as a paradigm change, since the liberal framework has not been challenged—market forces are still considered more efficient but new instruments are designed to mitigate the consequences of deregulation. In Hall's words, it is as a "second-order change" (Hall 1993). Contrary to the British case studied by Hall, key actors have been *societal rather than official*, and the changes appear as a response to social pressure. The main hauliers' associations have demanded new forms of regulation, and some of their claims have been supported by trade unions, whose influence increased in the wake of the 1992 roadblocks.

Organizational density alone does not always account for the relative strength of societal groupings given its relatively low level in the transport sector (only about 50 percent of sectoral enterprises belong to a professional organization, and union membership stands at about 7 percent). What is important is the willingness of enterprises to participate in group action meant to withhold important functions in order to defend their sectoral interest against the government. Moreover, in addition to the economic impact, the strikes of hauliers gained impetus from a diffuse public support acknowledging the poor working conditions in the sector. Both aspects helped shift the balance between the two advocacy coalitions in favor of the pro-reregulation coalition.

Hence, there are good empirical grounds for arguing that both the deregulation and the reregulation reforms in the French road haulage were the result of domestic factors. They were either caused by the failure of the former regulation and a change in the general attitude of civil servants and state economists in the mid-1980s or, from the early 1990s onward, generated by societal pressure expressed by industrial action by road hauliers and their interest organizations. Yet, we argue that in both reforms it is possible to trace a particular European influence that becomes apparent in the domestic arena by strengthening the position of either of the two advocacy coalitions.

With regard to the 1980s, the liberalization reforms were indeed linked with European projects such as the Single Market Program (SMP), as national reforms were presented as a necessary precondition for successful and competitive entry into the European single market (*Le Monde* 1985, 1986).[42] Thus, domestic reform factors were given additional European momentum, and an anticipatory strategy fueled reforms in France well before those of its main competitors in Europe, that is, Germany and the Netherlands. In the absence of any significant opposition by societal or political actors, the position of the pro-liberalization coalition revolving around the institutionally powerful administration was again strengthened by referring to competitive advantages that French hauliers might achieve in a single European market. Yet, what cannot be explained with reference to the liberal bias of European policies is the reregulation movement.

In this respect we are faced with a puzzling finding. Although since the late 1980s there was a complete fit between French policies and the requirements of a liberalized European transport market, the European policy had considerable impact on the politics in the domestic arena in France in the sense of strengthening the position of those actors opposing deregulated domestic markets. The position of the coalition of hauliers' associations and trade unions that was active in demanding a reregulation of domestic transport markets was strengthened by referring to European policies. Given the consequences of the domestic deregulation, that is, a marked increase of the competitive situation in the sector followed by a decrease of tariffs, incomes, and a massive tendency to self-exploitation of small hauliers, the "pro-regulation" coalition could successfully refer to a worsening scenario in liberalized European transport markets. It defended its claim for social regulation, for instance, on the grounds that the geographical position of France within Europe exposed it more to competition. Despite its marginal empirical effect, cabotage became the symbol of the threat of uncushioned market forces at both the domestic and European scale. Given the economic impact of their industrial action, the strategic position of hauliers and their associations in the domestic arena was significantly strengthened by European policies, thus promoting far-reaching reregulation activities in France.

Indeed, such an interpretation offers new insights into how European policies might impact domestic structures. Even if there is a broad fit between national policies and European policy requirements of liberalization but a country has moved on to deregulation, referring to Europe might help counterdevelopments. In France, this effect was due to a shifting balance in the domestic arena as a specific advocacy coalition found its strategic position strengthened by successfully using the threat deriving from European policies to back its arguments.

## Railway Policy: Following Europe by Opposing Its Policies

As has been shown, there are parallels between the reforms in the sectors of road haulage and rail. The changes in the 1970s and 1980s in the liberalization of road haulage and rail both took place in the context of a new, more market-oriented policy paradigm, whereas recent developments are specific answers to particular problems placed on the public agenda by organized industrial action in the sector. The reforms of the 1970s and 1980s were intended to make the SNCF more independent, and hence more commercially viable, but did not lead to a complete change of the policy framework as in the case of road haulage: state intervention, albeit reduced, is still high and competition between rail enterprises has simply not materialized. The paradigm change within the administration did not have as far-reaching consequences as in the road haulage case in terms of policy content. European perspectives did not provoke radical change either; Directives 91/440, 95/18, and 95/19 have been implemented, but the principles defended by the European Commission, such as open access, are not integrated into French legislation, and the SNCF's monopoly has in effect been preserved. The explanation for this lies in a strong opposition to such developments; the main veto positions derive from the adherence to the notion of public service.

The public service was a reference shared by all opponents of the reform, not only trade unions and left-wing parties that opposed the reform in the Parliament. Even the majority right-wing parties promoting the reform tended to limit liberalization on the basis of public-service principle, given the strong societal adherence to this notion. The way in which Directive 91/440 was implemented is another illustration of the cautiousness of right-wing parties on transport liberalization: this directive was only implemented in 1995, that is, two years after the 1993 deadline, and the decree was passed just before the end of government led by Balladur between the two rounds of presidential elections when it no longer feared a threat to its popularity.

A second factor diminishing the pressure for reform of the railways and the introduction of market forces was the railways themselves. The SNCF management, for example, was against further liberalization, preferring the "more fruitful" strategy of cooperation.[43] It only agreed to participate in the creation of European freeways on rail tracks because it was built to coordinate infrastructure and management rather than to step up competition.[44]

However, the SNCF viewed liberalization as premature rather than undesirable,[45] and the construction of a European rail market is seen as an opportunity, particularly for freight.[46] It is aware that if it does not participate in the construction of any freightway it will be isolated and therefore favors "cooperative freightways." Liberalization and competition are seen as unavoidable, and it is generally considered "suicidal" not to prepare for them, the SNCF's goal being to reduce its debts so as to better compete with the other European railway enterprises.[47] The need to reduce the number of railway employees, one of the arguments of the white paper, is also supported by the SNCF.[48] With regard to current forms of cooperation, the SNCF champions Eurostar and Thalys as successful examples of such initiatives.[49]

The trade unions put up greater resistance to European developments than the SNCF management. They criticized the commission's proposals as "ultra-liberalist," and all eight SNCF unions unanimously rejected them as a bad solution for the railways. They opposed liberalization, because they considered it a threat to their employment, wages, and status (Ribeill 1992), and argued that there was no need for intramodal competition since there was already (unfair) intermodal competition, mainly with road transport. The slow erosion of public-service principles, line closures, and redundancies was frequently cited as the cause of the decline of the railways. In their view, private companies would abandon unprofitable secondary lines, endangering the equitable distribution of rail transport, and the creation of the RFF constitutes a first step toward the introduction of such competition.[50] The unions also oppose the assigning of particular lines to freight transport and consider regionalization as a threat to SNCF's monopoly.

That the trade unions have been able to shape the reform of the French railways was not only due to the public and political support to the notion of public service, widely used by them. The importance of the unions as a veto actor in the reform process is also related to the relatively high rate of unionization within the SNCF.[51] Those rejecting the reform (CGT, CFDT, and SUD) represent more than 50 percent of rail employees (*Les Echos* 1996: 17), and even those unions that supported the general framework of the reform insisted on principles such as the unity of the enterprise. Results of the high degree of unionization and the conflictual tradition[52] of the main trade unions within the SNCF were effectively organized blockings of rail traffic and other industrial action in France and in Brussels. In addition to the domestic strikes of 1995, 1996, and 1997, in 1992 the representatives of six French rail unions went to Brussels to protest against the liberalization initiated by Directive 91/440, although there was no real threat to France at that time.

Thus, in rail policy we find a configuration of actors in the policymaking arena similar to that in road haulage. First, societal actors were able to establish themselves as key actors opposing European influences in the domestic arena even though the French political system does not grant them institutionalized veto points. In the railway case, sectoral resistance with its broad societal backing even constitutes a major constraint for the reform of rail policy.[53] Second, neither political parties nor governmental actors were the main promoters of domestic reforms. Even those in favor of a more far-reaching reform were hampered in the pursuit of a straightforward policy by massive social resistance. Finally, the administration once again played a decisive role in pushing the reform process.

The way in which particular senior civil servants slowly introduced liberal elements into the governance structure of the French railways reveals the basic mechanism linking domestic and European policymaking. European ideas entered French transport policy through the administration. However, the promoters of the reform had to take into account political opposition to the reform. These two elements gave the politics of reforming the railways its particular features. The two-level game between the domestic and European level was played in a division of labor between the administration and government, as shown below in more detail. Civil servants were the main promoters of liberalization in France, while French governments opposed the liberal orientation of the European Commission in order to reassure organized national interests and to tame their strong capacity to mobilize opposition.

*The Impact of the European Union on the 1997 Reform: Constraints and Solutions.* Although we have stated that national forces had put the 1997 reform of the railway on the national agenda by reinforcing the idea of a need for change, and despite the finding that French railway policies were already formally in line with EC provisions, the influence of European developments is undeniable in the sense that they were at the same time a "constraint" and a "source of inspiration." This influence can be illustrated by the way in which the French government tried to cope with the debts of the railways.

First, the SNCF's liabilities have simply been transferred to another public entity, thus leaving the question of how to finance current and future investments unresolved. The 1997 reform is therefore only a partial answer to the financial problems of the railways, and even among those who formulated the reform, its financial shortcomings are recognized.[54] However, the government did not want the state to bear SNCF's debts directly so as not to jeopardize compliance with the Maastricht criteria; it was indeed a "major constraint."[55] The rail debt transferred to the RFF accounted for more than 1.5 percent of GDP; had the state relieved the railways of all their liabilities, there would have been a risk of a public debt ratio of more than 60 percent. The creation of a public entity with a commercial income, not subject to the same state accounting rules, was a way to avoid these consequences.

Second, European policies not only limited the possible responses to the debt problem through the Maastricht criteria, but also provided a solution. A response to indebtedness could indeed have been to transfer part of the railway liabilities to a defeasance structure, which, as in 1991, would not have been calculated in public debts. The proposed solution was an institutional separation between infrastructure management and transport operations, as recommended by the European Commission. Indeed, possible changes had already been discussed in relation to European legislation and projects, and these debates had defined the possible solutions. An interesting point is that almost all the recent parliamentary reports made on the railways were written by the parliamentary delegations on European issues or in response to a European Commission Communication (Assemblée nationale 1994b, 1994c, 1994d, 1995, 1996a, 1996b; Sénat 1996a, 1996b, 1996c). In these reports and in those of select committees, the idea of creating a separate entity responsible for infrastructure is considered in relation to European recommendations (Assemblée nationale 1994a). Even before a reform was seriously considered, the idea of making a sharper distinction between infrastructure and operations was mentioned on account of the new European provisions. When the reform process was initiated, the European legislation had thus been discussed, and its content had been integrated by most actors. The supporters of the reform partly justify it by the need to fall into line with European rail provisions.[56]

Hence, there are grounds for arguing that the reform originated at the domestic level, but that its content was substantially influenced by European policies in general, here the prospect of monetary union with its financial criteria, and the European rail policies in particular, with its objective of introducing competitive elements in the rail sector. With respect to the latter aspect, the 1997 reform was not only inspired by European directives and recommendations, but also may produce long-term effects along the lines recommended by the European Commission.

*The Slow Introduction of the "European Logic."*    Although the creation of RFF is only a precondition for the introduction of competition, its creation and the process of regionalization are expected to generate a dynamic of their own, which may lead to a more liberalized system. First, the 1997 reform had a "ratchet effect," as shown by the change in attitude of former political opponents to the reforms: while having criticized the railway policy of the former conservative government, after its inauguration in 1997 the new left-wing government changed its attitude. Although the communist minister of transport, one of the then main opponents of the reform, announced he would "reform the reform," he did not abolish RFF and even upheld the principle of separation between ownership and planning (*Les Echos* 1997: 22).

Second, some civil servants consider it likely that transport services by new companies will be encouraged to create new sources of income. As admitted by the current president of the RFF, albeit reluctantly, even if the SNCF's unity has been preserved, there is now an entity responsible for infrastructure that does not have the same interests as the SNCF.[57] Indeed, RFF will need new sources of income, since the infrastructure charges paid by the SNCF and state contributions to infrastructure costs do not allow it to balance its budget.[58] Simultaneously, however, they state that the creation of RFF was not intended to allow other companies to carry out transport operations.[59]

Other developments in French rail policy are also expected to generate commitments to liberalization in the long term. For example, the creation of international groupings such as Eurostar and Thalys is considered a soft form of liberalization by French civil servants. They are expected to develop their own logic of development, thus obliging the SNCF to "react."[60] Similarly, regionalization is considered a threat to the monopoly of SNCF in rail transport.[61] Since the 1997 reform, the SNCF has been a service provider for regional authorities that agreed to experiment with regionalization, but it is difficult to assess empirically the impact that this part of the reform may have on the SNCF monopoly.[62]

In conclusion, even if the 1997 reform is very limited in scope and preserves the SNCF's monopoly, it has produced some institutional preconditions for a further liberalization, through the creation of RFF and regionalization. Moreover, the idea that in the future other rail enterprises will operate on the French networks seems to be commonly held not only within the RFF and the transport administration but also in the SNCF, where the management considers it "suicidal" not to prepare for competition. European principles regarding rail policy are therefore slowly defining a new organization of the railways in France. The specific interaction between policies at the domestic and European levels, however, led French policymakers to take an opposing role to any liberalization policy at the European level.

*The Refusal of European Orientations as a Solution to National Obstacles.* At the European level, since rail policy reappeared on the European Commission's agenda at the end of the 1980s, France has criticized and slowed down the movement toward a market-oriented organization of rail transport. The main bone of contention has been the extension of access rights to infrastructure. In 1991, France rejected a general liberalization of access and only agreed to open access rights to international transport, and it has been keen to prevent any further liberalization, especially when Directives 95/18 and 95/19 were discussed.[63] Later, in 1996, the French government took a stand against the white paper on the revitalization of the EC's railways, rejecting it as an "unconditional liberalization unconnected with reality" (*Le Monde* 1996b). The French position on freight freeways for rail transport also illustrates its rejection of the logic of liberalization. France initially rejected the idea as a way of extending access rights, and when it later agreed to facilitate freight transport along certain routes it was within the bounds of Directive 91/440. Contrary to the recommendations issued by the commission in May 1997, which insisted on nondiscriminatory conditions and the need to open freightways to international traffic and cabotage (*Bulletin Quotidien: Europe* 1997a, 1997b), the SNCF, the SNCB in Belgium, and the (CFL) in Luxembourg agreed to create a freightway on which international traffic, in particular, cabotage, will therefore not be free. France presented this decision as a way to improve cooperation between European networks, in opposition to the liberal "freeways."[64] One of the main lines of argument used by France to counterbalance the commission's "liberal proposals" is an insistence on cooperation and interoperability. When the commission's initial proposal was discussed in 1989,[65] under French chairmanship, France simultaneously proposed a resolution on high-speed networks and interoperability. During its 1995 mandate, France also gave greater importance to interoperability and therefore prepared the adoption of Directive 96/48.[66]

Hence, irrespective of the political color of the government, the positions held at the European level are therefore guided by the same principles: slowing down liberalization as much as possible. In so doing, the official French position was in line with the positions defended by the SNCF as a whole, and by the trade unions in particular.[67] The question is, however, how can such a consensus be commensurate with the introduction of European principles—which goes beyond the mere implementation of European legislation—into French policies? The answer is as surprising as it is intriguing: to refuse these principles is in fact a way of introducing them.

Left-wing parties and trade unions opposed the reform proposed by the right-wing government by negatively linking the project to European developments.[68] In this context, opposition to the European orientations helped make the reform acceptable; "Europe" acted as a kind of "decompression chamber" (Cohen 1996: 153). In response, the government and right-wing members of Parliament have adopted a highly critical stance vis-à-vis European developments, and opposition to the white paper was used to bolster the proposed reform as a way of guaranteeing their sincerity as far as liberalization and competition are concerned, in response to the fears expressed by trade unions. Such arguments were used during the parliamentary debates by right-wing members of parliament and the junior minister of transport (*La tribune des fossés* 1997). For some senior civil servants, opposition to recent European developments was necessary to get the reform through; the white paper was a constraint in the reform process and had to be criticized for this reason.[69] More generally, the French representative for transport in Brussels explains that France has to oppose European proposals because of industrial relations constraints, and has to *"calmer les ardeurs bruxelloises."*[70]

The reference to European policies within the French reform processes is often stressed as a way to promote liberal reforms.[71] Regarding the creation of RFF, European integration was not referred to as an important project that justified liberal reforms, but opposition to European liberalism was meant to show that the proposed reform was not as liberal as its opponents suggested. External pressure in the two-level politics was used in a twofold, contradictory way. There is a "division of labor" between political and administrative actors. Whereas members of Parliament and members of government, irrespective of political party, oppose the European rail policy, European principles are promoted by senior civil servants. A survey of French senior civil servants has shown that they usually have a good opinion of "Europe," with almost 90 percent stating that they were favorable or highly favorable toward European integration (Rouban 1993). They are indeed quite responsive to European orientations,[72] and civil servants working in Brussels constitute a special channel through which European orientations are explained and defended. The fact that many senior civil servants successively work at the national and the European levels helps impregnate the national arena with the European logic. Within the French administration we thus find a positive appreciation of European solutions for rail policy (Martinand 1996: 7), and, in line with Lesquesne's observations, some civil servants explicitly cite "Europe" as an opportunity to inaugurate a new policy.[73] It is these civil servants who are also the experts who prepared the rail reform, and who proposed solutions directly inspired by European orientations in their reports (Stoffaës, Bertold, and Feve 1995; Martinand 1996). The rejection of a European orientation by political actors was primarily a way to reassure the opponents of liberalization, trade unions, and left-wing parties, but also members of the then majority. In spite of this official discourse, there is a strong internalization of the European logic among most senior civil servants, who have sufficient weight to diffuse their ideas within the French polity, especially as "experts" (Jobert and Théret 1994).

To sum up, in comparison to the reforms in Britain, the Netherlands, and Germany, the French rail reform has been limited, as the SNCF's monopoly has been preserved for all rail transport services and the separation between infrastructure and transport operation is incomplete. Powerful national forces, primarily the trade unions but also a relatively strong political consensus (both opposition and majority parties), regard the notion of "public service" as sacrosanct and impede a more radical organizational change of the railways. In this context, opposition to the European Commission's proposals was a means to disconnect the French reform from the liberal European rail policy. However, within both the transport administration and the SNCF management, European developments tend to be considered as inescapable and are increasingly integrated into their strategies and regulatory reasoning. Both current and future EU legislation is likely to determine French rail policy. The creation of RFF itself tends to confirm this hypothesis. Indeed, even if changes were called for by internal forces, mainly because of the poor financial situation of the railways, the concrete shaping of the reform was directly influenced by European legislation: the idea of creating a separate entity responsible for infrastructure was discussed only after Directive 91/440 was issued, and many actors of the reform recognized that this directive was an element that mattered. The promoters of a rail policy in line with European orientations, more than the right-wing majority that proposed the 1997 reform, are senior civil servants, heavily immersed in the European logic and supporting the solutions advocated by the European institutions. They have had an impact that goes beyond governmental change, as shown by the de facto acceptance of the reform by a left-wing government.[74]

## CONCLUSION

Transport policymaking in France, as elsewhere, has undergone significant changes over the last two decades. The studies of the reforms in the road haulage and rail sectors identified a particular linking of endogenous factors and a European influence. These explanations provide us with significant insights into the differential impact of European policies on structures and policies of the EU member states by influencing the mechanisms of Europeanization and the ambiguous patterns of the two-level game between the French domestic and European levels.

With regard to the first, both sectors show that the impact of Europe is not due to any degree of institutional or policy pressure to which domestic structures and policies must be adapted. In neither of the two cases was the European influence felt through a hierarchical imposition of certain policies or economic pressure deriving from European decisions. Instead, endogenous factors brought French regulations broadly into line with European requirements. Nevertheless, we did trace a distinctive European influence, but with quite different consequences. In road haulage, "Europe" accelerated a reregulation countering the European liberalization of international transport markets. In the rail sector, the ideas of the European reform model made inroads into administrative thinking and policies despite all rhetorical refutations. If French policies were already in line with European policies, what, then, could explain this European influence on French transport policymaking?

We argue that three factors—the specific stage of the "liberalization–deregulation–reregulation circuit" in which France is located and the national policymaking arena with its institutional framework, its configuration of actors, and its socioeconomic belief system, that is, a certain preference for public interventions—constitute the key for tracing the influence of Europe. It is the specific domestic institutional configuration and the patterns of interaction where European influence is felt most. What characterized the domestic arena in the French transport sector was the existence of two clearly identifiable and opposing advocacy coalitions, one involving administrative actors, researchers, and state economists, the other comprising societal actors and interest organizations. Espousing free-market values, government economists backed up their position on foreign experiences with liberalization and deregulation, and their frequent contact with the European decision-making arena has immersed especially senior civil servants in the European logic. In opposition we find a strong coalition favoring the preservation or restoration of an interventionist regulatory framework. While this coalition was partly organized and represented by sectoral associations or by trade unions, it drew its strength not only from the degree of organization, but also from the economic impact of its industrial actions (road haulage), or from public support. Generally speaking, the socioeconomic coordinates in France have a marked disposition toward public intervention for social reasons, best expressed in the notion of "service public" which expressed the deeply rooted notion of solidarity and social equity. In the case of transport, the notion serves as a container for various arguments including the railways' obligation to guarantee universal passenger transport. If this sense of social rights is perceived as violated by public actors, either through intervention or uncushioned exposure to market forces, there is a high likelihood of massive resistance to public policies. Such a protest is often not restricted to the actors in a particular sector, but to some extent enjoys broad support of civil society. Hence, although the French political system offers very few institutionalized veto points, de facto societal actors have the chance to substantially shape policymaking.

The mechanisms in which European policies affected this domestic arena varied from modifying the institutional constraints and opportunities to altering the political climate at the national level in order to win support for European reform models—with road haulage being a case for the former and the railways for the latter.

In the case of road haulage, European policies brought about very different results. On the one hand, the general tenor of the SMP helped the emergence of the pro-liberalization coalition, but, given the absence of a homogeneous opposition, reference to European policies facilitated the implementation of the domestic liberalization of transport markets from 1986 onward. On the other hand, in the aftermath of the domestic regulation, the coalition favoring a reregulation began to consolidate. In this respect, referring to the European threat contributed significantly to the coordination and organization of sectoral interests favoring a reregulation of domestic transport markets in France. Hence, in the case of road haulage, European policies helped shift the balance between these two advocacy coalitions by providing either the one or the other with supportive arguments that could be used in domestic bargaining processes.

In the case of the railways, the situation was similar to that of road haulage. We were faced with two coalitions, both of which are strengthened by referring to European developments. Given that liberalization would imply far-reaching changes for the traditional regulatory approach in rail transport, the forces of resistance were stronger and actively hindered the introduction of competition. Although the European influence was not strong enough to tip the scales toward a more liberal rail policy, there was an important Europeanization mechanism at work, leading to a certain degree of convergence between European policy requirements and French railway regulation.

In explaining this slow convergence in the railway case in the face of strong opposition to the European model, we argue that it is not primarily by altering the domestic opportunity structure that European railway policies had an impact on French rail policies. Recruiting on studies that emphasize the importance of ideas, we take the analysis of the creation of RFF as an example for the influence of Europe via a cognitive mechanism (Jachtenfuchs1995; Kohler-Koch 1999; Knill and Lehmkuhl 2000; Wallace and Wallace 2000). In this respect, administrative actors with a positive appreciation of a European solution for rail policy increasingly permeate the national arena with the European logic. Despite the current strong resistance, it is probable that the "European logic" is slowly making inroads into regulatory practice. In addition, this positive assessment of the pervasive character of European policies can be backed up by an institutional change that has taken place. In this respect, the future developments allowed by the 1997 reform might induce a dynamic of their own in a double sense. On the one hand, the RFF is an institution with an interest in its persistence and development in institutional and financial terms. The pursuit of this interest might not only help create a corporate identity of those working for the RFF, but may also generate a conflictual constellation between the RFF and the SNCF. On the other hand, regionalization has upgraded the importance of regional actors with an interest in cost-effective transport. In some countries, such as Germany, it is primarily the regional level where the competitive elements are increasingly felt, and they not only challenge the monopoly of the former monopolist but also exert pressure on the overall regulatory framework (see Teutsch in this volume; Herr and Lehmkuhl 1997).

Finally, the studies of the reforms in the French transport sector provide insights into the peculiar interaction between the domestic and European level. In empirical terms, both cases tend to confirm well-known patterns. On the one hand, in the case of road haulage, the French government defended the position of its industry in the process of European policymaking by trying to integrate its position on social issues in European regulations. On the other hand, in the case of rail, European provisions bear the potential to constrain opposition at the national level. Yet, although to some extent in favor of the European model, national policymakers could not straightforwardly use European constraints as a lever for the modernization of rail regulation. Given the resistance of societal actors, they tried to disconnect the two levels as far as possible. In this respect, the opposition of French officials at the European level had a twofold objective: to slow down the process of liberalization at the European level, and to make the reform acceptable at the domestic level. But the two cases have more to offer than just a "thick description" of empirical developments.

In analytical terms, these French patterns of playing the two-level game allow us to draw some more general conclusions on both the supranational-to-domestic and domestic-to-supranational halves of the loop. Although this chapter—as most of the others in this volume—has focused on the first, we are quite aware that both halves are often so closely interlinked that to separate them bears the risk to dismiss their reciprocal causation. To capture the particular dynamics of European governance in a more encompassing way requires the relation of both dimensions to one another.

In this respect, a distinction between a "domestic security network" defending values related to "national security, cohesion, public service and occasionally safety and environmental concerns" and a "supranational regulatory network" governing the "now well-established rules affecting market access and competition in all modes" (Aspinwall 1999, 125ff.) only partly captures the dynamics of the patterns described above. What seems to be more promising is to follow the claim that the executive is not unified (Putnam 1988: 432; Parsons 2000). In so doing we have been able to show two things concerning the way the two-level game is played in France, that is, the division of labor between the administrative and the political executives.

On the one hand, we tend to confirm the neofunctionalist assumption that functionally specific bureaucracies at the national level are among the effective carriers of integration (Haas 1964: 49). Immersed into the process of European integration and its strong liberal bias by its frequent meetings with its European colleges, the transport administration was most active in implementing its concepts. It was the one that carried the ideas inherent in the European model into the domestic arena. On the other hand, this process was slowed down by the political executives. Given their need to follow the claims of their constituencies, political leaders were necessarily much more sensitive to the loud voice of social interests. Put differently, the logic of party politics made French governments play the part of the brakeman in the intergovernmental negotiations at the European level. In sum, the division of labor between the administrative and the political leadership represents a mechanism to solve a country's cognitive dissonance deriving from the need to accommodate the domestic and European influences.

# NOTES

1. Indeed, the interventionist policy in the road haulage sector did not always produce the expected results. In spite of price legislation, contracts were often made at 10 to 20 percent below the legal minimum rates, licenses were resold at high prices and did not stop the growth of long-distance road haulage, social regulations were not respected, and subcontracting sprouted up. As a way to escape legislation, own-account transport, which is not subject to quantitative limits and price controls, took off after 1975, as did truck-and-driver rentals as another way of avoiding legislative constraints. In addition, the former regulation proved insufficient to counter dramatic changes in the modal split that have been detrimental to the SNCF.

2. The licenses were abolished with the introduction of the "authorizations" provided for under the 1982 Law on Inland Transport.

3. Law 98-69 of 6 February 1998 (OJ 7/2/98) adjusted the French system to the European one by introducing licenses for categories of vehicles that do not have an EC license. The creation of this new type of license does not mean the reintroduction of quantitative restrictions.

4. Decree, 6 May 1988.

5. Law 90-369 of 11 May 1990 (OJ 15/5/90).

6. Decree 92-609 of 3 July 1992.

7. At least 21,000 FFr. for each vehicle of over 6 tons. A 1997 decree increased this to 100,000 FFr. for the first vehicle, 50,000 for the second, and 21,000 for any additional vehicle.

8. See Regulation 3820/85.

9. These provisions first only applied to the *grands routiers* who spend at least six nights away from home and were extended to all truck drivers in January 1998.

10. Law 92-1445, OJ 1/1/93, amended in July 1996.

11. In line with the 1994 agreement, 165 million FFr. were earmarked for groupings of road haulage companies in 1996, but according to UNICOOPTRANS, a private association promoting groupings and providing technical assistance, very few enterprises applied for this support. Most enterprises still employ only one or two workers.

12. See, for instance, *L'Officiel des Transporteurs,* 1–8 February 1996. The hauliers' association UNOSTRA demanded that these decrees be quashed by the Conseil d'Etat (*L'Officiel des Transporteurs,* 1–8 March 1997). The 1997 strikes highlighted the poor enforcement of the agreements and degrees adopted after the 1996 barricades.

13. The same movement occurred in the road haulage sector and is illustrated by the Nora and Guillaumat reports in 1968 and 1978.

14. There are now seven representatives of the state, compared with ten in 1982, and the six delegates of the personnel are elected by the workers and no longer nominated by the state.

15. Law 97-135 of 13 February 1997 (OJ 15/2/1997).

16. Decree 95-666 (OJ 10/5/1995).

17. Some argue that the legal nature of Eurostar and Thalys are international groupings (interviews RFF and MELTT1), whereas others contend that they are based on cooperative agreements (interviews DTT5 and SNCF3).

18. According to Voilland (1985), liberalization tries to create conditions for "safe" competition, whereas deregulation is simply the abolition of regulative constraints. Consequently, deregulation, which is a means, does not always lead to the goal of liberalization. The reforms adopted from the mid-1980s onward were to generate "safe" competition, and as such they can be called liberalization reforms using the instrument of deregulation, even if the results were not those originally anticipated.

19. According to the European Commission and the French Ministry of Transport, in 1995, 11.4 percent of the tkm of cabotage was done in France whereas French hauliers realized 11 percent of the tkm of cabotage. The figures for Germany and the Netherlands are 72.7 and 4 percent, and 0.5 and 35 percent, respectively (*Officiel des Transporteurs* 1997b: 21–23).

20. Interviews DTT4, DTT3, RP.

21. Whereas in 1989 and 1990, the SNCF had almost balanced its budget. The deficit reached 3.6 billion FFr. in 1992, subsequently leaping to 9 billion FFr. in 1994. Its liabilities also grew rapidly from 82 billion FFr. in 1991 to 131 billion in 1993, producing interest charges of around 14 billion FFr. in 1995. In 1996 the debts had risen to over 200 FFr. with a budget estimate of a 400 billion FFr. debt for 2005 (Commissariat Général du Plan 1995: 39–40).

22. Interview SNCF2.

23. The French road haulage sector is characterized by a high number of small firms. Today, more than 85 percent of haulage enterprises employ less than five workers.

24. This point of view is confirmed by the then principal private secretary of the minister of transport (interview MELTT1). One must, however, note that the suppression of rate controls was not taken into consideration.

25. According to Hall, a policy paradigm is "a framework of ideas and standards that specifies not only the goals of policy and the kind of instruments that can be used to attain them, but also the very nature of the problems that they are meant to be addressing" (Hall 1993: 279).

26. According to Jobert and Théret (1994), right-wing forces adopted neoliberal ideas when the socialists were in government.

27. Muller distinguishes between a "référentiel global" and "référentiel sectoriel" (Muller 1990: 47).

28. Interview DTT1.

29. See note 1.

30. In addition, two smaller associations, the CLTI (Chambre des louers et transporteurs) and the FFOCT (Fédération française des organisateurs et commissionnaires de transport), represent road hauliers and freight forwarders. They defend liberal positions and exert little pressure on public authorities.

31. Subsequently, it became the Conseil national des transports (CNT) as of 1982.

32. Interviews CFDT1 and DTT4.

33. Interviews FNTR2, UNOSTRA, CLTI, FNTR, RP, DTT4.

34. Interviews MELTT1, RP, DTT1, DTT3.

35. See also, interview FNTR2.

36. Interviews MELTT2 and DTT3. It should be noted that France has had eleven ministers or junior ministers of transport since 1980.

37. Sectoral statistics for 1986 indicate that liberalization was followed by a drop in prices, while problems such as subcontracting remained and even increased (OEST 1995: 33).

38. The position of hauliers' associations on subcontracting is indicative of their ambiguous stance on state intervention insofar as they demand controls to offset the drop in prices caused by subcontracting but are reluctant to impose them, because subcontracting is a solution to the problem of competitiveness.

39. Between 1986 and 1995, employment in the road haulage sector increased by almost 30 percent as compared to almost 3 percent for total employment (SES 1996). See also interview MELTT1.

40. Both associations organized *les états généraux du transport* in June 1996. The president of UNOSTRA would have liked a closer and more permanent association with FNTR, but his membership opposed the idea (*Officiel des Transporteurs* 1996b: 14).

41. The five main workers' organizations are the CFDT (*Confédération Française* Démocratique du Travail), the CGT (*Confédération Générale du Travail*), FO (*Force Ouvrière*), the FNCR (*Fédération National des Chauffeurs Routiers*), the CFTC (*Confédération Française des Travailleurs Chrétiens*), the CGC (*Confédération Générale des Cadres*).

42. See also interviews MELTT1, UNOSTRA, UNICOOPTRANS, and CLTI.

43. Interviews SNCF1 and SNCF3.

44. Interview SNCF1.

45. Interview SNCF1.

46. Interview SNCF3.

47. Interviews SNCF1, SNCF2, SNCF3.

48. Interview SNCF3.

49. Interview CGT.

50. Interviews CFDT2 and CGT.

51. This amounted to 33 percent in 1990, as compared with 26 percent in the public sector and 8 percent in the private sector (Ribeill 1994: 50; see also Siwek-Pouydesseau 1993: 111). After a period of decline, the rate of unionization appears to have risen, and the creation of SUD-rail is considered a possible factor of radicalization (interviews CFDT2 and RFF).

52. With less than 1 percent of the workforce, rail employees are considered accountable for 10 percent of strike days (*Le Monde* 1995b), and even 20 percent according to the Commissariat Général du Plan (1995).

53. Interviews DTT5 and RP.

54. Interview RFF.

55. Interviews MELTT1 and RFF.

56. Interviews FO, DTT5, and SNCF1.

57. Interview MELTT1.

58. Fixed, respectively, at around 6 billion FFr. and at around 12 billion FFr. for 1997 and 1998 (Article 11 of Decree 97/445 of 5 May 1997).

59. Interview DTT5. A former civil servant at the Ministry of Transport who went on to work for RFF also mentions the infrastructure charges payable by new entrants as part of the commercial income of RFF (interview RFF).

60. Interview RFF.

61. Interview SNCF3.

62. A subsidiary of one of the most important French groups and a significant experience in rail transport, the Compagnie Générale d'Enterprises Automobiles (CGEA) is a subsidiary of Vivendi (the former Compagnie Générale des Eaux, CGE) and participates in rail transport services in Indonesia, Britain, Germany, and the Netherlands. The contents of a February 1997 press release, making it clear that the agreement between the SNCF and CGE on telecommunications does not concern rail transport, is a clear indication that this group is seen as a potential threat to the SNCF's monopoly.

63. Interview RFF.

64. Another agreement was signed in March 1999 among the French, British, German, and Austrian railway enterprises for a new freightway with the same "cooperative" principles.

65. COM (89) 564.

66. Interview RFF.

67. We observed similar patterns in road haulage in at least three instances: when EC licenses were introduced in 1968, France tried to limit the increase in the number of such licenses and then attempted to delay the introduction of cabotage, although the French market had already been liberalized (*Le Figaro* 1989; *The Times* 1989); when the transitional system of cabotage was due for revision in 1992, France again delayed the final agreement and joined Germany in demanding prior tax harmonization (*Bulletin Quotidien: Europe* 1992b: 9, 1992c: 8, 9), despite having no special interest in the "Eurovignette" since it already had a toll system; and with Italy and Spain, France also rejected the 1997 deadline for the full liberalization of cabotage (*Bulletin Quotidien: Europe* 1992a: 7).

68. CGT and CFDT cited in *Le Monde* 1996a.

69. Interviews DTT5 and MELTT1.

70. Interview RP.

71. In the words of Cohen (1996: 151), "the fusing of free market policies represents the constraints employed by member states of the European Union, especially the Latin nations (France, Italy, Spain), to reform their policies in protected sectors, where there may be either a strong trade union presence or political consensus prohibiting major changes. . . . Brussels, perceived as a constraint mechanism, has thus progressively become a powerful lever towards modernization in spite of the resistance of concerned pressure groups."

72. "Generally speaking, the majority of senior French civil servants do not perceive the European construction as a great danger to be opposed. Even though this does not prevent regular outbursts of hostility, Europe is viewed as an exogenous constraint which encourages the state to fulfill its duties more efficiently. . . . In the surveys conducted between 1986 and 1993, the internal market was generally seen as a means to 'clean up' and rationalize outdated domestic public policies . . . ." (Lequesne 1996: 111–12).

73. This is illustrated by the following statement from the Stoffaës, Bertold, and Feve report (1995): "L'Europe est aujourd'hui l'argument du destin . . . , le fil directeur des réformes."

74. Such conclusions are not specific to the rail sector. In the case of telecommunications, the strength of the notion of public service within trade unions and in the "republican political culture" was also the main obstacle to deregulation, whereas initiative and leadership came from the administrative elite (Brenac 1994).

# 5

# Regulatory Reforms in the German Transport Sector: How to Overcome Multiple Veto Points

*Michael Teutsch*

German transport policy—long characterized by a high degree of state interventionism and extended responsibility for the supervision and active development of the sector—has undergone significant changes in recent years, with a series of reform steps designed to give market mechanisms more weight. These reforms have involved changes in three different dimensions: the problem-solving approaches of key actors; the abolition of protectionist or monopolist policy instruments and the introduction of more market-compatible forms of regulation; and, finally, the patterns of state–society relations as well as the relationship between state agencies.

The central focus of this analysis is the impact of European policymaking on the German reforms. Was it a decisive factor in explaining national developments? What were the mechanisms that made European policymaking important for domestic reforms? And how did national actors react to the emergence of a multilevel governance? Furthermore, what does this analysis tell us about the reform capacity of the national political system and sector under study?

As to Germany's reform capacity, the country is characterized by a highly differentiated political system, involving corporatist arrangements, coalition governments, and a specific form of federalism; factors that all favor incremental reforms rather than abrupt policy changes (see, e.g., Katzenstein 1987) and account for the slow progress made in public-sector reform (Dyson 1992; Benz and Goetz 1996). But despite this, and despite the fact that transport sector reforms had been discussed for decades before any concrete political decisions were taken, a breakthrough did finally occur in both cases under study, and it is this breakthrough in the context of potential deadlock that requires explanation.

My central hypothesis is that regulatory reforms in the German transport sector could be accomplished because of a combination of national and supranational reform pressure. In the case of road haulage, "Europeanization" was a decisive factor in overcoming national opposition insofar as the liberalization of European markets exerted pressure on the national industry and because some actors used the multilevel structure of European Community (EC) governance to shift the existing distribution of power at the domestic level (cf. Putnam 1988, Grande 1996). In rail policy, the economic and explicit legal pressure generated by EC policies was less pronounced. However, even without strict EC rules imposing specific solutions at the domestic level, German policymakers tried to develop the national railway system in congruence with the philosophy underlying the emerging European railway regime. But the main factor to explain how the domestic veto points standing in the way of the reform was eventually surmounted was the federal government's determination to push the reform through a difficult decisional process, which also implied massive side-payments to the opponents of the reform. Hence the German railway reform was brought about by a change in the dominant belief systems in the sector under study (cf. Hall 1993, Sabatier 1998) and by the German government's capacity to act in spite of a high number of institutional veto points.

## ROAD HAULAGE REGULATION: EUROPE
## AS A CATALYST FOR NATIONAL REFORMS

The recent developments in German road haulage policy are a good example of the new opportunities that the EU offers to domestic policy-makers. It would be inaccurate to interpret the domestic reforms as an implementation of decisions taken at the supranational level. Yet, it is unlikely that the existing institutional inertia could have been overcome without the effects of Europeanization. The actual impact of EC policies must be seen in a specific national context of protracted conflict over regulation and an existing demand for reform. Under such conditions European legislation did not impose new forms of regulation, but instead functioned as a catalyst for national reforms.

In road haulage, the German government has often taken a defensive stance in supranational negotiations, because its traditional interventionism conflicted with the central element of the Common Transport Policy (CTP), that of the liberalization of services. Furthermore, because of Germany's central geographical location and its economically attractive transport market, the opening of national markets to foreign hauliers was expected to open the doors to a large number of foreign competitors of the domestic transport enterprises that the government had been trying to protect. But at the same time, regulatory reforms were proposed at the national level, which brought the German regulatory approach closer to the EC model. Regulatory failure was one justification for a domestic reform. But whereas this problem had been known and discussed for years, it was European policymaking that was decisive in realizing the reform. In the first place, the opening up of EC markets increased the economic pressure to adapt the old regulatory system, and second supranational decision making provided new opportunities for certain national actors to act. These developments eventually led to a redefinition of the government's policy preferences and allowed it to overcome political resistance to regulatory reforms, which in turn left more room to pro-market forces.

The analysis starts with a presentation of the development of German road haulage regulation, its traditional characteristics, and recent changes. In a second step, the persistence of the old regulatory system is explained with reference to particular features of decision making in this sector. Finally, I examine how European policymaking helped overcome the strong domestic resistance to liberalization, and how it may affect traditional patterns of decision making in the German transport sector in the long run.

## The Regulatory Regime: Liberalization and Adaptation

Restrictive licensing procedures and rate controls were the two main instruments characterizing the interventionist character of the traditional system of road transport regulation in Germany. Both were introduced in the 1930s in the wake of the severe economic crisis that had affected transport operators, and when road transport started to represent serious competition for the state-owned railways (van Suntum 1986: 97ff.; Basedow 1989: 61ff.). Although these instruments were adapted over time, they were only abolished in the 1990s. This last step transformed the highly regulated German road transport regime into a liberal one.

Regarding the German licensing system, its restrictive nature consisted in the limitation of the number of licenses available for long-distance haulage. As could be seen from the existence of "gray" markets for licenses the demand for road transport services exceeded available capacity.[1] Quantitative licensing restrictions already lost practical importance due to a simplification of the system in 1991 and a high number of licenses issued in the East German regions at the same time.[2] They were finally abolished in 1998 parallel to the complete liberalization of cabotage, that is, the free access of foreign hauliers to domestic markets. Meanwhile, efforts have been made to raise the standards of individual licensing criteria, both at the national and the European levels, which require hauliers to meet specific professional and financial criteria. However, as this instrument is not as restrictive for market entry as a fixed maximum numbers of licenses, it does not constitute the reinstalling of the old regulatory system.

With respect to price regulation, road hauliers had to apply the same tariffs as the railways until 1961. Then, in a first liberalizing move, bracket tariffs and a large number of exceptional tariffs were introduced.[3] Moreover, the responsibility for rate setting was transferred from the minister of transport to tariff commissions composed of experts from associations operating in the sector of road transport. But transport prices were still not freely negotiable between individual hauliers and their clients. This only became possible at the beginning of 1994 when price controls were finally abolished.[4]

For Germany, the use of fiscal instruments was another important aspect affected by the creation of EU-wide markets. This is because Germany until 1995 only imposed vehicle excise duties on hauliers registered in Germany and fuel taxes. In contrast to countries such as Italy or France, Germany has not used the instrument of tolls, whereas, similar to Britain, the level of vehicle taxes was much higher than the European average (Committee of Enquiry 1994: 37). As this system led to very low contributions for foreign infrastructure users and gave the latter the competitive edge over their German counterparts,[5] the German legislator tried to adjust the system by introducing time-related charges for all infrastructure users and by reducing vehicle taxes simultaneously. A first unilateral attempt to do so was halted by the European Court of Justice in 1991. In June 1993 a compromise was eventually found by EC transport ministers,[6] which allowed the introduction of road-user charges for heavy vehicles (the "Eurovignette") and, by setting relatively low minimum levels, also allowed Germany to reduce its national vehicle taxes by 50 percent (Mückenhausen 1994). This implied a gradual shift from the principle of nationality to that of territoriality in German taxation. Moreover, the tax burden of German hauliers was brought closer to the European average.

In short, the latest developments regarding the regulation and taxation of road hauliers in Germany show the liberalization of the national policy regime and its adaptation to the common transport market. Instruments that hindered the application of market principles were abolished. Rules were introduced to put German and foreign hauliers on an equal footing regarding regulation and taxation. These changes try to adapt the national regulatory regime to supranational challenges, and attempt to defend the country's fiscal interests as well as the competitive position of national hauliers in the common transport market. However, it also implies the endorsement of a new regulatory approach. This means more than simply adjusting existing instruments to European requirements while leaving basic principles of regulation untouched. It instead stands for changes in the fundamental principles of regulation and in the regulators' core beliefs. But how exactly did these changes come about?

## Decision Making: Sectoral Corporatism and Conflicting Policy Coalitions

Political decision making in the German road haulage sector was traditionally characterized by the existence of two coalitions with contrasting views on economic regulation and a specific form of sectoral corporatism. The latter had once been created by the regulatory regime and placed the pro-regulation coalition in a dominant position.

## Problem-Solving Philosophies

As far as the goals of the regulatory regime and the theoretical assumptions about the functioning of the transport sector underlying it are concerned, Germany was a typical representative of the "continental" approach to transport policy (Button 1991).[7] The state was expected to protect a public good by safeguarding an efficient and "societally desirable" transport system; a long-term perspective on economic and social development was built into both regulation and infrastructure planning; and policy goals not only originated in the transport sector itself, but were often linked to policy fields such as regional, industrial, environmental, or social policy. With respect to road haulage, the main goals pursued by regulation were to defend the national railways, to protect small and medium-sized enterprises, and to avoid negative externalities.

The railways were the focal point around which the whole sectoral regime was built. This was motivated by the fiscal interests of the state following the nationalization of the railways in the late nineteenth century. Moreover, the ownership of the railways gave the state an important policy instrument to achieve regional, industrial, or social policy goals. To be used for these purposes, the railways needed to maintain a key position in transport markets. Therefore, since road haulage began emerging as a serious competitor of the railways in the 1920s, the state tried to intervene in intermodal competition by restricting market access for road hauliers and by initially subjecting them to the same tariff system as the railways (Laaser 1991: 136ff.; van Suntum 1986: 97ff.).

Regulation was furthermore legitimized by the intention to protect small and medium enterprises in the road haulage sector, to avoid cutthroat competition, to assure similar price levels for transport in the whole territory, and to reduce negative externalities regarding road safety, drivers' working time, or the environment. The need for regulation was deduced from the assumed "peculiarities" of transport markets, which presumably did not allow the application of pure market mechanisms (van Suntum 1986: 61ff.; Laaser 1991: 144ff.). In more recent years, a new demand for state intervention in transport market has been stipulated by a discussion about a possible "collapse" of the transport system with its concomitant negative impact on the economy and the environment (Brandt, Haack, and Törkel 1994). As road transport may arrive at the limit of its capacity one day, and as it is not regarded as an environmentally friendly mode of transport, the issue of shifting the modal split toward rail has gained new salience in domestic transport policy (Enquete-Kommission 1994).

These goals provided the interventionist regulatory regime with legitimacy, stabilized it, and defined the criteria that alternative forms of regulation had to match. They were shared by a majority of the actors directly or indirectly involved in regulation (civil servants, members of specialized parliamentary committees, professional associations, advisory bodies, and so on), and they became a part of the fundamental convictions about problem solving in the sector.

However, with the exception of the immediate postwar period, the interventionist paradigm in transport regulation also had its critics. In the 1950s there already were some supporters of liberal transport policies among academic observers as well as politicians. By the early 1970s, a majority of German transport economists rejected theories about the sector's "peculiarity" and called for the application of market mechanisms as applied in other parts of the economy (Willeke 1995). The transport economists' calls received increased attention with the general political move toward liberal market policies in the 1980s. Then, a vast number of studies, some of which were explicitly addressed and issued by policymakers, claimed that a liberalization of the regulatory system would lead to increasing economic efficiency without harming other transport-related goals (Hamm 1989; Basedow 1989; Laaser 1991; Deregulierungskommission 1991). Such studies had an impact that was felt beyond scientific circles, and they were part of a permanent and institutionalized dialogue between policy analysts and policymakers, helping to shape the long-term perception and definition of transport problems.[8]

The evidence presented by these studies as well as by different lobbyists undermined the legitimacy of the old regulatory regime. Even its traditional supporters recognized the need for reform,[9] mainly because the existing instruments were unable to achieve central goals underpinning regulation and also produced negative side effects. First, regulating road haulage could not prevent the yearly fall of the railways' markets shares. In 1995 road hauliers accounted for 57 percent of the ton-kilometers in long-distance transport, while the railways, once the dominant mode of transport in the freight sector, held a market share of only 20 percent.[10] Second, prices on German domestic transport markets were on average 20 to 30 percent higher than those for international destinations with liberal price regimes (Hamm 1989: 24–26; Laaser 1991: 41), which raised the protest of German industry and seaports. Third, regulation of hire-and-reward haulage led to a rise of own-account transport (Deregulierungskommission 1991: 47), a development in stark contrast with the goal of protecting small and medium-sized transport enterprises.[11] Fourth, the growing complexity of transport services made it difficult to handle the tariff system efficiently and moreover undermined its implementation, as it became common practice to make mixed price calculations between services that could be negotiated freely (e.g., logistics or international transport) and the portion of the services subject to regulation.[12]

In sum, scientific and practical evidence undermined the legitimacy of the old regulatory regime and provided the opponents of regulation with plausible arguments. However, policy failures and expertise could not challenge the persistence of the traditional mode of regulation. Some of the problems were already known and discussed twenty years before fundamental regulatory reforms were enacted. In order to explain the long-lasting stability and eventual change of the German regulatory system, political and institutional factors must be taken into consideration as well.

## The Administration, Parliament, and Their Interaction with Interest Groups

The political arena in the German road haulage sector was characterized by two opposing policy coalitions. For a long time, these two coalitions were not on an equal footing, as one of them, the pro-regulation side, was reinforced by a firmly established sectoral corporatism.

The most important public actors on the federal level were the Ministry of Transport and the Ministry of Economics. The two ministries held diverging conceptions regarding sectoral regulation: Whereas the Ministry of Transport has often taken a pro-regulation stand, the head of the transport division in the Ministry of the Economy defined its role as making sure that liberal views about transport policy counterbalanced those of the transport ministry.[13] The transport ministry was the main actor using the argument of railway protection to legitimize the regulatory system,[14] and according to some observers it also gave more attention to the hauliers' interests in terms of stable markets and high prices than to industry's and other transport users' plea for more flexibility and lower prices.[15] In contrast, the transport users' demands had much better standing in the Ministry of the Economy, with which they shared a liberal problem-solving philosophy. The identification of civil servants with their external partners' interests was not only based on similar regulatory ideas, but was also strengthened by regular personal contacts and services such as data gathering provided by the associations for "their" respective department.[16] Moreover, due to traditional recruitment mechanisms, there was a strong presence of ex-railway employees in the Ministry of Transport,[17] which further strengthened the general pro-regulation attitude of this department.

The Ministry of the Economy repeatedly intervened in decision-making processes concerning transport matters, but was confined to cojurisdiction. It could block some initiatives for new or stricter regulations, for example, regarding own-account transport or small vehicles[18] (Klenke 1995: 21, 79), but could not impose its views on the primarily responsible Ministry of Transport, which maintained its skepticism of the liberalization of transport markets. As a consequence of this constellation, the regulatory regime that the Federal Republic of Germany had inherited from the prewar period remained in force until the 1980s.

The pro-regulation stance of the Ministry of Transport can be explained at least in part by corporatist decision making, which implied a close relationship between the ministry and the major transport associations, that is, those demanding regulation. This was particularly visible in the implementation of the tariff system, where the concrete decision-making procedures moreover favored hauliers over transport users. From 1961 to 1994 tariffs were set by special commissions composed of experts representing hauliers on the one hand and industry, agriculture, and trade interests on the other. Tariffs kept their status as a ministerial decree, but in practice public authorities only ratified the outcome of negotiations between the associations.[19] Concerning short-distance transport, both sides enjoyed equal rights, while in long-distance transport haulier representatives could theoretically outvote transport users: according to the law, rate proposals were prepared by the hauliers alone, whereas the industry representatives only had to be consulted. Thus, to defend its interests in case of conflict, the industry had to rely on the brokering function of public authorities and in particular on threats to lobby the Ministry of the Economy, whose formal consent was necessary before the Ministry of Transport could finally set the tariffs. In fact, rate setting for long-distance transport was also a matter of compromise (Willeke 1995: 176), but the high prices for domestic transport in Germany provided some evidence that hauliers held a dominant position.

A second area where transport associations were involved in the implementation of the regulatory system was the control agency Bundesanstalt für den Güterfernverkehr (BAG). The BAG was founded in 1952 but largely based on a cartel that the state had imposed on road hauliers in 1935 (Linden 1952). It was in a somewhat ambiguous position with respect to transport operators and industry. On the one hand, it had to control whether hauliers and their clients applied the official tariffs. On the other hand, the latter were represented in the agency's administrative council, whose competences included, among others, decisions on the annual budget. Thus the controlled could exercise some influence from within.[20] However, industry representatives complained that the agency did not respect all interests equally, but tended to give most attention to the demands of hire-and-reward hauliers.[21] The unbalanced composition of the administrative council might have contributed to this tendency—ten of its twenty-seven members were representatives of the haulier or forwarder associations, whereas transport users (industry and agriculture) were represented with only four seats (BAG 1991: 7).[22] Furthermore, only a small portion of the controls was actually carried out by this agency. The greatest part was done by haulier cooperatives closely related to the main haulier association BDF (now BGL).[23] Thus, an analysis of the reasons for the opposition of this association to the abolition of tariffs cannot be limited to the arguments regarding the hauliers' economic situation. We must also take into account the fact that the BDF itself profited from its involvement in sectoral governance. A part of the power of this organization was linked to its expertise in the field of tariffs and to the fact that practically anyone asking for a special tariff had to contact this association. Financial interests may also have played a role, insofar as the fees for checking waybills and the correct application of tariffs constituted a significant source of income for hauliers' cooperatives.[24]

Corporatist decision making was one of the reasons for the dominant position of the pro-regulation side and for the persistence of the traditional regulatory regime. However, some of the central institutions stabilizing this mode of inter-action, for example, the tariff system, existed only as long as the legislator did not decide otherwise. As long as the Ministry of Transport shared the stance taken by the protectionist transport associations with which it collaborated in the imple-mentation of the regulatory regime, it did not take any major reform initiatives. However, the political preferences of a ministry or of powerful private actors could not have been put into practice without a majority in Parliament or, more specifically, in the committee in charge of transport policy. The latter must be in-cluded in the pro-regulation coalition; it actually was one of its main compo-nents.[25] The relevant sectoral associations gave great weight to lobbying activi-ties and permanent contacts with the members of the committee.[26] Moreover, the dominant sectoral division of viewpoints found in the Parliament was not coun-terbalanced by conflict along party lines. Partisan mobilization did not play a major role in the sector under study. Representatives of the relevant associations state that center-left, Green, and leftist parties (SPD, B'90/GRÜNE, PDS) are generally more in favor of regulation than Christian-Democrats (CDU/CSU) and Liberals (FDP), but do not deny that these differences are only slight and that variations tend to become blurred when discussing pro-railway attitudes or the in-troduction of new fiscal instruments.[27] Conflict, where it occurred, took place within different parties and mirrored a sectoral division of viewpoints instead of partisan lines (Klenke 1995: 27–28).

To conclude, policymaking in the German road haulage sector was character-ized by two opposing policy coalitions with sectoral corporatism placing the pro-regulation side in a dominant position. Specialized public and private actors formed coalitions built on normative goals and shared assumptions about the basic features of the sector and their institutionalized cooperation during the im-plementation of public policies. This led to close relationships, and at times to the identification of the public authorities with their respective clientele's policy goals, which would explain the long persistence of the traditional regulatory regime despite increasing evidence of regulatory failure.

In view of the presence of these entrenched institutions of sectoral governance, how were far-reaching changes achieved in the late 1980s and early 1990s? The domestic critique of regulation alone is not a sufficient precondition for recent de-velopments. Some of the negative effects of regulation were already well known, without any legislative consequences deriving from this. It is claimed here that the European integration process was the decisive factor that made the reforms possible, as it changed the basic economic and political conditions for policy-making in this sector.

### The Impact of European Integration on National Politics

The impact of European policymaking on the German regulatory reforms was twofold: the opening of markets by the EC produced economic pressure and thus provided the advocates of a reform with new arguments for an adaptation of domestic regulation. In the context of multilevel governance, the EC moreover created new channels of influence and new opportunities to form coalitions for these political actors. Thus, EC policymaking had an impact on the strategic options open to domestic political actors. Both factors contributed to changes in the relative strength of domestic actors and eventually favored a specific policy, that is, the liberalization of domestic regulation.

## Economic Pressure

In the German political debate, economic pressure deriving from the integration of EC transport markets was one of the main justifications for regulatory reforms. Deregulating domestic transport markets is not part of official EC legislation, but the opening of national markets to foreigners in practice undermines national capacity of regulation. Regarding capacity control, foreigners have had free access to national markets since 1998. Under these conditions, limiting the number of licenses for inland hauliers would simply have discriminated against the latter. Hence, the minister's early announcement that Germany's quantitative restrictions to market entry would be abolished parallel to the introduction of "cabotage," that is, the opening of domestic transport markets to foreign hauliers (Wissmann 1994: 430). With respect to price controls, foreign hauliers engaging in cabotage are required to respect the norms in force on the territory where they actually operate and may therefore be subject to national tariffs. In practice, it would have become increasingly difficult to enforce such a system. Controlling rates relies on access to detailed documents covering longer periods of time, which are only accessible in the operator's home country. That is, they are placed beyond the reach of national control authorities, while the authorities of the other countries regarded such controls as complicated, costly, and, in the last instance, superfluous. As the application of price controls to national enterprises alone would have again discriminated against the latter, and as the instrument moreover came in for severe domestic criticism, it was eventually abolished altogether.

As the full liberalization of cabotage only came into force in mid-1998, the economic pressure that the free access of foreign hauliers would actually exercise on domestic markets was unknown when the decisions for the German reforms were taken. However, given the attractiveness of German domestic transport markets to foreign hauliers and given that German hauliers were not doing very well on the already liberalized markets for crossborder transport (BDF 1995b: 47), the liberalization of cabotage was perceived as a threat for the national transport industry. This accounted for the initially defensive attitude of the German administration in supranational negotiations. But after the German government could no longer block the liberalization of EC transport markets in the Council of Ministers (see Kerwer and Teutsch in this volume), it pushed for domestic reforms in order to adapt national regulation to the new situation. The Ministry of Transport and the Parliament considered the abolition of rate controls by the end of 1993 and an increase in the number of available licenses necessary to "accustom" German road hauliers to a new regulatory regime, thus forcing hauliers to adapt to tougher competition before the effects of the final implementation of a single European transport market materialized (Bundestag 1993: 12,806 ff.).

In short, the economic pressure of liberalized European transport markets played an important role in the German reform process. Irrespective of its actual economic importance, the opening of EC markets provided the advocates of liberalization with new and convincing arguments they could use in domestic political battles. In addition, the new strategic opportunities offered by the EC did also include the creation of new access points to the political decision-making process.

*Multilevel Governance*

Institutional developments in the EC offered new channels of influence to some domestic actors. Moreover, the reference to European policies was used strategically to limit domestic policy options and to push through the liberalization of the national transport market. This did not only concern the above-mentioned economic pressure. For example, the decision taken by the Federal Parliament in 1993 to abolish compulsory tariffs was made in the expectation that the European Court of Justice (ECJ) would declare the German system of rate controls an infringement of European rules on competition. However, this expectation ironically did not materialize.[28] A German court had requested the ECJ to test the congruence of the national tariff system against European law when it had to decide in a case where an enterprise had been accused of not having respected the legally set rates. In referring the case to the ECJ under Article 177 (now Article 234) of the EC treaty, the national court followed the plea of the lawyer of the accused enterprise. EC law seemed much closer to the interests of the involved enterprise than national legislation. Moreover, the same lawyer was also employed by an industry association specialized in transport matters. Hence the reference to the EC legal framework was also a conscious political move designed to eliminate the national system of rate controls that this organization opposed.[29] The association's efforts became a political success despite their legal failure. German policymakers did not wait for the ECJ's verdict, as had been asked, for instance, by those who would have preferred to keep rate controls.[30] Similar to the almost unanimous support for regulation in the years before, the Parliament now hurried to abolish rate controls and declared this an adaptation to legal and economic pressure deriving from the supranational level (Bundestag 1993: 12,806 ff.). Then, to the surprise of most policymakers and many lawyers, the ECJ did not declare the German tariff system in contradiction to European law.[31] Even though some, in reaction to the verdict, did initially propose reintroducing price controls,[32] the overall impression remains that this was never seriously considered. Consequently, adaptation to legal impositions coming from the European level alone is not sufficient to explain this regulatory reform. Although German policymakers wrongly assumed the existence of legal restrictions in the case of rate control, this argument does neither sufficiently explain why they hurried to change legislation before the publication of the ECJ's verdict nor their unwillingness to reintroduce rate controls following that verdict. Instead, the evidence suggests that the old regulatory system had already lost much support on the national level. The Ministry of Transport and the Federal Parliament were prepared to reform the domestic system as a consequence of economic pressure and the negative experiences with regulation (see Sandhäger 1987). Thus, even though the ECJ ultimately adopted an unexpected legal point of view, the case constituted a political occasion to reform national regulation without taking full responsibility for this development with the policymakers' traditional clientele, which opposed such moves.

European policymaking constituted a strategic opportunity for those national policymakers bent on overcoming the resistance of the traditionally influential opponents of liberalization. The EC did not impose new forms of regulation for domestic road transport markets. But the economic consequences of open market access as well as the institutional setting provided incentives that clearly favored the liberalization of national markets with respect to other policy options, and German policymakers actually used these incentives to bring forward a major reform of domestic regulation. They could do so because the regulation of road haulage had long been a contested policy field. The old regulatory regime had long been the butt of fierce criticism from some actors, so that when it did eventually change its policy the government was able to exploit this long-standing opposition from industry and almost all transport economists, to strengthen its choices. In changing its stance on domestic regulation, the Ministry of Transport and the Parliament did not stand alone, but rather tipped the scales in favor of an alternative coalition.

*Institutional Changes and New Cleavages:*
*The End of Sectoral Corporatism?*

The reform of the regulatory system in German road haulage implied that transport policymakers took a distance with respect to the policy views of their traditional clientele. The question, then, is whether the shift to a liberal transport policy and the corresponding institutional reforms also mark the end of sectoral corporatism. This question becomes even more relevant as the reform of the regulatory regime is accompanied by the emergence of new political conflicts that cut across the traditional political divisions in the sector. Taken together, changes in the institutional setting as well as in the politically relevant cleavages may weaken the traditionally close links between public policymakers and a particular group of private actors, and transform sectoral corporatism into a looser relationship characterized by pluralist lobbying (Streeck and Schmitter 1991).

The traditionally close relationship between public and private actors in the German transport sector as well as the number and structure of private-interest associations had been shaped by the old regulatory system. Thus, the reform of the underlying system could lead to loosening the formerly close ties between certain public and private actors. The abolition of the tariff system, for example, implied the disappearance of some institutionalized forms of private–public coordination: the tariff commissions were dissolved, the haulier cooperatives lost their control function in the area of transport prices,[33] and the involvement of private-interest associations in financing and administrating the control agency BAG was removed. The agency—whose current tasks include controlling individual licenses and the compliance with social and technical regulation as well as market observation—is now directly subordinated to the Ministry of Transport and financed entirely by the state budget.[34] This structure was designed to make the BAG more independent of the attempts by private actors to exert pressure on the way the agency is run from within.

Regarding the structure of private-interest representation, the legal distinction between long- and short-distance haulage, and between hauliers and freight forwarders or between public haulage and own-account transport, with its connected procedural consequences in the case of licensing and rate control, was mirrored in the existence of separate associations representing their respective clienteles.[35] After liberalization, the background of associational diversity is changing, moving from a differentiation rooted in domestic legal provisions to one based on a new market situation. For example, in view of the abolition of the legal distinction between long- and short-distance transport, the two respective associations started talks about merging. After these talks failed in 1997, it is likely that only one of the two competing associations covering the whole range of haulage-related questions will survive in the long run. In the meantime, another association, the VKS, developed into a special forum for the representation of large transport enterprises.[36] The latter are generally considered to take the greatest advantage of the opening of transport markets, especially if they develop into suppliers of integrated transport services (including logistics, among others), which may sharply distinguish themselves from hauliers offering pure transport services (often as subcontractors of the first). These developments, reinforced by the deregulation of road-transport services (Boes 1997), highlight the distinct interests inherent in the transport sector. This leads to the emergence of new lines of conflicts within the sector that make it more difficult for its representatives to confront political decision makers with joint demands and thus eventually limit the transport association's political strength.

Such trends will, however, only become clear in the long run. Due to the long experience with close collaboration, the contacts between representatives of the Ministry of Transport, the control agency BAG, and the transport associations have remained very close until now.[37] The Ministry is still willing to cooperate with the sector in order to ensure a smooth implementation of national and supranational policies, and the hauliers indeed obtained concessions, but—this must be emphasized—lost the central conflict about the general principles of future transport policy. The ministry repeatedly affirmed its independence in defining the broad lines of German transport policy, that is, its goals and the type of instruments used to achieve them. Consequently, relations between the Ministry of Transport and transport associations were extremely strained in 1993, when the then minister, Matthias Wissmann, agreed to the introduction of cabotage and fiscal harmonization in the EC Council, and the domestic tariff system was abolished (BDF 1994: 12). Both measures had been fiercely opposed by the traditional clientele of the Ministry, especially by the haulier association BDF (now BGL). But, unlike Italy or France, the hauliers did not blackmail the state with strikes or similar actions, which, quite apart from being illegal and most probably illegitimate in the eyes of the general public, would have disrupted the established and routine-like consultations between the state and interest groups, historically also to the advantage of the latter. Since it took eight years to reach a compromise in the Council of Transport Ministers after the ECJ inactivity verdict and the Council's programmatic decision on the creation of a common transport market without quantitative restrictions of 1985, and since the complete liberalization of cabotage was only realized five more years later in 1998, German hauliers at least managed to delay the implementation of these decisions.[38] The haulier association BDF/BGL moreover claimed that it prevented the implementation of plans to increase the number of licenses during that period (BDF 1995a: 47). Thus, the minister may have compromised on certain details, but he rejected any attempts to make him step back from the recently established liberal approach to transport regulation. The transport minister and the presidents of the haulier and freight forwarder associations set up a common program to improve the competitiveness of the German road transport sector (BMV 1994, 1995a), but the minister was not ready to accept proposals such as to make the European crisis mechanism an effective instrument for the suppression of "exaggerated forms of competition," to establish new forms of quantitative entry controls at the national and the European level ("Flexible Capacity Control," BDF 1995c), or to give the haulier association a right to be heard when new licenses are issued on the basis of individual access criteria. Such proposals were declared a politically undesired effort to go back to the old interventionist regime (DVZ 1997a, 1997b). They also illustrate the limits within which the minister was ready to conciliate.

The observation that German transport policy is characterized by shifting lines of conflict is underlined by the growing political importance of environmental issues connected to the transport sector. Concerning the negative image of road transport with respect to environmental protection, transport associations that feel under heavy pressure from public opinion (BDF 1994: 18ff.; BSL 1994: 3ff., 1995: 5ff.; VKS 1995: 14f.) and political decision makers may actually be forced to react to such pressure. Given that the defense of a long-term goal such as environmental protection is a stance that is consistent with Germany's traditional Continental approach to transport policy, political decision makers could use environmental goals as a justification for new forms of regulation in the transport sector. But again, due to the recent changes of the regulatory approach, public policymakers are primarily oriented at searching for solutions consistent with market logic today. Thus, they also treat the environmental aspects of transport as a topic to be handled separately from that of market regulation. The demands by some environmentalists to drastically reduce transport in general and road transport in specific (Hesse 1993; Holzapfel and Schallaböck 1992) are unlikely to find a favorable majority among key policymakers. Instead, German policymakers support strict emission standards, they introduced tax incentives for the use of low-emission lorries in 1994, and they seek to improve the competitiveness of environmentally friendly modes of transport. Even environmental taxes seeking to internalize the presumed external costs of transport (cf. ECMT 1994; CEC 1995b) would fit the new dominant logic of regulation, and could be added to the existing set of instruments without contradicting the current regulatory philosophy. However, as neither representatives of transport enterprises nor of transport users want higher prices for road transport services imposed by the state, any attempt to do so invariably raises the opposition of both these groups and makes the introduction of such instruments a difficult political enterprise.

To sum up, state–society relations in the German road transport sector are currently in a phase of transition. Due to a changed institutional setting, public–private interaction will in the future be shaped to a greater extent by lobbying activities of a larger number of groups rather than the participation of only some private actors in sectoral governance. Together with a new constellation of societal interests and crosscutting cleavages this development makes it less likely that certain interests will gain or maintain privileged access to policymakers and stabilize such relations over a long period of time.

## Europe as a Catalyst for National Reforms

New strategic opportunities provided by multilevel policymaking and the economic consequences of EC rules worked as a catalyst, a sine qua non, for the reform of German road haulage regulation. Although the reform of purely national market regulation is not officially part of the EC agenda in transport policy, the liberalization of services in international road transport and, more specifically, the liberalization of cabotage facilitated domestic reforms that would not have taken place in this form and at this time had policymaking remained restricted to the national level alone.

Economic interdependencies were an important factor reinforcing the impact of supranational liberalization policies on Germany. They explain why the effects of EC policy in reality went beyond the narrow field of regulation as defined in the Official Journal. Only under such conditions would the opening of markets provide strong incentives for public policymakers to adapt domestic road haulage regulation in order to avoid economic disadvantages for German enterprises on domestic and international markets.

To explain why national policymakers actually took up these incentives and reacted to the changes in their environment, it is important to recall that the traditionally interventionist domestic approach to regulation had already lost support before the impact of European integration became evident. Domestic actors were pushing for long-desired reforms that were basically congruent with supranational policies. Supranational decision making provided these actors with new support and new access points to the political decision-making process. The Ministry of Transport, which moderated between opposing interests and itself initially skeptical of the concrete EC policies in its field of responsibility, eventually took the opportunity to reconcile national and supranational policies, to change its regulatory approach, and to push regulatory reforms through the political decision-making process. In doing so, the government was facilitated by the chance to point to economic threats to the sector, presumed legal obligations, the availability of a plausible alternative approach to regulation, and by the presence of alternative support groups in the domestic policy arena.

## THE RAILWAY REFORM: PAYING OFF THE OPPONENTS

Parallel to the changes in road haulage regulation, German policymakers were also working on a major railway reform.[39] When the reform passed the Federal Parliament in December 1993, both the governing parties and the opposition considered it a "milestone in the history of transport and industry in this country," "the largest privatization program which has ever been carried out," and "a historic project, a revolution in the transport sector and an urgently needed move to strengthen our national economy" (Deutsche Bahn 1994: 94). But was such enthusiasm really justifiable with regard to the content of the reform, or was it instead a sign of relief after a difficult political decision-making process had been brought to an end?

Similar to the shift in road haulage regulation, the German railway reform was inspired by liberal conceptions of economic regulation. The underlying philosophy was to improve the efficiency and the competitiveness of the sector by creating a regulatory framework that would provide more incentives that encourage those involved to act in line with market logic. Establishing a specific market for rail transport services was one task of the reform, but reorganizing the former public monopoly and clarifying its relationship with the state were equally important with respect to the principal goals of the reform, that is, the improvement of the railways' efficiency and their competitiveness with respect to other modes of transport.

Taking into account that rail policy has also become more important in the EC context, the two main questions to be pursued in the following analysis are, first, whether supranational incentives for reform played a role in the national decision-making process, and second, how the railway reform could be enacted despite the existence of a high number of veto points in the German political system and considerable opposition to elements of the government's reform plan. In what follows, I assess the range of the German reform and demonstrate how its output was shaped by typical domestic political structures and patterns of interaction. The railway case confirms the finding of the preceding section that the German federal government can pursue a reform agenda despite the existence of a high need of formal and informal veto points in the national political system. Mobilizing the support of specific domestic groups in favor of such a reform, however, comes at a price. In the case of the railways, the price to be paid by the federal government for getting the reform through the decision making process consisted in massive side-payments that made the reform costly with respect to its financial aspects and less radical than once intended with respect to the scope of regulatory and organizational change.

The analysis starts with a presentation of the main elements of German rail reform policy. The legislative output is then compared with the criteria laid down by supranational legislation. Then the response of those actors affected most by the European policy is investigated. In the subsequent section, the political reasons leading to this particular policy output are explained. The analysis comprises the driving forces behind the German railway reforms, the lines of conflict that emerged during the decision-making process, and finally the strategies used to overcome opposition.

**The Range of the Reform**

German policymakers see themselves in the forefront of rail reform policy in the EC. However, when the 1993 legislative package is compared to the whole range of alternatives discussed on the national and the supranational level, this judgment holds only true with respect to its fiscal and regulatory parts. As far as the railway's internal organization is concerned, the reform rather deserves the qualification as medium range.

*Corporatization without Privatization*

The core of the 1993 reforms was the transformation of the two German state railways, the western Deutsche Bundesbahn and the eastern Deutsche Reichsbahn, from setups resembling those of public administrations to a unified joint-stock company under private law, the Deutsche Bahn AG. For the proponents of the reform the new status as a joint-stock company was necessary to make the railways economically successful. Their main argument was that the new legal framework made the railways less dependent on government and gave them more freedom to behave as an economic actor, although the federal state remained the sole owner of the enterprise. It was hoped that the legal provisions regarding the division of competences between the management board, the supervisory board, and the shareholders of a joint-stock company would prevent repeated intervention by the state in the work of the railway management.

Previous political interference in the railway's business was regarded as a major disadvantage for the railways with respect to their competitors and a prime reason for their bad economic standing. The former legal framework, based on an unclear definition of the railway's duties and procedural rules that provided political actors with the opportunity to interfere in their operational decisions, had made such interventions possible. The State Railway Act, in force until 1993, stated that the Deutsche Bundesbahn (DB) should act as an economic enterprise,[40] but also stressed the railways' public-service obligations and restricted the freedom of the management board to act according to purely commercial criteria. The Ministry of Transport was called to use rail regulation to support the government's transport, economic, fiscal, and social policy goals, and the railways required ministerial authorization, for example, for their tariffs, budgetary plans, salaries, and the closure of track or other infrastructure facilities.[41] Furthermore, the organization of the old DB comprised an administrative council that assured participation in the railways' internal decision making to actors with an interest at stake in the sector but not necessarily in the railways' financial viability and economic success. Among these were the unions (i.e., representatives of the railway's employees), associations of industry and agriculture (the railway's clients), the Länder (which defended local and regional interests in public services), and representatives of the railway's commercial competitors such as inland shipping or road transport.[42] The minister of transport could raise objections to the decisions of the administrative council. However, his decisions were again influenced by lobbying activities of the actors represented in that council and pressure from members of the Federal Parliament who, for instance when it came to decide on line closures, feared that their specific constituencies would be cut off from the national rail network. As a consequence, according to the critics of the old regulatory framework, conflict between divergent logics of action in that sector was all too often resolved to the disadvantage of DB's economic viability. The railway management complained that decisions of major commercial importance, such as the introduction of automatic coupling in freight transport or the closure of nonprofitable regional infrastructure, were subject to lengthy discussions and eventually blocked for political reasons, while the railways were later blamed for inefficiency and growing debts.[43] There were simply too many actors ready and able to interfere in the railway's commercial decisions, while not accounting for the costs created by their policies. Moreover, there were few incentives to reduce politically motivated interventions, because their costs were not always obvious and because the most important of such incentives, the threat of bankruptcy, did not exist either, as it was taken for granted that the state would always cover the railway's debts. The new status was meant to change this situation (Dürr 1994; Regierungskommission 1991; BMV 1995b: 4, 6).

Furthermore, changing the legal footing of the railways also implied the abolition of the special rules regarding payment and promotion of those employees with civil servant status. This was expected to increase the flexibility of personnel management and to provide incentives for more ambitious employees who were promised better opportunities for individual careers according to personal abilities and performance after the reform.[44] Apart from providing such direct incentives, the image of being a private enterprise and the "new beginning" that the change of the legal status symbolized were used to promote new behavioral norms among rail employees, such as a more client-oriented approach and a more aggressive defense of the railway's economic interests. The new situation thus created new demands, but it could also motivate the staff, as they could now be regarded as members of a modern service enterprise with positive prospects for the future instead of the employees of a declining and inefficient public service.[45]

## Internal Reorganization and Open Market Access

The recent German rail legislation calls for a stepwise internal differentiation of the former public monopoly into different branches with separate profit centers to enhance the internal efficiency of *Deutsche Bahn AG (DB AG)*. Moreover, the separation of the track from the operational units should also provide fairer conditions for competition between different rail operators. German policymakers have opted for an organizational separation between track and operation, that is, a medium-range solution, but have been hesitant to completely dismantle the integrated structure of the railways. *DB AG* was obliged to introduce separate units and accounting at least between the division in charge of the infrastructure and those responsible for the operation of services in the fields of long-distance passenger transport, short-distance passenger transport, and freight transport.[46] It was further specified that *DB AG* had to transform these branches into separate joint-stock companies not later than five years after its foundation, itself becoming a holding company with the responsibility for coordinating these enterprises. The holding company may be dissolved at a later time, but this step—that would lead to a complete institutional separation of the different branches—has remained optional and would require further parliamentary approval (see Figure 5.1).[47]

Meanwhile, access to the German rail network has been opened to new operators. Since 1993 any national or foreign rail operator can purchase slots from

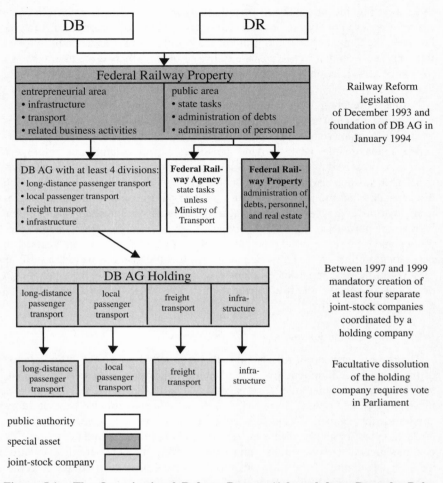

<table>
</table>

Railway Reform
legislation
of December 1993 and
foundation of DB AG in
January 1994

Between 1997 and 1999
mandatory creation of
at least four separate
joint-stock companies
coordinated by a
holding company

Facultative dissolution
of the holding
company requires vote
in Parliament

**Figure 5.1.  The Organizational Reform Process (Adapted from Deutsche Bahn 1994: 102)**

DB's infrastructure branch and run trains on its network, provided that the operator fulfills individual licensing criteria and that it opens its track to other German operators.[48] This reform had repercussions on the organization of the former rail monopolist. There is a certain risk that the infrastructure unit of *DB AG* discriminates against the competitors of its operational branch. For example, DB's first charging system for track use was heavily criticized for including high discounts for large demands by single clients, which, in practice, could have been used only by its own operational units (Aberle and Brenner 1994)—hence the demands to complete the separation between track and operations and to dissolve DB also as a holding company as soon as possible.[49] Furthermore, a new regulatory body, the Federal Railway Agency (EBA), took over supervisory functions previously carried out by the railways themselves. The EBA is responsible for licensing railway undertakings, for controlling the safety of technical equipment, and for specific tasks in the field of infrastructure planning. Moreover, rail operators that feel discriminated against by other railway companies can lodge a complaint with the EBA.[50] In contrast, the allocation of specific infrastructure using rights or slots, sometimes defined as a public task because it offers ample scope for discrimination, is carried out by the rail track companies themselves.[51]

### Subsidies

One of the distinct characteristics of the German railway reform was the state's generosity in providing the railways with a sound financial standing. The idea to strengthen market forces in the rail sector was not accompanied by a financial retreat of the state. First, *DB AG* could start its activities without any financial burdens from the past. The government relieved the railways of all their outstanding liabilities, including obligations incurred by the civil servant status of former rail employees in matters of pensions and social insurance,[52] and granted the railways special financial assistance to upgrade the outdated East German rail infrastructure. Apart from these exceptional measures, the state remains involved in financing regional rail services and infrastructure investment. The new railway legislation laid down the responsibility of the federal government for the development of rail infrastructure and exact sums that it must provide for regional passenger transport in the coming years.

Meanwhile, changes in the way financial transfers take place have increased the pressure on the railways to introduce more rigorous economic calculations across all fields of activity. The introduction of a contract-based regime in regional passenger transport is designed to increase the transparency of financial transfers between public authorities and the railways and to introduce competition for these funds. Whereas in the past the central government paid an annual lump sum to the national railway company in compensation for its public-service obligations, covering roughly only 80 percent of the calculated costs, today public actors pay for the specific service they retain desirable.[53] In addition, public transport has been opened for tendering. Regional and local authorities, which are responsible for this field as of the 1993 reform, can now decide independently and on the basis of the best offer in terms of cost and quality to whom they assign the operation of regional rail services in their respective areas.[54]

Regarding infrastructure investment, the specific solution that was agreed upon was, first, the introduction of a clause obliging the federal government to maintain and build rail track into the German Basic Law. Secondly, the federal government must keep a majority share of any future track operator (Article 87e, nos. 3–4 GG). Finally, after the reform, the greater part of investment in rail track is financed by means of interest-free loans that are granted on the condition that the railways' projects are in line with public infrastructure plans and that the state budget allows the investment. And if the railways consider a line commercially unviable and the state nevertheless wants to build it, the railways can, in exceptional circumstances, also request nonrefundable subsidies in addition to the loans.[55] Thus, the state remains strongly involved in infrastructure investment. However, the railways must reimburse public infrastructure funding according to the annual depreciation of the track's value, which implies that the infrastructure operator must normally gain sufficient revenue from track users to finance its full costs.

## The Reform in Light of European Requirements

Germany has, with its 1993 reform legislation, fulfilled and, in many respects, gone beyond the minimum requirements laid down in the European Community's central railway Directive 91/440. The German reform also goes further than the limited reform steps taken by France or Italy. However, concerning the internal reorganization of the state railways, Germany falls behind not of the EC's (modest) legal obligations, but of some options that had previously been discussed on the supranational as well as on the domestic level, and certainly far behind the British reforms.

In line with Directive 91/440, the independence of the railway management from the state was increased by transforming the former Bundesbahn and Reichsbahn into a joint-stock company. The total debt relief of this company was a far-reaching solution with respect to the demanded improvement of the railways' financial situation. And as concerns the right of new rail operators to obtain access to the national infrastructure, Directive 91/440 only obliges the member states to grant access rights to international groupings and combined transport while Germany's legislation does not contain this limitation. But whereas Germany has gone quite some way toward the implementation of these points, it only opted for a medium-range solution regarding the separation of infrastructure and operations. The German railways were forced to introduce organizational separation, whereas the decision over a complete institutional separation of the different branches was postponed. It is true that the EC directive only obliges member states to introduce separate accounting between the two branches while any more far-reaching solution is left to the discretion of the member states. Nevertheless, the EC directive does suggest going ahead with organizational and institutional separation, and whereas this was actually done in Britain, in Germany efforts to move into this direction were blocked in the domestic decision-making process.

But arguably more important than the legislative output is the fact that the 1993 reform has already had an impact on the orientation and behavior of many representatives of the German rail sector. In addition to the transposition of EC directives into national law, competition on a European scale has actually become a relevant dimension for the activity of these actors. For example, the German railways participate in international joint ventures such as NDX, DACH, and Thalys, the cargo division did not only extend its international business (Sinnecker 1997) but actually opted for a merger with the cargo division of the Dutch railways, and the government and the railways alike are in favor of extending access rights to foreign infrastructures beyond the sector of international groupings and combined transport within the EC.[56] Apart from such activities concerning international transport markets, DB AG encounters international competition on domestic markets, too. Foreign investors are already active on the German regional rail transport market—which has become economically attractive due to high public subsidies—either by directly applying for franchises or by investing in existing local operators, such as the Deutsche Eisenbahngesellschaft, DEG-Verkehrs-GmbH.

The railway reform of 1993 thus was the sign of a new, market-oriented regulatory philosophy in the German rail sector. However, the reach of the new approach is still contested. Discussions in the years following the reform have shown that its implementation and specifically the railways' primary orientation at economic profitability can still provoke political conflict. One of the remaining questions is whether the transformation of the railways into a state-owned joint-stock company is sufficient to achieve a division between commercial activities of the railways, on the one hand, and the pursuance of political goals under the *aegis* of government, on the other. The case of the magnetic levitation train Transrapid seems to show that the government can in extremis still intervene in major railway decisions. Although this new technical system is incompatible with the existing rail network and although the financial risks associated to the project are high, the central government in office until 1998—in its intention to promote a new technology "made in Germany"—could urge the *DB AG* to take the responsibility for operating this train on the planned route between Hamburg and Berlin.[57] And speaking about the reduction of personnel, a member of the DB AG's management board frankly admitted that four years after their transformation into a joint-stock company the railways were not yet a place as free of politics as other enterprises (Daubertshäuser 1997: 2).

Furthermore, it is an explicit part of the German rail reform concept—distinguishing it, for example, from the Swedish or the Dutch model—that the track must also be operated according to commercial criteria and cover its full costs. But this approach could run counter to remaining notions of public service as well as to efforts to shift traffic volumes from road to rail. Small railway undertakings frequently complain that the rates charged by DB's infrastructure branch for the use of its infrastructure are too high for new entrants to establish themselves in the market and to compete with road transport. In the meantime, under current financing conditions only relatively few principal lines can be financed completely through the fees they generate. A recent study revealed that revenue from fares cover only 56 percent of the costs of DB's rail network (DIW 1997). DB AG calculated that about a third of the existing track cannot be run profitably and is consequently threatened by closure. When this became generally known, it provoked an immediate public outcry.[58] It remains to be seen how the company and its owner, the central government, respond to this situation. Although public authorities must still be heard, it has generally become much easier for Deutsche Bahn to sell unprofitable lines to alternative operators or to close them altogether following the railway reform.[59] Thus, besides some efforts to reduce the costs of maintaining and operating its track, and besides the examples showing that regional railway enterprises can run formerly unprofitable lines with lower costs (JB 1996), DB AG may make greater use of these options, unless those demanding rail transport services in the public interest also pay for the costs.

In conclusion, the 1993 reform fired important developments in the German rail sector even though the new railway laws fell short of some proposals previously discussed both nationally and internationally. The next sections examine how this specific policy result came about in the political decision-making process. In other words, what was the impact of structural characteristics of the German political system and of distinct actor strategies on the reform output? This embraces two distinct aspects—first, given the generally high number of potential veto points in the German polity, how could the reform be carried out at all? And second, why did it not go further?

### Rail Reform Policies in the German Political System

How was the reform possible? In much the same way as road haulage, there were actors putting forward demands for fundamental railway reforms and an intellectual background from where concrete concepts for a new policy emerged. The latest reform was the result of the seventeenth major rail reform initiative since 1949 (Deutsche Bahn 1994: 8; Wissenbach 1994). The need for railway reforms had already been discussed in the Federal Parliament during the 1980s (Lehmkuhl and Herr 1994: 635). Industry had repeatedly called for better rail services and specifically for the introduction of more competitive elements in the railway sector (BDI 1987, 1989; DIHT 1991). Major enterprises had even founded an association, the German Transport Forum, to promote the development of new concepts for transport policy and for the rail sector in particular.[60] Moreover, there is a well developed academic discipline of transport economics in Germany that has been examining the railways and related problems for decades. And finally, the railway management and the government had already tried to improve the situation of DB and to strengthen economic thinking within the enterprise through internal reforms during the 1980s, without, however, achieving their main goals (König 1993; Wissenbach 1994).

However, even if the existence of economic and political actors demanding a reform satisfies a first condition for a possible reform, the seventeenth reform initiative might have again got stuck in the decision-making process. The transformation of Deutsche Bundesbahn and Deutsche Reichsbahn into a joint-stock company under private law required changes in the German Basic Law. Consequently, to be approved, the reform needed a two-thirds majority in the Bundestag, the Federal Parliament, as well as in the Bundesrat, the legislative body representing the regional governments at the federal level. Thus, the government had to put together an extraordinarily broad majority to get the reform through the political decision-making process: the government had to reach an agreement with the major opposition party, at that time the social democrats, and with the distinct interests of the Länder. Such a constellation is a typical feature of the German institutional setting, but tends to create "interlocking politics" and to make ambitious reform policy arduous (Scharpf 1988). In what follows I examine how the reform was nevertheless accomplished through the political entrepreneurship of the minister of transport and the railway management, and moreover how the interests of those actors whose dissent could have capsized the project, above all the opposition, the trade unions, and the regional governments, were accommodated. I start, however, with an analysis of the impact of the commission's and also the council's efforts to establish an EC railway policy on the German domestic reform.

## *The Impact of EC Legislation on the German Reform*

EC legislation was not the main cause for the German reform, but the parallel discussions over the establishment of an EC railway policy facilitated building a consensus over the national reform plans. The German reform plans did not originate in Brussels, but EC legislation put some specific regulatory issues on the decisional agenda and was at times used strategically to overcome domestic opposition to the reform. The implementation of Directive 91/440 was explicitly mentioned as one of the tasks of the German reform by the Federal Ministry of Transport (BMV 1995b: 4). However, the directive was neither the starting point nor the immediate reason for the domestic reform process. Supranational legislation was so indeterminate that it allowed a vast array of solutions. The need to adapt to EC legislation existed only in certain areas, whereas the German reform went beyond the EC rules. Moreover, railway reforms in general as well as most of the issues contained in Directive 91/440 had already been discussed by national experts for some time. According to one of its members, the expert commission appointed by the German government never referred to the directive, and some of its members did not even know that it was being prepared.[61] However, we can assume that the discussions held on the supranational level had at least an indirect impact on the parallel debates in the national arena. This derives from the fact that the representatives of the Ministry of Transport working on the German reform concept were certainly aware of the issues discussed in Brussels, that the German preferences with regard to rail regulation were not ultimately formulated at that time, and, finally, that the German minister of transport had long hoped to achieve coherence between European and national policies in this area.[62] Furthermore, European rail legislation could be used strategically on the national level. For example, the leadership of the German railway worker's union used the duty to implement EC policies as an argument to overcome the skepticism of its membership with regard to the German reforms, although the latter were more far-reaching than the member states were legally obliged to go under Directive 91/440.[63] To conclude, EC rail policies did not initiate the German reforms, but they reinforced existing domestic trends.[64]

## Agenda Setting and Problem Definition

The German rail reform would not have been possible had the advocates of reform not managed to convince other actors of the urgency of the problem, and had the consequences of German unification not opened a "window of opportunity" (Kingdon 1984) to proceed from analysis of the problem to concrete legislation. The agenda-setting phase already explains much of what could eventually be accomplished.

One of the main factors explaining how the German reform could get through the difficult domestic decision-making process is that the principal reform advocates, that is, central government and railway management, were able to build a large consensus about the need for fundamental railway reforms and a particular reform concept already at a very early stage of the decisional process. By presenting the railways' problems as acute and in urgent need of solution, maintaining the status quo became an unacceptable policy option. Consequently, outright opposition to the reform became difficult. Moreover, once a principal consensus on the need for reform was established, it also became much easier to find solutions for conflicts over detailed regulatory and fiscal issues.

A central element of the government's agenda-setting strategy was the establishment of an expert commission in 1989. In contrast to some of its predecessors, this commission had an enormous political impact. It focused public attention on the railways' financial crisis, put forward a comprehensive reform concept, and, given that the members of such a heterogeneous and prestigious group had agreed on a reform concept,[65] already established a preliminary consensus not only about the principal need for reform, but also on a particular solution to the railways' problems (see Regierungskommission 1991). All these factors were important for overcoming difficulties in subsequent negotiations over the details of the government's reform concept.[66]

To explain this further, in the eyes of most German policymakers the railways' rising annual deficits and accumulated debts were the key problem that made a fundamental reform indispensable.[67] Fiscal considerations had also stood at the center of the federal government's decision to establish its expert commission (Regierungskommission 1991: 4). However, as the deficit problem was anything but new for either politicians or the railway management (König 1993: 424), the very way in which it was discussed constitutes an important factor in the reform effort. Even more than the already negative development of current deficits—the railway commission pointed out that in normal commercial circumstances the railways would have already been bankrupt at the beginning of the 1990s (Regierungskommission 1991: 11)—it was the commission's forecast for the future development of the deficit and the railways' repeated warning that they might completely run out of money within a short period of time that convinced most policymakers of the indispensability and the urgency of a major reform effort. The estimated debts showed enormous growth rates for the future. As the owner, that is, the federal government, would have been called to cover the railways' deficits one day, their critical financial situation also became a potentially serious threat for the public budget.[68] Transport policymakers moreover argued that it was necessary to improve the financial situation of the railways and their competitiveness as soon as possible in order to prevent rail services from being radically cut back in the future for fiscal reasons (Deutsche Bahn 1994: 73). Furthermore, the railways' financial problems had already been serious in West Germany, but due to the poor state of the East German rail infrastructure, the high staffing levels of the Reichsbahn, and the immediate loss of their high market shares following the lifting of East Germany's rigorous limitations to road transport, these problems grew dramatically in the wake of German unification.[69] Thus, the impact of German unification—unknown when the railway commission was appointed in February 1989—increased the pressure for reform and provided its advocates with a "window of opportunity" (Kingdon 1984) to enact their legislative plans. Although the result of a reform could obviously not be known from the outset, carrying on with the old policies became a highly unattractive option and made policymakers more prepared to accept a new railway regime.

Given this effect of the commission's calculations, it was a further advantage of its report that it also presented a solution for the railways' problems. The commission, the government, and the railway management jointly argued that the transformation of the state railways into a joint-stock company and accompanying regulatory and financial measures would free the railways from preexisting burdens and reverse the described negative trends (Regierungskommission 1991; Dürr 1994). This admittedly was a highly speculative hope (see König 1993), but it fitted the dominant paradigm of economic regulation[70] and parallel discussions about the reform of other public utilities such as telecommunications, postal services, broadcasting, and health care (Deregulierungskommission 1991; Dyson 1992; Benz and Goetz 1996a). But above all, it provided the railways with a perspective for the future that they previously seemed to lose. The way the policy problem was shaped implied that although the reform created costs in the short term, it would create fiscal benefits in the long run, whereas not taking any action would actually lead to a "worst-case scenario." The presentation of such a "worst case-scenario" in combination with a concrete reform proposal turned out to be an agenda-setting strategy that attracted the utmost attention for the project and increased the chances of the reform to be accepted.

Finally, apart from focusing the attention on the present and future situation of the railways and on concrete policy proposals, the commission also showed an almost unanimous agreement among a group of highly respected figures from different professional backgrounds in business, science, and politics. The composition of the commission and the fact that it was completely free regarding the solutions that could be considered provided its proposals with legitimacy.[71] As such a heterogeneous and prestigious group could agree on a peculiar reform concept in an admittedly complex field, their recommendations represented an authoritative starting point for any succeeding discussion and made it much more difficult for the critics of the government's reform plans, which were largely based on the commission's recommendations, to defend their position afterward.[72]

This became visible in the succeeding conflict between the minister of transport and the minister of finance over the fiscal implications of the reform. The minister of finance holds a particularly strong position in the German cabinet.[73] His reservations regarding the railway reform can be explained by the already strained fiscal situation that came in the wake of German unification and the immediate costs of the reform concept presented by the Ministry of Transport, that is, the plan to relieve the railways of outstanding debts and extraordinary personnel costs. Moreover, the Länder demanded financial help in return for the transfer of regional passenger transport into its responsibility, and the federal government had to remain involved in financing rail infrastructure. The conflict between the two ministers was finally resolved with a compromise (Lehmkuhl 1996: 78–79). Still, the existing reform proposals were not fundamentally put into question again when their fiscal implications eventually came on the negotiation table. The sequential treatment of regulatory and financial issues, or the strategy to develop first a comprehensive reform concept and to settle its financial implications only afterward, had created a path dependency. Given that a preliminary consensus on the reform concept had already been reached in the governmental railway commission, the pressure to find solutions for related fiscal questions was much greater than would otherwise have been the case.[74]

In sum, the federal government's decision to establish an independent expert commission with the task of developing a concept for railway reforms instead of presenting such proposals itself must be considered a political move. Given that the intention to strengthen economic thinking in this sector could be expected to meet opposition, the backing of a reform by such a group increased the legitimacy of the government's project and the chances that it would go through the decision-making process. And as the commission only prepared a report, whereas the concrete legislative proposals were drafted by the bureaucracy itself, the Ministry of Transport still had ample opportunity to interfere in the decision-making process should its preferences not be fully mirrored by the conclusion of the appointed group. Moreover, the head of the railway department within the Ministry of Transport actively participated in every meeting of the commission, and thus most probably shaped its result as well. By contrast, some actors that might have been more skeptical of a reform concept based on business logic, such as, for instance, the single states in the German federation, were not represented in the commission. They entered the decision-making process at a later stage. The Länder could threaten to vote against the project in the Bundesrat and actually obtained important concessions. However, the relatively late appearance of these actors meant that they were restricted to negotiating on measures dealing with the consequences of a reform whose principle elements had already been defined.

## Compromises and Side-Payments

Despite the broad consensus on the need for a railway reform, the legislative process repeatedly risked failure when it came to decide on specific legislative provisions. Some regulatory as well as fiscal questions remained conflict loaded, while the planned changes in the constitution made the approval of the opposition as well as the regional states essential for the reform. Given the pressure to take action, these actors could not block the reforms. However, due to their institutional veto points, they succeeded in shaping the reform output according to their own preferences. This made the German reform particularly costly for the central government and, as far as regulatory and organizational issues are concerned, less clear-cut than was originally intended. The institutional structure of the German political system does not principally preclude any reform, but it favors cautious advances rather than the implementation of radical reform programs.

*The Major Opposition Party.* As can be seen from the parliamentary initiatives taken by the social democratic opposition during the 1980s (Lehmkuhl and Herr 1994: 635) and from the cooperative attitude they showed in the eyes of members of the administration,[75] there was a basic agreement between the government and the opposition on the general need for reforms in the rail sector. However, consent on the urgency of a particular policy does not preclude conflict over its details. Whereas the core of the government's reform concept was corporatization and the step-by-step introduction of market criteria into a former public monopoly, the social democrats stressed the comparative disadvantages of the railways with respect to competitive conditions and infrastructure investment, insisted on safeguarding the interests of the railways' employees, and called for the integration of the railway reforms into a more comprehensive concept of transport policy in general (Daubertshäuser in Deutsche Bahn 1994: 74). Whereas the integration of the railway reform in a comprehensive transport policy program was too ambitious a project, the SPD at least sought guarantees that would secure the state's duty to develop rail infrastructure after the privatization of the railways. That is, whereas there was a basic consent about introducing more competitive elements in the railway regime regarding the operation of trains, the regulatory philosophy in the area of infrastructure development remained contested. These demands of the social democrats were shared by the unions, the national association of chambers of industry and commerce, and the Länder.[76]

Given the need to obtain the approval of the opposition for the reform, the government accepted to insert a clause in the Basic Law that fixes the responsibility of the central government to develop rail infrastructure, and to create a law that put the construction of rail track on a similar legal footing as the construction of roads (Lehmkuhl 1996: 79–80). Thus, partisan conflict did not endanger the railway reform, but the need to win approval from the opposition party did shape its output.

*The Unions.*    Another factor ensuring that the social democrats agreed to the reform was the decision of the major railway union to side with the reforms. The social democratic parliamentary group had actually announced that the unions' approval would be a decisive precondition for their own consent. Thus, even without holding formal veto power, the sectoral unions held effective means to oppose the reform. Why did the unions, which have been a major obstacle to railway reforms in other countries and which opposed the reform of postal services in Germany, approve the German railway reforms?

The answer lies in the long-term strategic benefit of the reform for the major trade union. In the beginning, the report of the governmental railway commission and specifically its privatization concept was criticized by the unions. Whereas the two smaller unions, the GDBA and the GDL, were fully opposed to the concept of putting organizational privatization at the center of the reforms (DBB, GDBA, and GDL 1992),[77] the major railwaymen's union (the GdED)[78] decided it could best defend the interests of its members by actively participating in the decision-making process and by formulating conditions for its approval of the reform:

> We were faced with the question: Should the GdED reject the railway reform and thus lose the chance to influence and shape it, or should we collaborate in the formulation of the reform? . . . The painful experiences in other countries show that blunt refusal ends up in a dead end and finally in the insignificance of the unions. No single workplace can be defended with a retreat to old recipes and struggles against obvious economic constraints. On the contrary: the longer necessary reforms are delayed, the more workplaces are unnecessarily put at risk. This holds true for the private as well as for the public sector of our economy.
>
>                                         (GdED 1996: 13, author's translation)

The decision of the major union to actively participate in the decision-making process and to seek compromises was facilitated by procedural and material aspects of the policy development. Regarding procedures, the government's strategy to involve all actors with a say in the rail sector from the beginning in the consultation process facilitated the spread of a new, economically oriented view of the railways and the acceptance of the principal ideas underlying the government's reform concept. Although the GdED had initially been critical of the railway commission's privatization plans, in the course of deliberations its position began to move closer to that of the railway management with respect to the need for rationalization and the detrimental effects of governmental control over the railways.[79] Concerning specific measures, the government accepted the union's major demands. Those concerning regulatory issues were shared by actors with formal veto points in the decision-making process, such as the social democrats and the regional governments. But for the unions a central point was the material situation of the employees. Due to their and the social democrats' insistence, the formal privatization of the railways was indeed accomplished in such a way that the employees and specifically the former civil servants did not suffer any disadvantages with regard to pay-levels, promotion, health care, pensions, and so on. The (huge) costs of this strategy were taken on by the state. Thus, the unions could accept the reform because it opened the possibility for a better future of a declining industry without creating financial risks for their membership, that is, the railways' employees.

Finally, the reforms also implied long-term strategic benefits for the railway unions themselves. As a consequence of organizational privatization, their influence in negotiations on salaries and working conditions has increased. Before the reforms, the railway unions could only participate passively on issues negotiated for the entire civil service; now they can negotiate directly with the railways' management.[80] And whereas the old Bundesbahn required ministerial authorization for any wage agreement reached with the unions, this is no longer the case today.[81] Last but not least, following the transformation into a joint-stock company, the staff and the unions appoint half of the members of the railway's supervisory board, which is a final point that makes it easier to understand why the GdED eventually agreed to the privatization concept.

The enduring opposition of the two smaller unions, the GDBA and the GDL, can be explained by the fact that the privatization concept conflicted to a much greater degree with their traditional identity and organizational logic than it did in the case of the GdED. As the former have largely represented civil servants and are embedded in the overarching association of the German civil service (Deutscher Beamtenbund), it was much more difficult for these organizations to accept a reform that attributed the main responsibility for the failures of the past to the very concept of public service (DBB, GDBA, and GDL 1992). However, the two smaller organizations did not hold veto positions in the political decision-making process. They could not convince any of the political forces of their position after the major sectoral union had accepted the reform and, in contrast to Italy or France, were unable to blackmail political decision makers by strikes. According to German labor law, strikes are only admissible for questions dealt with in the collective contracts between employers and employees, whereas strikes for political goals are forbidden. The regulatory and organizational questions addressed in the railway reform lay outside this area. Thus, due to the division of the worker's representatives and due to the restrictive elements of the national traditions and regulations in collective bargaining, an aggressive opposition of a small group such as, for example, the train drivers would have been illegitimate in Germany.

*The Länder Regional Governments.*   A further line of conflict that put the reform seriously at risk and decisively shaped its output was that between the federal government and the regional states. Agreement between the Federation and the Länder was crucial, as the regional states had repeatedly threatened to veto the entire reform in the second legislative body at the federal level, the Bundesrat, if the agreement reached did not meet their demands. This was a unanimous position of all regional governments, independent of their partisan affiliation. The demands of the Länder were all directly or indirectly linked to the question of upholding public service in the transport sector. Specifically, they concerned (1) financial transfers in order to enable regional and local authorities to pay for public transport, (2) the security that local transport would not be driven out of business by the privatized railways because of the higher profitability of long-distance passenger transport and freight transport, (3) state responsibility for rail track, and (4) fixing a legal commitment of the federal government to maintain public-service obligations in the sector (Lehmkuhl 1996: 81–83; Deutsche Bahn 1994: 78–79).

Indeed, the bulk of the costs of public services in the transport sector arise, from the usually deficit-making regional and local transport in which regional and local authorities are obviously more interested than central government. Thus, it was much easier for the federal government to call for the introduction of free market mechanisms in the rail sector than it was for the Länder. While the federal government tried to reduce its expenditures through the introduction of new regulation, the latter were above all concerned about safeguarding high levels of service. Furthermore, the Länder has limited opportunities to raise taxes in order to pay for the services its respective governments regard adequate. Thus it is a common strategy of the Länder to create political links between policy decisions producing costs at the regional level with parallel provisions concerning the funding of these expenditures (see Scharpf 1988).

Some central government proposals indeed provided evidence for suspecting it of trying to roll back its commitment to public service in the rail sector. For example, the central government and the minister of finance in particular were reluctant to fix their commitment to finance rail infrastructure (Lehmkuhl 1996: 79). Furthermore, the central government's first draft proposal concerning the transfer of the responsibility for regional transport to the Länder did not contain any provisions about financial transfers from the central to the regional level to enable the latter to assume these new responsibilities. According to plans of the finance minister, even the subsidies that the central state had paid for regional rail transport up until that day would be stopped. This created a harsh reaction of the Länder and almost brought the reform process to a halt (Deutsche Bahn 1994: 61, 71–90; Lehmkuhl 1996: 74). The following negotiations resulted in a compromise as far as financial questions were concerned and far-reaching concessions by the federal government to the regions on procedural issues. The crucial point was that the Länder was guaranteed fixed tax transfers from the central government in order to finance public transport.[82] Moreover, in coalition with the social democrats and the unions, the regional states insisted on legal and procedural safeguards for upholding the central government's commitment to public services. Although not all Länder demands were met, the regional states did manage to water down some of the market-inspired elements of the central government's reform concept. This regards, first, a new passage in the Basic Law (Article 87e) stating that the future track company cannot be fully privatized (the state is obliged to keep a majority share) and that the federal government has a responsibility to defend the public interest by building and maintaining rail infrastructure. It can be seen, second, by the postponement of the final decision on the railways' holding company, that is, the institutional separation of the track from the operating branches. Whereas the government originally intended to fix a date for the dissolution of the holding company, it is now unclear when this step will be taken. Moreover, given the strong opposition of DB AG, which plans to assign a strong coordination and management function to its remaining central unit (*Süddeutsche Zeitung* 1997b), it is not certain that this will happen at all. Eventually, the Länder won far-reaching procedural guarantees about its future participation in transport-related decision-making processes. Any arrangement about financing public transport will depend on the approval of the Bundesrat as well as any decision concerning the federal railway administration, selling shares of the national railway undertakings to private investors, the institutional reorganization of the railways, leaving parts of the Deutsche Bahn's infrastructure to other owners, and laws concerning the closure of track lines or otherwise affecting public transport (Article 87e GG). Moreover, the Länder must be heard when the tariffs for public transport are set by transport operators.[83] This impressive list is a telling example for the perpetuation of the logic of joint decision making in the German federal polity (Scharpf 1988). It illustrates the institutional interest of the regional states to ensure their future participation in the decision-making process at the federal level and demonstrates the improbability of abrupt policy changes in the German political system.

## Entrepreneurship and Side-Payments

The 1993 reforms were not limited to details; they have introduced a new regulatory regime that is a sign for the emergence of a new approach in German rail policy. The German railway reform was only possible because a large consensus for the reform was actively sought out from the beginning and because the federal government was prepared to bear the costs of this strategy. Nevertheless, the German political structures shaped the policy output and were responsible for the medium range of the reforms with respect to privatization and specific organizational issues.

The work of the governmental railway commission is an example of successful political agenda setting. The commission's calculations about the railways' future were alarming. The fiscal risks became even more pressing when German unification added the disastrous conditions of the East German railways to existing problems. Thus, domestic problem pressure was high and reform concepts were developed at the national level that became authoritative departure points for the legislative process. European legislation was an additional incentive for reforms, but it was not its cause. Directive 91/440 pointed in a similar direction to the concepts being discussed at the domestic level. Consequently, the German railway reform fits the European framework and was favored by specific EU rules. But the latter were not one of the politically most important sources of the German reform.

The hesitancy to introduce a pure market regime and the prudent implementation of the reform can be explained by a number of factors. Doubts concerning the technical and organizational feasibility of such models, as well as their economic advantages in the rail sector, are widespread. But above all, the reduced scope of the German reforms and their high financial costs are a result of politics. Even though there was a broad understanding on the general need for reform, disagreement on important details remained. In the last instance, the ministries involved, the Länder, and the opposition agreed to compromise, which was indispensable for institutional reasons. The regional governments, the largest opposition party, and the trade unions held important veto points in the political decision-making process and used them to ensure that public-service obligations would not be completely abandoned by the federal legislator. Consequently, the central government got the reform, but it had to make far-reaching concessions on fiscal and procedural questions.

## CONCLUSION

The new German transport regime is characterized by a parallelism of increased room for the market alongside continued state activity. The economic efficiency of the sector has become the cornerstone of the regulatory regime. Transport-related goals linked to regional, social, or environmental policy still exist. Even a redistribution of transport volumes between the different modes of transport is still on the agenda. But in contrast to the beliefs underlying the traditional regulatory system, the pursuance of these long-term goals no longer implies a suppression of market mechanisms. Today, all the instruments used to achieve these goals must fit the dominant economic logic of regulation—hence the recent attention for fiscal instruments that provide incentives but leave a greater margin of action for individual behavior than, for example, quotas. A similar ideology is behind the efforts made to increase the economic efficiency of those transport modes destined, one hopes, to win additional market shares in the future. In sum, in German transport policy, far-reaching steering efforts have been replaced by piecemeal engineering of separate problems. Government has not retreated from transport regulation, but its policy has become more modest, more fragmented. It is eventually dominated by the idea that all regulation must be market conform.

Apart from the slow dissemination of more liberal policy approaches and of the advocacy of groups opposing the old regulatory system, a change in the political setting or a major turbulence in the sector was a necessary precondition for overcoming institutionally entrenched opposition to new forms of transport regulation. In the field of road haulage, European policymaking clearly played this role of a catalyst. Even if EC policies did not directly concern domestic rules, economic interdependencies and the mechanism of "competition among rules" in practice accentuated the problems faced by the German domestic system. What is more, the embeddedness of national policymaking in the wider EC framework changed the main actors' strategic opportunities in a way that favored the proponents of regulatory changes at the domestic level. Finally, the central government was not confronted with any actor with a formal or a de facto veto power. As a consequence of the introduction of a more liberal road haulage regime, the relations between the federal government and their traditional clienteles were strained, but the power of these groups was limited. The central government did not encounter any formal veto points for the introduction of a new domestic regime. Real or perceived legal and economic restrictions, as for example in the case of tariffs, only made interventionist policies more difficult, but not liberalization. And concerning political support for its policy, the central government was not dependent on its traditional clientele either, as there were sufficient alternative groups in favor of its new policy at the domestic and the supranational level.

European policymaking could not play a similar role in the railway sector, because supranational rail policy and the German reforms were discussed parallel to each other, because the discussions held at both levels were quite similar, and finally because the crucial EC railway Directive 91/440 gave domestic decision makers great leeway in matters of implementation. Thus, EC policy supported certain domestic trends, but it was not a novel point of reference to domestic policymakers in this field. Instead, a combination of a frightening assessment of the long-term fiscal threats deriving from the railway's financial situation, which was placed on the political agenda by the government and other policy entrepreneurs, and the unforeseen aggravation of this problem following German unification became the turning point in the case of German rail policy. They focused the attention of policymakers on that field and laid the foundation for a large political consensus over the need for reform. However, in the case of the railways, the central government was not as free to act as in the case of road haulage. For institutional reasons it was confronted with a number of veto points. Thus, in order to get the reform through the decision making process, the central government had to make far-reaching concessions in terms of the rules that were established as well as in terms of the financial resources that it had to invest in the rail sector. In this case, European policymaking only had a minor impact on the domestic reform process. However, it is one result of this reform that the programmatic ideas of the European Commission suit the regulatory philosophy of German policymakers and that the railways now push for a further development of the EC's railway policy, too.

In sum, German transport policy is affected by EC policymaking with both public and private actors participating in this two-level game. The enlargement of the institutional setting provides those actors that are in line with EU policies with new strategic opportunities and strengthens their position in domestic politics (Putnam 1988; Grande 1996). However, the EU does not automatically change fundamental preconditions for successful political action at the domestic level. The German transport reforms were possible because the central government was able to provide the crucial resources—it had the formal authority to set rules, independent expertise that supplied it with sufficient information, political support by relevant groups, and adequate financial resources to cover the costs created by the reforms and to compensate those actors who would otherwise have blocked them.

# NOTES

1. Officially, it was illegal to trade licenses unless whole companies or sufficiently independent parts of a company changed owners. In practice this rule was never enforced, and license trading at prices of around 200,000 deutsche mark (DM) per license was common (van Suntum 1986: 15; Basedow 1989: 127ff.).

2. In West Germany the number of available licenses increased by 46 percent between 1986 and 1993, whereas it had only grown by 9 percent between 1978 and 1986 (Aberle 1996a: 112).

3. With bracket tariffs prices could be set by the hauliers and their clients within a margin that was up to 8.5 percent above or below the officially set tariff in long-distance transport and up to 10 percent above and 30 percent below the official tariff in short-distance road transport.

4. *Tarifaufhebungsgesetz* 13.8.1993, BGBl. I, p. 1,489.

5. Their cost coverage rate has been calculated at approximately 14 percent, as compared to 50 to 65 percent of German hauliers (DIW 1994: 70).

6. Council Directive 93/89/EEC.

7. For many years, all governments have regarded transport as a field for legitimate political intervention rather than a market (interview BGA, 31 January 1996).

8. Willeke 1995; interviews ex-DG VII, 22 May 1996; and BMWi, 26 January 1995.

9. Interview BMV, 30 January 1996.

10. Inland navigation, 18 percent; and pipelines, 5 percent (BMV 1996: 237).

11. The above-mentioned regulations only applied to hire-and-reward hauliers. Own-account transport has never been subject to quantitative limits and by its very nature cannot be submitted to price controls. Thus, it offered the chance to escape them despite repeated efforts to introduce strict limitations for this sector (Klenke 1995: 21, 79).

12. Interviews BAG, 20 February 1996; BDI, 12 July 1995; BMV, 30 January 1996; BMWi, 26 January 1995.

13. Interview BMWi, 26 January 1995.

14. Interview DG VII, 22 May 1996; Advisory Council BMV, 29 January 1996.

15. Interviews BMWi, 26 January 1995; BDI, 12 July 1995; BWV, 30 January 1996; ex-DG VII, 22 May 1996.

16. Interviews BGA, 31 January 1996; BDF, 26 January 1995.

17. Interview BMV, 30 January 1996; see also Garlichs and Müller 1977: 346.

18. Interview DIHT, 21 November 1995.

19. Interview BMWi, 26 January 1995.

20. Interview BAG, 20 February 1996.

21. Interview BWV, 30 January 1996.

22. Others were the railways (one), insurance (one), trade-unions (five), regional state authorities (six).

23. The national organization of the cooperatives is a member of the haulage association BDF/BGL, and at times the same people have run both organizations (BDF 1995a: 95–96).

24. Interview ex-DG VII, 22 May 1996.

25. Interviews BMV, 30 January 1996; and BMWi, 26 January 1995.

26. Interviews MP/CDU, 11 May 1995; MP/SPD, 22 June 1995; MP/CSU, 11 May 1995; BDF, 26 January 1995.

27. BDF 1994: 10. Interviews DIHT, 21 November 1995; BDI, 12 July 1995; BDN, 21 February 1996; BSL, 31 January 1996; BGA, 31 January 1996; VKS, 30 January 1996.

28. Interviews BDI, 12 July 1995; BWV, 30 January 1996; BMWi, 26 January 1995. See also Basedow 1989; Lammich 1991; Herber 1992.

29. Interview BWV, 30 January 1996.

30. Interview BDF, 26 January 1995.

31. Case C185/91 (*Bundesanstalt für den Güterfernverkehr* v. *Gebr. Reiff GmbH & Co.KG*), [1993] ECJ I–5801.

32. Interview BWV, 30 January 1996.

33. The cooperatives continue to offer services to their members, which are, however, no longer related to public policies.

34. In this context the agency was also renamed. It is now called Bundesamt für Güterverkehr instead of Bundesanstalt für den Güterfernverkehr.

35. Hauliers have been represented by the Bundesverband des Deutschen Güterfernverkehrs (BDF), renamed Bundesverband Güterverkehr und Logistik (BGL) in 1997, traditionally responsible for questions of long-distance haulage, and by the Bundesverband des Deutschen Güternahverkehrs (BDN), specialized in short-distance haulage. Freight forwarders have been represented by the Bundesverband Spedition und Lagerei (BSL), renamed Bundesverband Spedition und Logistik, as well as by the Vereinigung Deutscher Kraftwagenspediteure (VKS). Firms active in own-account transport have the Bundesverband Werkverkehr und Verlader (BWV). Finally, the demand side on transport markets has been represented by the major associations of industry and trade, above all the Bundesverband der Deutschen Industrie (BDI), the Deutscher Industrie- und Handelstag (DIHT), and the Bundesverband des Deutschen Groß- und Außenhandels (BGA).

36. The VKS has also started to build strategic alliances with associations in other EU member states that mainly represent larger enterprises (interviews VKS, 30 January 1996; and BSL, 31 January 1996).

37. Interview BAG, 20 February 1996.

38. Interviews DG VII, 22 May 1996; and BDF, 19 April 1996.

39. *Gesetz zur Änderung des Grundgesetzes vom 20. Dezember 1993*, BGBl. I, 22.12.1993, p. 2089 f., and *Eisenbahnneuordnungsgesetz*, BGBl. I, 30.12.1993, p. 2378 ff.

40. § 28 *Bundesbahngesetz*.

41. §§ 14ff., 50 *Bundesbahngesetz.*

42. §§ 10 and 12 *Bundesbahngesetz.*

43. Laaser 1991: 33–34; Basedow 1989: 58. Interview DB, 13 February 1997.

44. Interviews DB, 13 February 1997; GdED 12 February 1997. See also Dürr 1994.

45. Informally, some of the recently recruited staff interviewed for this project pointed out that they would not have joined the railways had the DB remained a traditional public-service undertaking.

46. § 25 *Deutsche Bahn Gründungsgesetz* (Art. 2 *Eisenbahnneuordnungsgesetz*).

47. § 2 *Deutsche Bahn Gründungsgesetz* (Art. 2 *Eisenbahnneuordnungsgesetz).*

48. See § 14 *Allgemeines Eisenbahngesetz* (Art. 5 *Eisenbahnneuordnungsgesetz).*

49. Interview Regierungskommission, 29 January 1996. See also Laaser 1994: 21–23.

50. The EBA decides cases where technical or railway specific questions are at the center of the dispute, whereas questions related to discrimination by commercial means fall under the competence of the antitrust authorities (interview EBA, 14 February 1997). See *Gesetz über die Eisenbahnverkehrsverwaltung des Bundes* (Art. 3 *Eisenbahnneuordnungsgesetz).*

51. The only provision specifiying allocation procedures in case the demand for certain slots exceeds the available capacity is contained in § 14 *Allgemeines Eisenbahngesetz* (Art. 5 *Eisenbahnneuordnungsgesetz*), which says that the specific necessities of trains that are integrated in a coordinated network of operations should be respected in the allocation of slots.

52. They were taken over by a special asset, the Bundeseisenbahnvermögen.

53. Interview DB, 13 February 1997. These changes are also suggested by Regulations 1191/69/EC and 1893/91/EC.

54. *Regionalisierungsgesetz* (Art. 4 of the *Eisenbahnneuordnungsgesetz*); see Herr and Lehmkuhl 1997.

55. As a result of the two different forms of public funding, there may be conflicts between the state, specifically the minister of finance, and the railways about the economic profitability of certain projects. In case such disputes occur, the Federal Railway Agency (EBA) is called to check the different calculations and to assess the sums each part must bear (EBA 1995: Art. 4; interview EBA, 14 February 1997). See § 3 (2) 5 *Gesetz über die Eisenbahnverwaltung des Bundes* (Art. 3 *Eisenbahnneuordnungsgesetz*), and § 9 *Schienenwegeausbaugesetz.*

56 Interview BMV, 25 November 1996. See also Henke 1997 and Deutsche Bahn 1996.

57. The new government taking office after the 1998 elections, however, stopped this project altogether.

58. "Railways switch the points towards road" (*Süddeutsche Zeitung* 1997a), "Demolition Enterprise" (*Die Zeit,* 14 March 1997).

59. § 11 *Allgemeines Eisenbahngesetz*, AEG (Art. 5 *Eisenbahnneuordnungsgesetz*).

60. Interview Deutsches Verkehrsforum 17 February 1997, Deutsche Bahn 1994: 41.

61. Interview *Regierungskommission*, 29 January 1996.

62. Interview BMV, 25 November 1996; and interview GdED, 12 February 1997.

63. Interview GdED, 12 February 1997; and GdED 1996: 12.

64. Interviews BMV, 25 November 1996; and Deutsches Verkehrsforum, 17 February 1997.

65. Only one member of the commission, a representative of the public-sector trade unions, voted against the final report.

66. Interviews BMV, 25 November 1996; GdED, 12 February 1997; Deutsches Verkehrsforum, 17 February 1997.

67. Interviews BMV, 25 November 1996; GdED, 12 February 1997; DB, 13 February 1997; EBA, 14 February 1997; Deutsches Verkehrsforum, 17 February 1997; BMV 1995b: 1.

68. Interview BMV, 25 November 1996.

69. The railway commission calculated that the combined annual deficits of Deutsche Bundesbahn and Deutsche Reichsbahn would rise from deutsche mark (DM) 27 billion in 1991 to DM 64 billion in 2000, amounting to a total deficit of DM 417 billion in 2000 (Regierungskommission 1991: 12). To compare, the central government's overall expenditure in the transport sector was worth DM 35 billion in 1991 when the report was published and 52 billion in 1995 (BMV 1996: 125).

70. Interview Deutsches Verkehrsforum, 17 February 1997.

71. Interviews BMV, 25 November 1996; Regierungskommission, 29 January 1996; and GdED, 12 February 1997.

72. The consensus-seeking function of the commission with respect to its function in gathering information on the technical aspects of a railway reform is also underlined by the fact that not all members of that commission had previously been known as rail experts.

73. See § 26 *Geschäftsordnung der Bundesregierung.*

74. Interviews BMV, 25 November 1996; GdED, 12 February 1997; and Deutsches Verkehrsforum, 17 February 1997.

75. Interview with BMV, 25 November 1996.

76. Interviews BMV, 25 November 1996; and GdED, 12 February 1997. See also DIHT 1991, 1992: and Lehmkuhl and Herr 1994: 646–47.

77. GDBA (Gewerkschaft Deutscher Bundesbahnbeamten, Arbeiter und Angestellten) (mainly public servants), GDL (Gewerkschaft Deutscher Lokomotivführer und Anwärter) (train drivers).

78. The GdED (*Gewerkschaft der Eisenbahner Deutschlands*) represents roughly 80 percent of national railways' employees.

79. Interview GdED, 12 February 1997.

80. Interview BMV, 25 November 1996. See also Lehmkuhl 1996: 77–78.

81. In the past, there have been examples when agreements between the railways' management and the railwaymen's unions about higher wages for specific groups of employees were vetoed by the minister of transport, because the government feared that any pay raises in one sector could influence the coming negotiations about the public sector in general (interview GdED, 12 February 1997).

82. These amounted to DM 8.7 billion in 1996 and thereafter DM 12 billion annually until 2001, when the transfer system will be revised (§ 5 *Regionalisierungsgesetz*) (Art. 4 of the *Eisenbahnneuordnungsgesetz*). Ironically, the revision clause was introduced at the request of the Länder. But whereas the regional states had feared that the sums at their disposal would not be sufficient in the future, the costs in the field of regional passenger transport have actually developed in the opposite direction. Thus, the federal government will probably insist on a reduction of its subsidies (Girnau 1997).

83. § 12 *Allgemeines Eisenbahngesetz*, AEG (Art. 5 *Eisenbahnneuordnungsgesetz*).

# 6

# Going through the Motions: The Modest Impact of Europe on Italian Transport Policy

*Dieter Kerwer*

## THE "EUROPEANIZATION" OF ITALIAN TRANSPORT POLICY?

The traditional Italian transport policy is based on extensive public intervention to reduce or replace market mechanisms. It stands in stark contrast to the European Common Transport Policy's (CTP's) long-term goal of building a common market for transport services. Research on European integration would predict that Europe would have a rather strong impact on Italian transport policy. First, it has often been observed that the European Union (EU) has been extraordinarily successful in the area of market liberalization. The Single Market Program launched in the mid-1980s is generally regarded as a success story. In this, once the center of policy formulation shifts to the European level, it is likely to bring about policy convergence and even the structural adjustment of the political system (Mény, Muller, and Quermonne 1996). Policy convergence is promoted by two powerful mechanisms. European law has a strong impact on the member states because of the mechanism of judicial review (Weiler 1991). If deficits in the implementation of EU law prevail, affected parties can use national administrative courts to force authorities to comply. Another powerful source of change is the regulatory competition unleashed by market integration (Woolcock 1996). The single market has increased possibilities for firms to leave jurisdictions they dislike, thus constraining the available policy choices. Hence, judicial review and regulatory competition in the EU exert considerable pressure on member states. Second, it has often been remarked that national governments use the external constraint of European policies to promote reforms unpopular with entrenched national interest groups (Putnam 1988; Moravcsik 1993; Grande 1996). One of the reasons why European Community (EC) membership enjoys such widespread popular support in Italy is

that it is widely expected that it will provide increased leverage for national reformers (Dyson and Featherstone 1996). Since there is a broad consensus on the
need for reform in transport, European policy may be seen as supplying readily
accepted solutions to national problems.

Another reason for assuming that the European transport liberalization has had a
strong impact in Italy is the favorable change in the regulatory landscape. The apparent potential for policy convergence due to Europeanization has improved considerably over the last decade or so because of changes in the patterns of economic
policymaking in general and in the transport sector in particular. For most of the
postwar period, the Italian economy has been characterized by a vast public sector
with state holdings such as the Istituto per la ricostruzione industriale (IRI), the
Ente nazionale per l'energia elettrica (ENEL), and the Ente nazionale di idrocarburi
(ENI), which have dominated the industrial and service sectors. State intervention
is particularly ubiquitous in the transport sector, where the provision and operation
of the infrastructure (such as roads, railway terminals, ports, airports) and the transport of passengers and freight in the various modes have been publicly controlled.
Railways have been nationalized for most of the century. The crisis-ridden Italian
air carrier Alitalia is state-owned and heavily dependent on public subsidies. State
enterprises such as Tirrenia have dominated shipping to the Italian islands for most
of the postwar period. However, over the last ten years, there have been signs of a
change in the intervention style in many areas of the economy, which may have improved the prospects for Europeanization. At least legally, Italy has also been affected by the worldwide move toward privatization and deregulation and away
from state intervention (Cassese 1995). A long-standing tradition of interventionism by means of state ownership and detailed regulation is increasingly being challenged by legal measures privatizing public enterprises and introducing new rules
for competition. In the transport sector this tendency is especially visible in the
1992 privatization of the state-owned railways. In addition, Alitalia's monopoly on
air transport services for the most important domestic routes was abolished in 1996,
and there are plans to privatize airport and air-traffic operating companies. Similar
signs of change in the style of intervention may also be seen in the area of shipping,
where infrastructure operations are also being privatized and port authorities formerly responsible for the provision of all port services must now limit their activities to the long-term planning and control of the services offered by private companies. The transport sector abounds in recent examples of privatization and
deregulation, and this is reflected in the academic debate regarding the role of state
intervention in the economy (Reviglio 1994; Necci and Normann 1994; Sylos-
Labini 1995). It has even been argued that the trend is redefining the Italian
"economic constitution" (Cassese 1995). Thus there are several theoretical and empirical reasons suggesting that the European transport policy has had a strong
impact on the national level.

If one is correct in assuming that the potential for the Europeanization of Italian transport policy has increased, the empirical results of the two case studies are

surprising. They show that, despite the potential for policy congruence, in Italy the dynamics of domestic policies for road haulage and railways is largely characterized by inertia. In the last ten years, decision making has remained on the traditional path, and Italian transport policy in the sector of road and rail has been "going through the motions" with old routines still dominating, despite widespread dissatisfaction with the results. In a nutshell, the paradoxical coexistence of the CTP at the European level and policy inertia at the domestic level is due to the strong tradition of state interventionism and the resistance of particularistic private interests in the transport sector that have undermined the capacity of public actors to introduce those key changes necessary for convergence.

## ROAD HAULAGE POLICY DRIFTING AWAY FROM EUROPE

Since the mid-1980s a primary goal of the European CTP has been to create a single market for road haulage services offered throughout the EC irrespective of the nationality of the road haulage enterprise. Cutting prices and increasing the quality of services were supposed to enhance the competitiveness of the European economies and the efficiency of the transport sector. But Italy was not prepared for a single road haulage market, and Italian hauliers, as the declining share in the international transport market had shown, were not ready for competition with their EC rivals (Ministero dei Trasporti 1992: 16). Furthermore, the administration of the road haulage sector had always been heavily biased toward interventionism, and the regulatory framework with its strict control of market access and fixed prices for transport services was ill-suited to accommodate intra-European competition.

The EC reform project thus posed a formidable economic challenge. Transport enterprises would have to devise strategies to adapt to the new competitive situation. The challenge, however, was also political. The liberalization of road haulage presented a unique opportunity for Italy to reform the administration of the sector that, even according to the Ministry of Transport, never achieved its major goals of balancing the modal split and preventing cut-throat competition among hauliers. An adaptation to the rules of the common road haulage market could have been accompanied by measures to improve the low productivity in the industry. Surprisingly, Italy did not take up the challenge. Instead of introducing widespread regulatory reform—as had countries in a comparable situation such as France and Germany—Italy opted for regulatory inertia, and instead of adopting an effective industrial policy—as in the Netherlands—it opted for fiscal benefits that were not even designed to improve the productivity of the sector and that led to an ever-widening gap between the Italian road haulage policy and the CTP. In an attempt to understand why Italian road haulage policy has drifted away from Europe despite the European effort to establish a CTP, the following sections identify and examine those factors at the national and European levels that contributed to policy inertia, that discouraged convergence, and that, in some cases, even increased the divergence between national and EC road haulage policy.

## A Decade of Road Haulage Policy

The development of regulation and fiscal instruments led to a continual increase in state intervention with protectionist tendencies that increasingly eclipsed market coordination within the road haulage sector,[1] despite perpetual regulatory failure and despite the objectives of the CTP.[2]

### Regulation

The history of road haulage regulation in Italy started in 1935 with the introduction of two instruments to control market processes (Fontanella 1974: 138). Qualitative standards for market access were defined so that firms wishing to offer transport services had to prove technical and financial soundness and professional reliability, and a licensing procedure was introduced that permitted the administration to control the number of vehicles circulating and thus the transport capacity of road haulage. By the 1960s it became clear that the market was not under effective control. A liberal policy of issuing licenses combined with entrepreneurial strategies to beat access restrictions inevitably led to cut-throat competition (Santoro 1974: 212). Subsequently, in 1974 a regulatory reform in the road haulage sector was introduced that shifted the regulatory framework toward increased interventionism.[3] The major change in the range of instruments was the introduction of a particularly complicated system of compulsory tariff brackets for the pricing of transport services subject to maximum and minimum limits.[4]

In the nine years that elapsed between the decision to introduce the tariff system in 1974 and its implementation in 1983, a substitute for bracket tariffs developed for certain types of goods such as cement, petroleum products, liquid chemicals, containers, and vehicles (Cozzi and Govoni 1989: 237ff.).[5] These so-called collective economic agreements, which, unlike the compulsory tariff rates, were influenced by shippers as well as by hauliers, came within the framework of the 1974 law and were formally recognized as legitimate exemptions from the tariff system in 1983.[6] The outcome of these collective agreements is also relevant for the stipulation of the general compulsory tariffs,[7] making price setting the result of a multitude of different negotiation systems that offer ample opportunities for interest groups to exercise their muscle. They indicate the strong politicization of the sector, which leaves little room for market coordination.

The reform was only moderately successful in controlling prices on the road haulage market, despite the inflexible application of the instruments. In 1985 the

Ministry of Transport decided to freeze the capacity of the transport market—no new licenses were issued, and new enterprises could only access the market by buying a license from a firm that left the market[8]—and market entry was further complicated by new EC regulation on qualitative access criteria such as "financial soundness." From the outset the tariff system suffered from a lack of compliance, with prices for transport services falling well below the lower limit of the tariff system. The imposition of legal sanctions for such infringements did not change the situation given the difficulty of detecting fraud. In 1993 an attempt was made to enforce compliance by extending the range of validity of the tariffs to contracts covering nontransport services,[9] and by allowing road hauliers to claim the difference between the price set in the contract and the lower minimum of the tariff bracket.[10] This regulatory revision effectively meant that market processes played an ever-decreasing role in the control of transport operations. To sum up, the regulatory reform of 1974, in particular the introduction of compulsory tariff brackets and their subsequent amendment, led to a sharp rise in regulatory intervention, unleashing an avalanche of detailed rules.

*Fiscal Measures*

To decide if the development of road haulage taxation has led to convergence with the reform model of the EU, one needs to examine the principle by which taxation is levied. Taxation and charges are more congruent with a liberalized EC market when levied according to the principle of territoriality where road hauliers are subject to the taxes and charges of the state in which transport takes place rather than that of nationality where hauliers contribute to the revenue of their country of registration (Rommerskirchen 1985: 217–18). For example, in Germany roads are mainly financed through vehicle taxes, which only apply to vehicles registered in Germany. Under the principle of nationality, nonnational road users do not contribute to the financing of infrastructure. Other countries such as France and Italy have a system of motorway tolls, which applies the principle of territoriality, charging all motorway users irrespective of nationality. The viability of a common market for road haulage increases with the shift from the principle of nationality to that of territoriality, thus decreasing the distortion of competition between hauliers from different countries.

At the time of the first key Commission proposal to establish a single market for road haulage in 1986, the Italian system of taxation and charges was already relatively well adapted to liberalization, because the major taxes and charges were levied according to the principle of territoriality. Motorway tolls had been introduced when the first motorways were built, and taxes levied according to the principle of nationality—mainly acquisition and ownership of vehicles—were low in comparison with taxes on petroleum products. Table 6.1 indicates the importance of the principle of territoriality in the Italian system of tax revenues where market entry, registration, and ownership account for a quarter of total

**Table 6.1.  Distribution of Tax Revenue in Freight and Public Transport on Roads (figures in %)**

| Principle | Activity | 1983 | 1994 |
|-----------|----------|------|------|
| Nationality | Market entry | 16.56 | 8.48 |
|  | Registration | 0.42 | 1.10 |
|  | Ownership | 7.28 | 13.06 |
| Territoriality | Operation* | 75.75 | 77.35 |
|  | Total | 100.00 | 100.00 |

*Source*: Centro Europa Ricerche 1996
*Operation includes taxes on fuel, lubricants, and road user charges; road user charges as such are excluded.

revenue and operations for three-quarters,[11] with a slight additional shift towards the principle of territoriality during 1983 to 1994.

To sum up, the general system of taxation was compatible with the EU policy from the start of the reform process in the mid-1980s, and the minor changes subsequently introduced confirmed the principle of territoriality. The structure and development of road haulage taxation differ from those of regulation. In contrast to the latter, there has been a slight policy convergence.[12]

This system of taxation is modified by another fiscal instrument used in Italy. Since 1990 tax credits are granted to professional road hauliers. From 1990 to 1994 a yearly budget ranging from 422,000 to 725,000 million lire was provided to compensate road hauliers for fuel taxes.[13] Road hauliers wishing to benefit from this scheme had to calculate their expenditure for fuel and lubricants for each of their vehicles. A tax-deductible benefit was granted as a certain percentage of that expenditure (namely income tax, municipal tax, or value-added tax [VAT]). The scheme has been the object of repeated intervention by the European Commission and has led to the initiation of a procedure at the European Court of Justice in 1995. The European Commission considers the tax credit scheme to be an illegal state aid because of discriminatory consequences for non-Italian EC hauliers.[14] Despite these interventions, the practice has been continued in 1996 by a modified scheme (*Il Sole 24 Ore,* 20 February 1996).[15] The introduction of the tax credit scheme is the most extreme case of divergence from the European model and constitutes a clear infringement of EC law.

Fiscal instruments have also been employed for industrial policy. A first attempt to improve the economic structure of the transport sector was made in 1980,[16] when the government provided a contribution for small hauliers to purchase new vehicles. Payments were stopped after these measures were contested by the Commission and a new law was introduced that linked payments tightly with the restructuring activities of small hauliers.[17] The law was replaced by a more ambitious project in 1992 that offered financial aid to back mergers, consortia and cooperatives, the introduction of electronic data processing, and that encouraged single-vehicle enterprises to leave the market (Stornelli and Battistoni 1994: 61–79).[18] Although the law contained detailed procedural provisions, it was never applied because of doubts on the part of the European Commission that the incentives for retirement could effectively reduce market capacity.[19] The contentious procedure initiated by the European Commission that led to a recent ultimatum would seem to be firm evidence of further divergence.[20] However, EC rules on state aids allow subsidies as long as they are not given as an operating aid but are part of a serious effort to restructure industry or to promote regional cohesion (Bellamy and Child 1993: 926).[21] Therefore, the measures to restructure the sector are not contrary to the Treaty per se;[22] unlike the Italian tax credit scheme that imposed no obligations on the profiting enterprises, the attempt to restructure the sector constitutes a relatively minor divergence from the CTP.

Taken separately, the instruments of Italian transport policy differ in the extent to which they diverge from the CTP, with divergence being low in the case of industrial policy, medium in regulation, and high in the case of the tax credit scheme.[23] But one should take the impact of the *simultaneous* use of the various instruments into account—when treated as components of a system of governance, the concrete policy outcome is "market protectionism in the interests of the hauliers and against the interests of the collectivity" (Munari 1994: 904). This is so for two reasons. First, the fact that the minimum official tariff is always well above the market price is a strong disincentive for existing hauliers to leave the market. Second, the tax credit scheme increases revenues for hauliers irrespective of the market and thus acts in the same way as a compulsory tariff. The protectionist effect of road haulage policy is confirmed by the failure of industrial policy, not only because of the resistance of the European Commission, but also because hauliers simply did not take advantage of the benefits granted to firms intending to merge.[24] There is strong reason to believe that government contributed to the lack of a sense of urgency among hauliers by sheltering them from national and international competition. If this view is correct, the verdict of protectionism may well be extended to the use of the whole range of instruments governing the road haulage sector in Italy. This result of the development of the road haulage regime is in stark contrast not only to the CTP, but also to developments in other member states. The question thus arises as to why the Italian policy developed along a path that steadily diverged from the EC model despite external influences of change.

## State Structure

The structure of the Italian state is the first explanatory factor for the inertia of the governance of road haulage. The likelihood of comprehensive administrative reform increases with the state's capacity to formulate *"autonomous policy goals"* that do not merely mirror societal demands and the *"possibility to implement"* these, even against societal interests (Skocpol 1985: 9–20).[25] Thus defined,

Italy has a *low state capacity* in the transport sector. Autonomy from private interests is low, since Parliament has largely fallen prey to the onslaught of the road haulage lobby, and the influence of the small haulier association has increased with the increasingly prominent role played by the Central Committee of the National Register of Professional Road Hauliers.[26] Finally, the potential to implement reforms is jeopardized by a high degree of horizontal fragmentation of the ministerial bureaucracy, which is detrimental to policy coordination.

In the decade since the beginning of the CTP the Italian Parliament has not enhanced state autonomy. No proposals involving a fundamental reform of the sector have been proposed. A more recent initiative by a member of the Transport Commission of the Chamber of Deputies, Paolo Oberti of Forza Italia, would not lead to restructuring of the regulatory regime for road haulage (Oberti 1995). In fact, neither the traditional restriction of market access nor the compulsory tariffs are touched. Moreover, recent provisions such as the tax credits or the reinforcement of the protectionist market regulation were approved, despite some criticism (*Il Sole 24 Ore*, 5 December 1997). In effect, Parliament put up little resistance to the old transport policy routines.[27]

The National Register of Professional Hauliers has also been particularly decisive for the low degree of state autonomy. This body has increasingly offered a means to transfer decision making from the public administration to the interest groups representing small hauliers. This has been meticulously demonstrated for the mandatory tariffs in a case before the European Court of Justice.[28] The legality of the mandatory tariff system was challenged on the grounds that the tariff setting was no longer controlled by public authority. Apart from the civil servants present, members of the Central Committee are presidents or general secretaries of road haulage associations rather than independent experts on tariffs. The minutes of the negotiations show that they speak openly on behalf of their association, and contain complaints by the civil servants that they are only free to rubber-stamp decisions already taken among road hauliers, without taking into consideration any general economic reasoning, and indicate that the minister of transport actually delegated the power to control tariffs to the Central Committee by agreeing to a new procedure on tariff setting. Instead of taking an autonomous decision, the minister of transport issues the agreement reached among the hauliers as a ministerial decree with the sole purpose of converting it into a legal norm. In 1993 the power of the hauliers' representatives within the central committee was guaranteed by allocating them a majority of seats.[29] The conclusion drawn, therefore, is that with respect to tariffs the public interest is no longer taken into consideration (Dani, Conte, and Giacomini 1994: 19). The colonization of the state by interest groups via the central committee on vital issues such as the determination of tariffs is the most extreme example of a low state capacity blocks reform for the road haulage sector.

Another handicap for the action capacity of the state is the problem of policy coordination within a highly fragmented administrative context. Although the

Italian transport administration is centralized and does not experience the co-ordination problems typical of a federal system (Scharpf 1994), the high degree of horizontal fragmentation leads to coordination problems that are no less se-vere. Administrative competence is divided among a number of different min-istries, the most important being the Ministry of Transport, the Ministry of Pub-lic Works, and until 1993 the Ministry of Merchant Shipping (Russo Frattasi 1984: 31ff.). The list has to be expanded if other tasks are included: the Ministry of Finance, which is responsible for customs, the Ministry of the Interior, which deals with traffic safety, the Ministry of Health for safety standards, the Ministry of Labor for the regulation of the professions, and the Ministry of the Environ-ment for transport-related environmental regulation (Strati, Franci, and Ferroni 1996: 98).

A series of administrative reforms have attempted to reduce horizontal frag-mentation, starting in 1965 with the creation of the Directorate General for Plan-ing, Organization and Coordination. The directorate's job was to improve inter-modal coordination within the Ministry of Transport, but at no stage during its thirty years' existence did it effectively fulfill its task (Sanviti 1992: 58). Since it was at the same hierarchical level as the other directorate generals it could not contribute to coordination without a close collaboration with the minister's cabi-net, but the cabinet rarely consulted the directorate general.[30] Intermodal co-ordination is not easily achieved at the cabinet level, either, because the contact offices to the various ministries are themselves organized by mode of transport (Sanviti 1992: 57).

Since the beginning of the 1990s several measures have been adopted to reduce horizontal fragmentation across ministries. In 1993 the Ministry of Merchant Shipping was incorporated into the Ministry of Transport (Costa 1994) as a first step toward concentrating transport competences.[31] Formal integration has not yet enhanced actual cooperation; another reform attempt started in 1991 was rap-idly abandoned.[32] In 1991 the Interministerial Commission for Economic Plan-ning of Transport (CIPET) was abolished after less than two years, during which time it never managed to influence the ministries. One of its main powers was the ability to exert influence on a common transport budget, including all the relevant transport expenditure, but the budget was never enacted (Fontanella 1993). A more recent proposal has been the creation of an independent regulatory agency for transport to safeguard competition in the sector after privatization and liber-alization (*Il Sole 24 Ore*: 12 May 1995, 13 May 1995). By the end of 1997 the matter was still undecided. The overwhelming impression is that administrative reforms did not significantly improve the coordination capacities.

**Interest Intermediation**

Alongside the low state capacity in the transport sector, the structure of the re-lationship between the state and interest groups is a related factor impeding reform. In the period from the beginning of the 1980s until the present, the different road haulage associations, formerly united in a single association before 1985 (Crespi 1986: 249ff.), went through a period of secession and split into two opposing blocks with relatively homogeneous memberships and distinct interest profiles. The Coordinamento, a joint venture of Unione imprese trasporti automobilistici Italiana (UNITAI)[33] and Associazione nazionale imprese trasporti automobilistici (ANITA), represents the bigger enterprises that are determined to face the challenge of the common market and are therefore opposed to protectionism. Unatras, on the other hand is formed by the key interest groups representing the small road haulage enterprises.[34] This coalition feels ill-prepared for a common market and demands that liberalization be preceded by measures to improve the competitiveness of the small hauliers, until which time the protectionist regime should be kept in place. In terms of numbers, Unatras is more representative than the Coordinamento. From the general political declarations and the strategies employed, there can be no doubt that there has been an increase in the polarization of interests between large and small hauliers.[35]

*Interaction between Interest Groups and the State*

The two blocks of interest associations represented by Unatras and the Coordinamento not only differ in membership structure and interests, but also in the strategies used to pursue their goals, which create two distinct patterns of interaction with the state. *Lobbying* mainly aims at influencing policy formulation and addresses Parliament and the government, and is thus concerned with more important legislative proposals. *Administrative interest intermediation* on the other hand is the process where interest groups interact with the state at the lower level of public administration, influencing its problem definitions and future policy proposals (Lehmbruch 1987).[36] Unatras defends the interests of its clientele predominantly by lobbying and resorts much less to a long-term cooperation with the public administration. However, for a characterization of the activities of Unatras, "pressurizing" is more apt than "lobbying" since it pursues its objectives mainly by mobilizing its members to participate in strikes, a powerful instrument that threatens to paralyze the entire economy. They are primarily addressed to the government. Parties, the parliamentary transport commissions, and the public administration do not play a role.[37] The pattern by now is familiar: demands such as tax credits or legislative changes are listed, followed by a strike threat if the proposals are not met. The result depends on the outcome of negotiations with the government. With or without a strike, an agreement is inevitable. The government then issues a decree, which is usually a copy of the agreement reached with the association. This strategy has become self-enforcing since it is the prime source of new occasions to strike. The wide range of demands is more than the frequently changing governments can cope with, and any unfulfilled promises offer ample reason to threaten a new strike to remind the government of its obligations and to add new demands.[38] In contrast to the lobbying activities, collaboration with the administration is rare, giving rise to complaints on the part of the association about lack of information (Scazzocchio 1995: 4).

The interest groups within the Coordinamento interact in a different way with the public institutions. On the one hand, they collaborate closely with the ministries on technical questions. One example is Confetra's participation with the Ministry of Public Works in the reform of the Road Traffic Act.[39] Another example is the reform of the regulation of special-load transport where it took part in a working group of the Ministry of the Interior to resolve the problem of lorry theft in the Italian *mezzogiorno*. This type of collaboration is based on close personal contacts between civil servants and association officials. Confetra was the only association of the transport sector consulted for the first financial law of the Dini government. However, the *canale preferenziale*, which exists with the administration, does not exist with the government.[40] The Coordinamento does not have the means to counter the power of Unatras, which means that governments are obliged to yield to the demands of the latter. In case of conflict the interest groups of the Coordinamento do not resort to strikes but try to negotiate with the public administration or, in the last instance, take legal action.[41]

The question remains as to how these developments relate to the lack of regulatory reform on the part of Italy and to the increasing divergence from the model of the CTP. The double structure of interest intermediation has detrimental effects on the capacity of the state to reform the regulatory regime of the sector.[42] First, there is an imbalance between lobbying and administrative interest intermediation, because many issues that have to be dealt with at the highest level such as tariff levels could be treated as technical issues and dealt with at lower administrative levels. Given limited time and resources, there is less room for a general reform effort. Furthermore, the lobbying component of the interest intermediation structure is dominated by interest groups representing the clientelistic interests of (small) road hauliers rather than the more generalized interests of the transport sector as a whole. The main influences on decision making by interest groups are therefore particularistic demands amplified by the strategic use of blackmailing power not only to influence the government but also to marginalize the representatives of more general sectoral interests.

Concerning the influence of the interest-intermediation structure the question is how the new polarized structure, with the Coordinamento on the one hand and Unatras on the other, compares with the former more unified structure of the Comitato Permanente d'Intesa that represented all hauliers? That is, has reform capacity improved, deteriorated, or remained the same? The prospects of convergence would appear to have improved when one considers that the establishment of the Coordinamento produced a clearly delimited group in favor of the CTP and its reform model for the road haulage sector, whereas formerly there were merely factions within individual interest groups.[43] But this advantage has to be weighed against serious disadvantages. The proponents of liberalization are much less influential than the proponents of protectionism. Furthermore, because the interests are split into two

different coalitions there is less chance of mediating conflict. Finally, the administration has lost routine contact with a large part of the sector. In effect it has become
more difficult for the Confindustria to promote a liberalization in the sector:

> The conflict of interest has become more radical. Whereas in the past, artisan
> hauliers had been members of ANITA and a first mediation of interests took place
> within the association, now these have become external and opposed to their former
> association and they have radicalized their opposition. This has made things more
> difficult. In the past, we managed to negotiate the tariffs amongst ourselves, that is
> Confindustria and all the transport associations. The minister just formalized the
> agreement reached. This does not work anymore.
>
> (Interview Confindustria, 3 May 1996)

This opinion is in line with all recent regulatory developments in the sector that
provide numerous benefits for small hauliers such as the advantages granted in
legal litigation over transport contracts that infringe the mandatory tariff system or
the tax credit scheme. Until now no signs of regulatory reforms can be seen.

### National and European Policies

The explanation of the inertia of the Italian road haulage policy—the continental policy paradigm, a low state capacity to design and implement reform, and
a polarized system of interest intermediation—has so far been focused on the national level.[44] These *internal* factors, however, are not alone in exerting influence
on national policy. Why did the *external* influence by the European CTP not contribute to policy convergence? This question is pursued in two directions. Italian
*participation in EC policy formulation* is analyzed to understand the extend to
which Italy managed to shape the CTP in the area of road haulage; that is,
whether Italy managed to influence the EC decision-making process so as to reduce the impact of the CTP for its national policy and thus mitigate external
forces of change. Second, the strength of the influence of the European level at
the national level, regarding road haulage policy directly together with the factors
contributing to its inertia or change, is assessed.

### National Participation in European Policymaking

The major outcome of the CTP for road haulage has been the decision to liberalize in order to create a single market in this sector. This decision process
reached a conclusion only after years of bargaining among the member states.
The main source of contention was the degree of harmonization of taxation and
road user charges necessary for a single market without distorting competition. In
this situation one can anticipate that every country will try to contain the potentially detrimental impact of liberalization on its road hauliers.[45] For Italy, the low
competitiveness of its road hauliers and the gloomy prospects of an improvement
for the short or medium term make it rational to oppose the liberalization project.

In the case of the liberalization of cabotage, Italy did indeed define and defend its national interest in this way.[46] Since outright opposition to the liberalization was not feasible, Italy joined the coalition of countries, under the leadership of Germany, demanding a high level of harmonization as a prerequisite for liberalization (see Teutsch in this volume). The Italian opposition to liberalization remained unaltered during the entire negotiation period, trying to prevent harm for the domestic road haulage industry. "Our policy is a policy of control . . . we believed and still believe today, that it would be better to keep the market under control, especially to prevent ruinous competition among hauliers."[47] However, the Italian influence on the outcome of the 1993 package deal did not make institutional adaptation superfluous. It just had the effect of gaining time to adjust.

This lack of influence on the CTP for road haulage is primarily due to the fact that the definition of the Italian national interest was not the result of careful economic and political calculations and subsequent clear instructions from the minister for the Italian representative in the *group question transports* of the Council of Ministers, but emanated instead from the educated guesses of the national representative who had to deduce from the ministers' general national policy what he would be prepared to sign as a European compromise:

> The point of reference is rather the general policy of the Minister as embodied by the provisions he promotes nationally and within the Council of Ministers. The representative cannot ask every other week what the Minister thinks about this and that but it is his responsibility to interpret Minister's policy that he develops independently of the initiatives in Brussels on the national level.
>
> (Interview Ministero dei Trasporti, 2 May 1996)

This is by no means the standard operating procedure for all the members of the Transport Group. Other members were continually receiving instructions from their national ministries and would not participate in negotiations without them. One of the major obstacles to tighter coordination is the high turnover of ministers,[48] and the consequent inability to develop a coherent strategy toward the EC. A final characteristic is the fact that Italian strategy was poorly co-ordinated even within the Ministry of Transport. Evidence for this is provided by the problem of the harmonization of taxes. In the opinion of the transport expert of the Italian Permanent Representation and member of the Transport Group of the Council of Ministers, taxation issues were not at the heart of the Italian national interest that had to be defended. Other issues were more important:

> Of course, the fiscal problem was relevant for the liberalization process, but we put the accent more than on other matters, on the technical harmonization and the harmonization of access to the profession. From our point of view, the fiscal problem was less important. This was first of all a German concern.
>
> (Interview Ministero dei Trasporti, 2 May 1996)

This is in outright contradiction to the opinion of the civil servant involved with the administration of the tax credit scheme for road hauliers. The main justification given for this credit scheme is based on the argument that it helps mitigate the gross disadvantage of Italian hauliers vis-à-vis their EC competitors arising from a lack of harmonization of taxation:

> The reason why tax credits are justified is that the price of diesel fuel in Italy is the highest in the European Community. Taxes on diesel fuel are determined by fiscal needs and taking into consideration the situation of public finance, no reduction is in sight. The tax credits are important to mitigate the disadvantages of the Italian hauliers that have to compete with the Community hauliers.
>
> (Interview Ministero dei Trasporti, 3 January 1996, No. 2)

The participation of the Italian government in the EC decision-making process may be summed up as the pursuit of national interest in a predictable way albeit with a low strategic capacity and thus with a low possibility to influence the course of events by leadership. The participation of the member state is not restricted to national governments and their representatives. Lobbying by interest groups is another way by which national interests may assert themselves in the EC decision-making process. To compensate for some of the deficiencies of government, Italian industry is represented by a large number of well-organized offices in Brussels. The transport sector is not part of this success story. First of all, conforming with the general pattern for Italy, smaller interest groups are not represented at the European level (Bardi, Bindi, and Tarchi 1993: 104–5). Neither Unatras nor any of the other interest groups representing small hauliers have established offices in Brussels.[49] ANITA as part of Confindustria is represented at the European level by the Confederation of European Industries, Unice. Within this representation of the European industry, transport policy was not influenced in any noticeable way by the Confindustria.[50] The only office that exclusively represents interests of the transport sector is the Rappresentanza permanente CONFETRA presso le Comunità Europee. Whenever the Commission asks for an assessment of a legislative proposal IRU consults its members and Confetra then expresses its views on behalf of its national members.[51]

An example of successful lobbying by the Confetra office is the action taken against the lack of implementation of Directive 92/106/EEC on combined transport in Italy. In a letter to the Commission the office claimed that despite the directive the Italian authorities were not issuing new licenses for combined transport. Since the Commission did not reply within a brief period of time because of procedural requirements when dealing with a member state, the office sought a parliamentary hearing on the matter.[52] Apart from major problems such as the implementation of a directive, more technical issues are on the agenda—for example, the funds provided by the EU to compensate haulage contractors for loss of revenue caused by the creation of a single market and their restructuring operations. As the closing date draws near, the likelihood that some Italian firms will miss out on this aid because the Italian authorities have simply been unable to distribute the funds among enterprises increases. The strategy of the Confetra office was to extend the period in which funds would be available to the Italian administration.[53]

In general, the potential to influence is lower than in other European countries. DG VII seems to be more open to other countries than to Italian interests. Furthermore the interests of the national members of Confetra are not easily aggregated to a more general interest, and are therefore difficult to transform into policy propositions.[54] If one takes into consideration the complete absence of the interest groups representing small hauliers, the weak Italian influence on the policy process appears inevitable. The Italian interest groups and the public institutions thus did not reduce the gap between Italy and Europe by changing the EC reform project. This leads to the question of why the influence of the EC policy on national policy did not cause convergence.

## The Influence of European on National Transport Policy

The CTP aims to influence national road haulage policy primarily by changing the range and use of regulatory and fiscal instruments. The supremacy of EC law over national law would appear to guarantee changes, because implementation is compulsory. Less visible but still important is the European influence on the factors that determine regulatory persistence or change, the problem-solving philosophy, the structure of the administration, and interest intermediation. The following analysis examines why the influence of the EU not only failed to achieve convergence of the Italian road haulage policy with the CTP, but in some instances actually *increased divergence*.

To explain why the CTP did not significantly change the Italian road haulage policy, it is important to note the very limited influence of the 1993 package deal on national regulation. By liberalizing, cabotage national markets were opened to foreign hauliers, but the impact on national regulation was limited. Indeed, the EC drive toward a single market for road haulage had the paradoxical effect of increasing divergence by strengthening the interventionist market regulation.[55] In Italy the stricter qualitative standards for market access combined with the block on new licenses since 1985 raised the protectionist barriers to market access. In this instance the small hauliers' associations therefore defended a strict implementation of EC provisions on market access, whereas the Ministry of Transport pursued a softer strategy (*Tuttotrasporti* 1988).

Furthermore, the mandatory tariff system, which is an important element of the protectionist regulatory framework, cannot be considered a contradiction to liberalization. The legality of mandatory tariffs at the national level was forcefully underlined by three decisions of the ECJ.[56] Contrary to the expectations of the Confindustria and the freight forwarder association federazione nazionale spedizionieri (FEDERSPEDI), the ECJ does not even consider the way in which tariffs are fixed in Italy a contradiction to EC competition law, although the process is dominated by haulier interest groups (Dani, Conte, and Giacomini 1994). This decision enhanced the legitimacy of the antiliberalization lobby, which now cites the ECJ decisions as an argument against deregulation.[57]

In the case of regulatory instruments, the CTP did not introduce any significant changes but left it up to the discretion of the member states to adapt domestic regulation to the situation after the liberalization of cabotage. In this case the EC influence failed to bring about convergence. The most visible impact of the EC on the national management of the road haulage sector, however, was the action taken by the European Commission against the Italian tax credit scheme for road hauliers. In this case the EC not only failed to align national and European policies but even fostered divergence between the two. The European Commission has repeatedly condemned the tax credit scheme as a *state aid* incompatible with the Treaty provisions because it is an "operating aid" that helps firms in financial difficulties without improving the sector.[58] The European Commission decided to refer the matter to the ECJ, and proceedings were formally opened in August 1995.[59]

This resistance of the European Commission is not a fact that may be dismissed lightly by the Italian authorities. The power of the Commission in the control of state aids is as exceptional as in the area of competition policy. Whereas the commission's legislative proposals have to stand the test of the Council of Ministers and the European Parliament, in matters of state aid control it may issue decisions that are directly binding on member states. The commission enjoys a wide margin of discretion in determining what is considered a state aid distorting competition (Bellamy and Child 1993: 946).[60] Few regulations have been issued subsequently specifying the application of the Treaty provisions on state aids.[61] One exception, Council Regulation 1107/70 and subsequent amendments, does apply to road haulage but its taming effect remains modest.[62]

In spite of the exceptional competences the European Commission enjoys in the matter, to this day it has not achieved its objectives. The Italian government made no attempt to recoup the money already distributed due to technical difficulties,[63] and reactions at the national level to the verdict of the commission led to the modification of the tax credit scheme but not its abolition. The only change that the Italian administration introduced strikes any observer as highly peculiar. The aid scheme was formally extended to foreign hauliers operating on Italian territory.[64] This involved complicated technical changes. The yearly budget had to be split between foreigners and domestic hauliers. Furthermore, a new calculation formula and new procedure had to be invented for foreign hauliers. This part of the scheme ceased to be a tax credit, because foreign hauliers do not pay the taxes in Italy via which the discount on fuel and lubricants was granted. Its implementation would have involved direct payments to foreign hauliers, similar to the present procedure for the re-reimbursement of VAT on fuel. No procedure has been worked out, however. The necessary cooperation between the Ministry of Transport and the Ministry of Finance failed.[65]

At first glance it would seem that the European Commission achieved at least one of its objectives in the long run, namely the abolition of Italy's aid scheme. In fact, in 1995 no extension of the aid was legislated. A closer look at more recent developments may suggest quite a different conclusion. By the end of 1995 Unatras announced a strike, if motorway tolls, ownership tax, and the cost of work (welfare taxation) were not reduced (*Il Sole 24 Ore*, 14 December 1995: 13). The government's inevitable surrender to prevent the strike involved finding new funds to the tune of 470,000 million lire and even changing the yearly financial law, two very delicate problems. However, it is highly doubtful if secretary of state for transport, Giovanni Puoti, was correct when he maintained that "the agreement signed with *Unatras* means a break with the protectionist policy tradition that has been pursued in the sector" (*Il Sole 24 Ore*, 17 December 1995: 5). The subsequent decree contains no evidence to support this view.[66] On the contrary, two of the three measures adopted are not linked to any restructuring effect, and would appear to be just another operating aid in the form of a tax credit. The first measure, the reduction of automobile taxes for hauliers, coincides with a decision to raise automobile taxes for private car owners. In fact, the discount was decided by the same financial law that had to be changed for the tax credit (*Il Sole 24 Ore*, 8 January 1996: 3). The same holds true for the reduction of motorway tolls. While hauliers have to pay less, motorways will be more expensive for private users (*Il Sole 24 Ore,* 8 January 1996: 3). Recent developments do not seem to put the European Commission in a winning position. On the contrary, the future is likely to see yet another contentious procedure against illegal state aid.

## Conclusion

Since the mid-1980s the CTP has had significant consequences for the road haulage policies of the member states, but in the ten years since the CTP gained momentum the gap between the Italian road haulage policy and the CTP has actually widened. The reinforcement of protectionist policy and the consequent increase in divergence was not the result of a conscious government decision to defend the domestic market against foreign competitors, but rather the result of policy "drift." The internal factors that prevented Italy from abandoning its policy trajectory were the continental policy paradigm, low state capacity, and the polarized structure of interest intermediation. Even more surprising than the magnitude of the internal obstacle to change was the influence of the external factors from the European level. Wherever they did exert influence on the national setting, as in the case of market access regulation, the tax credit scheme, or the structure of interest intermediation, they only reinforced divergence, and it is only in the case of the policy paradigm that we can observe a weak influence favoring convergence.

With the complete liberalization of cabotage in 1998 every haulier in the EC will have unlimited access to national markets, making the instruments on which the Italian protectionist policy depends obsolete. With free access to the national market by foreign hauliers, the tight control of the transport market capacity by freezing the issue of new transport licenses for national hauliers will constitute a discrimination of national vis-à-vis foreign hauliers. The same holds true for the mandatory tariff system. Legally, there is no discrimination between national and nonnational hauliers, as both are obliged to apply the tariffs valid of the territory on which they operate, but in practice, the control of nonnationals is much more difficult to guarantee. The functionalist hope that in the long run market pressures will accomplish the policy switch that politics was unable to achieve may be altogether too optimistic.

## REFUSING THE EUROPEAN "RAILWAY RAGOUT"

The impact of the European Common Railway Policy (CRP) on Italian railway policy is more complex than in the case of road haulage. In Italy, CRP encountered a national railway reform that had already started in 1985. An analysis of the impact of the former raises the question about their relationship. In the first section, the question will be pursued, if the national reform contradicts the goals of the European reform or if they follow a common strategy and common goals. The analysis shows that during the last decade, a difference between the two policies exists and that this difference has not been reduced substantially. European policy did not cause policy convergence with regard to its most fundamental concern, the introduction of competition between different railway companies within and between member states. The subsequent section offers an explanation for this lack of policy convergence. In Italy, the organizational fragmentation of the railways that this policy implies has been called the "railway ragout." It was refused by the trade unions as well as the railway management. Once again, as in the case of road haulage, government and administration have been too weak to overcome entrenched interests.

### Italian and European Railway Reform Projects Compared

At first glance, the Italian railway policy is an entirely different case to that of road haulage. The Italian railway reform project appears to be a case of spontaneous convergence of a national with a European policy, characterized by political reform rather than policy inertia. However, important differences remain that challenge the claim of policy convergence. Recent reforms aim to change significantly the way railways have been run in Italy for most of the century (Ministero dei Trasporti 1996: 27–30). Ever since 1905, when the three main private railway companies were nationalized to form the Ferrovie dello stato (FS), the railways were a part of the public administration. Developing and maintaining the railways and running trains to transport people and goods was a task of the state. In the postwar period, mainly as a reaction to the increasing financial difficulties, the legal status of the state railways changed several times. These reforms were concerned with the problem of how to define the autonomy of the state railways.[67] The general tendency was to increase the railways' autonomy in relation to the public administration. This process has accelerated since the early 1980s. In 1985, the FS acquired the status of *ente pubblico economico,* thus acquiring new management competences. In 1992, after almost ninety years of being part of the public administration, the state railways were legally privatized, and although the public administration is still the sole owner, the railways now have the status of a joint-stock company.

On a formal institutional level, the change in the legal status of the railways has had two types of consequences for their administration. Firstly, *hierarchical coordination* has been abolished as the decision-making powers of management have been increased and the role of the public administration (the Ministry of Transport and the Treasury) have become merely supervisory. Second, hierarchical coordination has been replaced by *contractual coordination.* Within the general framework of an "act of concession" giving the FS the exclusive right to run the railways, two contracts define mutual rights and obligations for a shorter time period: the "program contract" for investments in rail infrastructure and rolling-stock; and the "service contract" for railway services.[68]

The analysis of the legal development leads to the conclusion that the reform efforts of the last decade gradually reversed the nationalization at the beginning of the century. The significance of the political reform has been reinforced by signs of reform and innovation in the railway sector. On several occasions, the FS has modified its organizational structure to enhance performance. Measures were adopted to promote the freight transport unit—generally believed to be among the biggest problems of the FS—supplemented by initiatives in the area of intermodal transport. Finally, the most visible sign of progress is the development of the high-speed railway network,[69] with new trains and the demanding upgrading of the infrastructure. These changes are most visibly reflected in the new organizational structure of the railways. Whereas before the legal privatization of 1992, the activities of the railways have been integrated into a single organization, the FS is now a holding consisting of more than a hundred separate firms carrying out diverse activities in transport, tourism, and other services.[70]

However, the reform was entirely focused on the organizational dimension. By redefining the relationship between the state and the railway and by internal restructuring, it attempted to improve performance. In contrast to the Italian railway reform, the CRP moves a decisive step beyond that with the idea of reforming railways by introducing intramodal competition.[71] Intramodal competition is a radical idea, since it contradicts the widely accepted belief that, for technical and economic reasons, railways are natural monopolies, that is, sectors that by their basic characteristics cannot be organized as competitive markets and that need protection from competition from other modes of transport, especially road transport. As has been pointed out, this aim is pursued by organizational changes and the setting up of market rules. Therefore, if the view is correct that the Italian railway reform revolves around the question of how to reconcile autonomy with institutional control, the reform is not simply equal or contrary to, but a subset of the CRP. A new definition of the relationship between the administration and the railways is an important prerequisite of the market-making goals of European policy. In the area of organizational reform, mutual reinforcement of the Italian and European reform programs makes progress at the national level more likely. The market-making ambitions of the CRP on the other hand do not have a national counterpart. Here, success depends on the implementation of EC obligations. In the following section, the organizational reform and the progress toward a (single/liberalized) market are analyzed in more detail to find out whether the national policy has converged with European policy. The first of the following sections analyzes the implementation of the congruent goals of organizational reform, while the second examines whether Italian policy converges with the European model in the area of market building.

## *Organizational Autonomy*

European and Italian reform projects have been concerned with various aspects of organizational autonomy. My contention is that despite policy congruence in this area, the administrative practices have not changed significantly compared to the outset of the reform. This can be shown for the independence of management and for the redefinition of financial relations. The 1985 railway reform was the first attempt to enhance the decision-making power of railway management by redefining its organizational structure and competences (Correale 1989: 2). However, these reforms did not change old decision-making routines. The fact that the reform has remained on a symbolic level can be illustrated by examining the way in which the prices of railway fares were set. The FS, unlike private firms, did not enjoy the right to determine the price of its services freely. For passenger transport, it had to adhere to *compulsory tariffs* fixed by the administration (Di Miceli 1985).[72] Before the reform, the criteria by which they were calculated, the decision-making procedure by which they were fixed, and the general policy pursued were all indicative of a low degree of managerial autonomy. The only area where the FS had some price-setting autonomy was, and is, in the freight sector. The 1985 railway reform introduced some changes that increased the complexity of the tariff system but not managerial autonomy, as envisaged by EC policy and national law (Di Miceli 1985: 360). The new procedure for determining tariffs envisages the introduction of an "economic tariff" by the railways to cover the cost of services provided, but with no obligation to compensate for lower "political tariffs." To date, the new procedure has not led to any subsequent change in the actual policy of modest, and politically determined, tariff increases (*Il Sole 24 Ore*, 3 September 1996: 13), and a more recent reform proposal makes no mention of increased decision-making autonomy in this area.[73]

A second dimension of the railway reform concerns the redefinition of financial relations between the state and the railways. In the past, this relationship, common to many European countries, was structured in a mutually unsatisfactory way: the railway management was obliged to take economically nonviable decisions, such as procurement from national champions and the maintenance of unprofitable lines, without any clear compensation, while government had to finance ever-increasing losses. Thus, financial responsibility was blurred insofar as one cannot know whether a loss is caused by low productivity of the railways or by a political decision not based on economic criteria. Similarly to many other European countries, Italy introduced the instrument of contracts regulating the relationship between the administration and the railways to resolve this lack of financial transparency (Amati 1991: 231–32). The first contract of this kind was designed to restructure the railways and to make them economically viable. Tariffs were to be raised to cover costs and compensation paid for unprofitable services, such as the construction, maintenance, and operation of unprofitable lines. The long-term objective was to reduce state transfer payments to precisely the amount of the public-service obligations and no more.

These contracts are only a very modest move toward the increased financial transparency and responsibility envisaged by the CRP (Pezzoli 1995: 226). They remove the system of indiscriminate cross-subsidies between infrastructure financing and the operation of services, but without reinforcing notions of economic viability, because the contracts do not stipulate sanctions in the case of negative business results. This allowed the FS to increase its investments in recent years in spite of massive debts (*Mondo Economico* 1996a: 86–88). Furthermore, they do not prevent interference in the economic decision making of the railways. The Italian Parliament made its approval of contracts dependent on an exhaustive list of amendments, mostly concerning the maintenance or even construction of unprofitable regional lines (Corte dei Conti 1996: 44–47). This clientelistic intervention by the Italian Parliament ran counter to the objective of the contractualization between the administration and the railways (Corte dei Conti 1996: 48–49).

Given the modest results concerning management autonomy and contractualization, it is safe to conclude that despite the congruence of national and EC reform, the goal of organizational autonomy was not achieved. The following section shows that this also holds true for the more radical market-building goal of CRP.

*Market Making*

Transforming national railway monopolies into a European market for railway services ideally requires free access by any European railway enterprise to any railway network in Europe. As with other network utilities such as telecommunications and energy, the liberalization of network access in the case of railways is pursued in two steps. First, the CRP prescribes that the management of

infrastructure be separated from the provision of services to prevent former monopolies from discriminating against new competitors by erecting obstacles to
network access. Second, the conditions for market access and market operation
have to be specified, that is, under what conditions may a new company gain network access and how may it provide its railway services?

## Building a European Market for Railway Services?

In Italy, the separation of infrastructure management and operation has been
implemented by organizational separation, assigning them to two separate divisions within a common holding.[74] The second step within this separation has not
been achieved yet. The divisions producing services (Area trasporto) does not yet
buy railway capacity from the division managing infrastructure (Area rete).[75]
Compensation is paid according to estimations, and an experimental system of
calculating costs has yet to be implemented within the FS. A complete separation
between the accounts for railway network and the provision of services will still
take considerable time (*Il Sole 24 Ore,* 15 March 1997: 9).

The second element of the CRP, the implementation of market regulation, is
even less developed. In Italy, no enterprise other than the FS can access the railway network. According to European rules, a hypothetical enterprise planning to
offer railway services in a member state would have to go through a step-by-step
procedure to obtain access to the market. At the time of writing, none of these
could be taken in Italy (Communauté des Chemins de Fer Européenes 1995:
75–77). At the end of 1997, a new enterprise independent of the FS wanting to
offer railway services would not be able to obtain a license to certify that its
rolling stock, the qualification of its personnel, and its security standards were up
to the required level. Furthermore, it is still impossible to buy railway line capacity, or have access to installations such as depots.

The backwardness in relation to European developments is mainly attributable
to a lack of initiative on the part of the management and its political supervision
rather than to technical problems. For example, the system of calculation of costs
of train paths had already been developed following the first railway reform in
1985 at a stage when this had not been discussed at the European level.[76] A further sign of reluctance is the fact that an independent authority to distribute infrastructure capacity has not been established, thus reducing the probability of a
neutral way of dealing with this problem. Instead, the railways still claim to be a
coordinator rather than just any operator (Beltrami 1995: 11).

The prospects for intramodal competition in the near future are not clear. Potential domestic competitors for the FS do not include the independent railways
that are mainly engaged in local passenger transport. Their economic condition is
so precarious and their management capabilities so low that from 1997 onward
they have been assigned to the FS for three years for an organizational reform
(*Il Sole 24 Ore,* 29 September 1996). Even the most successful, the Ferrovie Nord

Milano, cannot be considered a potential competitor in the immediate future.[77] However, the advent of intramodal competition is not such a remote prospect to the Italian policy community (Spirito 1996a: 4ff.). In freight transport, frequently cited examples of the genesis of a market are the access of a U.S. company offering rail transport services in Britain, and two European consortia (European Rail Shuttle and NDX Inter-modal) planning to offer intermodal transport services to and from the ports of Northern Europe, especially Rotterdam.[78] In the passenger sector, the first modest signs of new operators are, for example, the interest shown by SwissAir in investing in an operator in that sector. Whereas one group argues that the advent of a market is inevitable and urges policymakers to anticipate changes actively rather than submitting to them passively, others consider that the development is dependent on the way the European reform is implemented—that is, whether the French model excluding competition, or the British model allowing a wide margin of competition, will prevail (Beltrami 1995: 9).

The analysis of the two dimensions of the CRP—organizational autonomy and market building—leads to the conclusion that although some progress has been made on the formal level, change in decision-making routines has been both modest and symbolic.[79] This is evident in the case of the contractualization of the relationship between rail and administration. From a legal point of view this constitutes a fundamental change, as it replaces hierarchy with a contract between equal subjects, whereas the analysis shows that in actual fact decision-making routines have not changed fundamentally but have simply been accommodated by the new structure.

There is reason to believe that the lack of any progress toward the CRP may be mainly due to passenger transport where public intervention to keep tariffs low and unprofitable lines operational is justified by the notion of the railways being a "public service." For freight transport, on the other hand, these types of considerations are irrelevant. Although transport is a vital infrastructure for the economy, the customers of freight transport services are firms, not individuals, making the likelihood of success for the CRP greater in freight transport. Moreover, liberalization has advanced further in freight sector than in passenger services. Rail freight is crucial in the sense that if there are no developments toward market building in this area, there is little likelihood of progress in passenger transport.

### Reforming Rail Freight: Toward a Competitive Market?

Shortly after the first reform of the FS in early 1986, a major reform of its freight activities was launched. In this period, freight transport was facing great difficulties throughout Europe, but in Italy the problems were especially severe. Geographically speaking, Italy is particularly suited to rail transport, but despite this, its share of the freight transported is one of the lowest in Europe.[80] The type of service offered by Italian railways simply did not create market demand, and rail freight was of poor quality.[81] The aim of the major reform of the freight sector launched shortly after the first FS reform in early 1986 was to remedy this situation. The underlying belief was that the FS should not just offer rail freight transport but should become a link in a chain of *intermodal transport* (see Pinna 1997; Ferretti 1996: 375ff.). In Italy this idea made particular sense, because both Switzerland and Austria have adopted measures to curb road transit through the Alps. Intermodal transport can thus offer a vital additional transport link between Italy and northern Europe.

The relaunching of the freight sector of the railways was based on the strategy of *societarizzazione*, that is, the transformation of a formerly homogeneous organization into an organizational network. This strategy was pursued in two ways. The first was to separate organizationally freight transport activities from passenger transport, and the second was to look for strategic alliances in other modes of transport to facilitate intermodal coordination (Eurolog 1996: 1). The organizational separation of freight from passenger transport was considered an important precondition for ending the discrimination of freight versus passenger transport. The list of disadvantages for freight within the Italian railways is indeed long.[82] When a freight timetable was finally established, freight was still secondary to passenger transport, and investment in freight-specific infrastructure and rolling stock was still only considered after passenger transport. For example, until recently the high-speed train involving major investments in infrastructure and rolling stock was not designed to include freight transport. Moreover, locomotives operating in the freight sector are often those considered too old for passenger transport—the fact that their technical characteristics also made them less suitable for freight trains was not considered important. The hope was that an independent freight company would remedy this situation more effectively because it could defend its interest better[83] and that the introduction of industrial accounting would increase the efficiency of the freight division.

The second way to boost the freight business of the FS was to launch intermodal transport by creating independent companies or establishing alliances with independent companies involved in multimodal transport. These companies were partly owned by the FS but with the involvement of private capital. The strategy of alliances aimed to offer intermodal services that could compete at the European level (Ferrovie dello stato 1996a: 17–18). These consisted in cooperation with key companies in intermodal transport. A good example is Cemat, a group of terminal operators for combined road and rail transport, which is a public–private joint venture with the FS holding the greatest amount of shares, thus allowing considerable control of enterprise strategy (Pinna 1997: 4). Another example is the alliance with Sinport, a company engaged in running container terminals in ports (Barbati 1992). This strategy of engaging in alliances with operators was supplemented by the establishment of the Freight Leaders Club, an exclusive organization grouping together the most important clients of the railways and interested in intermodal services, designed to involve users in the development of combined transport (Necci 1992). The strategy of *societariz-zazione* led to a complex network of continually changing alliances. These maneuvers were supposed to facilitate intermodal transport and to increase the share of the railways in this sector.

Nearly ten years after the reform, transport users seem to appreciate the effort undertaken and acknowledge the structural limitations imposed by infrastructure and rolling stock, but are less enthusiastic about the end results: the customer orientation of the railways still falls far short of expectations.[84] The reformers themselves have reason to be disappointed. The new accountancy system has not yet been implemented and, what is worse, neither has the organizational separation of freight from the rest of the railways.[85] The first task was to set up an independent company for freight. Although some progress has been made toward increasing autonomy with the creation of Eurolog as an independent railfreight company in 1996, the final step toward a subholding has not been completed.[86] The second step of transferring the entire freight division to the railways was never even started, and there is no prospect of its happening in the near future (Eurolog 1996: 11). One of the main prerequisites for the strengthening of freight versus passenger transport remains unrealized. The second aspect of the strategy, that is, the system of strategic alliances, was discredited because the financial transactions of one of these alliances triggered the political scandal that led to the downfall of the former head of the Italian state railways, Necci. The new management, therefore, has announced a return to the core business that seems to exclude the expansive strategy of *societarizzazione*, without specifying clearly what the new reform would look like. According to one of the main protagonists of the *progetto merci*, this jeopardizes the whole reform of converting rail freight into a part of intermodal transport:

> If the present railway management and the present transport minister do not realize that they have to separate the freight division from the other activities and to face competition on a European level, the Italian railways will be marginalized. Transport policy will then be about local transport, about who will do the public works, about who gives money to the road hauliers. But it will not be about a system of logistics.
>
> (Interview Italcontainer, 6 March 1997)

How does the experience of Italian freight transport relate to Europe? Certainly there can be no doubt that the reformers have used "Europe" to justify their strategy. On the one hand, Europe's positive declarations regarding intermodal transport were used to justify the orientation toward intermodal services (Eurolog 1996: 9) On the other hand, the threat of competition on a European scale was highlighted (Spirito 1996a),[87] making inertia appear riskier than reform. Undoubtedly, Europe has also been used by opponents of the radical reform to emphasize that privatization was being inflicted by national governments and *not* by European decisions, and that less radical adaptations, as for example in France, were indeed possible (Beltrami 1995). Furthermore, the Italian Antitrust, the competition watchdog, has had doubts about the FS strategy of forming alliances at the national level to compete on a European scale, arguing that an alliance with one company operating in another mode of transport may undermine the chances for other companies to compete with the FS in intermodal transport (Pezzoli and Venanzetti 1996: 4). The overall impression is that there is a considerable controversy within the policy community as to how the experience relates to Europe.

If one takes the standard of evaluation proposed at the beginning of this chapter—that convergence occurs when a member state embarks on a process of reform and searches out new opportunities by confronting the challenge of competition—then the Italian experience in the freight sector was indeed a move toward Europe. However, two very important shortcomings modify this verdict. First, no stable solution has yet been found: Eurolog remains an empty box after the reform stopped halfway, making it difficult to draw any conclusions from the Italian experience, and there does not seem to be an irreversible development toward a new type of rail freight service as an independent company. And second, even the rationale of the strategy is increasingly being called into question by the new management with its emphasis on a return to the core business.

### Conclusion

Unlike road haulage, the national railway policy shared some objectives with its European counterpart. This is true for both dimensions of the EC reform, the objective of organizational autonomy and, albeit to a lesser extent, that of market building. The result of the analysis in both cases has been that changes have remained on a formal level. Intervention in the "railways business" has not been reduced substantially, and even in freight transport, no significant development toward a market has taken place.

## EXPLAINING THE LACK OF POLICY CONVERGENCE

The main reason for the limited impact of the CRP on the national railway reform, and why the implementation of neither the objectives of the Italian nor of the European policies were achieved, are evidenced by the lack of convergence between the two policies. The Italian reform was limited to the objective of organizational autonomy. This was possible because the directives generated by the CRP (see Kerwer and Teutsch in this volume) only cautiously introduce compulsory elements of competition. The public administration was concerned about the risk of losing control over the railways. The railways were simply converted from a public monopoly to a private monopoly, sidestepping any risk of competition. The central question for an explanation of the modest consequences of reforms to date is why the European railway reform has not been adopted by national reformers. Why has a solution developed on a European level not been applied to a pressing domestic problem?

A first answer is that the European reform would have involved questioning an entrenched idea in Italy: the railways as a public service to be provided by government.[88] However, in comparative perspective, this is not a satisfactory explanation. In the United States, in spite of a traditional concept of transport as natural monopoly, radical reform of state intervention took place (Derthick and Quirk 1985). The same holds true for the British railway reform (see Knill in this volume). In both cases, public actors played a major role in reforming the transport sector. Therefore, the first question is whether government and the public administration tried to redefine the concept of railways to introduce competition, and if so, why they failed to translate it into a railway policy. Subsequently, the preferences and strategies of the other two major groups of actors likely to oppose the European reform, the railway management, and the trade unions are analyzed. The former are bound to lose their privileged position as a public monopoly, the latter are bound to lose their traditional power because of organizational disintegration.

## Government and Administration

Unlike Britain, the government and the administration in Italy had no clear preference for the abolition of the national railway monopoly until very recently. The first attempt ever to achieve policy convergence with Europe dates back to early 1997. The so-called *Prodi directive* reads like a catalogue of past EC decisions and proposals: organizational separation between infrastructure and operation, that is, to abolish a single railway company and to follow the English model; financial restructuring to increase managerial responsibility and to reduce state transfer payments.[89] Even a reform of the tariff system has been planned (*Il Sole 24 Ore,* 1 February 1997: 13). However, it is still not clear whether this plan will lead to a new railway policy in the future. Although it contained fundamental changes, no consultation process with either the railway management or the trade unions preceded the directive. Furthermore, its author, the minister of finance, seems to have launched the directive without even consulting the minister of transport (*Il Sole 24 Ore,* 5 February 1997: 10). The directive seems to be an ad hoc answer to the problem of how to resolve the Italian budget deficit and was probably triggered by the announcement of new and heavy losses in the year 1996. The ad hoc nature of the plan is in stark contrast with its ambitions. Not surprisingly, the intentions of the government met with strong opposition from all the trade unions—the only immediate consequence of the government proposal being to unify the railway trade unions in a common opposition against the so-called *spezzatino ferroviario*, the "railway ragout." Their main objection referred to the plan to abolish the unity of the railway organization within the span of one year, by creating one company for the railways and many others for their operation. After only two weeks, the negotiations effectively neutralized the directive. Organizational separation ceased to be a short-term policy objective, the financial

restructuring of the railways would not be carried out at the expense of the workers, and the autonomy of negotiating wages was underlined. The direttiva Prodi
remains in force but is relegated to a long-term policy plan (*Il Sole 24 Ore,* 13
February 1997: 3).

The episode is nevertheless typical of the whole of the decade of railway reforms analyzed in this chapter. Government simply never managed to play a crucial role in the railway reform process. The major promoters of the first reform of
1985 were the trade unions, and the protagonist of privatization in 1992 was railway management. Government was mainly preoccupied with mediating between
the two. The perspective has been short-term indeed: how to avoid the next strike.

Considering the magnitude of the financial problems of the railways, the finding that the government has never been the protagonist of a reform is something
of a surprise. The low strategic capacity of government has to be explained by institutional factors. Among the most important institutional factors weakening
government is the fact that Italian governments are very unstable and cabinets
highly conflict-prone in comparison to their European counterparts (Ministero dei
Trasporti 1996: 425).[90] This reduces the relevant time horizon for action considerably. Under these circumstances, any successful reform will most probably add
to the reputation of the successor. Policy is restricted to managing emergencies.

A second institutional factor is the condition of the administration, the Ministry
of Transport. It has to rely exclusively on the FS for information about them.
There is no independent source of information that could be used to counter the
information monopoly of the railways (Ponti 1996a). In fact, the Court of Audi-
tors has criticized the Ministry of Transport for not establishing an adequate control structure to follow the complicated task of surveillance (Corte dei Conti
1996). Although the railways were formally privatized in 1985, by 1997 there
was still no division responsible for developing a railway policy within the ministry.[91] Furthermore, no such structure exists within the minister's cabinet.[92] The
only source of independent expertise appears to be external advisers (see Ponti
1996b). Therefore, one may conclude that even more fundamental prerequisites
for autonomous action based on independent expertise, economic critique, and
mechanisms for their translation into policy are missing.

The institutional weakness of the government and its administration is not the
only reason for the failure to draw up a comprehensive reform. Other institutional
factors, which would allow policymakers to question the notion of public service,
are absent. In the United States, one of the important prerequisites for the success
of deregulation policy in spite of the resistance of the target industry was the powerful criticism of the protectionist regulatory regime by economic theory
(Derthick and Quirk 1985: 246–52). All the necessary prerequisites for such a
mechanism to work seem to be absent in Italy. The economic analysis of transport has never produced a coherent and overwhelming set of arguments against
public ownership as their American counterparts about deregulation. The major
coherent research effort in Italy by the Italian national science foundation, the

Progetto finalizzato trasporti, focuses on new technical solutions for vehicles and traffic control systems (Bianco 1996), but excludes economic analysis. Economic transport research seems to be limited to academia, and if it does criticize public ownership it seems to be ineffective.[93] This may be because in Italy a second important prerequisite unfolding the power of economic ideas is missing. The mechanisms that transformed economic ideas into policies in the United States are less well developed in Italy. Recruitment patterns in the public administration in Italy do not favor the entrance of innovative economists (Bilotta 1983). Furthermore, there are no specialized and influential advisory organizations to advise policy-makers, thereby translating scientific knowledge into policy (Regonini and Giuliani: 1994 138–39).

The lack of institutional prerequisites for reform explains an interesting detail of the Prodi directive. Although it is a close translation of the CRP, the reference to Europe has not been used to overcome national resistance. Since the beginning of the Italian railway reform process, it was the best opportunity to use the EC as an excuse to introduce unpopular measures. Its provisions came very close to the CRP, and opposition from the trade unions was stiff. Taking these circumstances into consideration, it is surprising that this directive has not been justified by reference to EC obligations at all. On the contrary, EC obligations were camouflaged as national decisions. In fact, in the ensuing debate the Prodi directive was treated as a national decision and the trade unions complained that the government did not try to follow the CRP but rather the problematic British model.[94] This is partly explained by poor political management on the part of decision makers, but it may also be due to the fact that the CRP is ambiguous and leaves ample room for interpretation of what constitutes compliance. Therefore, it is more difficult to use the reference to European obligations as a substitute for a low strategic capacity of government.

To conclude, government and the administration have not yet become promoters of the reform process of the railways. The weakness of the government due to several institutional factors is a first step in the explanation of why there has been no sustained reform effort by government in spite of the severe financial problems of the railways. This explanation shall be supplemented by an analysis of the role of private actors, railway management, and the trade unions.

## Management

During the last decade, the railway management has itself been an agent of organizational reform in various different ways, but has never been a promoter of policy convergence with Europe. A closer look at the various management strategies of this period shows that recipes other than intramodal competition were tried to overcome the economic difficulties.

Since 1986, the railways have had four different managers: Ligato (1986–1988), Schimberni (1988–1989), Necci (1989–1996), and Cimoli (since

1996). These four different management periods correspond to two different problem-solving approaches concerning the economic difficulties of the railways (Ponti 1992: 130–36; *La Repubblica,* 23 September 1996). The first type, pursued by Schimberni and Cimoli, consists of a strategy of cutting costs and personnel to reduce the railways' deficit. Schimberni, for example, decided to abandon plans for building a high-speed railway network in Italy until the FS has tackled its deficit. Similarly, Cimoli wants to improve the railways by cutting costs (*La Repubblica,* 18 September 1996). The second and contrasting problem-solving approach pursued by Necci,[95] the most ambitious management style analyzed, has been to improve the economic performance of the railways by expanding their activities and by conquering new markets. Unlike Schimberni, Necci decided to go ahead with the high-speed train and planned huge investments in new infrastructure and rolling stock despite existing railway deficits (*Mondo Economico* 1996b: 10–15). Unlike Cimoli, he decided not to concentrate on the traditional task of providing transport services only but to diversify the activity of the railways. To allow this, the so-called strategy of *societarizzazione* had been pursued. This involved the founding of more than one hundred subenterprises that allowed the railways to involve private partners and to expand their activities into other modes of transport (Ministero dei Trasporti 1996: 88).

The two major managerial strategies of the railways both welcomed the tendency of the Italian reform to increase organizational autonomy. During the first period until the end of Schimberni, the railways tried to boost their autonomy by a generous interpretation of a newly acquired power to abolish obsolete ministerial decrees. This gave rise to continual conflicts, with the Ministry of Transport opposing this strategy (Correale 1989: 5; Colacito 1989: 7). Under Necci's leadership, the defense of the railways' autonomy even increased. First, legal privatization and contractualization were actively promoted by the railway management (*Il Sole 24 Ore,* 1 May 1992: 22), and again opposed by the minister of transport (*Il Sole 24 Ore,* 17 May 1992: 15), but was successful as part of the general privatization program launched by the Amato government to deal with a severe economic and political crisis (Claudiani 1996: 7). In particular, during the negotiations over the program contract for the period 1994 to 2000, the railways stubbornly refused any measures to enhance state control over the ever-increasing public investments into the railways (Ponti 1996b).

Just as the public railway policy, neither of the two management strategies promoted the market-building intentions of the CRP. This is more visible with the first type of strategy. The organizational reform did not include any consideration about the transformation of the monopoly as such. On the contrary, this approach is more likely to see the introduction of intramodal competition as detrimental to a basically noncompetitive organization (Di Miceli 1990: 358). The second type of strategy pursued by Necci did include a vision of a competitive operational environment. However, unlike the European model, it emphasizes competition between different intermodal alliances on a European market. Intramodal competition between different railways seems to be only a weakening of the railway mode, especially in the face of a transport policy that distorts intermodal competition by favoring road transport. In his capacity as head of the UIC, Necci clearly voiced his doubts about the CRP:

> [a] tendency is emerging to introduce competition between the infrastructures and between the enterprises of rail transport; if an orientation of this nature prevailed, the outcome would be a further strategic weakening of the railways with respect to the other modes of transport, consolidating . . . the process of marginalization of the European railway system versus road transport.
>
> (Necci 1994: 4)

Under Necci's management, the strategic capacity of the railways and hence the chance to determine the direction of the railway reform easily exceeded that of the government or public administration. The frequent attempts to regain control over railway financing failed, not only because Necci remained in power much longer than the transport ministers, but because he had developed a vision of how to reform the railways that was shared by a large coalition of interests (*La Repubblica* 1996b). His idea of relaunching the railways by investments and by conquering new markets was much more attractive to the interests involved than the strategy of downsizing his predecessor Schimberni. In particular, the high-speed train promised to be profitable business for the many private investors and firms that would have been involved in constructing the infrastructure and the new trains. The reform was acceptable to the trade unions because growth promised job security. And finally, for the government, the promise of severely reducing debts was attractive, too. Even though the Necci era came to an end due to a corruption scandal in 1996, it is still acknowledged that his leadership was based on a coherent vision of how to reform the state railways unrivaled during the last decade.[96] This is also mirrored by the fact that he managed to motivate his collaborators and staff of the railways beyond the usual level (Ponti 1996b: 18).

To conclude, at no stage during the last decade did the management of the railways actively promote a reform that included the introduction of intramodal competition. Especially during the Necci era, this would have seemed to be an exceptionally difficult task for any government to pursue, since it would have meant overcoming a coherent reform strategy supported by large coalition of interests.

## Trade Unions

In searching for explanatory factors for the development of the railway reform in Italy, the overwhelming impression is that railway trade unions constitute one of the major obstacles for a convergence of national and European policies.

Fierce trade union resistance followed hot on the heels of the government's declaration on future railway policy in the beginning of 1997. It was widely held that the outcome of subsequent negotiations was a victory of the trade unions.[97] However, the role of the trade unions may not be reduced to merely blocking reform initiatives by the management. In fact, the trade unions were among the active promoters of the first legal privatization in 1985. They had tenaciously pushed the reform process ahead, when a deadlock formed in the beginning of the 1980s (Coletti 1985: 339). In the view of the CISL, trade unions had played a fundamental role in promoting the reform at a time when privatization was not yet prominent in Europe (Claudiani 1996: 4). The major interest of the trade unions in promoting the reform was due to the fact that the change in legal status would formally ratify the achievements of contractual bargaining achieved previously but could not be institutionalized because of the legal status of *azienda autonoma*.[98] A second reason for the promotion of the reform was that it was in the trade unions' vital interest that the economic crisis of the railways would be overcome.

This constructive role of the trade unions changed after the first reform law of 1985 had been passed. The trade unions started to resist the efforts of the management to restructure the railways and to slow down the reform process.[99] This fundamental change in interest requires some explanation, also because it is linked to factors that are important for the future prospects of the railway reform.

With the railway reform, the management had acquired increased financial responsibility. As a consequence, the high costs of excess manpower in comparison to other European railways became one of the major problems of the railway reform. This problem was a legacy from the past, when the railways were still a part of the public administration and shared its common fate of being used to reduce unemployment.[100] Another problem was the simplification of the classification system of professions and wage levels, which was a very complex system due to the wide range of activities pursued by the former state railways (Bordogna 1992: 80–86). As a consequence of the salience of these problems within the general railway reform, the constructive collaboration of the trade unions was decisive for its success.

The first test for the pro-reform strategy adopted by the trade unions was the negotiations for the collective contract under the new regime of autonomous industrial relations that had been part of the railway reform in 1985. The major trade unions agreed to the fundamental prerequisites of the reform that concerned them. They negotiated over a new professional classification system and were willing to trade a decrease in manpower against an increase in salary.[101] However, the proposals advanced by the major trade unions led to widespread dissatisfaction among the membership, especially the train drivers who felt that their specific status within the system of the railways had been neglected. In 1987 they founded a new trade union, the Coordinamento dei macchinisti uniti

(COMU), which changed the character of the industrial relations within the railways. At the beginning of the reform, representation was spread among the transport sections of the four national confederate trade unions that collaborated closely in the negotiations of the National Labor Contract (CCNL) (Bordogna 1992: 86–88).[102] The principle of these trade unions was that they were not organized according to professions but had shares of each professional group within the railways. For various reasons it was difficult to integrate this new trade into the established industrial relations system of the railways. COMU did not respect the principle of general representation of the workers but spoke for a specific professional group only. Furthermore, it did not want to be integrated into the system itself; instead it accused the trade unions of collaboration with the management and antidemocratic behavior (Bordogna 1991: 157). The protest of COMU was effective because of several factors that combined to give it considerable bargaining power. Among the most important is the fact that the small number of train drivers may easily paralyze the circulation of trains. As in all public-sector strikes, those made by train drivers are effective because they harm not only the organization but all potential users (Ferner and Hyman 1992: 578). In the past, COMU has frequently managed to mobilize its members for strikes.

The rise of COMU and the end of the unity of the railway trade unions had a seriously detrimental effect on the railway reform. The frequent strikes inflicted considerable economic damage on the railways. Moreover, the level of conflict between the confederate trade unions and the COMU was high, because of the fierce attacks of the latter and because the established trade unions had different opinions about admitting the COMU as a bargaining partner at the national contract level, making any agreement between the several parties involved about the major reform questions of the restructuring of the sector very difficult to reach.

In the first half of the 1990s several factors combined to solve the problem of excessive trade union activities in the railway sector. After COMU had been admitted to the bargaining table and after most of its other demands had been met, its strikes became less frequent. Furthermore, Necci was much more successful in winning over the trade unions by adopting a new strategy of financial restructuring of the railways. His strategy of relaunching the railways especially by starting up the project of the high-speed train promised the substantial development needed to secure higher salaries and prevent further job losses. In this period the trade unions seemed to return to their former more constructive role. It was with their basic consent that the number of employees was reduced by more than 40 percent, thus putting the Italian railways on a European level of productivity per labor unit. However, this undisputed success of the era of the management of Necci came at a high price. Whereas the number of employees dropped, the cost-per-unit labor rose sharply, so that in the short and medium term the reduction of the workforce did not lead to a significant alleviation of railway finances

(*Il Sole 24 Ore*, 19 December 1997: 11).[103] Nevertheless, the established trade unions still feel that they have done their part and blame management for not having achieved the growth rates that would have countered this unfavorable development (Claudiani 1996).

Quite apart from the resistance to the reduction of the labor force, trade unions also retarded the process in other ways. Their opposition to any form of privatization of railway activities prevented efficiency gains by outsourcing of activities and the chance to increase income. For example, resistance to the privatization of the data-processing section of the railways (TSF) (*Il Sole 24 Ore*, 11 June 1996) not only prevented a potential profit for the railways and impaired customer services, but also had negative repercussions on the reform of rail freight insofar as the telematic infrastructure necessary for the modernization of combined transport was not available.[104] The opposition of the trade unions was because workers would no longer be covered by the CCNL after privatization.[105]

It is reasonable to conclude that although the national railway reform process was started by the trade unions, they later slowed down the reform process and increased the costs, and they were still opposed to the organizational division of the FS at the time of writing (*Il Sole 24 Ore*, 3 December 1997), because this would severely restrict their bargaining power. It is important to note that with the rise of the small trade unions such as COMU, the structural conditions for including the trade unions in the reform processes have become more difficult. An agreement reached with the major trade unions is now worth less than before the reform process started, because the small autonomous unions may effectively strike against any compromise that excludes them.

# CONCLUSION

The analysis of Italian transport policy presented here shows that despite the advent of a European CRP, convergence has not yet been achieved. Italian railway policy and management have so far not embraced the goal of converting the railways from a state monopoly into a unit of a European market for competition. The explanations offered here centered on the reasons why government did not apply the European solution to a pressing national problem. The findings suggest that *the government's capacity to develop an alternative policy is too low.* During the Necci era (roughly half of the period examined), a change toward market building was prevented by the higher strategic capacity of the railway management, which viewed the prospect of competition with skepticism. Furthermore, trade unions have opposed any European reforms that threaten to severely limit their power. However, in the future, policy convergence may become more likely if the following conditions are met. First, the present regime transition toward the so-called *seconda repubblica* has led to more stable government and to an administrative reform in the transport sector. Second, the success of policy convergence will depend on the progress of the CRP. If the compulsory liberalization of markets progresses, the capacity of the government to change policy may increase. At this stage, the prospects for implementation of such a policy in Italy seem to be entirely uncertain.

## TRUCKS AND TRAINS: A COMPARATIVE CONCLUSION

The analysis of the policy dynamics in the road haulage and railway sectors indicates that national policies have not converged toward a European model, but have instead remained within traditional boundaries, despite widespread dissatisfaction. However, the impact of the CTP on the two sectors has been different. In the railway sector, the differences between the two policies at the end of the period studied had not been significantly reduced. The Italian railway policy did not adopt the policy goal of converting the monopoly-dominated railway sector into a market. In contrast to the national railway policy, road haulage policy even increased the differences from the European policy. At the end of 1997, barriers to market access were higher than in 1985, and the compulsory tariff system was better enforced. Furthermore, since 1990, state aids contrary to EU law have been introduced. Whereas the Italian railway policy may be considered a case of persistence, in the case of Italian road haulage policy it is justifiable to speak of divergence.

These differences allow us to check the explanations given for the policy developments in this sector. A first striking observation is that in Italy, policy divergence has occurred in areas in which it was less likely to occur according to the structural properties of the sector. Liberalization in the road haulage sector is easier to achieve, since the structure of the sector already resembles a competitive market (OECD 1990: 7). This is confirmed by the other cases presented in this volume. In France, policy convergence with Europe has been achieved in road haulage, but not in the case of the railways. In Britain, road haulage liberalization preceded the railway reform by nearly two decades. On the other hand, in Italy the rail sector is the only area where modest progress toward the CTP has been achieved even though the introduction of competition there was an unfamiliar idea until recently. This allows us to conclude that the economic structure of the two sectors is not a sufficient explanatory factor for the policy dynamics in Italy. It is therefore justified to concentrate on political variables.

The second confirmation of the explanatory approach chosen here regards the treatment of, and relationship between, public and private actors in accounting for policy dynamics. A focus on state capacity alone does not explain the differences between the policy outcomes. In both the road and the rail sectors, state capacity has been low, and yet policy outcomes differed. The same result would have been reached had only the structure of the interest group representation been examined. In the past decade, both road haulage associations and railway trade unions have increased in number and have been divided by a polarization process into two camps: one that collaborates with public actors and another that frequently jeopardizes compromises by strikes. For example, with respect to their blackmailing strategy, the train drivers' union, COMU, is similar to the association of the small hauliers, Unatras. However, the interaction between the public and private has been different in the two sectors. In the case of railways, under Necci it was possible to substantially reduce the opposition of the autonomous railway unions and to strike a bargain with the major trade unions. This was an important precondition for promoting the national railway reform and introducing elements of conversion. By contrast, neither the Ministry of Transport nor the government ever managed to launch a comprehensive reform and to turn resistance into acquiescence, let alone support.

This chapter examines how the advent of a European CTP has affected Italian transport policy in the road haulage and railway sectors. Two questions arise in this context. First, has European policy influenced national policy traditions in a significant and sustained way? In other words, has there been a Europeanization of Italian transport policy? And second, if so, what kind of effects has it had in Italy? Did Europeanization lead to policy *convergence*, that is, to policy instruments and policy goals that conform with Europe's? The empirical results of the two case studies indicate that this did not occur, despite the expectation that it would. They show that, despite the potential for policy congruence, in Italy the dynamics of domestic policies for road haulage and railways is largely characterized by inertia. Italian transport policy in the sector of road and rail has been "going through the motions," with old routines still dominating, despite widespread dissatisfaction with the results. In a nutshell, the paradoxical coexistence of the CTP at the European level and policy inertia at the domestic level is due to the strong tradition of state interventionism and the resistance to particularistic private interests in the transport sector, which have undermined the capacity of public actors to introduce those key changes necessary for convergence.

Comparing the two cases does not merely reveal differences, but also one striking similarity. In both instances the administrative capacity to introduce reform was too low. In the case of road, decision making was largely colonized by the association of small hauliers. In the case of rail, the management of the state railways was the most important policy entrepreneur. Public actors have been frequently observed to have similar structural weaknesses, thus this does not come as a surprise, especially in Italy. However, as is pointed out in the introduction to this chapter, in the EU, powerful Europeanization mechanisms can create considerable pressure for member states to adapt by forcing them to implement EU law or to respond to increasing competition. External pressure of this kind allows national governments to "cut national interests slack" (Moravcsik 1993) and to advance reforms more successfully. In the cases analyzed here, the EU failed to provide an external boost, sufficient for reform, for the national state capacity. In road haulage policy the competitive pressure resulting from a liberalized market was not initially strong enough to overcome the fierce resistance of the small hauliers. In the case of rail, the limited external constraint provided by the CRP was even more obvious. Even though the Prodi directive was very close to the CRP, the government was not able to easily defend it against the onslaught of the trade unions, because many aspects of the CRP have not become legally binding. Of course, it is impossible to conclude from this case that the mechanisms of Europeanization are generally ineffective. But the analysis presented here suggests that the functioning of these mechanisms depends on preconditions at the national level. Thus, it confirms an approach to Europeanization research that emphasizes the importance of national institutional dynamics (Olsen 1996).

## NOTES

1. However, the case of the Netherlands shows that an increase in state intervention need not necessarily mean less market, and may actually foster market processes (see Lehmkuhl in this volume).

2. Several internal reports by the Ministry of Transport had already come to the conclusion that the transport sector was in crisis (Ministero dei Trasporti 1977, n.d.(a), n.d.(b).

3. Law of 6 June 1974, n. 298 (G.U. n. 200, 31 July 1974). For an overview, see Lepore (1993).

4. Other changes involved the improvement of instruments already in use, such as a revised distinction between own-account operators excluded from restrictive market access regulation and professional hauliers, and the issuing of licenses according to transport capacity rather than number of vehicles (Ministero dei Trasporti 1977: 127–29.).

5. Interview ANITA, 1 March 1996.

6. The transport of petroleum products is far more sensitive to strikes than, for example, the transport of glass, and the bargaining power of the small hauliers varies accordingly (interview ANITA, 1 March 1996).

7. The representatives of the hauliers' associations who sign the collective economic agreements also negotiate the mandatory tariffs (Dani, Conte, and Giacomini 1994: 16).

8. In 1996 a license for a medium-size vehicle for professional road haulage cost about Lit. 40,000,000 (interview Confindustria, 3 May 1996).

9. Law of 27 May 1993, n. 162 (G.U., 28 May 1993, n. 123).

10. Since the law came into force road hauliers have made recourse to the courts and, given the extension of the period of validity, the industry has been sued for considerable amounts of money (interview Ministero dei Trasporti, 11 May 1995). But other provisions of the law, such as the fact that only written contracts are valid from 1993 onward as a basis for claiming the legal price, will restrict this possibility in the future (interview ANITA, 1 March 1996).

11. This conclusion should be treated with some caution, since the taxes for operation are not all levied according to the principle of territoriality. Foreign road hauliers

are entitled to a reimbursement of VAT on petroleum products whereas domestic hauliers are not. Furthermore, fuel is not always bought where it is used. These considerations are important when comparing the difference in costs that EC road hauliers might have when competing with each other (Rommerskirchen 1985: 235–36). Another limitation of the table is that it does not only include freight transport but also public transport by road. The table, therefore, is only sufficient to illustrate the salience of the principle of territoriality.

12. This conclusion is only true for market regulation but not for the incorporation of environmental considerations into taxation.

13. Ministero dei Trasporti, *decreto* of 19 October 1990 (G.U. n. 246, 20 October 1990) and *decreto* of 15 February 1991 (G.U. n. 42, 19 February 1991).

14. OJ L 233, 16 September 1993, p. 10.

15 . *Decreto legge* (DL), 20 February 1996, n. 67 (GURI n. 42, 20 February 1996).

16. Law n. 815, 27 November 1980.

17. Interview Ministero dei Trasporti, 30 January 1996, No. 2; Law n. 404, 30 July 1985.

18. Law n. 68, 5 February 1992.

19. Interview Ministero dei Trasporti, 30 January 1996, No. 2; interview Confcooperative, 16 February 1996.

20. The recent extension of the period of validity of Law 68/1992 and the assignment of an annual budget for 1995, 1996, and 1997 (Art. 3 of the Law of 5 January 1996, n. 11 GURI n. 9, 12 January 1996) has been challenged by the European Commission (*Il Sole 24 Ore*: 1 May 1996).

21. Interview European Commission, DG VII, 16 April 1996.

22. The case of the Netherlands shows that a proactive industrial policy in the road haulage sector need not run counter to EU competition law (see Lehmkuhl in this volume).

23. General corporate taxes valid for all enterprises are excluded here for the sake of simplicity.

24. Interview Ministero dei Trasporti, 30 January 1996, No. 2.

25. Autonomy in this context does not imply perfect independence but the ability of the state to manage its dependence on the environment for resources according to its own principles (Luhmann 1991: 156). Thus defined, the concept does not contradict a model of policymaking and implementation based on networks of public and private actors (Mayntz 1993).

26. The official name of the institution is albo nazionale degli autotrasportatori di cose per conto di terzi. Title I of the Law of 6 June 1974, n. 298 (GURI n. 200, 31 July 1974).

27. Interview Camera dei Deputati, April 1996.

28. Case C–96/94, *Centro Servizi Spediporto Srl* v. *Spedizioni Marittima del Golfo Srl*, [1995] ECR I–2883. See Dani, Conte, and Giacomini (1994).

29. Article 9, *decreto legge* (DL), 29 March 1993, n. 82 (GURI, n. 73, 29 March 1993).

30. Interview *Ministero dei Trasporti*, 9 May 1995.

31. An ambitious reform proposed by the most important governmental advisory body, the Consiglio nazionale di economia e del lavoro (CNEL) in 1994 included the transfer of competence in the area of infrastructure and the breaking up of the organization according to different modes of transport.

32. Interview Ministero dei Trasporti, 2 May 1996.

33. UNITAI has replaced FAI as the haulier association belonging to Confetra. FAI left the comitato permanente d'intesa as well as Confetra by 1986.

34. That is, the Federazione autotrasportatori Italiani (FAI), Federazione Italiana trasportatori professionali (FIAP) for industrial enterprises, Federazione Italiana trasportatori artigiari (FITA), CONFARTIGIANATO TRASPORTI, and Sindacato nazionale autotrasportatori confederazione di artigianato (SNA/CASA) for artisan enterprises.

35. Polarization has not yet put an end to all forms of cooperation. An example of collaboration of Unatras and Coordinamento is the foundation of the consortium Unione autotrasportatori toscani alta velocità (UNATAV) among members of Unatras and ANITA to participate at the works for the high-speed railway line between Florence and Bologna (*La Nazione* 1996).

36. This is only an analytical distinction, since the two phases of the policy cycle are closely interrelated.

37. In the words of Unatras, "we always negotiate with the government" (interview Unatras, 16 February 1996). The exclusive aim to influence government decision making is shown by the fact that strikes are not called in periods of political crisis when the government is unable to react to their demands.

38. Interview ANITA, 1 March 1996.

39. Interview Confetra, 4 December 1995.

40. Interview Confetra, 4 December 1995.

41. A case in point is the decision by the Ministry of Finance to abolish a number of customs offices that disrupted transport operations. Confetra responded to this decision by a letter to the ministry and was considering legal action, but at no point was a strike considered (*Il Sole 24 Ore,* 24 August 1995, and 31 August 1995).

42. In the case of road haulage the structure of interest intermediation does not correspond to either of the ideal types proposed by LaPalombara in his analysis of Italy (La-Palombara 1964). The absence of a *parentela* relationship between haulier associations and a dominant party that offers specific promotion of the haulier interests is obvious. But even a *clientelistic* relationship where an interest group of a sector is treated by the administration as its exclusive representative does not fit the situation well, since the candidates for such a relationship, Confetra or the Coordinamento, did not effectively monopolize their influence on the administration.

43. Interview ANITA, 1 March 1996.

44. Another factor contributing to policy inertia in Italy could have been that the liberalization of cabotage was not a major problem due to the country's peripheral geographic location. Compared to Germany, which has a much higher percentage of transit traffic, the pressure of liberalization in Italy may indeed be inferior. Still, cabotage was *perceived* as a serious problem. As early as 1985 it was a topic in an important annual transport conference (Conferenza di Varese 1985: 287), and even as far south as Naples freight forwarders are prepared to work with foreign hauliers (interview Sticco-sped, 12 May 1995).

45. There is considerable ambiguity as to what precisely constitutes a "level playing field." When do differences in taxation according to the principle of nationality matter? And how can disadvantages in one area be traded off against advantages in others?

46. This runs counter to the usual portrayal of Italian participation in EC policy formulation as the "ceremonial heart of Europe" (Willis 1971: vii), where Italian governments assent to the greater part of European policy propositions but do not implement them (Noël

1988; Giuliani 1992). Another exception to this image is telecommunications policy (Natalicchi 1996: 332–34). For the formal structure used by Italy to coordinate its input in European policy formulation, see Franchini (1993: 92ff.).

47. Interview Ministero dei Trasporti, 2 May 1996.

48. In the period 1985–1996 there were ten different Ministers of Transport.

49. Confartigianato Trasporti and FITA/CNA may be represented by their respective peak associations at the European level, but their influence on policy formulation has not been felt yet. The same holds true for Confcooperative and the Lega delle cooperative. Therefore, no further investigations on the subject have been made.

50. Interview Freight Transport Association, 17 April 1996.

51. Interview Confetra, 16 April 1996.

52. This initiative shows the close cooperation among the haulier associations that are part of the Coordinamento, since the complaint versus the Italian government was formulated by the road haulier association of Confetra together with ANITA from Confindustria (interview Confetra, 16 April 1996). Further evidence for their close cooperation is their recently published joint publication on transport (Confetra 1996; interview ANITA, 1 March 1996).

53. Interview Confetra, 16 April 1996.

54. Interview Confetra, 16 April 1996.

55. Ironically the EC transport policy was a major factor in Italy's expansion of its instruments of intervention. The introduction of mandatory tariffs for the domestic market in 1974 was favored by a compulsory tariff system for EC transport (Santoro 1974: 174–75; interview Ministero dei Trasporti, 11 May 1995).

56. Case C–185/91, *Bundesanstalt für den Güterfernverkehr* v. *Gebr. Reiff GmbH & Co. KG* [1993] ECR I–5801; Case C–153/93, *Federal Republic of Germany* v. *Delta Schiffahrts- und Speditionsgesellschaft mbH* [1994] Ecr I–2517, p. 2525; and Case C–96/94, *Centro Servizi Spediporto Srl* v. *Spedizioni Marittima del Golfo Srl* [1995] ECR I–2883.

57. Interview Ministero dei Trasporti, 30 January 1996, No. 1; interview Unatras, 16 February 1996.

58. OJ L 233, 16 September 1993, and OJ C–3/2, 6 January 1996.

59. Case C–280/95, *Commission* v. *Italian Republic* [1998] ECR I–259.

60. Interview European Commission, DG VII, 16 April 1996.

61. The state aid policy pursued by the EC is specified mostly by the commission itself through directives and communications by letters to the member states (CEC 1995a).

62. Interview European Commission, DG VII, 16 April 1996.

63. The credit has been granted on a wide range of different taxes. According to EC law, however, the Italian government may only use this excuse once it has made a serious attempt to recover the aid (Bellamy and Child 1993: 938–39).

64. *Decreto legge* (DL) of 29 March 1993, n. 82 (GURI n. 73, 29 March 1993).

65. Interview *Ministero dei Trasporti*, 30 January 1996, No. 2.

66. *Ministero dei Trasporti*, *decreto legge* (DL) of 20 February 1996 (GURI n. 42, 20 February 1996).

67. This has been a general concern ever since widespread nationalization in Europe has occurred. The question was how could the railways be oriented toward goals such as regional development or the provision of mass public transport, while operating efficiently? The answer was that the desired trade-off between social goals and economic efficiency should be institutionalized by a correct balance between the influence of the administration and the autonomy of the railways (Witte 1932).

68. A reform has also been started in the area of local rail transport. By definition, this type of transport (mostly commuter transport) is provided by small private companies not part of the FS. As a first step to increase their economic viability, the management of these companies has been assigned to the FS with the task to restructure them. Subsequently, it is planned to reorganize local transport at a regional level (Spirito 1996b). The reform of local transport is not dealt with here since it is not a main concern of the European railway reform.

69. For a description of the high-speed train in Italy, see Strohl 1993, ch. 6.

70. Examples of the activities pursued by these new companies that are part of FS are CIT, a travel agency with at least a dozen international partners, EFESO, which publishes railway advertising material, and the like, and ISFORT, which deals with general transport-related management training (Corte dei Conti 1996: 78ff.).

71. For details of the railway reform, see Kerwer and Teutsch in this volume.

72. For freight transport the determination of tariffs was free before and after the reform. Economically this activity is much less important for the railways.

73. Interview Ferrovie dello stato, 6 March 1997.

74. For the organizational transformation into a holding at the end of 1992, see *Collegio Amministrativo Ferroviario Italiano* (1996). This has been prepared by the introduction of an accountancy system according to industrial norms, which, however, did not yet distinguish between infrastructure and operation (Fiorentino n.d.: 32–33). A first distinction in the accounts of subunits was introduced in 1990 (Bilancia 1992: 4), but at that time, infrastructure was not a separate division from operation.

75. The program contract 1994–2000 obliges the FS to adopt a system of infrastructure pricing that completes the separation of infrastructure and operation in the following accounting year (Corte dei Conti 1996: 37). Due to a lengthy debate in Parliament, however, the "program contract" only came into being in March 1996, and was binding as of January 1997 (Ferrovie dello stato 1996c: 9).

76. Interview Ferrovie dello stato, Area rete, 28 February 1997.

77. Interview Ferrovie dello stato, Area rete, 28 February 1997. For a list of these enterprises and their economic performance, see Ministero dei Trasporti (1994).

78. Interview Italcontainer, 6 March 1997; interview Ferrovie dello stato, Area rete, 28 February 1997.

79. Symbolic adaptation in organizations in the sense that a change of self presentation does not result in a change of daily working routines is a well-known phenomenon (Meyer and Rowan 1991).

80. Distances between the north and south of Italy and between Italy and northern and central Europe are long enough to make railways competitive with road transport, which has a structural advantage over short and medium distances.

81. There was, for example, no timetable for freight trains, making it impossible to predict the time of arrival for goods in transit. A more anecdotal indicator of the poor level of services is that, until recently, the FS did not accept checks so that "the user had to go around with a little suitcase full of money to pay for his transport" (interview Confindustrua, 3 May 1996).

82. Interview Italcontainer, 6 March 1997. See also Gelosi 1995: 23–24.

83. Interview Italcontainer, 6 March 1997.

84. Interview Confindustria, 3 May 1996.

85. Interview Italcontainer, 6 March 1997.

86. The railway reform may be interpreted as a steady increase of autonomy in the production of railfreight services. Immediately after the 1985 railway reform, the FS was organized along functional lines; the production of freight and passenger transport was included in one unit (Fragolino and Rossi 1987). In 1990, the production of services was organized according to market segments, and passenger and freight transport became two separate divisions (Bilancia 1992: 4). After the conversion into a joint-stock company in 1992, a further reorganization ensued, but the two separate divisions were still part of the Area Trasporti distinct from the Area rete (Ferrovie dello stato 1993: allegato 4). In 1996, freight was put on the same level of hierarchy as passenger transport and the management of the infrastructure (Ferrovie dello stato 1996b). Although the minor organizational changes introduced early in 1997 by the new head of the railways, Cimoli, mainly regarded the holding but not the individual subdivisions, attempts are being made to end decentralization by defining the tasks and objectives of each unit more precisely (*Il Sole 24 Ore,* 20 February 1997: 9).

87. Interview Ferrovie dello stato, ASA rete, 28 February 1997.

88. For a broad definition of public service in the Italian context that includes all transport sectors and justifies virtually any state intervention, see Di Miceli (1989: 5–7).

89. This directive is not a government decree with immediate binding effect and which must later be turned into law by Parliament. It only has binding effects for the responsible ministers (Merlini 1994: 456). It may also be considered a proposal that may be turned into law at some time in the future (interview Camera dei Deputati, 27 February 1997).

90. Government instability is one of the most frequently cited explanations for the lack of reform of the sector given by practitioners working in the field.

91. The unit where one would expect to find such a section on railway policy is called '*Programmazione, Organizzazione e Coordinamento*'. The organigramme contains no reference to a section dealing specifically with the railways.

92. Interview, *Ministero dei Transporti*, 25 November 1996.

93. In Germany, a liberal approach to transport economics has become increasingly influential (Willeke 1995) in sharp contrast to the Italian situation (Loraschi 1984).

94. Interview CISL, 28 February 1997; interview FISAFS/CISAL, 6 March 1997.

95. The management period of Ligato is excluded from the analysis. He left no particular mark on policy in the short time before he was swept away by a corruption scandal.

96. Interview FISAFS/CISAL, 6 March 1997.

97. Interview Freight Leaders Club, 18 March 1997. It is interesting to note that the trade union protest was not directed against the CRP (interview FIT/CISL, 28 February 1997; interview FISAFS/CISAL, 6 March 1997). Most of the unions argued that the government was proposing the British model of reform and not the European model. Since this is only partly correct (a European Commission proposal includes the mandatory introduction of separation in two independent companies), the question is why this has not been highlighted by the trade union protest. The unions seem to take the introduction of intramodal competition for granted but think that a reorganization according to the British model is not a good strategy to deal with this situation.

98. This view is supported by the observation that industrial relations existed, albeit informally, before the reform of 1985 as a negotiation of agreements between workers and management. The reform changed the formal status of the system of industrial relations by introducing a system of collective bargaining (Stocchi and De Angelis 1992).

99. Interview FISAFS/CISAL, 6 March 1997.

100. Interview CISL, 28 February 1997.

101. Interview CISL, 28 February 1997.

102. FILT/CIGL, FIT/CISL, UILTRASPORTI, and FISAFS/CISAL.

103. Train drivers were much less affected than other groups and managed, for example, to defend the use of two drivers on trains in contrast to the one employed in many other European countries.

104. Interview Italcontainer, 6 March 1997.

105. Interview FISAFS/CISAL, 6 March 1997.

# 7

# From Regulation to Stimulation: Dutch Transport Policy in Europe

*Dirk Lehmkuhl*

## EUROPE AND THE FLEXIBILITY OF EXISTING INSTITUTIONS

Does the process of political and economic integration in Europe necessarily imply a loss of the member states' capacity to govern their economies? Does European Community (EC) legislation lead to a convergence of administrative structures, instruments, and forms of administrative interest intermediation? And does European policymaking crowd out traditional or newly emerging concerns from national agendas? With respect to the Common European Transport Policy and the reform of the transport markets in the Netherlands the response to all three questions is clearly negative. Without sacrificing its guiding function vis-à-vis socioeconomic developments, Dutch governments matched their domestic policies with European policy demands calling for the liberalization and deregulation of international transport. European integration in general, and the reform of transport regulation in particular, actually reinforced characteristic features of the Dutch institutional context and led to a strengthening of corporatist patterns of concertation and consultation. The functional content of concertation shifted from the regulation of market access to the stimulation of market forces and industrial competition. Moreover, this shift strengthened the social responsibility and self-regulation of economic actors and allows policymakers to incorporate emerging objectives, such as environmental issues, into the national agenda.

Three factors explain why the transformation of Dutch transport markets was neither a hard-core, pro-competitive disengagement of the state as in Britain, nor an Italian-style refusal of reform by private actors: the functional change of existing institutions of interest intermediation, the compatibility of policies at the national and the European level, and the mutual reinforcement of the policies of the two levels. First, at the heart of the overall developments in the Netherlands was the rude awakening of the Dutch political and economic elites to the competitiveness of the Dutch economy in general and the functioning of the institutionalized forms of administrative interest intermediation in particular. Instead of guaranteeing a capacity to adjust politically to economic change (Katzenstein 1985), corporatist structures proved too immobile to adapt to the changes in the environment of the Dutch economy. Public–private interaction was characterized by institutional sclerosis rather than a high degree of reform capacity (Hemerijck 1995). By increasing the general willingness to reconsider established political positions, the perception of crisis paved the way for a restructuring of industrial relations in the Netherlands, which eventually fueled the "Dutch miracle," that is, the widely admired virtues of economic performance under conditions of economic internationalization (Visser and Hemerijck 1997). As the competitiveness of the transport sector is frequently equated with the prosperity of the Dutch economy in general, it comes as no surprise that the sector was affected by the general mode of change. A strengthening of market forces and a redefinition of the role of the state in deregulated transport markets were considered the best way to prepare the industry for the increased competition in European transport markets. The distinctive framework of consensus seeking between public and private actors allowed for a problem-solving-oriented transformation of the regulatory framework accommodating market-making policies with policies aimed at curbing negative externalities of market processes.

Second, the emphasis on liberal policies at the national level was largely compatible with the strong liberal bias of European policy demands. The landmark ruling of the European Court of Justice against the Council of Ministers (1985), the Single Market Program (1985), and the Single European Act (1987) with its introduction of qualified majority voting (QMV), broke open the three-decade-long deadlock and sparked the take-off of the Common European Transport Policy. The objective of this policy was not primarily a convergence or harmonization of national regimes, but their mutual compatibility and the removal of direct and indirect barriers to the free flow of goods and services. This admittedly rather weak approach (Kerwer and Teutsch in this volume) granted national governments sufficient latitude to take into account country-specific concerns. In the Dutch case, it allowed the reconciliation of the contradicting values of liberal business practices and legitimate state intervention rooted in Dutch political culture. Instead of sacrificing the claim of public actors to guide socioeconomic behavior on the altar of efficiency, the government developed a medium-term to long-term approach to the restructuring of the transport sector. The creation of "win-win strategies" constituted a key mechanism for achieving integrated political leadership. By accompanying competitive deregulation with a host of compensatory policies, policymakers were able to unite public and private forces in a coalition to strengthen the competitiveness of the industry, and to take into account other policy goals such as growing public concern about environmental damage.

Finally, the mutual reinforcement of reforms at the domestic level and the demands of EC policy at the European level are a striking feature in the national response to European policy challenges. In road haulage, the transformation at the national level started *before* European policies took shape, with public and private Dutch actors actively promoting the liberalization of international transport. At the same time, the perception of enhanced competition increased the willingness of economic actors to abide by policies designed to boost the competitiveness of the sector. In the case of the railways, the Dutch government joined the European reform process once it had already started. While European policies were initially used as a way to secure the cooperation of potential opponents at the national level, their implementation in the Netherlands actually outstrips the demands imposed by European policies, and the Dutch government is actively engaged in achieving integrated railway markets in Europe. In sum, the changes emanating from the implementation of the reform concepts are more radical in the case of the railways than in that of road haulage.

The transformation of the Dutch transport sector is a succinct example of how regulatory reform may occur in the context of European integration, and how the challenges generated by European policies may be successfully incorporated at the domestic level. This chapter examines how the development and implementation of a new problem-solving approach took place in two interrelated subsectors, and how the advent of the Common Transport Policy impacted upon policymaking in the Dutch road haulage and railway sector.

## THE REFORM OF ROAD TRANSPORT POLICYMAKING: NEOCORPORATISM ALIVE AND KICKING

The most striking aspect of the developments in Dutch transport markets in the 1980s and early 1990s was the establishment of what one might call a new division of labor between state and economic actors. Traditionally, it is claimed that Dutch transport markets are governed by an essentially commercial, or quasi-commercial, approach that places emphasis on the internal efficiency of the transport system (Button 1993b; Kerwer and Teutsch in this volume). But if one takes a look at the preexisting regulations governing road haulage, inland waterways, and the railways, it becomes clear that this description requires some qualification. Dutch transport markets were not exempt from the distinctive feature of state-economy relations in the Netherlands, characterized by the reconciliation between a commitment to the liberal values of free trade on the one hand, and the legitimacy of active state intervention in civil society on the other (Andeweg and Irwin 1993; Daalder 1996: 194; van Waarden 1992: 146). The government's approach to the coordination of intermodal (*between* modes of transport) and intramodal (*within* a mode of transport) transport was to establish restrictive regulations that intervened rigorously in market processes, undermining the appearance of a liberal approach to market policies. However, the government decided to reconsider its policies in the face of a crisis generated by the failure of the existing regulatory regime and the advent of the process of European integration in the sector.[1]

The revision of the regulatory framework did not prompt the retreat of the state, which, rather than sacrifice its right to intervene in the actions of societal and economic actors, simply changed its style of intervention. On the one hand, instruments of market conformity and a strengthening of market forces were considered the best ways to promote efficiency in the road haulage industry. In anticipation of the liberalization of international transport markets within Europe, access to Dutch road haulage markets was subject to a far-reaching process of liberalization. On the other hand, more competition does not necessarily mean less government intervention. Instead, the government overhauled its tools, by reinforcing its monitoring capacity so as to emphasize its role as a guardian of competition, and developing a host of supplementary policies to fortify a proactive governmental role. At the domestic level the latter include the promotion of restructuring activities and the initiation of research and development schemes. At the international level they cover information to help promote the image of Dutch transport abroad, and intensified support for the pro-liberalization lobby in Brussels and the opening up of international transport markets. This section analyzes how this change from the regulation of market access to the stimulation of market dynamics took place, how the shift in intervention style led to a strengthening of the patterns of public–private interaction, and how European policies impact on this development.

## Changes in the Regulatory Framework

As in most other European countries, the Dutch regulation of transport after World War II maintained certain elements of the prewar regulatory regime, such as the control of market entry, the use of tariffs, and the application of fiscal instruments. The following sections concentrate on those developments that best illustrate the changes that took place in Dutch transport policy: the transformation of the market access regime, and the strategic use of fiscal instruments. These examples throw light on the way in which the shift away from a market regulating measures enabled the government to stimulate efforts to increase the competitiveness of the industry while simultaneously incorporating other policy objectives into transport policymaking.

### Market Access

In the Netherlands, the first regulation of road transport, the Vehicle Freight Act (Wet Autovervoer Goederen, WAG), was introduced in 1951. The proliferation of legislation, especially in the 1950s, was designed to ensure a balanced road transport market and the coordination of different modes of transport by regulating capacity. The approach used to achieve this did not include a quota system of licenses for hire-and-reward services, but instead provided methods for controlling market access via unit capacity. While own-account transport was relatively unrestricted, the WAG distinguished two categories of transport for hire-and-reward operations that required different authorization procedures: *regular* and *occasional* (or demand-responsive) transport services. The consequences of the two regimes can be summarized as follows. The intensity of the regulation of market access for regular transport, that is, scheduled services or collection and delivery, gave this segment a public-service character, where the obligation to operate was rewarded by protection from competition (Bernadet 1991: 14). The procedure for access to the occasional transport market was more sophisticated. In order to exercise strict control over haulier capacity, the Transport Licence Commission (Commissie Vergunningen Wegvervoer) and the State Traffic Inspectorate (Rijksverkeersinspectie) examined applications for market entry or for extension of a firm's capacity. Licenses were granted or extended on the basis of a proof of transport necessity, that is, by assessing the equilibrium of the goods transport market, taking into account estimated overall capacity requirements. In order to obtain a license for a ten-year period or to increase loading capacity, the claimant had to furnish proof of a "general transport necessity." As international markets were not deemed to contribute to overall capacity in the national market, international permits were regarded as an upgrading of domestic permits and were consequently easier to obtain than the latter. A compulsory tariff system was introduced to ensure the financial health of the sector, in the sense of fair competition, and in addition, a mechanism was established that allowed the closure of the domestic market in the event of high levels of overcapacity.

The recession in the 1970s highlighted the failure of these measures to match market supply and demand; the sector suffered from overcapacity and cutthroat competition. The ineffective system of compulsory tariffs was abolished, and the government tightened restrictions to cope with oversupply by fixing a maximum loading capacity for single firms in 1975 ("tonnage-stop"). However, the new system used to regulate capacity proved insufficient, impractical, and a hindrance for economic activities and innovation.[2] Moreover, the implementation and control of the entire regulatory system was cost-intensive (ECMT 1987: 57). The lack of flexibility in the provision of transport services caused by capacity restrictions for single enterprises, the increase in the number of own-account operations, and the expense of implementing the current legislation—now inadequate given that the separation between regular and occasional services de facto no longer existed—all figured prominently on the list of disadvantages experienced by transport-related actors. The experience with the liberalized Benelux traffic and examples in the international context, such as the United States and Britain, were proof that it was indeed possible to match the increase of transport demand more efficiently.[3] By the early 1980s, all transport-related actors in the Netherlands, that is, government, regulatory agencies, industry, carriers and forwarders, were deeply dissatisfied with the existing regulatory arrangements.[4]

In 1982 a new Dutch center-right government came to power and in 1984 began to adopt a fundamental reorientation of Dutch transport policy.[5] Following the recommendations of an advisory committee,[6] and in accordance with all transport-related actors, the agenda was set for a shift toward liberalized transport markets. In 1985, the "tonnage-stop" was lifted, and the government signed an agreement with hauliers and own-account operators, trade unions, and forwarders stipulating a four-year transitional period for the introduction of a liberalized and deregulated regime (Covenant Toekomstig Wegvervoerbeleid). The preparation of the new legislation based on "Community ideas, . . . liberal ideas, and fed by the market-force thinking of the government"[7] was prepared by a steering group that presented the main lines of the future legislation. In 1988 the existing law was amended in order to introduce elements of liberalization with respect to market access for hire-and-reward services and own-account operations. The new legislation, the Road Freight Act (*Wet goederenvervoer over de weg*, Wgw), represents the logical final agreement of the fundamental about-turn experienced in the 1980s (Keus and Tweel 1991: 625) and came into force in 1992. It is fully in line with European legislation concerning the use of leased vehicles, the liberalization of cabotage, and adherence to international requirements such as the specific aspects of the Benelux agreements. The main aspects can be summarized as follows. The act abolished the distinction between regular and occasional transport and, more generally, all quantitative restrictions of market access. Instead, the conditions governing access to the sector relate to occupational qualifications, solvency, and reliability. In order to obtain a license for national transport, the claimant must meet three qualitative requirements: a certificate of reliability issued by a local authority, a certificate of professional skill based on a written examination, and a certificate of good financial standing issued by the Stichting Nationale en Internationale (NIWO).[8] Licenses for international transport are granted by the NIWO to companies holding a license for national transport. Foreign companies enjoy equal treatment with domestic firms insofar as obtaining a license for international transport from the Netherlands is not linked with registration in that country and only a complementary certificate proving professional competence in international road haulage operations is required. The Own-Account Transport Registration Foundation (SIEV), an independent governing body similar to the NIWO, is responsible for the registration of lorries—there are no license requirements for own-account transport. Apart from this regulation of market access, the new law contains a system of conditions for competition, entailing the stringent control of violations of laws on transport, road traffic, and resting and driving times in order to combat unfair competition. Severe infringements are punishable with fines or the confiscation of an operator's license.

Finally, hire-and-reward transport between the Netherlands, Belgium, and Luxembourg has undergone an accelerated process of liberalization, which took place in three steps, starting in October 1962, when the Committee of Ministers of the Benelux Economic Union eliminated quantitative restrictions on Benelux traffic; subsequently, with the liberalization of third-country traffic, that is, transport between the territory of two states or transit through a state; and finally, with the establishment of cabotage between the Benelux countries when the Wgw came into effect (Keus and Tweel 1991: 624ff.). An interesting difference between the Benelux agreements and European legislation is that while the former stipulate the country-of-origin principle with respect to wage and working conditions, general intra-EC transport is governed by the principle of territoriality (Jacobs and Herk 1995: 168).

*Fiscal Instruments*

In the Netherlands freight transport constitutes a trunk industry that is vitally important for the Dutch economy. Road transport performs a key function in national logistics, and its higher share of revenues, as opposed to other modes of freight transport, creates a vested interest in a strong road freight industry (Gwilliam 1991: 272). Given the importance of the competitive position of Dutch road hauliers in Europe, one would expect a correspondingly favorable taxation structure, but—at least at first glance—this is not the case. The reason for this is the successful attempts made by the Dutch government to reconcile fiscal imperatives with policies that stimulate the sector's efficiency and, for example, environmental objectives.

In the Netherlands, petrol and diesel taxation has been raised several times since the late 1980s and ranks above the European average, and above the agreed minimum tax stipulated by the Council of Ministers. Moreover, there is a fuel surcharge, based half on the carbon and half on the energy content of fuel. The tax is the result of a restructuring of previously separate elements of environmental legislation under the umbrella legislation of the 1993 Environmental Control Act (Wet Milieubeheer), which laid down procedures, competences, and a number of normative elements, such as the drive for the reduction of pollution levels.[9] Tax revenues are mainly transferred to the general budget, although some, including a progressive vehicle tax based on empty vehicle weight,[10] are fed into the "infrastructure fund" set up in January 1994 to provide a framework for an integrated transport infrastructure policy. The system of taxation is completed by the "Eurovignette," a road-user charging system introduced in 1996 and agreed to by Germany, Belgium, Denmark, Luxembourg, and the Netherlands in accordance with European legislation.[11]

The apparent inconsistency between comparatively high levels of taxation on the one hand, and attempts to give industry a competitive edge on the other, can be explained as follows. The Dutch government has developed two ways to reconcile the need to raise general revenues in order to reduce the budget deficit, with the need to avoid disadvantages for the Dutch transport industry, and the need to achieve political goals such as environment-friendly transport techniques. The first strategy takes the form of a simple compensation for increases in diesel tax through lower vehicle tax rates.[12] In much the same way, the Dutch Parliament agreed to raise the diesel levy by five cents as of 1 July 1997 when it agreed to compensation for heavy goods vehicles. However, the Dutch government has been increasingly forced to coordinate the compromises reached at the national level in negotiations with hauliers' associations at the European level, as in the case of the 1997 compensation that was long contested by Belgium and Luxembourg.[13] In general, the growing awareness of the European Commission concerning the illegal use of state aids or the distortion of competition restricts the established routine of compensating an increase in one form of taxation with a reduction in another. Within its policy of a "variabilization" of transport taxation, that is, an increase in variable taxation (e.g., diesel fuel and, in the longer run, road charging) and a lowering of fixed costs (e.g., vehicle taxes), the Dutch government supports an increase of the minimum excise duty at the European level.

The second strategy to compensate industry for an increase of financial burdens is more sophisticated. By developing subsidy schemes, the government was frequently able to kill two birds with one stone. Tax increases are motivated both by the general need for deficit cutting and—in the case of transport—by a need to raise variable costs. By linking a partial refunding of a tax increase to specific behavior, such as the use of environmentally friendly vehicles, the government was able to achieve additional political objectives. One example is the introduction of the "contribution scheme for low-sulfur fuel" in 1993 in anticipation of a planned reduction in the maximum permitted sulfur content in diesel fuel, subsequently terminated in 1996 when the new European directive on the sulfur content of diesel came into force. The second example is the introduction, also in 1993, of the "contribution scheme for lean-burn, low-noise truck engines" in anticipation of the implementation of Euro-2 standards for engines, which was designed to reduce the additional costs incurred by the planned legislation by providing an incentive for a rapid introduction of the new technology (Centrum voor eenergiebesparing en schone technologie 1996: 47ff.). These temporary subsidies, fueled by previous tax increases, were designed to reduce transport-related pollution and help contribute to the fact that the Dutch truck fleet is currently the cleanest in Europe (Centrum voor energiebesparing en schone technologie 1996: 49).[14]

## Changes in the Administrative Organization

The shift from regulation to stimulation not only had consequences for the use of instruments, but also brought about change in the administrative structure. Both intraministerial organization and implementation procedures were subject to reform in order to enhance the coordination and effectiveness of policymaking. The failure of the old regulatory system, the growing problems caused by inadequate infrastructure capacity, and the advent of the conflict between economic necessity (access to infrastructure) and public concern for the quality of life (livability) exposed the procedural and structural deficiencies within the Ministry of Transport and Public Works: lengthy and inflexible planning procedures, rigid hierarchical structures, and shortcomings in coordination. The ministry was arranged in what can best be described as loosely coupled units with formal rather than concrete contact (Ministerie VenW 1991: 10). The competitive relationship between units within the General Directorate for Transport expressed what was referred to as "reproduction of the substitutive relation between transport modes" (Lehmbruch 1992). Since the early 1990s, the distribution of competences within the ministry were reallocated several times, one consequence being the integration of all freight-related competences in a General Directorate for Freight Transport in May 1997,[15] which combined sea shipping, inland waterways, road, and rail transport in an attempt to approach transport policymaking in a more *coordinated* manner. Efforts were also made to reduce departmental fragmentation by increasing the coordination between the ministries, as, for example, in the 1989 National Environmental Plan.[16]

With respect to implementation, the State Traffic Inspectorate (Rijksverkeersinspectie, RVI), which has overall control responsibility for transport by road, rail, and inland waterways, is a good example of the extent to which changes in the regulatory framework are reflected in organization and procedure. Despite earlier plans, the RVI was not subject to the government's general "privatization-to-increase-efficiency" program. Instead, its autonomy was strengthened and more emphasis was placed on its participation in the policy process, so that it developed new instruments, methods, and techniques to improve control efficiency.[17] The basic idea was to intensify cooperation between the controller and the controlled in order to foster voluntary legal compliance in a "negotiation-oriented enforcement style." (RVI 1995: 3) where direct hierarchical intervention would be partly replaced by "communicative action" between public actors and their respective target groups (Grin and van de Graaf 1996).[18]

A further characteristic of the developments in Dutch road haulage is the strengthening of the self-responsibility of the industry by upgrading privatized or delegated public responsibilities such as registration (carried out by the Rijksdienst voor het Wegvervoer) or licensing. For hire-and-reward transport licensing is carried out by the National and International Road Transport Organization (Stichting Nationale en Internationale Wegvervoer Organisatie, NIWO).[19] The NIWO was founded in 1946 as a nonprofit-making interest association whose main objective was to promote Dutch international road transport. Its activities have always been public and private, covering licensing, administration, analysis of data, and participation in bilateral negotiations between the Dutch government and governments of other countries in the field of road haulage.[20] Since the early 1990s, according to the new domestic transport legislation, the formerly public body responsible for national transport licensing (Commissie Vergunningen Wegvervoer) became part of the NIWO. This left the granting of licenses for international and for national transport to the industry, so that licensing was in effect privatized, while inspection remained a public competence carried out by the Rijksverkeersinspectie. In this way the shift from strict market regulation to a liberal regime led to a reduction of government intervention and simultaneously increased the responsibility of the transport industry.

Given the growing concern about the prospects of the Dutch transport industry, both government and industry increased their common involvement in activities designed to promote the "ondernemen Nederland" ("the Dutch business firm"). In 1987, on the basis of a McKinsey report on how the Netherlands should position itself in international transport and distribution, the Ministry of Transport and Public Works, the Ministry of Economic Affairs, and the Dutch transport industry helped finance the creation of a new institution, the Dutch International Distribution Council (Stichting Nederland Distributieland, NDL),[21] with the task—transferred from the NIWO—of promoting the Dutch road transport industry and the Netherlands as the "gateway to Europe."[22]

### From Regulation to Stimulation

To sum up, the transformation of Dutch transport market regulation represents an innovative response to the impending crisis caused by the failure of existing national regulation and the advent of the Common European Transport Policy. The shift from regulating market access to stimulating innovative market dynamics reflects a change in the sectoral problem-solving philosophy. On the one hand, market mechanisms constitute the dominant mode of governing economic-exchange processes, which in turn strengthens both the self-regulation of the industry and the individual responsibility of the single firm. On the other hand, liberalization and deregulation do not automatically imply a retreat of the state, but rather a reformulation of its tasks in liberalized markets. The state, apart from safeguarding competition, took an active part in preparing the industry for future developments.

The impact of European policy demands on the use of instruments and administrative structure requires a differentiated assessment. In general, the impact on the Dutch road haulage regulation was indirect. This is not surprising when taking into account that the purpose of the Common European Transport Policy was primarily to guarantee the compatibility of national and international regulations, and not to intervene in national regulatory regimes. In the case of taxation, however, the objective of European policies was to harmonize the national systems.[23] The adaptation of the Dutch taxation system had two dimensions. The first is a rather technical one, as the divergence between the reference unit of taxation in the Dutch and the European approach required a general overhaul of the Dutch system. Second, the introduction of road user charges represented a new element for the Dutch system. The mode of adaptation to European policies can be described as *innovation*, as the harmonization and the new element were incorporated into a new approach based on a variabilization of transport taxation, that is, a reduction of fixed costs (e.g., vehicle taxes), and an increase in variable costs (e.g., diesel fuel and road charges). With respect to the liberalization of market access, the influence of Europe was also more indirect. To prepare the Dutch transport industry and to avoid a discrepancy between a liberal international regime and restrictive domestic regulations required a change in the default conditions of Dutch transport regulation. The twofold impacts were an elimination of quantitative restrictions and *institutional absorption*, as the administrative unit responsible for granting domestic licenses (CVW), was dissolved into the private institution responsible for international transport (NIWO). Finally, while the creation of an agency to promote the Dutch transport industry might indirectly be linked to the Single Market Program rather than to the advent of the Common Transport Policy, the changes in the ministerial organization were generated exclusively by national factors. But precisely what factors triggered the change in the problem-solving philosophy, and which factors explain how internal and external influences were processed?

## EXPLAINING CHANGE: DUTCH NEOCORPORATISM MEETS NEOLIBERALISM

The developments in the Dutch transport sector are characterized by the change in the problem-solving philosophy (Hall 1993). It is claimed that domestic institutional conditions mediated endogenous and exogenous pressures so as to pave the way for a reconciliation of diverging economic, political, and societal objectives such as increase of efficiency, intrasectoral and intersectoral coordination, and environmental protection and to combine them in a consistent approach. The system of interest mediation represented the decisive element for understanding exactly how the transformation of road transport regulation occurred. Before shedding light on the interaction between public and private actors that led to a change in the preferences and specific policy choices, we will sketch out the socioeconomic embeddedness of the transport sector to provide the background to these developments.

### Economic Interests

It is generally assumed that actors' preferences emanate from their position in the international and domestic economy (Gourevitch 1986, chap. 3), so that changes in the economic environment may contribute to changes in the policy preferences of the latter. In order to understand why the failure of the existing market regulation was perceived as a dramatic threat for the Netherlands, we need to understand the role of the sector in the economic and political context. As a country of traders, the Netherlands traditionally accounts for a disproportionately high share of international transport and trade relative to the small size of the country and its small domestic market. From the end of World War II until the mid-1990s, Rotterdam developed into the largest port in Europe, in terms of both size and the volume of through trade (Port of Rotterdam 1996). Today, the transport flows to and from the Netherlands that both the Port of Rotterdam and Amsterdam Schiphol Airport originate lay the basis for the development of an transport industry that has a share in intra-European transport of about 27 percent. The slogan "Nederland Distributieland" reflects the commitment of the country to the export of goods and services. Cross-border transport has been growing at a significant rate for about a decade. In 1995, the contribution of companies active in transport, distribution, warehousing, and communication to (GDP) was about 8 percent,[24] of which road haulage accounted for about 25 percent (Transport en Logistiek Nederland 1996: 21). With respect to the labor market, transport and communications contribute more than 6 percent to the total workforce, of which hire-and-reward transport accounts for about 32 percent (Transport en Logistiek Nederland 1996: 20). The Dutch road haulage industry benefited from the constant increase of goods to be transported from the country's main ports, and the industry reflected the strong international orientation of the Dutch economy and was generally considered to be highly competitive.

But since the early 1980s, the existing system of capacity restriction has proved too rigid to cope with the significant increase in the volume of transport. In particular, regulation limiting the growth of firms was perceived as a threat of the international competitiveness of the industry.[25] In addition to the shortcomings of the regulatory framework at the domestic level, the existing system of bilateral quotas governing cross-border transportation was frequently the subject of complaint. On behalf of its road haulage industry the government had to negotiate with neighboring countries, especially Germany, for an increase of the quotas for Dutch hauliers. The inconvenience caused by the existing regulation in combination with the forecasted increase of volumes to be transported internally and the development of the economic integration in Europe provoked a change in the preferences of both public and private actors. However, there was no automatic link about the path of policy and institutional change after the redefinition of preferences. As the following examples show, the patterns of interest mediation represent the connection between policy and choice, or, in other words, "between what could be done and the various factors that shape what decision-makers actually choose to do" (Gourevitch 1986: 54).

## Administrative Interest Intermediation

What is striking about the Dutch case is that the changes did not so much affect the basic form of institutionalized interactions between public and private actors, as that neocorporatist structures successfully adapted to the neoliberal context and allowed for a substantive policy change. In general, the changes in the regulation of Dutch transport markets are best conceived as a process in which public actors successfully welded together various actors into a coalition able to consider different policy objectives simultaneously. In the case of road haulage, the sectoral neocorporatism and the principles of interaction between public and private actors provide the clue for understanding the way in which the internal and external influences are processed. In what follows, the important role of state actors in establishing what can be called integrated political leadership will be described with respect to the revision of intervention style, the restructuring of the associational landscape, and the incorporation of environmental issues.

## The Revision of Transport Regulation

At the heart of the changes that characterize industrial relations in the Netherlands since the early 1980s was the awareness that the previous institutional constellation and in particular the established patterns of public–private interactions were unable to cope with the "Dutch disease," that is, the discovery of natural gas yielded a temporary income which was used to finance permanent expenditure. As a response, the "Reconsideration Program" of the first conservative–liberal government under Lubbers (1982–1986) supported a strengthening of market forces and a cutback of state intervention as the only efficient way to increase the profitability of the Dutch industry. The starting point of a general restructuring was a path-breaking agreement in which trade unions and employers' associations, under the auspices of the state, gave up obsolete and outdated positions (Visser and Hemerijck 1997). The Wassenaar Accord of 1982 unleashed energies that spread rapidly into sectors not directly linked to labor issues. Given the twofold importance of the transport sector as an infrastructure for the exchange of goods and services and as an industry in its own right, it comes as no surprise that the sector was also subject to a general overhaul in the early 1980s.

In its efforts to orchestrate the search process,[26] the Ministry for Transport and Public Works relied strongly on the participation of private actors. A key document for the development of a new division of labor between state and economic actors, or in other words, for the shift from regulating to stimulating, was the Convenant Toekomstig Wegvervoerbeleid of September 1985 and the subsequent protocol agreement signed in November 1985. The covenant and the protocol were the fruit of lengthy negotiations in which the government and all actors related to road freight transport came together to think about the future transport policy.[27] The resistance of the smaller hauliers and their associations to deregulation and liberalization diminished as the government agreed to provide the industry with enough time to prepare for a deregulated market and to accompany its competitive deregulation with a significant state guidance.[28] A whole host of supportive measures was developed that aim at the production side of enterprises, that is, the quality of transport services, the skills, and the capacities of the individual firm. Hence, the government found a strategy to reconcile two opposing concepts, that of market on the one hand and industrial policies on the other (de Bandt 1994). This was not only the starting signal for a revision of government intervention in road transport markets, but it also prompted the restructuring of the road hauliers' representation.

*The Changing Associational Landscape*

The active involvement of the government in restructuring the road haulage sector was not limited to the industry or individual firms, but also addressed its collective representation. A statement by a former minister of transport underlines this point and illustrates how the government pushed to enhance the international competitiveness of the transport industry. In an interview, Mrs. Smit-Kroes criticized both the industry and its interest organization, which asked for protectionism while at the same time making no attempt, either on an individual or collective level, to adapt to a more competitive environment. Given the government's policy mixture of financial incentives and persuasion, a significant change in the organization of interests paralleled the restructuring within the road freight sector. What characterizes the associational landscape today is first of all a high degree of concentration and well-established structures of interorganizational coordination.[29] After a number of mergers, the supply side of the transport sector is organized by two associations: the Dutch Transport and Logistics (Transport en Logistiek Nederland, TLN), representing roughly 70 percent of all hauliers, and the Royal Dutch Transport (Koninklijk Nederlands Vervoer, KNV), which organizes large companies active in freight transport by road and logistics. At the transport demand side of industry, commerce and agriculture are represented by the Employers Organization of Industry and Own-Account-Operations (Algemene Verladers en Eigen Vervoer Organisatie, EVO).

The concentration in the associational landscape was not only an important contribution to securing the transformation of Dutch transport regulation, but was also a necessary precondition for the development of an integrated problem-solving approach in the transport sector. The modus of transformation within the existing neocorporatist patterns of interaction between public and private actors would have been impossible without the centralization of interest representation and the commitment of the industry to their associations. Without this concentration the application of voluntary agreements stating the main policy targets would have been impossible. In institutional terms, voluntary agreements require, first, a state that is strong enough to replace hierarchical forms of influencing societal developments by nonhierarchical means and, second, an organization of interests sufficiently centralized to assure commitment of their constituency to binding agreements.[30] A decisive factor for the relatively smooth way in which the transformation occurred was the high level of credibility of public actors with regard to their ability to compensate potential losers (Frieden and Rogowski 1996). In general, it is assumed that potential to compensate is related to the size of a country. Small states with open and vulnerable markets have few opportunities to export or preempt the costs of change. This constraint, combined with the position of international marginality, facilitates the consensus building necessary to adapt to turbulent environments. Hence, economic openness facilitates the emergence of corporatist structures, and political and economic compensations are the currency that makes this institutional mechanism work (Katzenstein 1985).

To sum up, the search for efficiency and the concomitant change of policy preferences triggered the perceived need for change in the regulatory regime. But the actual transformation of the transport regulation took place in a process characterized by close interaction between public and private actors. Public actors, with their high level of credibility to compensate for potential losses, were able to guide a restructuring not only of the transport industry, but also of the industry's collective representation and self-regulation. The government initiated a discussion on the future of the transport industry incorporating all transport related actors. The outcome of the 'harmony-oriented' style of policymaking was a broad consensus which established the basis for a shift towards 'supply-side economics' and a parallelization between Dutch and European transport policymaking. Important prerequisites for this developments were, first, the government's acceptance of its triple function as guardian of a liberal regulation, stimulator of quality improvements, and advocate of the interests of the domestic industry at the European level. Second, the concentration process in the representation of interest contributed significantly to mode of transformation as negotiating and implementing the new approach was possible only on the basis of a representative and sufficiently well-organized counterpart. This way, the concentration of the interest representation and the government's credibility to compensate enabled the development of a medium-term approach to transport policymaking that takes into account contradicting policy objectives such as economic growth and sustainability. Thus, existing patterns of public-private interaction were strengthened rather than weakened by the application of neo-liberal policies and the advent of the Common Transport Policy. In what follows we take a closer look at the reciprocity of national—Dutch—and European policymaking.

# EUROPE AND THE TRANSFORMATION OF ROAD TRANSPORT POLICIES

## The Impact of Europe on Dutch Road Transport Policymaking

The relation between Dutch policymaking in road haulage and its European counterpart was characterized by parallelization and mutual reinforcement. Given this reciprocal influence, a short description of the Dutch attempts to influence the European level precedes the considerations of how European policies impact upon the national level. As one of the founding members of the European Economic Community (EEC), the Netherlands had always been in favor of liberalizing intra-EC road freight transport. The Port of Rotterdam and Amsterdam's Schiphol Airport were considered the engines of the Dutch economy and also play a key role in determining the "attractiveness" of the country as a location for business and industry.[31] The main objective of the Dutch government at the European level was the liberalization of international transport, in particular cabotage. To achieve this objectives, or at least to get the most out of the bargaining process, the Dutch pursued several strategies. The government engaged actively in European Court of Justice (ECJ) trials, it was busy in setting up a blocking minority,[32] it used the opportunity to send civil servants to the European Commission to monitor or push topics of specific interest for the Netherlands such as the regulation of qualitative criteria for access to transport markets, and it pushed the need to harmonize the implementation of European legislation.[33] In addition to public actors, the association of road hauliers tried to influence the policymaking process at the European level via their Brussels offices.[34] But how did European policies affect policymaking and societal structures at the domestic level?

Broadly speaking, one might say that the Dutch appeared to be the winners of European policymaking. With respect to the deregulation of international road freight transport, the Dutch achieved their main objective because quantitative restrictions for international transport have been abolished as of July 1998. The advantages for the Netherlands are twofold. First, the position of Dutch ports as "gateways to Europe" has been strengthened as intra-EC transport has been facilitated. Second, cabotage allows the Dutch to extend their activities to foreign markets, especially the German one. However, when painting the picture of the impact of European transport policies on transport policymaking in the Netherlands in more detail, the assessment has to be differentiated in the sense that there is both a direct and indirect impact. Apart from the advantages emanating from liberalized international transport, the Dutch had to make concessions on many other issues, and the introduction of user charges based on the principle of territoriality was a particularly bitter pill to swallow. As one senior civil servant put it, "We didn't succeed. We lost this struggle" (interview Ministerie VenW, December 1995). Both the Dutch government and branch associations had long opposed the introduction of road user charges based on the principle of territoriality. Resistance to charging on the basis of territoriality constituted a new component for Dutch hauliers, accustomed to a well-established routine of taxation/compensation developed between the public administration and the transport industry in the Netherlands. After the decision was taken, however, the Dutch incorporated the regulation within the approach aiming at a variabilization of transport costs.

Of key importance are effects related to European competition rules on the provision of state aids. As the description of the interaction between public and private actors has shown, compensation for costly consequences of policymaking and the use of subsidy schemes to achieve certain policy objectives were part and parcel of Dutch consensual political and administrative culture. But the more the European Commission focuses on the application of competition rules and the illegal use of state aids, the more the Dutch government is obliged to replace these traditional instruments to compensate the industry for certain policy measures by other means. Thus, while liberalization favors the international position of Dutch hauliers, competition policy impedes well-established patterns of policymaking at the national level. This brings us to the question of the impact of European integration on societal structures at the domestic level. There is good reason to assume that the progressive Europeanization of road freight transport had an impact on the concentration process of the interest-representation structures in the Netherlands. The many smaller associations would not have been able to undertake the time- and cost-intensive lobbying on a great variety of topics at the national as well as at the European level. The pressure on the internal legitimacy turned out to be strong enough to help surmount sociocultural boundaries between different associations and led to a merging of resources.[35]

Finally, the advent of the Common Transport Policy impacted only indirectly on the reform of Dutch road haulage regulation. This is not surprising when taking into account that European policymaking is mainly concerned with the liberalization of international transport and leaves national regimes virtually untouched. Neither European legislation on the liberalization of international transport and cabotage nor the power of market forces in an integrated and liberalized market creates pressure that requires an adaptation of national legislation. Rather, the reference to Europe has a persuasive quality, and the knowledge that "in Brussels they were thinking along other lines" (interview Ministerie VenW, November 1995) strengthened the governments argument concerning the need to reform and redirect existing legislation. At the same time, the prospect of economics gains emanating from the liberalization of European transport markets eased the negotiating and compromising between public and private actors at the national level. In this respect it is interesting to note that the 1985 agreement between public and private actors on the transformation of the Dutch transport regulation included not only a shift from regulation to stimulation, but also the government's commitment to assume the role of advocate and guardian of road hauliers' interests in the European negotiation process. Hence, the "Europe-as-a-resource" argument may be interpreted not only as a way for governmental actors to pursue unpopular policy at the domestic level, but also as an amplifier of national policy objectives—that is, as a mechanism for exporting domestic policy preferences (Kassim and Menon 1996: 6; Héritier, Knill, and Mingers 1996).[36]

## The Transformation of Dutch Road Freight Policy

The striking feature of this shift from regulation to stimulation is that neither the execution of neoliberal policies nor the advent of European transport regulations led to a weakening of the neocorporatist patterns of public–private interaction. Rather, the government succeeded in bundling all relevant forces into a consultative and consensual decision-making process with the overarching objective of maintaining the competitiveness of the road haulage industry. The national actors perceived the emerging European regime as a potential economic gain and strategically chose to anticipate the liberalization. The perspective of a potential gain emanating from liberalization facilitated government efforts to unite the transport industry behind its policy objectives and to compensate potential losers in the process. In this general atmosphere of trust in the interaction with private actors and given the government's proved credibility, it was able to develop a medium-term perspective for the development of the sector.

The transformation of road haulage regulation in the Netherlands is characterized by a new contract between public and private actors. On the one hand, the market is accepted as the basic mechanism governing interaction of private actors. On the other hand, deregulation and liberalization did not equate to a retreat of the state. Running alongside the liberalization of market access and the deregulation of market functioning went a revision of the tools and instruments used by government. First, the subsequent strengthening of the monitoring function documented that competition is a fragile system that requires protection. Second, the launching of promotion and development schemes either to back the competitiveness of the Dutch transport industry or to curb the negative effects of road transport shows that deregulation and liberalization need not necessarily mean less government intervention.

Essential elements of these plans were an increasing incorporation of environmental issues and, last but not least, a modal shift from road to rail. It was this context in which the reform of the Dutch railways took place in the late 1980s.

## THE REFORM OF THE DUTCH RAILWAYS: FOSTERING THE NEGLECTED CHILD

As has been shown, a separation of public and private responsibilities was at the heart of the regulatory reform of Dutch road haulage markets. This also holds true for the core of the reform of the Dutch railways (Nederlandse Spoorwegen, NS). The decision to end the monopoly of the NS by separating infrastructure-related issues from operations laid the basis for a general distinction between the public and the private sphere, between public responsibilities and private business, and between state intervention and market competition. The development can be seen less as a withdrawal of government and more as a reallocation of responsibilities in order to reduce the tension between a predilection for free trade and an active role on the part of government. Thus, in much the same way as for road haulage, the future role of government is not restricted to guaranteeing the framework within which competition operates, but implies a guiding of socioeconomic behavior.

Comparing the reform of the road and the railways, one has to say that the changes in the rail sector were more radical than in road haulage. This is due to the fact that the application of the new approach to transport policymaking to the rail sector turned out to be more complicated and witnessed significantly more far-reaching consequences than in the road case. In particular, the institutionalized involvement of the state in both the daily and the strategic business of the railways hampered the disentanglement of private and public functions and responsibilities.

The purpose of the following analysis is to display the complexity of the problem constellation and the solutions found to resolve this, to analyze what structured and influenced both process and outcome of the reform, and to assess the impact of European policies on the Dutch reform process. The proposition is that, faced with a failure of existing regulation, the Dutch government selected a model proposed in the European context and integrated it into a far-reaching reform concept that, in turn, serves as a reference model for future European railway policies. Hence, similar to road haulage, parallelism and mutual reinforcement characterize Dutch and European railway policies. This section analyzes the reform of the railways first by presenting the changes in the regulatory framework, by offering an explanation for the change, and, finally, by assessing the impact of European policies on the Dutch reform.

## The Regulatory Framework

### Past History

In the Netherlands, a state-owned public limited liability company, N.V. Nederlandse Spoorwegen (NS), was traditionally responsible for freight and passenger rail transport. NS was owned by the state, and the company was under control of the Ministry of Transport and Public Works. Direct control of the NS was exercised not on the basis of statute but on certain provisions in its articles of association and a contract that imposed a universal transport obligation on the NS and stipulated the right of the ministry to set transport rates and conditions.

After World War II, passenger and freight transport by rail developed along different lines. The heterogeneous development was best expressed by an internal NS decision in 1967 to consider passenger transport as the "main product" and freight transport as a "by-product" (Zijderveld 1989: 271).[37] The differentiation between passenger and freight transport was underlined by a separation of accounting from 1967 onward. In consequence, the passenger transport of the NS developed into a kind of nationwide operating public transport undertaking with a dense timetable of regular departures,[38] whereas freight transport simply cut all loss-making services and operates on a strictly commercial basis. While this strategy could forestall the accumulation of new debts, it could not stop the declining share of the railways in the modal split. The increasing financial demand for passenger transport contributes to a continuation of the negative trend—an important reason for the Dutch reform.[39]

Fiscal considerations aside, efforts to revitalize freight transport by rail were to a large extent due to pressure that stemmed from economic and social actors at the domestic level. On the one hand, the limitations of the existing infrastructure tended to endanger the transit of goods via the ports Rotterdam and Schiphol. Thus, bottlenecks and road congestion were perceived as a threat for the Netherlands as the "gateway to Europe." On the other hand, in a general atmosphere of growing environmental consciousness, the public awareness of the negative effects of freight transport by road increased and exerted pressure on political actors. Pressure at the domestic level was reinforced by international developments as some countries, especially Austria and Switzerland, demonstrated an increased political willingness to shift freight transport from road to rail.[40]

Given this problem constellation, a broad consensus for a strengthening of the railways emerged and was absorbed by the Dutch government. The Ministry of Economic Affairs favored rail, as it improves the access to the main harbors and as it is an additional option for the providers of logistics and distribution services. The Ministry of Environment and Spatial Planing took a pro-rail stance on the grounds that it contributes to the sustainability of transport. The Ministry of Transport and Public Works incorporates the pro-rail position in the face of increasing environmental concerns, dramatically increased congestion problems on roads, and bottom-up pressure from congested provinces and municipalities.[41] While the NS made use of the pro-rail tailwind and offered offensive reorganization plans that would have left the NS as a integrative unit, Parliament and government followed the recommendations of two commissions (the "van der Plas Commission" of 1989 and the "Wijffels Commission" of 1992), which lay the foundation for a general restructuring of the Dutch railways.[42]

## The New Structure

The reorganization of the Dutch railways followed the general principles laid down in the 1992 Wijffels report. As of January 1996, Netherlands Railways is now formed of independent legal entities.[43] There has been a debt release, and, with the exception of infrastructure, the property rights have been shifted to the NS. Organizationally, two main groups have been established. The first comprises the *government-commissioned sector* in which the so-called task organizations or agencies perform infrastructure-related activities. The three divisions—capacity management and licensing (Railned), traffic control (NS Verkeersleiding), and rail infrastructure maintenance and construction (NS Railinfrabeheer)—perform public functions, that is, they operate as instructed by, and for, the account of central government.

The second pillar of the grouping encompasses the *market-oriented components*. The commercial part of the NS, the NS Groep, is characterized by three main types of business. The first type consists of four core activities: freight (NS Cargo), passenger (NS Reiziger), real estate (NS Vastgoed), and stations (NS Stations). The business units are the main revenue-generating activities and operate on a return-for-investment basis. To underline this status several financial arrangements have been made to reduce the government's operating grant to zero by the end of the 1990s. The second type consists of the support services to the four core activities, including rolling stock maintenance, personnel, research, training, and ancillary companies. The third category compromises a number of subsidiary companies in which the NS Groep is a majority shareholder.

## Preparing for Competition

The description of the reorganization scheme shows that the disentanglement between public and private responsibilities and tasks is the underlying theme of the Dutch railway reform. In institutional terms, this means a vertical and horizontal separation of functions with each segment embedded within a regulatory framework appropriate to its politically assigned function. On the one hand, all infrastructure-related tasks are assigned to the government-commissioned sector to reinforce their public character and to ensure governmental influence for reasons of coordination. On the other hand, the horizontal separation of operations has been regarded as a precondition to set the agenda for competition. Provided with an increased managerial autonomy and financially put on an even keel, the main products of the NS—passenger and freight transport—are now, though to a different degree, subject to competitive environments.

### The Vertical Dimension

The decision to split up the formerly integrated railway organization and to institutionalize the vertical separation of infrastructure and operations in the Netherlands goes beyond the requirements of EC Directive 91/440 and its daughter directives (EC Directives 95/18 and 95/19). This caused a number of problems; nevertheless, the decision to keep infrastructure-related questions under public auspices was seen as an important precondition for the simultaneous presence of public intervention alongside competition. The solutions found were related to the problems of how to administer the infrastructure, how to allocate and charge for the use of the railtracks, and how to deal with the question of property rights and responsibility for infrastructure investments.

*Management of the Infrastructure.* To underline their public character, all infrastructure-related issues are assigned to the task organization of the government-commissioned sector, consisting of Railned, NS Infrabeheer, NS Verkeersleiding and NS Railinfratrust. Within these organizations, Railned as the body responsible for the allocation of infrastructure, licensing, and charging caused the major discussions. Railned is responsible for the capacity management and the safety of the rail infrastructure and shares responsibility for capacity management with NS Verkeersleiding.[44] According to the government's claim, a restrictive policy is applied to new licenses for transport by rail. For a transitional period, licenses for passenger transport are granted only if there is free infrastructure capacity and the new services "add significantly" to existing supply by the NS (NRC Handelsblad 1997a: 1).[45]

Railned is part of the government-commissioned task-organizations under the umbrella of the NS. To ensure a nondiscriminatory performance, it has to report to a special supervisory board appointed by the government. After a transitional period of five years ending in 1999, there will be a revision of the performance and positioning of Railned. Both the ministry and Railned were convinced that after the transitional five-year period Railned will be taken out of the NS organ-ization.[46] In late autumn of 1999, however, there were clear signs that the transi-tional period for the final positioning of the regulator would be extended for at least one year.

*Allocation Principles and Charging.*    The ministry considers the task organi-zations as "extensions of government."[47] which operate as instructed by, and on account of, central government. Railned is responsible for the allocation of the in-frastructure and charging and has to execute government decisions relating to them. With respect to the allocation function, this implies that Railned has to de-velop principles consonant with government policies, that is, boosting the num-ber of passengers while simultaneously encouraging a modal shift for freight transport from road to rail. Passenger transport has traditionally enjoyed prefer-ential treatment, but this is due to change under the new regime. The problem of allocating existing infrastructure either to passenger or to goods transport has proved extremely difficult to resolve given the consequent clash of public inter-ests. Help is expected to come from the Betuwe line, a new freight-only railway running from Rotterdam to the German border.[48] But until its completion in 2004, the allocation of scarce infrastructure resources will mean permanent compro-mising between conflicting interests (Ranke 1996).

Concerning infrastructure charging, the ministry's decision to suspend the levying of charges until the year 2000, is a way of gaining time. A transitional pe-riod is necessary for the rail transport companies to adapt to, or prepare for, the new market situation, and for Railned to develop a differentiated charging scheme. The criteria of the new charging system will have to extend to other modes of transport, using a similar approach for road, rail, and inland waterways, with the Ministry of Transport developing a framework for an integrated ap-proach to infrastructure charging, with the added difficulty that this must be in line with an—as yet undefined—European approach.

*Property Rights and Investments.*    A further point of discussion between the Ministry of Transport and the NS has been the question of how to handle infra-structure property rights. The former argued that as the existing infrastructure had been built up with public money it should stay within the public realm, whereas the latter saw the private ownership of the means of production as an indispensa-ble precondition for the commercial management of the railways. The final com-promise assigned responsibility for the existing infrastructure to the government-commissioned sector but separated the legal ownership (assigned to NS Railinfratrust) and economic ownership (assigned to NS Railinfrabeheer).[49] NS Railinfrabeheer is responsible for the rail infrastructure maintenance and con-struction of new infrastructure. Funding for the construction of new tracks is to be provided by government. For the purpose of an integrated infrastructure pol-icy, a separated infrastructure budget (the infrastructure fund) was introduced in January 1994 and is partly funded by levies of the transport sector (e.g., taxes on vehicles, oil, and infrastructure use).

The creation of the infrastructure fund is indicative of the government's intention of controlling future developments. It is obliged to finance new infrastructures for all modes of transport, thus stressing the public responsibility for infrastructure investments. Moreover, it represents a step toward a more integrated transport policymaking that accepts the decisive impact of infrastructure investments on the modal split (Ostrowski 1993). In this respect, the fund allows government to exert a legitimate influence on future developments. As direct intervention in favor of a certain mode is not in accordance with free-market approach, the government exerts a guiding or steering influence more indirectly by supporting measures. These measures range from decisions on infrastructure investments—with the freight-only Betuwe line as an extreme example—to measures such as the stimulation of intermodal cooperation by means of fiscal incentives, by stimulating research, or by providing financial support for investments.

## The Horizontal Dimension

The separation of the main operation related functions is one of the basic ingredients of the Dutch railway reorganization. A holding company within the NS, the NS Groep NV, consists of several formerly integrated units separated into a number of activities in order to increase their task related profile, to increase the transparency of their accounting, and to improve their responsiveness to market requirements in qualitative and quantitative terms. Though there are several interesting developments in some units with respect to cost-consciousness, inspired not least by European procurement provisions (van Empel 1997), the following description concentrates on the freight and passenger segments, which both illustrate the specific problems related to the transformation of the railways in general and the introduction of competition in particular.

*The Freight Sector.* The relaunching of the rail freight sector was helped by two important prior developments. First, NS had laid the basis for an internal reform with its plan, "RAIL 21 CARGO," which changed the long-standing product-oriented approach dominant in NS customer relations to one emphasizing the ability to respond flexibly to market and customer requirements (*Railway Gazette International* 1994: 663). Second, the need to invest in rail infrastructure had already been emphasized by the "van der Plas Commission" as the sine quo non for a revival of the railways, and the NS had integrated this recommendation in its plans. Strong economic and social pressure paved the way for the incorporation of both ideas into the Second Structural Traffic Transport Plan presented by the government in June 1990. While the Betuwe line has for a long time been the subject of an intensive public debate on its cost and the environmental damage, the main parts of the "RAIL 21 CARGO" represented the starting point of the negotiations between the Ministry of Transport and the NS.

NS Cargo was given the legal status of a shareholder company, allowing it to enter into contracts with third parties and allowing third parties to buy shares of the freight company. Though the final report that the working party handed in

October 1994 did not give answers to all the questions, the NS Cargo has been established as a joint-stock company with a healthy balance sheet (in January 1995). Only after lengthy negotiations and after McKinsey & Company made an evaluation of the NS business plan[50] did the government and the NS agree at the end of 1996 on the amount of the final donation (about Dfl. 190 million). But increased managerial freedom is only one part of the efficiency coin, risk being the other. The more radical school of thought within the ministry considered that rail freight did not automatically have to remain in the hands of the NS,[51] and that private, domestic or foreign, interests to purchase the ownership of the rail freight company may be a possible option in the future.[52]

The first competitors for the NS Cargo appeared in 1997, but the absence of binding regulations for market access hampered the development of the Bentheimer Eisenbahn, ACTS, and ShortLines (NRC Handelsblad 1997b: 7). NS Cargo had developed two forms of cooperative strategy to take the wind out of new operators' sails. An example of the first is the "European Rail Shuttle," a co-operation of three shipping companies—Sealand, Nedlloyd, P&P Containers, and the NS Cargo, which connects Rotterdam and Milan on a daily basis. An example of the second form of cooperation is the NDX, consisting of NS Cargo, the rail freight unit of the Deutsche Bahn AG and the U.S. railway company CXS, the parent company of the shipping company Sealand.

*The Passenger Sector.* The *passenger segment* has not been subjected to a strict transformation in the same way as the freight unit. Rather, the peculiarities of the subsector led to a rather timid preparation for a competitive environment. Given the higher share of passenger transport by rail in the modal split, the large number of public and private actors involved, and the uncertain consequences of a more liberal regime, the government was relatively cautious about introducing market mechanisms. Indeed, it has frequently been stated that despite all the former efforts to increase its efficiency, the NS is neither prepared for competition *for* the tracks or for competition *on* the tracks.

Although NS Reizigers was not given the same legal status as the NS Cargo, the reform agenda envisaged making passenger transport as commercial as possible. The relation between the government and the NS was transformed in such a way as to significantly increase the independence of the company and to drastically cut back on the opportunities for government intervention in its management. This applies, for example, to the tariff structure that is now fixed by the NS and no longer requires ministerial approval, and for all redistributive objectives for which government had previously instrumentalized the NS.[53] With the introduction of the "user pays principle," the NS must be paid for all politically imposed services—public-service obligations, exceptional travel conditions, or the operation and frequency of departures[54]—and, according to the private legal status of the NS, these agreements with the Ministry of Transport or an other public entity and the NS must take the form of civil law contracts.

A characteristic of this framework is the distinction between a "contract sector" and a "noncontract sector." The former comprises all transport that is not profitable but that must be maintained for political reasons. In this segment there will be competition *for* the tracks in which the NS or new companies, either Dutch or foreign, with or without participation of the NS, compete for concessions on certain lines or in specific regions (Ministerie VenW 1997, Bijlage 1: 2). Such a system would be in line with the proposal made in the European Commission's green paper on "The Citizens' Network" (CEC 1995c: 8). The legal framework in the "noncontract sector" is still undefined,[55] but there is a consensus that there should be competition between private companies *on* the tracks with no subsidies payable by government (Ministerie VenW 1997, Bijlage 1: 1–2).

For a transitional stage, that is, until the year 2000, market access to the passenger transport sector will be handled restrictively. Whereas in the freight sector open competition on the tracks is—at least theoretically—possible, NS Reizigers enjoys special treatment in preparation for the introduction of unhampered competition in public transport from the year 2000 onward (Ministerie VenW 1997: 4). Until that time, arrangements will be governed by an interim contract between the government and NS, and a restrictive licensing policy will only allow a limited and phased market access for new competitors.

In 1996, the first enterprise appeared that is testing the ministry's declared intention to liberalize the rail network and establish competition. The company Lovers is challenging the monopoly of the NS by running a service on tracks abandoned by the railway more than a decade ago. In March 1997, Lovers was given a concession on the core network of the NS, a frequently used line between Amsterdam and Haarlem (NRC Handelsblad 1997: 3). In its attempt to obtain further concessions on the core network, Lovers is backed by its major shareholder, the French Compagnie Générale d'Entreprises Automobiles (CGEA).[56]

To sum up, at the heart of the railway reform in the Netherlands lies the disentanglement of the public and private spheres. An organizational splitting up of the railways along vertical and horizontal lines allows policymakers to reconcile opposing concepts. On the one hand, keeping infrastructure-related tasks in the public domain, that is, under the control of the government, is indicative of the ability of public actors to coordinate future developments. On the other hand, the market principle will govern the relation between railway operations of freight and passenger transport. For that purpose, the managerial autonomy of the NS and its subunits has been strengthened and their financial situation improved. The internal organization of the railways, that is, the distinction between transport of passengers and freight, facilitated the horizontal splitting up of the operational services. However, the introduction of competition occurred to different degrees across the two sectors.[57] In the freight sector, there has been an uncompromising market approach, which gave NS Cargo the greatest possible freedom. In this respect, rail freight is put on the same private footing as any road freight company.

It was, however, far more difficult to transfer the market philosophy to rail passenger transport, mainly due to the sector's high political salience, the involvement of a huge variety of actors, considerable public sensitivity, and the uncertainty arising from the lack of experience with independently operating rail companies. Hence, competition in the rail passenger market was not introduced immediately, but took place but in a typically Dutch way, that is, limited and guided by the administration (Ministerie VenW 1997: 9).

Having said this, it is apparent that the reform of the Dutch railways did not follow the path taken by liberalization and commercialization in Britain, but assumed elements characteristic of the Netherlands. The following section examines what triggered the reform and how the outcome was linked to the Dutch institutional context and to European policies.

## EXPLAINING CHANGE: DOMESTIC PROBLEMS MEET THE EUROPEAN MODEL

The failure of the domestic regulatory regime fueled intensive interaction between public and private actors on the future railway regulation in much the same way as road haulage. The process revealed analogies between the two subsectors in terms of outcomes. As the new regulations allow policymakers to pursue different objectives simultaneously, an efficiency-oriented revitalization of the railways was regarded as an opportunity to tackle the economic transport demand without relinquishing the right to coordinate development.

The history of the reform underlines the broad consensus among political, economic, and societal actors in favor of a strengthening of the railways. Key economic actors such as the Port of Rotterdam—feared for its competitiveness in comparison to its European rivals—pleaded for a strengthening of the railways as a supporting mode of transport. Furthermore, increasing public concern about the negative external effects of freight transport fueled significant environmental concern and, given the relative openness of the Dutch political system,[58] placed environmental issues squarely on the political agenda from the mid-1980s onward. Finally, in order to tackle infrastructure and environment-related problems, governments in the Netherlands had always supported a fully developed system of public transport, but the success of these efforts have been limited. The increase of mass private mobility continued apace, while the deficit caused by unprofitable public rail transport increased constantly. This constellation endangered not only the government's attempts to curb public spending at the national level, but, given the advent of the European Monetary Union with its strict financial criteria, also threatened to have a negative impact on the position of the Netherlands at the European level in its efforts "to green" the European Monetary Union's policies.

Given these pressures and the awareness that road transport alone would not be able to cope with an ever-increasing volume of freight transport, the government started to revise its policies from the mid-1980s onward and fostered the long neglected child of freight rail transport. The major feature of the new policymaking approach was the drive to take the interdependence of different modes of transport and their interaction more into account. *Coordination* became a major theme of an approach striving to integrate different subsystems.[59] But the integration of passenger and freight transport into the same organization and their dependence on the same infrastructure hampered the development of a solution aiming exclusively at resolving the problems of one subsector.

In view of the undisputed need to strengthen the role of the NS, the government drew strength from a European policy model. The model proposed by EC Directive 91/440 fell on fertile ground, as it matched proposals made earlier in the Netherlands by the "van der Plas Commission" (1989), the Sociaal Economische Raad, and the Voorlopige Raad voor het Vervoer (1990).[60] Most important, the model entailed the splitting up of the complex problem structure related to the railways and allowed policymakers to deal with specific problems sequentially. Moreover, it fitted well with the emerging Dutch approach of integrated transport policymaking, as the provisions enshrined in the regulation left sufficient room for the Dutch government to incorporate its own policy views while transforming the provisions into national legislation.

The directive and its daughter directives (EC Directives 95/18 and 95/19) were the result of a negotiation process characterized by the resistance of some members states—notably Belgium, France, and Spain—to a far-reaching liberalization of rail transport (Kerwer and Teutsch in this volume). Consequently, the directive only stipulated a limited number of binding provisions regarding the four key issues that emerge after the transformation of a former public utility: the relation between regulator and the regulated; the political determination of objectives for the regulator; a fixing of competences and resources of the regulator; and the control of the regulator (Grande 1997: 587ff.). Answers to all four aspects had to be found at the national level in the interaction of the Dutch government and its prime interlocutor, the Dutch railways.

## The Government and the NS: A Fighting Cooperation

The outcome of the railway reform was to a great extent shaped by the interaction between the Ministry of Transport and the NS. Compared to the road haulage reform, the transformation was much more controversial, and the interaction took the shape of a "fighting cooperation."[61] Although the ministry and the NS shared the same broad objective, that of boosting the railways, their concrete approaches to that objective differed significantly. The recommendations of the "van der Plas Commission" marked a decisive step toward a reorientation of Dutch railway policy. The negative environmental consequences of individual mass mobility and freight transport by road created a broad consensus among social and economic actors that passenger and freight transport by rail should be strengthened. The NS took up this rail renaissance with the publication in 1988 of a plan setting out the main objectives for passenger transport by rail and subsequently integrated in the Second Traffic and Transport Scheme published in 1990 (Ministerie VenW 1990).[62] In 1990, it followed suit with a plan to increase market share by internal reorganization, "RAIL 21 CARGO." Freight transport was to be incorporated into a separate company responsible to an NS holding company. But this time the government did not refer to the NS proposals for a cautious move toward the organizational separation of different tasks without destroying the structural unit of the railway company, but instead followed the more radical scheme proposed by the "Wijffels Commission," whose recommendations were more in line with the new regulatory approach of the government toward transport markets, that is, to establish the market principle wherever possible while maintaining government's prerogative to intervene where necessary. The more the new concept to approach different subsectors of transport in a similar and integrated fashion took shape, the more the government became convinced that any watering down of its ideas would mean falling short of its declared objectives.

Hence, the starting points of the negotiations diverged significantly for the two parties. On the one hand, the NS had a relatively strong position based on successful internal reforms, experience in drawing up plans, and strong public support for the railways. The railway unions contributed to the strong role of the NS. The unions also supported the reform because they foresaw a possible strengthening of the railways. Faced with the European legislation, they accepted the need to restructure but, like the NS, opposed a splitting up of the railways. This accord between the unions and the NS ended, however, when the issue of staff reductions was touched. Though the, almost unavoidable, staff reductions were cushioned by social plans including early retirement plans, there was unease at various locations within the NS.[63] The strong position of the NS, on the other hand, met the government as a very powerful interlocutor with specific interests and resources. The government was striving to curb its regulatory intervention in transport markets, had a more clearly developed concept of how to approach transport-related problems, and could cite European legislation. In addition, as in the case of the business plan of the NS, the government referred to external expertise of independent consultancies to evaluate the internal calculations of the NS management (see above).

Given this constellation, the negotiations between the government and the railways proved relatively difficult. Both the deeply rooted delineation of political and societal actors in the Netherlands to solve their conflicts peacefully rather than adversarially and the de facto impossibility of pushing through individuals' position against the resistance of the respective interlocutor generated compromises that smoothed the process of transformation. The outcome of the reform, an interim agreement between the government and NS, made it easier not only for the NS but also for the railway unions to participate in the restructuring of the railways. It largely conserved the existing arrangements between the state and the NS and imposed a restrictive licensing policy until the year 2000. Nevertheless, the agreement signed in 1995 between the government and the NS put the relationship between the two parties on a new footing. Despite the need to compromise, the outcome reflects the main features of the new Dutch approach to transport markets: the disentanglement of private and public functions, and a maintained governmental prerogative to coordinate in order to achieve intramodal and intermodal objectives.

For example, one important element of the reform was the allocation of infrastructure-related questions to a government-commissioned sector, which enabled the government to retain development under its own control. Although the government had to compromise, at least for a transitional period, with regard to the positioning of Railned as the body responsible for capacity allocation and licensing, the basic principles remained intact. These were, first, to remove this key function from the influence of the operational services and, second, to place it in sufficiently close proximity to government to be able to exert influence on the management. Although Railned and the other functional organizations are not part of the Ministry of Transport, they are seen as "extensions of government." Thus, the principles of allocation, charging, and infrastructure building are to a large extent prescribed by government. This applies to the transitional period in which all actors have to adapt to, or prepare for, the new framework. It is not yet clear what answers will be found to the four questions regarding the role, objectives, competences, and control of the regulator in the highly probable event that Railned will be completely removed from the NS organization after 1999. However, there is little doubt that this removal will occur and that there will be some governmental influence on Railned.[64] In any case, the introduction of a regulator is a new element in Dutch railway policy, while the fact that this newly created regulator was located within the organizational structure of the regulated industry is as such remarkable.

Regarding the field of operation, it turned out to be much more difficult to transfer the market philosophy to rail passenger transport. This is mainly due to the sector's high political salience, the clash of two different policy objectives, that is, to shift individual mobility from road to rail and to strengthen the market principle in passenger transport by rail, and finally, the uncertainty arising from the lack of experience with independently operating rail companies. These considerations together with the strong position of the NS, its social backing, and its marketing concepts in the negotiations with government may explain why the question of competition has been dealt only with relative caution in the rail passenger segment. This, however, does not mean that the government sacrificed its concept of separating public and private responsibilities. The example of what is known as the "contract sector" may illustrate two things. First, public actors at the national or subnational level bear a clear financial responsibility for the provision of required services. Second, the attempt to introduce competition for a certain line or region, in other words, the competitive battle for the network, suggests that public financial responsibility and the competition between private actors are not mutually exclusive. The situation in the "noncontract sector" is to some extent easier, as a market for services will be established by the application of the competition-on-the-tracks principle.

## The Impact of Europe on Dutch Railway Policymaking

Over time, the impact of Europe appears to have shifted from secondary to primary importance in the shaping of railway policymaking in the Netherlands. Despite their limited legal impact, European policies serve as a point of reference for the Dutch reform, and one can justifiably describe the relation between the European and the Dutch approach to the regulation of the railways as one of parallelization. However, it is necessary to explain the, at times subtle, influence of the European level in a more differentiated manner.

In contrast to the director of the NS, Robert van Besteu, who states that "it all started in Brussels" (*Railway Gazette International* 1994: 663), there is indeed good reason to place the origins of the reorganization of the railways at the national level and to assume that international and European developments only played a secondary role in the early phase. However, the argument changes when one looks at the reform model chosen in the Netherlands. Here, one has to agree with his description of the Netherlands as "always a star pupil in the European class . . . quick to respond to the directive" (*Railway Gazette International* 1994: 663). Indeed, the Dutch not only transposed the directive but went even further by establishing vertical institutional separation. The model finally chosen in the Netherlands is a mixture of market-oriented and welfare-state-oriented elements, not dissimilar to an earlier Swedish model established in 1988.[65] This illustrates the close relationship between the flow of ideas and concepts at the domestic and the European level, national and supranational bodies, and EC member states and the international context. The mutual exchange and fertilization between different levels and actors make it difficult to isolate single causal explanations or to define the direction of influence. In contrast to the liberalization of international road freight and cabotage, the European provisions concerning the railways intervened directly in existing national legislation and require implementation by the national governments. Nevertheless, the content of the European legislation is far too weak to prescribe a specific model of transposition. In the Dutch case, Europe neither functioned as a catalyst for a reform nor prescribed a specific form of implementation, but constituted a *focal point* for a basic reform model. In the last instance, it was domestic factors that determined the specific national application.

In relation to the developments at the domestic level, the European dimension played a minor role until the end of the 1980s. Whereas one can reasonably rule out a European impact for the initiation of the railway reform, it is justified to presume a certain European impact for the concrete shaping of the reform. Both the "Wijffels Commission" and the government had compared the ideas and models current in the European context and finally selected that most appropriate to the Dutch institutional context. Moreover, within the process of transformation the "Europe-as-a-resource phenomenon" could have been observed. Either to justify the dimensions of the reform steps taken or to overcome resistance, actors exploited the European legislation as a resource to back their arguments in interaction with other actors at the domestic level. This applies to the Ministry of Transport in the negotiations with the NS and the railway unions, and to the latter, which hid behind EC Directive 91/440 when faced with the need to explain the expected reorganization and redundancies to their members.[66] In both cases, the reference to the European legislation either legitimized a declared position or shifted the buck to European institutions.

### Summing Up the Reform of the Dutch Railways

The existing regulatory framework for the Dutch railways failed in a twofold sense. It could not prevent the steady decline of the share of freight transport by rail in relation to road transport and inland waterways, and it was unable to halt the steady increase in the public transport deficit. Faced with a multiple problem structure revolving around economic and environmental concerns, a broad consensus emerged in favor of strengthening the railway system. Under the influence of European ideas and with Europe as a point of reference, national efforts to reinforce the railway system led to a far-reaching reform concept that went beyond the European legislation, whose main elements were a splitting up of the until then integrated unity along vertical and horizontal lines. In institutional terms, the ending of the railway monopoly brought about a clear separation of private business and public responsibilities. While passenger and freight transport were to be governed by the market principle with quality, pricing, and services as the currency of competition, all infrastructure-related tasks were to be performed in the public domain. In terms of process, a consensus-oriented approach brought about a number of consequences that smoothened the transformation process, such as the transitional period that postponed the final decision on the positioning of Railned as the newly created regulator, the controlled introduction of competition in the passenger segment, and the use of social measures to cushion redundancies.

## CONCLUSION

The final reflections on the reform of the Dutch regulatory regime in the transport sector address two issues: What characterizes the new approach to transport policymaking? And how has European political integration impacted on the content of the new approach and the way in which it has been achieved?

An important finding that emerges from the case studies is that the liberalization and deregulation of transport markets in the Netherlands are managed as a "continuous program" based on a relatively "consistent approach." The term *continuous program* refers, first and foremost, to the specific way in which the reform of a given subsector is pursued. In general, single reform packages do not initiate immediate, radical change. In order to smoothen the transformation process and to avoid the situation where acceptable proposals are made hostage to more controversial ones, the transformation processes are stretched and the introduction of radical measures takes places in a controlled way. Examples include the seven years that elapsed between the general agreement, on the part of the government and the road haulage industry, the realization of a liberalized market in 1992, and the introduction of "managed competition" in railway passenger transport. Moreover, the term *continuous program* indicates how a reform of the entire transport system requires a coordinated reform of the various subsectors of which it consists. Starting with aviation and road haulage, government reformed, or plans to reform, the framework for the railways and inland waterways (until the year 2000), while the deregulation of public passenger transport and taxicab markets is currently under consideration. While taking into account the subsectoral characteristics, the reforms always follow the same principles, which leads us to the underlying "consistent approach."

Since the mid-1990s, Dutch governments have continuously reworked their approach to tackle the perennial problems of transport: congestion, accidents, and pollution (Gibbs 1997). The basic elements of the new approach are a disentanglement of public and private responsibilities and a sustained governmental claim for intersectoral and intrasectoral coordination. In both areas, competition between private suppliers of transport services was considered the best way to realize an efficient transport system. Moreover, in both areas the retreat of the state cannot be equated with its complete withdrawal. Rather, the maintained guiding or steering claim of government is no longer exercised by state presence or other forms of direct intervention but by the use of supporting measures of which investment infrastructure is the most obvious and long-term form. In the case of road haulage, backing financial loans or initiating research are examples of a shift from regulation to stimulation.

An interesting aspect of the transformation process in Dutch transport policy is that the governmental approach to "control at arm's length" or to "steer from a distance" (Cath et al. 1994; Kickert 1993) implied a strengthening of the sector-specific patterns of interest mediation. In road haulage the long established interaction between administration and interest associations together with the centralization of interest representation allow them to reach voluntary agreements. Given the particular status of the NS and specific constellations characterizing the transformation of an interbureaucratic interaction to a more familiar interaction between public and private actors, this is dominated by contract-based arrangements. Common to both patterns of formalized interaction between private and public actors is the fact that they simultaneously guarantee two things — the (managerial) autonomy of economic actors, and a governmental guiding option.

The transformation of both road transport regulation and the railway reform demonstrated that the social and institutional embededdness of the Dutch economy is the major factor explaining how influences from the domestic and European levels are processed into a specific outcome. While geopolitical factors and culturally or economically rooted ideologies may contribute to certain policy preferences, it is the domestic sociopolitical configuration that constitutes the decisive element linking policy preferences and outcomes. The way in which influences are processed is precisely the "junction where the quality or style of a political economy makes a difference" (Willke 1995: 342). Furthermore, although there are few de jure veto points in the "decentralized unitary state" (Toonen 1987), a hierarchical imposition of policies is alien to the Dutch policymaking tradition where cooperation and compromise characterize policymaking and implementation is frequently delegated to the respective branch of industry. Neither the wave of neoliberalism nor the Europeanization of transport policymaking meant a weakening of the consensual style of public–private interaction. On the contrary, the institutionalized forms of public–private interaction were actually strengthened in the road freight sector. In the Dutch system the interaction between public and private actors, or, in the case of the railways, between public and semipublic interlocutors, turned out to be of the utmost importance in explaining the characteristic outcomes of the reform process: the *disentanglement* of public and private functions and responsibilities, and intrasectoral and intersectoral *coordination*.

To conclude, two aspects are of utmost importance for the assessment of the Dutch transport regulation in a Europeanized environment. On the one hand, the Dutch system exhibited a distinctive framework of concerted action and consensus seeking between public and private actors that facilitated a smooth and problem-solving-oriented transformation in which change followed a cumulative negotiated path. The realization of the new problem-solving approach led to a new mode of governance expressed in three components, that is, the market principle governing the interaction between private actors, forms of self-governance guaranteed by public–private agreements, and government intervention in questions concerning the public good.

On the other hand, both the way in which the transformation took place and the new mode of governance itself indicate that the role of government is still of key importance in the Netherlands. Neither the increasing economic interdependence nor the ongoing process of European integration has contributed significantly to an erosion of the traditional intervention by Dutch public actors in economic processes and societal developments. The government was able to sustain its claim by bringing its policies into line with European ones. In a situation where the existing national regulatory regimes for road and rail increasingly ran counter to the reality of modern transport markets, the search process at the domestic level was influenced not only by the national context, but also by emerging European legislation and by ideas, concepts, and models present in the European or international sphere. But as the road haulage reform has shown, the convergence of European and national policies was *bilateral* in nature rather than unilateral. Dutch public and private actors did not follow "international developments haphazardly" (Hulsink 1996: 384), as had been the case in the early days of the telecommunications reform, but instead learned how to parallel domestic and European policies and to use Europe as a resource for their own economic and political interests.

With respect to the process of Europeanization, one may say that in the Dutch case government policies to sustain economic performance remained important even where their methods and function have changed (Hirst and Thompson 1996: 144ff.). Given its ability to orchestrate social consensus and to compensate for the effects of both a shift from protectionist to market-fostering policies and Europeanization, governments can set the course of socioeconomic developments. In other words, the general problemsolving capacity of the Dutch state has not diminished but has been maintained in light of changes in the political and economic environment, allowing us to take the Dutch case as a good example of how, within the context of European policymaking, "member governments can set the course of their own national policies" (Kohler-Koch 1996b: 195). For the case of freight transport this holds, although both Europe's policies of "negative integration" and the downward pressure of regulatory competition have ruled out a certain range of options related either to market protection or other competition distorting policies.

These considerations have two important implications for the interpretation of the European impact on domestic policies. First, European policies impacted on the distribution of power and resources in the domestic arena. Instead of prescribing a concrete institutional model—as is often the case in regulations to curb the negative externalities of market processes—European market-making policies in road haulage left a good degree of leeway for adjusting domestic arrangements in light of particular domestic constellations. The development of "win-win-strategies" allowed both users and the suppliers of transport services to reap the benefits from the national and international process of liberalization. The German and the French cases, in contrast, provide us with examples for more uneven changes in the domestic opportunity structure (Douillet and Lehmkuhl in this volume; Teutsch in this volume). Second, the railway case exhibited a further aspect of Europe's potential impact on domestic policies. Rather than prescribing a concrete institutional model or altering directly the domestic opportunity structure, European railway policies both lent support to domestic changes by providing a concept of reform to solve specific problems— the disentanglement of public and private responsibilities—and altered the expectations of actors with the potential to oppose the reform, in the present case the railway unions. In theoretical terms, these empirical findings imply that one look at the differential impact of Europe not only in terms of a differential policy impact. In addition, it is necessary to sharpen the analytical tools to account systematically for the domestic impact of European policies. As there is no single approach to explain policymaking at the European level (Schmidt 1997; Wallace 2000), to analyze and interpret the differential impact of Europe requires more different approaches. This chapter has—as the others in this volume—added some insights to this enterprise.

# NOTES

1. It comes as no surprise that the reconsideration of transport regulation started with the road haulage sector, which, although representing a relatively young mode of transport in relation to inland waterways or the railways, is the mode of transportation that benefited most from the general development of production and manufacturing (e.g., the decline of bulk volumes at the expense of smaller units, containerization, the advent of sophisticated logistical services, and the extension of the freeway network). Today, the share of road haulage in the modal split of the Netherlands is about 80 percent (TLN 1996).

2. Interview with the EVO, December 1995.

3. Interview with the EVO, December 1995. See also Keus and Tweel 1991: 622.

4. Interviews with the Ministerie VenW and the Transport en Logistiek Nederland (TLN) in November 1995 and with the EVO in December 1995.

5. *Tweede Kamer der Staaten-Generaal* 1983/1984, 17 931, No. 39, p. 14.

6. Commissie Geelhoed, "Deregulering overheidsregelingen," The Hague.

7. Interview with the EVO in December 1995 and with the Ministerie VenW in November 1995.

8. At the time of writing, a working capital of Dfl. 7,500 for each truck and a minimum of Dfl. 40,000 for an enterprise was required. The Commissie Vergunnigen Wegvervoer was incorporated into the NIWO by the new act.

9. One of these is the "as-low-as-reasonable-achievable-principle" where the best available technology is applied for the protection of the environment when reasonable normative elements exist; otherwise the best practicable means are practiced.

10. The Dutch taxation system was transformed in July 1997 for two reasons. First, the European legislation on minimum levels for vehicle taxes relates to gross vehicle weights, that is, vehicle weight plus maximum load, whereas the Dutch system is based on empty lorry weight. Second, the basis of taxation according to the European legislation is vehicle ownership, whereas in the Netherlands it was the use of the public roads. The transformation of the Dutch system was not only a "rather technical story" requiring a great deal of assistance on the part of the associations (interview with the TLN, June 1997), but also required a general overhaul of the existing system.

11. Sweden opted to join the system in 1997.

12. As in 1992 and 1994, although it should be noted that the first compensation was reversed after the intervention of the European Commission and Germany.

13. Both countries finally agreed to the Dutch scheme based on a refund of the five-cent increase of diesel fuel for vehicles weighing more than 12 tons.

14. It should be noted that the government did not limit its fiscal policies to environmental issues. For instance, to increase the international orientation of its transport industry, international freight transport enjoyed a favorable taxation regime compared to domestic transport.

15. The objective of the new Directoraat-Generaal Goederen is to "actively contribute to a safe, competitive, high-quality and sustainable transport system," which, given the limitation of hierarchical forms of steering, the department seeks to achieve in "an active partnership with the industry" (B. Westerduin, Directeur-Generaal Goederen, in an interview with the *Nieuwsblad Transport* of 12 June 1997; translation [DL]).

16. The NMPP was co-signed by four ministries, and elements of this environmental framework plan were incorporated into the Second Structural Traffic and Transport Plan in 1990.

17. Efforts to improve the effectiveness of legislation, generally known as the "chain approach," allow for the participation of relevant actors in the integrated policy process of formulation, implementation, and evaluation (interview with the RVI, November 1995).

18. Consequently, the recruitment policy of the RVI changed from the practice of hiring former policemen to recruiting personnel with a higher level of education and more flexible working attitudes (interview with the RVI, November 1995).

19. The National Registration for Own Account Transport (*Stichting Inschrijving Eigen Vervoer*, SIEV) is responsible for own-account transport licensing.

20. The board of the NIWO consists of representatives of two employers' organizations, two trade unions, and of the transport users' organization, with two representatives of the government entitled to attend the board meetings as observers.

21. The creation of the NDL was financed 30 percent by the ministries and 70 percent by the Dutch transport industry. It includes employers' organizations, road transport associations, the authorities of Rotterdam Port and Schiphol Airport, and individual firms.

22. The "promotion of the Netherlands as the gateway to Europe and the ideal location for a centralized European distribution center" (interview with the NDL, November 1995). The NDL is concerned with lobbying for transport-related issues (e.g., infrastructure) at the national level and with promoting the Dutch transport and logistics industry in general, such as the promotion of "Centralized European Distribution," "value-added logistics," and the global advantages to be gained from locating business in the Netherlands (*Nederland Distributieland* 1993: 3).

23. In addition, technical standards and social regulations were subject to Europe-wide harmonization policies.

24. Thus, the transportation sector was more important than agriculture and fisheries, which accounted for circa 4 percent to both national income and total domestic employment.

25. Indeed, after the relaxation and final removal of the capacity restricting system, the average size of road haulage firms increased significantly, and by the end of the 1980s the average loading capacity of Dutch companies was the highest in Europe (Husmann 1989; Sleuwaegen 1993).

26. "A process whereby sectoral actors pursue their interests within a variety of constraints and eventually *select* a new governance regime by combining in intended and unintended ways their individual strategies for coping with dilemmas of production and exchange" (Campbell and Lindberg 1991: 328).

27. "We ask them to participate in thinking how the policy will be in the future" (interview with the Ministerie VenW, December 1995).

28. Interview with the Ministerie VenW, February 1997; Bernadet 1991: 19.

29. For a more detailed examination of the Dutch associational landscape and the current centrifugal developments, see Lehmkuhl 1999.

30. Starting with gentlemen's agreements, voluntary cooperation in the form of covenants are now highly formalized with respect to procedure and content. Covenants, which have more frequently been used in environmental policies, either prepare legislation or are seen as a complement to existing legislation (Bastmeijer 1997; van der Burgh 1994; OECD 1995:130ff.).

31. In the words of one civil servant, who has for many years been a member of the European Commission, "The Netherlands do what they can to help the development of Rotterdam to play its role as European Port and at the same time as the biggest port in the world" (Erdmenger 1983: 8).

32. For example, by transnational coordination with foreign ministries of other countries (Ministerie VenW 1990, No. 12).

33. Interview with the RVI, November 1995.

34. After the German hauliers association for long-distance transport, a predecessor of the TLN was the second association to establishment an office in Brussels

35. Interviews with the TLN, November 1995; EVO December 1995; Nederlands Vervoersoverleg, December 1995.

36. Especially in environmental policies the Netherlands have a reputation as net exporter of policy concepts (Liefferink 1997).

37. This decision could be seen as a response to the decreasing share of the railways in the modal split in both segments. This development was due to an enormous increase of individual mobility that on the one hand led to a decline of public transport in the period between 1960 and 1970 from 47 percent to 18 percent (Harstrick 1994: 22); with respect to freight transport, it was the closing of the coal mining at Limburg at the end of the 1960s that was responsible for a dramatic fall in transport demand (about 50 percent) (Mulder 1992).

38. According to Directive 69/1191/EEC, the government was to bear the costs for public-service obligations.

39. Interview with the Ministerie VenW, February 1997.

40. In interviews it became evident that actors in Dutch transport policymaking perceived the impact of the Swiss referendum of 1992 concerning the shift for the most part of cross-Alpine freight transport from road to rail within a ten-year period as dramatic (interview with the CE, November 1994; Ministerie VenW, November 1994 and November 1995).

41. Interviews with the Ministerie VenW, November 1994; the Ministry of Transport, November 1994 and February 1997; see European Centre for Infrastructure Studies 1996: 159ff.

42. In 1989, the report of the "van der Plas Commission" marked the crucial point in the Dutch railway policy. The report, called Strategy for Freight Transport by Rail, made a quite gloomy forecast concerning the competitive situation of the Port of Rotterdam and the development of the railways in the future. The missing of railways as a high-quality transport alternative would be "disastrous" and a "serious handicap for the Netherlands as a gateway to Europe." In 1992, the report of the Wijffels Commission made concrete recommendations for a future organization of the railways; for example, a vertical and horizontal

splitting up of different railway units. Moreover, the government was required to develop a clear and coherent transport policy, including infrastructure planning for all transport modes, and to set up an infrastructure fund that should pay for the construction and maintenance of the infrastructure and that should receive fees from users.

43. The units NS Cargo NV, NS Stations BV, and NS Real Estate BV have been separate legal entities since 1 January 1995, a status that was attained by the several units of the government-commissioned sector during the same year. All remaining units followed this development in 1996.

44. Railned is responsible for capacity up to twenty-four hours before trains depart, at which point NS Verkeersleiding takes over.

45. The reliance on information of the NS in the question whether or not there is free infrastructure capacity is a tricky point. In September 1997, for instance, the NS announced to extant its inter-city services in the Randstad though it before had denied the existence of free capacity. Due to this negative judgment of the NS, a private competitor did not obtain a license. After the announcement of the NS, however, this competitor complained immediately at Railned (NRC Handelsblad 1997a: 1).

46. Interviews with the Ministerie VenW and with Railned, February 1997.

47. The Ministerie VenW, written answer to a questionnaire on the "Restructuring of Railway Undertakings" drawn up by the ECMT Group on Railways (no author, no year).

48. Despite the government's 1995 decision to build the Betuwe line, both increasing costs of construction and doubts of its profitability paved the way for serious discussions since the summer of 1999.

49. For a new infrastructure that is built with the participation of private interests, new companies have to be established. An example is provided by the case of the Betuwe line, which is funded 78 percent by public means, 18 percent by private participation, and 4 percent by the European Commission. The ownership and operation will be assigned to the "Betuwe line ownership company" (*"Betwuelijn Eigendom Maatschaapij"*).

50. The former was considered to have been "completely wishful thinking" (interview Ministerie VenW, February 1997).

51. The second school of thought within the freight unit of the Ministry of Transport has a more patriotic attitude (interview with NS International Affairs, February 1997).

52. Interviews Ministerie VenW and NS International Affairs, February 1997. In June 1998, NS Cargo and the freight unit of the German railways, DB Cargo, announced the merger of their freight operations in an entity called Rail Cargo Europe (RCE), based in Mainz and due to begin operations in the second half of 1999 (NRC Handelsblad 1998: 17–21; *Financial Times* 1998: 1).

53. For a detailed account of the former government–NS relations, see van Kolk, Kuik, and Onverzaagt 1991.

54. This is in accordance with Directive 91/1893/EC, which amended Directive 69/1191/EC.

55. The field includes what NS Reizigers has declared as its core (i.e., profit-making) network.

56. Apart from France and the Netherlands, the CGEA is active in Britain, Germany, and Portugal. In this respect, the CGEA represents a clear signal for a Europeanization of the supply side of railway services (Herr and Lehmkuhl 1997: 412).

57. The distinctive degree of competitive orientation in the reform is expressed in the different legal status of the two segments. While NS Cargo as a joint-stock company is open for external investment, NS Reizigers is a limited liability company.

58. Due to the fact that there is no special electoral threshold that a party must cross to achieve representation in Parliament, the Dutch electoral system is not only one of the most proportional systems of the world. Political parties are also forced to watch carefully new themes growing in society in order to absorb these themes to avoid a loss of votes to newly emerging "one-issue parties" (Andeweg and Irwin 1993; van Waarden 1992).

59. One of the first documents expressing the new approach was the "ondernemend vervoer" published by the Ministry of Transport and Public Works in 1987. A key document expressing ideas, concepts, and developments that have taken place since the late 1980s was the "Tweede Structuurschema Verkeer en Vervoer" (SVV II) of 1990 in combination with the Nationaal Milieubeleidsplan (NMP2), and the Vierde Nota Ruimtelijke Ordering Extra (VINEX).

60. Interview with the Raad voor het Vervoer, June 1997.

61. Interview with the Ministerie VenW, February 1997.

62. "*Rail 21—Spoor naar een nieuwe eeuw*" ("Railways for the Next Century").

63. Interviews with Vervoersbond FNV and Federatie Spoorweg Vakvereniging (FSV), June 1997.

64. Interviews with the Ministerie VenW and Railned, February 1997.

65. See, for example, the Swedish model (Brandborn and Hellsvik 1990; Hansson and Nilsson 1991; Larsson and Ekström 1993).

66. Interviews with the Ministerie VenW, NS International Affairs, and FNV; FSV, February 1997.

# 8

# Differential Responses to European Policies: A Comparison

*Adrienne Héritier and Christoph Knill*

What is puzzling about member states' policies is that they respond so differently to identical European policy demands and similar external and internal conditions, such as the internationalization of markets or fiscal pressure. While Britain has radically liberalized its transport sector, France has been hesitant in privatizing its railways, while simultaneously carrying out a step-by-step deregulation and reregulation of road haulage. In the Netherlands, a mixed strategy of market liberalization and state intervention has been applied in both sectors. Germany reveals a significant degree of transformation in both sectors. And Italy has made only very modest reforms in either. How can these different responses to the same challenges be explained? In other words, how and why do the responses to European policy stimuli vary?

## COMPARATIVE EXPLANATORY SCHEME

We argue that the differences in reform policy output and structural adjustment are a function of three factors: the stage of liberalization prevailing in a given country; the dominant belief system or problem-solving approach, and national reform capacity. Those influences that are basically the same for all countries studied, such as the impact of worldwide liberalization in both sectors, pronounced fiscal strain in the rail sector, and the need for a functioning transport system as a central precondition for an efficient economy, are defined as contextual factors.

Concerning the first explanatory variable, the specific stage in which a country finds itself with respect to the liberalization of utilities when faced with European policy demands, we distinguish between the phases of pre-liberalization, liberalization, and post-liberalization. The stage of pre-liberalization is defined by the prevailing use of policy instruments that are still of a clearly interventionist nature, that is, fixing tariffs by administrative decision; applying quantitative limits to market access in road haulage; maintaining public ownership of track, rolling stock, and the operation of services; and the tax funding of infrastructure and service operations in the railways. We claim that a country will respond differently to Europe's demands: for liberalization depending upon the stage it has reached. For a member state at the stage of pre-liberalization, more will be expected of it in terms of policy transformation so as to comply with European policy expectations, and domestic actors supporting a reform will be strengthened. If, by contrast, a member state has already embarked on the path of liberalization, less will be required of it in terms of policy changes. Yet another possibility is that if a country has already entered the stage of post-liberalization, European requirements will trigger different responses, which are likely to strengthen opposition to European Community (EC) demands. In other words, the stage reflects the degree of congruence with Europe's liberalizing demands: the policy match or mismatch.

While constituting an important factor accounting for a specific response to European liberalization policies, stage in relation to liberalization takes for granted that reform can take place in the presence of a mismatch between national and European policies. This is not, however, the case. Instead, what we term *"reform capacity"* is needed to bring about a policy change. This is determined by the number of formal and factual veto positions that need to be overcome in order to realize a decision, and by the degree to which that country enjoys politically integrated leadership. Regarding the first component, we distinguish between member states with a high number of formal and factual veto positions and countries with few formal and factual veto positions. Many formal veto positions exist in federalist or decentralized political systems, with multiple-party coalition governments, a high degree of ministerial autonomy, an independent constitutional court, and an independent central bank. Factual veto positions have to be taken into account where there is a participation of associations in decision making, such as in corporatist sectoral decision-making arrangements. Countries with few formal and factual veto positions tend to be unitary states with a single-party majority government and administrative decentralization but no bipartite or multipartite decision-making structures.

With respect to the component of integrated political leadership, this can be provided by a formal majoritarian hierarchical government, or by a long-standing and successful practice of consensual bipartite, tripartite, or multipartite decision making that incorporates or reconciles diverging interests. Thus, we find that even in the face of multiple formal and factual veto points a consensual capacity develops in bipartite and multipartite decision-making practices that allows the integration of political and societal forces. A country may also be characterized by a high number of veto positions and a simultaneous lack of consensual political leadership, in which case reform capacity will be low.

In analyzing the impact of European policy inputs, it would be wrong to make a static or mechanistic link between the number of veto positions and existing types of integrated political leadership and the probability of reform. The relationship is neither so static nor so linear as to allow us to predict from numerous formal and factual veto positions and weak integrated political leadership to the probability or unlikeliness of reform. It is, instead, a dynamic process. European policy inputs can be understood as a political resource that may be exploited by some domestic actors, in order to improve their relative positions in the domestic political conflicts, and not by others. This may lead to a transformation of the political opportunities in the domestic sectoral arena. At a structural level, political opportunities are defined as the number of available coalition partners and target points that can be addressed in order to shift the arena of decision making to, for example, the level of the European Court of Justice, or to obtain new policy parameters for the domestic arena of action by, for example, addressing the European Commission. The use of such opportunities alters the conditions for building the integrated national leadership needed to bring about change. The relative importance of individual veto positions may be reduced, while others may increase in weight. In brief, the distribution of power among actors in the domestic arena, which is determined by the fallback options in case of nonagreement with other domestic actors, is affected by the entrance of new actors.

The ability to generate a capacity for reform is not indicative per se of the direction that this capacity will take. While the direction of European policy influence is taken as given, that is, pressure for liberalization, our second explanatory variable, the prevailing belief system in a member state (which exists quite independent of the overall influence of the international liberalization ideology), determines the direction in which reform capacity will materialize. The dominant belief system is defined as the values prevailing regarding the role of road and rail transport in that member state. In a country where there are still strong ideological elements of an interventionist or "public service" tradition, the responses to European policymaking processes in the domestic political arena will be different from the responses in a country with a very weak interventionist tradition.

On the side of the explanandum, we analyze policy outputs, that is, legislative changes in the countries under investigation that have occurred in the context of European policymaking and the structural administrative changes immediately linked with them, together with the transformations in structures and patterns of interest intermediation. These changes are qualified as high, medium, and low. A high degree of change is defined as a large-scale change of overall problem-solving ideology, that is, liberal or interventionist, and an abolition of all instruments linked with this overall belief system. In the case of road haulage, this implies the elimination of quantitative barriers to market access, the administrative setting of tariffs, and the use of market-incompatible taxes. In the case of the railways, it means the full privatization of infrastructure, rolling stock and service operations, the full institutional separation of network and services, the opening up of access to the network for train operators, and an end to public subsidies for network and service operators. A medium-range change is defined as a mixture of old and new policy elements combined in about equal parts. In road haulage this may mean a mixture of quantitative access restriction with free tariffs or vice versa. In the railways it may involve partial privatization—that is, of operations, but not of the network that remains under state ownership—the maintenance of state subsidies, and an organizational separation of infrastructure and services (or a separation in accounting). A low degree of change is defined as a minimal degree of application of market instruments that are introduced in both sectors, while leaving the old interventionist measures in place.

On the basis of the above comparative explanation based on three explanatory factors, contextual influences are held constant. Moreover, the factor "stage" is held constant by forming two categories of countries for the purpose of comparison. In road haulage, one category of countries was at the pre-liberalization stage (Germany and Italy), and another category (the Netherlands, France, and Britain), at the stage of liberalization when faced with European policy demands. In the case of rail, all countries were starting to liberalize when faced with European policy demands. This leaves us with two systematic explanatory variables in both sectors in each group. How then did European policies in the two sectors specifically affect policies and structures in the five countries examined?

## COUNTRY COMPARISON

The case studies presented in this book reveal that the impact of European policy requirements on domestic arrangements varies considerably across countries. This differential impact of European road haulage and railways policies on corresponding regulatory activities and structures at the national level can be understood in light of the distinctive configuration of our explanatory variables given for each country and policy sector under investigation.

### Road Haulage

The project to establish a liberal transport market throughout the EC has made significant progress since the mid-1980s, with the most crucial issue concerning the establishment of a single European transport market being the introduction of cabotage—the operation of nonresident hauliers in foreign domestic markets—by regulations in 1990 and 1993. A key characteristic of European road haulage policy is that its domestic impact emerges from a restricted "positive" definition of requirements for domestic market policy regulation, and the provision of new strategic opportunities and constraints for domestic actors. Thus, the liberalization of cabotage removed the protection of national transport markets, so that states were no longer able to restrict the access of nonresident operators to their domestic markets. Apart from these restrictions, however, European legislation allowed for the maintenance of quantitative restrictions and price controls, that is, the coexistence of highly regulated domestic markets alongside a deregulated international market that includes the right to provide domestic transport for nonresidents. In this way, European policies required only limited instrumental and institutional changes in the domestic regulation of road haulage.

On the other hand, the liberalization of cabotage opened domestic markets up to international competition, hence affecting the strategic opportunities and constraints of domestic actors and challenging well-established regulatory arrangements. The introduction of cabotage, which limited the opportunity for member states to protect their markets from foreign competition, created new strategic options for certain groups of actors, such as users of transport services (e.g., companies can decide whether they have their goods transported by foreign or domestic hauliers), while reducing the number of feasible options for others (e.g., in light of European competition domestic tariff regimes for road transport are no longer sufficient to promote the market position of national hauliers). In other words, the European liberalization of cabotage operates through the mechanism of "regulatory competition," putting pressure on the member states to redesign domestic market regulations in order to avoid regulatory burdens restricting the competitiveness of domestic industries.

As revealed by our case studies, European road haulage policy triggered highly different patterns of regulatory change in the five countries examined. While the persistence of existing arrangements reflects the dominant scenario in the British case, patterns of change range from liberalization in Germany to social reregulation in France, liberalization and economic stimulation in the Netherlands, and increased interventionism in Italy.

At first glance, this variance is highly surprising. The member states were faced to a similar extent with new opportunities and constraints implied by European liberalization activities, and one would consequently have expected an overall pattern of converging approaches in domestic market regulation. Moreover, road haulage policy in all five countries was characterized by, and subject to, similar social, economic, and political context conditions. Notwithstanding minor differences in degree, the transport sector is considered to be of key economic importance in all five countries examined. The same applies with respect to the overall economic, and industrial development, population density, standard of living and social services, liberal–democratic politics with the participation of (political) parties and interest groups in policymaking, together with well-developed administrative systems. As a consequence, the five countries were confronted with the potential impact of the European liberalization of cabotage to much the same degree.

How can we explain the difference in domestic responses to European Union (EU) policy? Which factors account for the fact that new strategic opportunities and constraints implied by European arrangements did not lead to converging regulatory trends at the domestic level, notwithstanding similar European requirements and domestic context conditions? As we have pointed out, the varying impact of Europe on domestic road haulage policy can be understood in terms of three explanatory factors, namely the stage of liberalization in which domestic haulage policy was faced with the demands of European legislation, the capacity for sectoral reform, and the prevailing belief systems of a country with respect to transport regulation.

The significant differences in domestic regulatory change and persistence in light of preexisting policies, new opportunities, and constraints created by European liberalization are reflected in distinctive configurations of these explanatory factors in each country under study, as summarized in table 8.1. Before investigating the linkage between variable configuration and domestic adjustment patterns from a comparative perspective, we will elaborate on our classification of cases with respect to these variables.

With respect to the stage of liberalization in which domestic haulage policy was exposed to European liberalization, the five countries can be divided into two groups. The countries in the first group, Germany and Italy, were at the pre-liberalization stage, pursuing an interventionist approach of market regulation, at the time of European liberalization. Notwithstanding certain regulatory differences across the two countries, their haulage policies had shared some key characteristics: the regulation of market access by quantitative licensing restrictions, and the regulation of market operation by a differentiated system of maximum and minimum rate levels. Although the objectives initially associated with the interventionist approach (in particular, the protection of railway freight transport and the provision of an efficient transport system) had not been achieved in either Germany or Italy, these regulatory failures did not imply a fundamental departure from the established approach.

By contrast, the second group, consisting of Britain, France, and the Netherlands, had liberalized domestic market regulation already before corresponding legislation at the European level was enacted. While Britain had liberalized its haulage sector already in 1968, similar reforms took place in France and the Netherlands in the mid-1980s. In view of the failures associated with previous interventionist approaches to regulation, these countries abolished rate regulations and quantitative restrictions, with market access being solely dependent upon individual qualitative conditions.

Different conditions also exist in terms of the domestic institutional context, that is, the institutional capacity for sectoral reform. What are the distinctive institutional opportunities and constraints for sectoral actors wishing to push through their interests? To what extent are sectoral reform initiatives confronted with formal and factual veto points? In the British case, the capacity for sectoral reform can be considered to be very high. On the one hand, this can be traced to general aspects characterizing the British political system, which put the government in a relatively strong position when initiating and putting through political

**Table 8.1. Explanatory Factors and Policy/Structural Change in Road Haulage Policy**

| | Germany | Italy | Britain | Netherlands | France |
|---|---|---|---|---|---|
| Liberalization Stage | Pre-liberalization | Pre-liberalization | Liberalization | Liberalization | Liberalization |
| Ideology | Interventionist | Interventionist | Pro-liberal | Liberal + state | Contested pro-liberal/interventionist |
| Reform Capacity | Medium:<br>- mult. formal veto points<br>- mult. factual veto points<br>- weak formal leadership<br>- strong factual leadership | Low:<br>- mult. formal veto points<br>- mult. factual veto points<br>- weak formal and factual leadership | High:<br>- few formal veto points<br><br>- strong formal and factual leadership | Medium:<br>- few formal veto points<br>- mult. factual veto points<br>- strong formal partnership and factual leadership | Medium:<br>- few formal veto points<br>- mult. factual veto points<br>- strong formal pol. leadership |
| Change in Regulation | High: liberalization | Low: increased intervention | Low: no change | Medium: reregulation through public/private partnership | Medium: social reregulation |
| Domestic/European Origin | Domestic: +<br>European: + | Domestic: -<br>European: + | Domestic: -<br>European: - | Domestic: +<br>European: + | Domestic: +<br>European: + |

reforms. Opposing actors have limited opportunities to block or reduce the scope and scale of governmental reform proposals, given the low number of institutional veto points in the political decision-making process. On the other hand, the reluctance of Britain to intervene in the haulage sector did not imply any particular need for a specialized organization of private interests to demand specific forms of state intervention advantageous to them. Given the lack of a differentiated system of administrative interest intermediation, no particular veto positions emerge from institutionalized exchange relationships between public and private actors, which could reduce the potential for far-reaching reforms within the British haulage sector.

While reform capacity can hence be classified as very high in Britain, the potential for fundamental sectoral policy changes is very low in the Italian case. From a general perspective, the highly fragmented political–administrative system is characterized by numerous institutional veto points that significantly reduce the potential for enacting far-reaching reforms. Moreover, the lack of integrated political leadership becomes apparent in Italy's series of short-lived, conflict-ridden, multiparty governments. In addition to these general characteristics, the factual veto positions linked with the polarized system of administrative interest intermediation (large versus small haulage companies) reduced the potential for political consensus on regulatory reforms at the sectoral level.

In contrast to Britain and Italy, which reflect opposite ends of the same spectrum, the capacity for sectoral reform in France, Germany, and the Netherlands lies somewhat in between. In France, the medium level of reform capacity can be traced to a combination of strong political leadership within a unitary state, and the adversarial tradition of state–society relations. The potential of government to realize political reforms is restricted by the high societal capacity for political mobilization. In the haulage sector, the adversarial tradition is apparent in a strong social movement that led to the massive strikes of 1995.

In Germany and the Netherlands, by contrast, the medium level of sectoral reform capacity can be explained by the ambiguous impact of corporatist arrangements. On the one hand, corporatist patterns of interaction between public and private actors, together with the delegation of powers to private associations, increase the government's need to bargain and accommodate different societal interests when formulating and implementing political reforms. The relevance of these corporatist patterns is reinforced by the emergence of representational monopolies, that is, the existence of peak associations enjoying broad political support and the strong linkages between associations and political parties (Schmitter and Lehmbruch 1979; Dyson 1992). In this way, the potential for path-breaking regulatory reforms is significantly reduced. On the other hand, the corporatist mediation of diverse interests allows for considerable adaptational flexibility and ample opportunities to adjust political strategies in the light of differing problems, although such adjustments are unlikely to imply radical reforms, given the variety of preferences of the numerous actors involved (Benz and Goetz 1996).

Turning to our third explanatory variable, dominant belief system, we again find important differences across the five countries examined. Thus, both British and Dutch road haulage policy are characterized by a liberal ideology that is rooted in the beliefs and ideas of dominant actor coalitions. According to this philosophy, which is often referred to as the "Anglo-Saxon tradition" (Button 1993), the achievement of policy goals is left to market forces, with state intervention playing a minor role. In this context, the dominant British ideology, which views market liberalization and state regulation as mutually exclusive, can be considered as even more "radical" than the Dutch approach, which views market liberalization and parallel state activities to enhance international competitiveness as compatible rather than contradictory concepts.

Germany and Italy, by contrast, were characterized by the dominance of an interventionist ideology. Notwithstanding the fact that this orientation was hotly contested by advocates of a more liberal approach, particularly in Germany, the dominant actor coalition in both countries pursued an interventionist notion of transport regulation. Strong economic regulation was expected to deliver an effective and socially desirable transport system by protecting the national railways and smaller haulage companies and by avoiding negative externalities. Moreover, transport was not seen as the mere provision of a service, but was linked to other regional, social, industrial, and environmental policy objectives.

While all the countries mentioned were characterized by the existence of a dominant—either liberal or interventionist—ideological orientation in the approach to political problems in the road haulage sector, the French case reveals a more ambiguous pattern. Although France had liberalized its road haulage sector during the 1980s, this did not imply a reduced influence of actor coalitions favoring a pro-regulatory approach. Instead, the political influence of liberalizers and interventionists can be considered well balanced, with no coalition playing a dominating role. This strong contestedness and the balance of ideological orientations can be traced to the deeply rooted tradition of state intervention and the state provision of public services, on the one hand, and the increasing acceptance of neoliberal ideas within the ministerial bureaucracy, on the other.

Turning to the scope and direction of regulatory change in national road haulage policy, that is, our dependent variable, we once again find highly varying patterns across the five countries. Thus, regulatory change remained at a very low level in Britain and Italy. While in Britain neither domestic nor European factors implied a departure from the liberal approach to market regulation, the European liberalization of cabotage had—until very recently—only minor implications on haulage regulation in Italy. In view of the challenges emerging from European liberalization, Italy gradually increased its interventionist approach in order to protect the domestic market from European competition. A medium level of regulatory change, by contrast, can be observed in France and the Netherlands. In France, both political pressure emerging from the domestic level and European policy activities triggered a development of social reregulation of the national haulage market, albeit without questioning the dominant liberal approach. A similar mixture of liberalization and state intervention can be observed in the Netherlands. In the Dutch case, national and European developments led to the emergence of a new approach to domestic haulage regulation, combining a liberalized transport market with an active industrial policy promoting the international competitiveness of the domestic industry through public/private partnerships. Finally, in Germany the abolition of the highly interventionist regulation in favor of a liberal approach implies a fundamental departure from existing patterns. In this context, the high level of regulatory change in Germany can be traced to the mutual reinforcement of national and Europe-induced reform pressures.

In sum, the classification of the five countries along the three variables accounting for the domestic impact of European road haulage policy reflects a highly differentiated picture revealing marked variations across countries with respect to all explanatory variables, with each country being characterized by a distinctive variable configuration. Given these differences, the identification of a distinctive pattern of regulatory change for each country is hardly surprising. In examining regulatory developments, this marked variation in variable configurations, however, does not imply that each variable is of similar importance. We are able to identify pairs of most similar cases which allow for the reduction of explanatory factors.

To this end, the five countries under study can be grouped according to the different stage of domestic liberalization at the time of European liberalization. While Germany and Italy belong to the group of "pre-liberalizers," Britain, France, and the Netherlands had liberalized their domestic haulage markets already before corresponding legislation at the European level was enacted.

These differences in national starting position when faced with European liberalization have to be understood in terms of the distinctive ideological orientations and capacities for regulatory reform at the domestic level. Thus, all countries initially pursued a highly interventionist approach to haulage regulation in order to protect railway freight transport and to avoid cutthroat competition within the haulage sector. Moreover, in all five countries, the strong economic regulation of the haulage market, including quantitative licensing criteria and the definition of maximum and minimum rates, soon turned out to be a major failure with respect to the achievement of the initial objectives.

Notwithstanding these similar developments and experiences, the corresponding regulatory responses in the five countries reflect a rather different picture. Given the experience of previous regulatory approaches, steps to liberalize the British transport market had already been taken at the end of the 1960s. Instead of being linked to liberal ideas (which entered the general political discourse much later), the British reforms must be understood in light of the high institutional capacity for regulatory reform. The low number of institutional veto points and the strong capacity for integrated leadership characteristic of the British political system allowed for a swift regulatory reform in view of the experience with earlier approaches (see Knill in this volume).

While Britain reformed its transport policy at a relatively early stage, similar developments only began to take place in France and the Netherlands—the two other countries belonging to the "liberalizer" group—from the mid-1980s onward. Not only did France and the Netherlands liberalize their domestic haulage markets at a later stage, but they also introduced the regulatory changes in a more incremental way. In their chapter on France (this volume), Douillet and Lehmkuhl show that these differences in the pace and timing of liberalization can be traced to institutional and ideological peculiarities. Notwithstanding the powerful position of the French government within a unitary state, both the strong embeddedness of antiliberal beliefs and the strong societal capacity for political mobilization posed significant constraints on the French administration in order to put through a more liberal approach to transport policy. As a consequence, liberalization occurred on the basis of incremental reform phased in over several years. In the Netherlands, by contrast, the corporatist tradition implied the need for a consensual decision-making process. The abolition of the interventionist regime was only possible by compensating potential losers. In this context, the liberal orientation that characterized the Dutch approach (which, in contrast to Britain, did not, however, impede active state intervention) facilitated consensus building within the corporatist structures (see Lehmkuhl in this volume).

While the specific constellation of ideological orientations and institutional capacities for regulatory reform found in Britain, France, and the Netherlands had already provided the basis for the liberalization of domestic haulage markets before corresponding European measures were enacted, both Germany and Italy were still at the stage of pre-liberalization at the time of European liberalization. In his chapter on Germany (this volume), Teutsch indicates how the advocates of liberal reforms were unable to overcome the factual veto position of domestic hauliers benefiting from the existing approach. The corporatist pattern of sectoral regulation was characterized by an interventionist bias, providing the haulage industry with privileged access to the formulation and implementation of German transport policy. In the Italian case, Kerwer (this volume) demonstrates that the combination of a highly fragmented political leadership and the factual veto position of the small hauliers inhibited any attempt to challenge the dominant interventionist approach until very recently.

In sum, the different regulatory developments in the five countries under study allow us to distinguish between three different stages during which domestic haulage policy was faced with the demands of European liberalization. As is apparent from the comparison of the countries at the same stage of liberalization, the classification of a country as a liberalizer, pre-liberalizer, or post-liberalizer with respect to road haulage policy is not sufficient to understand the varying impact of European legislation at the domestic level, particularly so when comparing the countries in the pre-liberalization group, namely Germany and Italy, where the constellation of explanatory variables for both countries reveals a high degree of similarity. In addition to a similar liberalization stage, German and Italian road haulage policy was characterized by an interventionist ideology. In view of this constellation, the strikingly different patterns of regulatory adjustment—liberalization in Germany versus increased interventionism in Italy—have to be explained by the level of sectoral reform capacity, the only variable where the two countries differ.

Instead of liberalizing the domestic market, Italy sought to protect domestic hauliers from the increased competition emerging from a liberalized European market by increasing state intervention (see Kerwer in this volume). It opted for more rather than less economic regulation, thus increasing the gap between domestic transport policy and European market liberalization. Instead of introducing widespread regulatory reform, Italy continued its traditionally interventionist approach to regulating market access and operation in the domestic haulage market. Moreover, instead of adopting measures to promote the international competitiveness of the sector, Italy attempted to protect domestic hauliers from international competition by offering them specific loans and social tax credits. In view of the persistent pattern of increasing state intervention in the sector, the relationship between public and private actors remained largely unaffected by European legislation. Thus, the association of small hauliers (Unatras) continues to defend its pro-regulation position by a combination of lobbying and "extortionist" practices. In this way, the association exerts a strong influence on Italian transport policy. By contrast, the association representing the larger enterprises (Coordinamento), which favors a more liberal approach, pursues a less aggressive strategy in defending the interests of its members and seeks to cooperate with the administration, but since the larger companies do not resort to strikes, they are politically less influential than Unatras.

Given the low institutional capacity for sectoral reform in Italy, European liberalization policy did not imply the sort of changes in domestic opportunity structures necessary to overcome existing institutional veto positions. The generally low capacity for integrated political leadership and the highly influential position of actor coalitions in favor of market intervention significantly reduced the opportunities for advocates of liberalization to trigger domestic reforms. In this context, it was in particular the factual veto position of the small hauliers that inhibited corresponding reforms. This group of actors often resorts to contortionist practices and calls strikes, in order to press the Ministry of Transport for new tax subsidies and to prevent deregulation, and their attempts are usually successful. Given these institutional constraints, the larger hauliers, which are basically in favor of a more liberal regime, were not able to successfully challenge the existing regulatory arrangements, not even with the support and new opportunities provided by European liberalization policy.

As Teutsch points out in his chapter (this volume), Germany by contrast completely abandoned its interventionist regime of market regulation in favor of a liberal approach. The German approach to liberalization is apparent in the abolition of restrictive licensing procedures and rate controls that traditionally characterized the system of transport regulation. The regulatory changes are also reflected in changed patterns of administrative interest intermediation. The former arrangements were characterized by a " biased" sectoral corporatism. Actors in favor of state intervention, such as haulier associations, were in a privileged position. Decisions were taken jointly by the Ministry for Transport and the major haulier associations, while consumer and producer organizations supporting a more liberal approach played a less important role. Haulier associations also played a dominant role in setting tariffs and in the implementation and monitoring of compliance by the federal agency (BAG). With the introduction of a more liberal regime, these old institutionalized forms of public/private interaction became less important. As tariffs are now subject to market processes, haulier associations became less influential in determining transport rates. Moreover, the formal participation of the haulier association in the BAG was abolished. Instead, new informal modes of cooperation between haulier associations and the Ministry of Transport emerged, with the common objective of improving the competitiveness of the German haulage sector. In contrast to the former arrangements, however, these modes of public/private interaction no longer imply a privileged position on the part of haulier associations.

The capacity for integrated leadership provided by the corporatist relationship between administration and transport associations facilitated regulatory changes under the impact of European legislation (see Teutsch in this volume). Although these arrangements were biased in favor of domestic hauliers, they provided a much weaker veto position against liberal reforms than the position enjoyed by the small hauliers in Italy. Given the well-established patterns of corporatist relationships with the transport administration, contortionist practices and strikes were not a feasible option for German hauliers wanting to push through their interests. Hence, in contrast to Italy, in the political contest between pro-liberalizers and anti-liberalizers, the European reform policies played a decisive role. They helped to overcome the de facto veto points by strengthening the position of the liberalizer coalition, that is, the opposition of the road hauliers with their vested interests in maintaining market regulation, tipping the scales in favor of the pro-liberalization coalition.

The number of explanatory variables can also be reduced when comparing the different patterns of regulatory change in the group of liberalizers, namely Britain, France, and the Netherlands. Considering the configuration of variables for France and the Netherlands, it becomes apparent that differences in regulatory adjustment (social reregulation in France versus economic stimulation in the Netherlands) can be traced to differences in the dominant belief systems of both countries.

In the French case, Douillet and Lehmkuhl argue that liberalization at the European level coincided with a strong tendency toward social reregulation in the wake of the liberalization of the domestic haulage market. Reregulation included not only the strengthening of professional requirements and working time limitations for hauliers, but also the regulation of minimum prices for transport services so as to protect small haulage companies and subcontractors from cutthroat competition. The introduction of new policy instruments was accompanied by substantial changes in patterns of administrative interest intermediation. In response to increasing problems and conflicts emerging from the liberal approach to market regulation, the government set up a corporatist reform commission, consisting of representatives of the state, haulier associations, and trade unions. These corporatist arrangements not only provided the basis for the development of reregulatory policies, but also helped strengthen the rather weak organization of trade unions and haulier associations.

As revealed by the French case study, the liberalization of the domestic haulage sector did not imply the emergence of a dominant ideological orientation in favor of a liberal approach. Instead, the strong embeddedness of the transport system as a public service provided and regulated by the state implied a constellation of highly contested and equally relevant ideological orientations. The—apparently paradoxical—domestic impact of European liberalization should be understood in view of an already liberalized domestic market, on the one hand, and the renewed emphasis on reregulation, on the other. While the pro-liberalization coalition had already achieved its core objectives as a result of domestic market liberalization prior to European reforms, European liberalization policy constituted a strategic resource for the reregulation coalition in order to increase its political influence. By emphasizing the fact that European liberalization may aggravate the social and political problems emerging in the newly liberalized domestic market, European legislation provided an important opportunity for these actors to promote their social reregulation proposals. In other words, the domestic actors opposing European developments were politically more influential than those actor coalitions supporting European liberalization policy.

In the case of the Netherlands, Lehmkuhl observes a quite different approach to promoting the competitive position of the haulage industry within a liberalized European market. Here, where the haulage sector was liberalized already during the 1980s, the role of the state is not restricted to safeguarding competition, as in Britain, but instead plays an active role in preparing the industry for future developments by strengthening the social responsibility and self-regulation of economic actors, promoting an innovative and high-quality-oriented transport industry. These changes in the regulatory approach had a marked impact on the patterns of administrative interest intermediation. While sectoral corporatism remains the basic characteristic of institutionalized interactions between public and private actors, the concrete form of corporatist arrangements underwent significant changes. First, the shift from regulation to stimulation was accompanied by organizational changes within the transport administration and interest associations. Attempts to overcome bureaucratic fragmentation were paralleled by a process of centralization of organized interests and a restructuring of the road haulage industry. These attempts were financially supported by the government in order to improve the international competitiveness of Dutch road hauliers. Second, the direction of the meso-corporatist arrangements at the sectoral level underwent significant changes from a "demand side" to a "supply side" corporatism, where state actors seek to provide a favorable economic framework for economic activities. While the market is seen as the dominant principle of coordination, the state insists on defining the overall objectives of this new mode of governance and, in addition to market efficiency, tries to integrate other goals such as, for example, the protection of the environment.

In contrast to France, the liberalization of the Dutch transport market coincided with the emergence of a dominant anti-interventionist ideological orientation. Although this does not mean that policy objectives often pursued with state intervention, such as environmental protection, are no longer taken into account, there is an overall consensus that the self-regulation of economic actors is a better way of achieving these objectives. In view of these ideological peculiarities, the strengthening of the competitive position of the haulage industry with an active role played by the state in promoting innovation and the self-regulation of economic actors was considered the best way to prepare the industry for the increased competition in European transport markets. Once again, in contrast to France, where the persistence of interventionist ideas in the wake of liberalization implied that European liberalization strengthened actor coalitions in favor of re-regulation, the particular beliefs system in the Dutch case favored the adoption of policies to stimulate the economy.

Ideological differences also explain the varying regulatory developments in Britain as opposed to France and the Netherlands. Britain is the only country out of the five cases examined where the impact of European road haulage policy may be considered negligible; that is, the persistence of regulatory arrangements is the dominant pattern in the British case. In his chapter, Knill shows that EU policy basically confirmed the liberal approach of market regulation, implying only minor adjustments in the setting of policy instruments, but without questioning their basic characteristics. As a consequence, well-established patterns of interaction between public and private actors remained largely unaffected by European developments.

In contrast to the British pattern of persistence, the tendency toward social reregulation in France can be traced to an enduring ideological orientation, where state intervention is considered necessary in order to resolve those political and social problems emerging from a liberalized domestic market. In Britain, such perceptions did not emerge, given the strongly anti-interventionist ideology characterizing the country's approach to transport policy. Notwithstanding the high institutional potential for sectoral reform, demonstrated by the early liberalization of the British transport market, European liberalization did not imply a departure from existing arrangements for the regulation of the domestic haulage market. In much the same way, the radical liberal philosophy dominant in Britain, which views market coordination and state involvement as contradictory activities, inhibited forms of active economic stimulation observable in the Dutch case, which is characterized by a more pragmatic liberal philosophy to transport regulation.

In sum, the analysis of domestic regulatory adjustment to European liberalization policy in the road haulage sector reveals distinctive patterns of change and persistence in all five countries. While the persistence of existing arrangements reflects the dominant scenario in the British case, patterns of change range from liberalization in Germany to social reregulation in France, economic stimulation in the Netherlands, and increased interventionism in Italy. This marked variance in domestic adjustment patterns indicates that the new strategic constraints and opportunities created by European policies had a highly diverging impact in different national context constellations.

## The Railways

The EC had long made proposals to liberalize the European ways, but it was only in the early 1990s that member states supported such attempts at reform at the European level. The reasons are twofold: the European Commission's approach to railway policy shifted from being detailed and legalistic to being more framework-oriented (see Kerwer and Teutsch in this volume; Knill and Lehmkuhl 1999). The loss in market shares by the railways in intermodal competition deepened the financial crisis in the rail sector, making the need to act increasingly urgent. As a consequence, in 1991 the Council of Transport Ministers agreed to a directive on the development of the EC's railways. Directive 91/440 prescribes the separation of accounting of infrastructure networks and service operation; the raising of tariffs to cover costs and the payment of compensation for unprofitable services (e.g., the construction, maintenance, and operation of unprofitable lines); and an overall, long-term objective of reducing state transfers to precisely the amount of public-service obligations. Directives 97/18 and 97/19 provide for the optional introduction of intramodal competition, that is, competition between different railway companies within, and between, member states and, linked to them, the liberalization of market access to national networks for all international undertakings and combined freight transport. In view of these requirements, why is it that member-state responses to the European policy inputs vary to a great extent from countries, such as Britain, which opted for radical reforms, to others, such as France, where incremental changes have been preferred. In view of the fiscal crisis currently hitting the railways combined with the pressure from intermodal competition, the extent of this differential response to identical pressure and identical—albeit loosely defined—European policy expectations, is puzzling. Classified along the explanatory variables accounting for the extent, mode, and nature of change and the dependent variables reflecting the nature, extent, and origin of change, the five countries present a varied picture of domestic variable constellations.

The regulatory reforms range from high in Britain, to medium-range in the Netherlands and Germany, to low in France and Italy. Britain, France, and Italy, represent the opposite ends of the continuum. While Britain opted for an extensive reform—privatizing the infrastructure and operation of services, introducing institutional separation, opening network access up to competition, but to some extent maintaining state subsidies for infrastructure and services—France realized an organizational separation of infrastructure and service operation, has maintained state ownership, but did not open up the access to the network. The same applies to Italy, which has, at least in principle, decided to introduce an organizational separation together with intramodal competition in the freight sector, but has not subsequently implemented it. The medium-range reforms in the Netherlands and Germany brought about a privatization of services, while infrastructure remains under state ownership. The rail networks are, at least in theory, accessible to competitors of the incumbents in both countries. Finally, state subsidies are still granted for infrastructure, and the state continues to play an important role in infrastructure planning. The variables accounting for the specific turns that reform has taken in the five countries are summarized in table 8.2.

The contextual variables, the influence of the worldwide ideology of liberalization and fiscal pressure, are the same for all five countries. In terms of this ideology, the theory of contested markets is advocated for natural monopolies under public ownership. Reform proposals called for a separation of the network infrastructure from the operation of services, at least in accounting, or by organizational separation (under the roof of one company), or better still, by establishing separate companies, that is, institutional separation. Measures were formulated to increase the managerial autonomy of the railways vis-à-vis the government, to reduce their fiscal dependency on the state, and to introduce intramodal competition, that is, access to the track for competing service operators. Privatization of the newly developed infrastructure and service operation companies were recommended. With respect to the second contextual condition, all national railways had lost out in intermodal competition, that is, their market share in passenger and freight transport had diminished as compared to road haulage and air transport. Due to this loss in business and general budget restrictions, the national railway companies in all countries came under strong fiscal pressure. In Germany, this was exacerbated by German unification and the ensuing need to incorporate the East German Deutsche Reichsbahn into the Deutsche Bahn AG.

The specific stage with respect to liberalization in which a country finds itself when faced with European policy requirements, our first explanatory variable, is the same for all five countries examined. All of them had begun to reform their railways when confronted with European legislation. They took their first steps towards changing public ownership, transforming the state companies into private stock companies; they attempted to make railway managers more independent of state intervention and tried to render the financial relations between the state and railways more transparent. None, however, with the exception of

**Table 8.2. Explanatory Factors and Policy/Structural Change in Railways Policy**

| | Germany | Italy | Britain | Netherlands | France |
|---|---|---|---|---|---|
| Ideology | Contested: interventionist versus pro-liberal | Interventionist | Pro-liberal | Liberal + state | Interventionist |
| Reform Capacity | Medium:<br>- mult. formal veto points<br>- mult. factual veto points<br>- weak formal leadership<br>- strong factual leadership | Low:<br>- mult. formal veto points<br>- mult. factual veto points<br>- weak formal and factual leadership | High:<br>- few formal veto points<br><br>- strong formal and factual leadership | Medium:<br>- few formal veto points<br>- mult. factual veto points<br>- strong formal and factual leadership | Medium:<br>- few formal veto points<br>- mult. factual veto points<br>- strong formal pol. leadership |
| Change in Regulation | Medium:<br>- part. priv.<br>- inst. sep.<br>- open access<br>less state credits | Low:<br>- state owner<br>- org. sep.<br>- no open access<br>- state subs. | High:<br>- full priv.<br>- inst. sep.<br>- open access to networks<br>- state subs. | Medium:<br>- priv. serv.<br>- inst. sep.<br>- open access<br>- state subs. | Low:<br>- state owner<br>- org. sep.<br>- no open access<br>- state subs. |
| Domestic/European Origin | Domestic: +<br>European: + | Domestic: -<br>European: + | Domestic: +<br>European: - | Domestic: +<br>European: + | Domestic: -<br>European: + |

Britain, had introduced intramodal competition for access to the track. In view of these more or less extensive reform measures, they all may be positioned in the stage of pre-liberalization reaching into liberalization.

With respect to the prevailing belief system, at one end of the continuum, Britain adheres to a vigorous neoliberal ideology according to which rail transport must be governed by market principles and serves as an instrument of the economy. At the other end, France and Italy postulate that rail transport must serve the public interest and, on account of the natural monopoly features of the sector, that the state should continue to play a dominant role. The Netherlands and Germany occupy a middle-range position. The Dutch have always maintained that market-liberal principles can be reconciled with state interventionism in order to safeguard public-interest goals. In Germany, the problem-solving approach dominant in the rail sector, while traditionally public-service-oriented, has come under increasing fire from transport economists calling for the introduction of a contested market in the railways.

Whereas the dominant sectoral belief system marks the direction in which national reforms are likely to develop when changes are being shaped, it cannot offer any insights into the process of change as such. It is our second explanatory variable, reform capacity, that accounts for the process of change as such. Britain commands a high reform capacity as a result of few formal veto positions and a high degree of formal integrated political leadership based on majoritarian, hierarchical, single-party government and represents one end of the continuum. Italy, with its multiple factual veto positions and a lack of integrated political leadership due to formal horizontal and vertical fragmentation and the short-term duration of governments, stands at the other. The Netherlands, France, and Germany are characterized by a medium-range reform capacity. When faced with multiple de facto sectoral veto positions, the Netherlands can rely on formal majoritarian government, but also on a successful sectoral tradition of consensual corporatist decision making. France is confronted by multiple factual veto positions that can, in principle, be overcome by formal majoritarian hierarchical government. However, decision making is embedded in a tradition of adversarial antistate politics, which makes consensus building difficult. Finally, Germany has to prevail over multiple de facto veto actors in the sector, without, as a federalist state, being able to rely on formal majoritarian hierarchical governmental powers. However, Germany's long tradition of sectoral corporatist decision making allows the necessary consensual capacity for reform to be developed.

As has been shown, the individual countries are classified very differently along the two explanatory variables "belief systems" and "reform capacity." Each country reveals a distinctive configuration of the two variables and their qualifications. It is therefore not surprising that countries have followed different paths of change in response to the European policy input. Still, as the comparison will show, there are commonalities and differences that offer more general insights.

In analyzing the reform policies of individual member states in the context of the European influence, several combinations of countries are conceivable, since the constellation of variables in the various member states is highly distinctive. Thus, France and Italy are both characterized by an interventionist belief system and multiple de facto veto actors, but differ with respect to formal veto points and the formal preconditions of integrated leadership. Germany and France, to a great extent, share the same philosophy and have to face multiple factual veto positions, but are distinctive regarding formal veto points and the formal basis of integrated leadership. Given this range of possibilities, for the purposes of comparison we have settled for categories where most variables may be held constant. Accordingly, we distinguish two categories of countries, with Germany and Italy with multiple formal and factual veto positions on the one hand, and Britain, the Netherlands, and France with few formal veto positions, on the other.

Examining the outcomes of the reform, we measure them along the four requirements of European legislation: the separation of infrastructure and service operation, managerial autonomy, the fiscal relations between the state and the railways, and intramodal competition. In addition, we have analyzed administrative changes linked to the reform and changes in administrative interest intermediation. The category of countries, Italy and Germany, with multiple formal and factual veto positions and weak integrated political leadership, which are expected to produce modest reforms, reveals only a limited output in Italy, but medium-range output in Germany. With respect organizational reform, Italy has taken some steps toward a formal reorganization of the railways. The Ferrovie dello stato (FS) is now a holding company consisting of more than a hundred separate firms carrying out a range of activities in transport and tourism. However, the separation of infrastructure and service operation has only been decided in principle, but has not been implemented. In Germany, the public monopoly was transformed into a joint-stock company under private law with the state as the sole stock owner. The operation of infrastructure was separated from the provision of services at an organizational and accounting level, and different types of transport (long-distance, short-distance, and freight) were also divided, but steps toward institutional separation with completely independent companies have not yet been taken.

With respect to managerial autonomy, Italy has decided to enhance, at least in principle, the organizational autonomy of the railway management vis-à-vis the state. In practical terms, however, these reforms have not amounted to much. Thus, the freedom to set passenger transport tariffs did not increase, but has instead remained under political control. Moreover, the Italian Parliament agreed to guarantee the maintenance, and even (re)construction, of unprofitable regional lines. In Germany, the granting of interest-free state loans for infrastructure allows the federal government to continue exerting political influence insofar as loans are conditional upon whether the railways' projects are in line with overall infrastructure planning. Moreover, the responsibility of the state for network development has been inserted into the Basic Law.

In regulating the financial relations between the state and the railways, Italy introduced the instrument of contracts that define the relationship between the administration and the railways. These contracts, however, are only a very modest move toward increased financial transparency and responsibility. While removing cross-subsidies between infrastructure financing and the operation of services, they do not sanction unprofitability. In addition, the FS is still dependent on sizable public subsidies. In Germany, the state maintains a supportive financial role: it took over all debts including obligations for outstanding pension and social security liabilities for personnel; and it remains financially involved in regional passenger transport and network investment. In order to increase financial transparency, a regime of contracts was established between regional authorities and service providers. In principle, the tracks must be operated according to commercial criteria and cover their full costs. However, if the public authorities require the maintenance of unprofitable lines that serve the public interest, they compensate the service providers for these functions.

As to intramodal competition, the first step—that is, the separation of infrastructure (area rete) and provision of services (area trasporto)—has been taken in Italy by introducing an organizational separation under the same holding. However, implementation once again lags behind intent. The service division does not yet buy railway capacity from the division managing infrastructure. The second important step, the opening up of the network for access for competing service operators, has not been accomplished either. Apart from FS, no railway company has access to the network. In Germany, access to tracks has formally been opened up to any operator who meets individual licensing criteria, but in practice the Deutsche Bahn AG discriminates against competitors, facilitated by the fact that the allocation of network slots is within the remit of the new railway company. However, a new regulatory body, the Federal Railway Agency, monitors possible discrimination against new entrants seeking access to the tracks.

The more limited reforms in Italy and their more extensive counterparts in Germany can to a great extent be accounted for by our two explanatory variables: belief systems and reform capacity. With respect to the first factor, it may be said that, despite the overall market liberalization ideology prevailing in both countries, sectoral ideologies still hold that railways must serve public-service goals. This belief is particularly pronounced in Germany with respect to regional public transport and reflected in the fact that substantial public subsidies are maintained in regional transport, and the continued responsibility of the state for infrastructure planning and its role as the sole stockowner of Deutsche Bahn AG. In Italy, this public-service orientation is attested to by the public ownership of FS, and far-reaching political intervention in management decisions. What distinguishes the two countries with respect to policy ideas is that in Germany there has been a long tradition of transport economics as a field of research, which, starting in the 1970s, discussed possibilities of liberalizing natural monopolies, but that in Italy no such independent scientific expertise exists that could be referred to in order to promote a process of reform.

The direction of reform is defined by the specific mix of existing belief systems and the overall pressure to liberalize in a country, whereas the ease or cumbersomeness of reform is accounted for by second the factor, that is, reform capacity as defined by the number of formal and factual veto positions and the existence and type of integrated political leadership. Both countries are basically characterized by multiple formal and factual veto positions in rail policymaking. The striking difference between the two countries is the capacity for building a reform consensus and a political coalition that supports it, together with the deployment of implementation capacity once decisions have been made. Italian governments are characterized by a fragmented, as opposed to integrated, political leadership, at both the horizontal and vertical level. Thus, the Ministry of Finance proposed a large-scale reform of the railways along the lines proposed by the EC, the "direttiva Prodi," without previously consulting the Ministry of Transport. Moreover, Italian governments have tended to be more unstable, more conflict-prone, and more short-lived than their German counterparts, effectively restricting the time horizon of political decision makers. With the exception of the "direttiva Prodi," itself a surprise to the other ministries, the government has not proposed long-term reform concepts and initiatives regarding railway development, but has instead left this to other actors, particularly the unions and the FS. When partial reform decisions were made in the past, such as the decision to realize an organizational separation of infrastructure and services, they have not been followed up by implementation.

The railway unions, which had previously presented their own plans for reform, particularly in view of the general push for market liberalization, have now become hard-line opponents of deregulation and privatization. At present they constitute the most important veto player in whatever reforms are proposed. Thus, the "direttiva Prodi" met with stiff resistance from all railway unions and was quickly brought to a halt. More specifically, the unions objected to the abolition of the unity of the railway organization and, since the end of 1997, were still opposed to an organizational reform. They also objected to the attempt to strengthen the financial responsibility of the railways in the belief that it would lead to cuts in the excessive manpower of the railways, previously been used by the state as a means to reduce unemployment. In much the same way, attempts to reclassify the system of job types and wage levels stirred up union opposition. This led to the emergence of a new train drivers' union, the Coordinamento macchinisti uniti (COMO), which in turn brought an end to the unity of railway trade unions and made coordinated decision making among the unions in the reform process even more difficult to achieve. In the newly founded union the train drivers repeatedly used their key functions and called strikes to achieve their goals.

The railway company itself, the FS, and the Ministry of Transport constitute two additional key actors who have tended to veto each other in their respective reform initiatives. The Ministry of Transport, which does not have a railways division of its own, houses staff from the FS and depends on the information provided by the railway company in assessing the efficiency of the railways. Obviously, the FS is unlikely to provide information testifying to its own inefficiency. At the same time, the ministry opposed attempts by the FS to have a greater degree of autonomy and less political intervention in its financial management and frequently intervenes in the setting of rail fares. One FS railway manager, Necci, however, actively developed reform initiatives that were not directed toward market liberalization, but instead advocated European intermodal cooperation in freight transport, while at the same time refusing to introduce intramodal competition as suggested by EC legislation.

In sum, Italian reform capacity is limited by multiple factual veto actors and a lack of horizontal and vertical coordination. This is reflected in a lack of government initiatives and a lack of capacity to build supportive coalitions to overcome the resistance of veto actors, and in the inability to guarantee compliance with existing legislation, once a decision has been made. Europe was used as a resource in an ad hoc manner by one ministry when proposing the "direttiva Prodi" and was not accompanied by a systematic attempt to tie diverse interests together in support of a reform; as a consequence, it was rapidly neutralized.

The German sectoral decision-making system is also characterized by a multiplicity of veto positions, but, in contrast to Italy, among the responsible actors there are some, above all the Ministry of Transport and the railway management, who are strong advocates of a reform and sought to put it on the federal government's political agenda. These actors also successfully mobilized the support of scientific expertise, in the shape of transport economists, who had long been advocating a liberalization of the rail sector. Their attempts were supported by the activities of a well-respected commission instituted to develop a reform proposal and which became very influential in building a consensus in the process of reform. An exogenous factor, German unification that exacerbated the pressing fiscal problems, made the need to act even more apparent. Furthermore, the reformers cited the authority of EU legislation and the European railways program when indicating the direction in which rail policies should develop.

The initial consensus established by the expert commission among the diverse actors in business, science and politics, regarding the principles governing the reform, helped overcome veto positions. Other key actors, such as the Länder and the unions, supported by the Social Democratic Party, only entered the negotiating process of the reform later when its central elements of reform had already been defined. However, due to their veto positions they still wielded considerable power and shaped the contents of the reform accordingly. Thus, the social democrats insisted that the interests of the railway employees be safeguarded and that the power of the state to take influence on infrastructure planning be maintained. This led to the insertion of a clause in the Basic Law mentioned above, which stipulates the responsibility of the central government to develop rail infrastructure.

The largest railway union decided to side with the reform for two reasons: it wanted to play a role in the shaping of the reform; and it obtained the concession of the above-mentioned guarantee, avoiding all disadvantages with regard to pay-levels, promotion, health care, and pensions that could have been linked with a reform. The huge costs of this compensation strategy were taken over by the state. Furthermore, new powers were won. By negotiating directly with the railway management instead of going through the civil service unions, the railway unions gained bargaining power and were no longer dependent on ministerial authorization of the negotiated wages. Additionally, under the new rules the staff and the unions appoint half of the railways' supervisory board. The two smaller unions, one of which organized the train drivers who opposed the reform, did not win over political key actors and, as opposed to Italy, were not able to resort to strike because under German labor law, industrial action is not allowed for political reasons.

In order to realize the reform, another group of important veto actors had to be won over, the regional governments, which could have blocked the reform in the second chamber representing subnational governments. They obtained important corrections of the reform such as the maintaining of public-service goals, the granting of financial transfers to regional and local authorities to enable them to pay for public transport, and the maintaining of state responsibility for the building and maintaining of railway infrastructure. Furthermore, the regional states secured competences regarding future structural railways decisions. The consensus was achieved because the federal government was prepared to pay the compensation costs for those who saw themselves as the losers of the reform.

In comparing Italy and Germany, it is striking to see that in the German case the capacity to coordinate diverse interests and to compensate opponents of the reform in exchange for their support is carefully "socially engineered." The support of a newly instituted and highly respected commission and the use of scientific expertise (and of course, the aid of an exogenous event, unification) and Europe, is used to push the reform through. In Italy, by contrast, while there are individual initiatives of reform, they are not incorporated in any coordinative attempts to balance the diverse interests that are involved, and therefore failed.

Looking at the outcomes of reform in the second group of countries, that is, Britain, the Netherlands, and France, we are faced with a far-reaching reform in Britain, a medium-range reform in the Netherlands, and a modest change in France. Britain has gone furthest with regard to regulatory reform (see Knill in this volume). At the level of organizational reform, a radical separation of infrastructure and service operation was carried through that goes beyond what was demanded by Europe. Railtrack was privatized and has become a private monopoly. It was separated from service operation, which has been taken over by twenty-five passenger service operating companies, on an institutional basis, and an independent private organization was established for rolling stock. All these undertakings are linked by contracts. Passenger and freight operators have to pay for access to the network and lease rolling stock from the rolling stock companies. In the Netherlands, organizational reform has not gone as far (see Lehmkuhl in this volume). Independent legal units were created to separate private from public tasks: a private, market-oriented component for freight, passenger services, real estate, and stations was created; at the same time a government-commissioned public sector was maintained for infrastructure tasks. At the vertical level, transport was regionalized. In France, where the reform is the least far-reaching (see Douillet and Lehmkuhl in this volume), no step was taken toward privatization, but a separate public entity the Réseau ferré de France (RFF) was created for infrastructure, which has taken over a large part of the Société Nationale des Chemins de Fer's (SNCF's) debts, owns the infrastructure, and is responsible for developing the rail network and for setting charges for the usage of the rail network. The SNCF is responsible for service operation, but is also responsible for managing and maintaining infrastructure on behalf of the RFF. Furthermore, a horizontal division of transport, that is, regionalization, was introduced: under the monopoly of the SNCF, regions are now responsible for local passenger rail transport.

Managerial autonomy varies significantly, in line with the different scope of reform in the three countries. Direct political intervention in the management of the privately operated track, rolling stock, and service companies no longer exists in Britain. However, the new private companies are subject to the intensive control by independent regulatory agencies, the Rail Regulator's Office and the Office for Rail Passenger Franchising, now merged into the Strategic Rail Authority. The latter concluded contracts with the service operators setting performance requirements that in turn are controlled by the agency. The fares for services into London are subject to price regulation. In the Netherlands, managerial autonomy was introduced to a considerable extent in the commercial sector. Thus, the tariff structure is now fixed by Nederlandse Spoorwegen and no longer requires ministerial approval. The public network company, by contrast, is under political instruction to follow specific principles, such as increasing the number of passengers and encouraging a shift of freight transport from road to rail for environmental reasons. In France, state intervention is still dominant, although it has been somewhat reduced through prior reforms. It is reflected in the still dominating policies in favor of the *grands projets*, that is, the "trains à grande vitesse." Public-service obligations are still considered important and, in consequence, political intervention also prevails in rate setting in passenger transport, as opposed to the freight sector, which is completely free in its decisions. Wage negotiations between the SNCF and the RFF and the unions and employment decisions must be confirmed by government officials. Concerning infrastructure decisions, the government is engaged in long-term planning.

The extent of political intervention is closely related with the nature of the fiscal relations between the state and the private companies in all countries. In

Britain, Railtrack and most service operators still receive, albeit decreasingly, public subsidies in order to maintain a minimum level of service. In exchange they are subject to the power of the regulatory authorities, which monitor performance as measured by the criteria defined in the contracts. In the Netherlands, the railway company is paid by the government for all politically imposed services which are stipulated in specific contracts. The tracks have remained under public ownership; hence they are fully subject to political decisions. As the state took over part of the SNCF's debt, it can insist on concessions being made by the SNCF with respect to, for example, employment. The SNCF is free to borrow on the capital market, and in order to finance the large projects, it has continued to build up debts that have subsequently been transferred to the RFF.

Concerning intramodal competition, a key feature of the liberalization project, Britain has subjected passenger services to competitive bidding for the operation on individual lines and applies yardstick competition among the different service operators. In freight services there is free access to all lines. But again, the reform is less far-reaching in the other two countries. In the Netherlands, all charges for the use of infrastructure have been suspended until 2000 so that rail service companies can gradually adjust to the new market situation. By contrast, market competition has been fully introduced in the freight sector. In France, there is at present no free access to the network. The SNCF is still responsible for all transport operations. However, international groupings and international combined transport enterprises do in principle have access to the French network, although these rights have not yet been exercised. Nevertheless, one can expect other lines to operate on the French network in the future, since the RFF will develop an interest in opening up access to the network in order to gain new customers as a source of income. Regionalization may speed up this process of opening up the market.

The scope and nature of the reforms in the three countries are reflected in corresponding structural administrative changes and transformations of interest intermediation patterns. The British reform completely changed the preexisting administrative structures. Instead of the public monopoly of British Rail, a new system of interlocked contracts of private companies was established, which are, however, subject to newly created regulatory bodies. This will create new patterns of administrative interest intermediation in the dealings between the regulatory bodies and the regulated industry, the shape of which is only beginning to emerge. The two regulatory bodies have been criticized for being too close to the interests of the rail industry. In the Netherlands, the scope of direct administrative action has been reduced in the commercial sector. However, the reform in sticking to the specifically Dutch "at arms' length" type of steering did not abolish traditional patterns of interest intermediation, but modified them. In France, by creating the RFF and introducing regionalization, new administrative structures have been created.

How can one account for these differences of a large-scale (British), medium-range (Dutch), and modest reform in France? All three countries are characterized by formally integrated political leadership, two of them are confronted with multiple de facto veto positions, and yet they deal with them in very different ways. One factor is that the traditional belief systems existing alongside the overall liberalization pressure vary strongly in the three countries.

Britain clearly adheres to an ideology of market liberalization. More specifically, the dominating ideology in Britain is purely neoliberal and pro-market. Under the impact of American deregulation and privatization, put into practical policies by the Thatcher government, this belief system has permeated almost all of the British public utilities, which have gradually been deregulated and privatized. While there is no explicit public-service goal in British utilities, the notion of consumer responsiveness, anchored in the consumer charter, plays an important role and is part of the passenger service operation contracts. In France, by contrast, the prevailing ideology is to view transport as an instrument in a wider social framework that also pursues distributive objectives with high levels of state intervention and a strong notion of public service. The tradition of public service, supported by all political parties and the trade unions, unified opponents during the reform process and effectively limited the scope of the reform. In the case of the Netherlands, the dominant ideology has always been a peculiar mixture of market liberalism and state intervention, which are not considered mutually exclusive as such, but to be reconciled. These attempts were buttressed by the mobilization of scientific expertise in commissions instituted for the purpose of reform.

The prevailing ideas regarding reform are borne out in the domestic political processes. The reform capacity is constituted by the formal possibilities of integrated political leadership, which is, however, confronted with opposition. In Britain, the goals of the far-reaching reform were easily translated into practical policies. This capacity for change is based on integrated political leadership derived from the presence of a majority party in government that is not confronted with formal veto points. Opponents of the reform, such as the railway unions, were split in their view of liberalization and hence were weakened in their political resistance. Labour, the opposition party, although very critical of the reform at the time, was outvoted. The former public monopoly, British Rail, had paradoxically weakened its position as a potential opponent by previously carrying through significant steps of internal organizational reform. What is most interesting in the British case is that, although there was opposition, the government in power did not have to take it into account, but could, as a result of majority rule, simply go ahead and push it through in spite of massive criticism. In this context Europe did not play much of a role, as it was not needed as a political resource to realize the reform legislation.

The Netherlands has not been faced with many formal veto positions in rail politics either. Nonetheless, the Dutch tradition of corporatist policymaking implies that factual veto actors, such as the unions, are taken into account. The key political actors in the reform process, Nederlandse Spoorwegen, the ministries of

Economic Affairs, Transport, and the Environment, together with the unions, (eventually) took a pro-reform stance. The main reason was that urgent action to shift transport to the railways was seen to be needed in order to safeguard the role of Rotterdam and Schiphol as the "gateways to Europe" by avoiding a transport bottleneck on Dutch roads. Hence, reorganization plans proposed by Nederlandse Spoorwegen met with interest. In order to put the reform discussion on a more objective footing, two committees were established that submitted reform proposals laying the foundation for a general restructuring of the Dutch railways. The actual reform was subsequently shaped in negotiations between Nederlandse Spoorwegen and the Ministry of Transport. Despite much controversy, or what has been termed "fighting cooperation," compromises were reached. Thus, a period of transition in licensing access to the networks was allowed for in order to smooth the way to liberalization.

The unions as potential veto players did not oppose the reform in general, but had some reservations regarding organizational separation. However, they supported the reform because they expected in general a strengthening of the railways. In exchange for their political support, they were offered compensation so that staff reductions were cushioned by social plans, including early retirement plans. The European reform initiative was used in order to accelerate the domestic reform process. The program of a Common European Railway Policy lent political decision makers legitimacy to enact their policy ideas.

France, too, as the other two countries, can formally rely on majoritarian integrated political leadership, but in contrast to the Netherlands, adversarial politics has been a pervasive feature of the reform process. With the exception of the governing party and senior civil servants who were open to policy initiatives from Brussels, and in part the SNCF management, the liberalization plans met with opposition. The railway unions protested against the reform of their pension scheme. They also demanded the full maintenance of public-service functions and argue that the introduction of market principles into the rail sector, already subject to stiff intermodal competition, jeopardizes public-interest services. Similarly, regionalization is considered to be a threat to the SNCF's monopoly. In order to underline their protest, they repeatedly organized strikes. In response to the first extensive three-week strike in 1995, the government appointed committees to discuss the problems of the railways. The outcome was the creation of a separate organizational unit for the network, the RFF. Under the impression of renewed strikes in 1996 and 1997 and demonstrations in Brussels against the European Commission white paper, the government hesitated with the implementation of Directive 91/440. Similarly, Directives 97/18 and 97/19 on access rights were implemented well past the deadline and further concessions made to the railway unions to the effect that amount of the SNCF debt taken over by the RFF was increased and the status of railways employees guaranteed. The opposition, which had much criticized the 1997 reform, did not abolish the RFF after coming into office.

Interestingly, the pro-reform coalition in France, consisting of the government and, in part, the SNCF management, did not use the European legislation in order to reinforce its domestic position in a positive sense. On the contrary, it criticized Brussels for its reform policy and used it in the domestic arena as a "decompression chamber," blaming Brussels and arguing that its own reform plans were not as bad as those of Brussels. Opposition to the European Commission's proposals and disconnecting the French reform from the liberal European rail policy are functional at the domestic level and improve the pro-reform coalition's chances of domestic support.

In brief, the comparison of Britain, the Netherlands, and France shows that while all three can rely on formal preconditions for integrated political leadership, they are all faced with multiple factual veto positions. The mode in which the latter are overcome differs largely in the three countries. The British government can rely on formal, hierarchical, single-party majority government rule; so can France, but, in contrast to Britain, it is embedded in an adversarial political culture and has to yield to the popular pressure that insists on preserving the values of the old culture of public service. The Netherlands could exercise integrated political leadership based on formal majoritarian authority, however prefers to rely to a large extent on a tradition of sectoral consensual corporatist decision making that easily reconciles market-liberal values with state intervention.

To what extent may the changes observed in the five countries examined here be attributed to European policy requirements? While Europe plays a nonnegligible role in some countries (France, the Netherlands, Germany, and, to some extent, Italy), it hardly matters in Britain, where the change originated entirely in a domestic reform process. In the other countries—with the exception of France, where the nationally initiated changes are minor but may prepare the grounds for further liberalization—the endogenously initiated process of reform went hand in hand with the European reform policy, where the second positively supports the first, as in Germany and the Netherlands. In France, by contrast, scapegoating Europe for "ultraliberal" reforms was used as a means to pass minimal reforms.

## CONCLUSION: EUROPEANIZATION AND DOMESTIC CHANGE

What general conclusions can be drawn from the above considerations? What are the implications of our analytical considerations for the field of Europeanization research? Notwithstanding the growing number of studies in this area, there is still a limited understanding of the processes and effects of Europeanization (see chapter 1 in this book; Radaelli 2000). In view of these deficits, our analysis not only contributes to improving the empirical knowledge on the impact of Europe at the national level. Given its comparative focus (across different policy subsectors and member states), it also offers new theoretical insights to account for the different national responses to European policies, which help to improve and qualify existing explanatory approaches. In this context, several aspects deserve particular attention.

## Convergence versus Divergence

While it is often claimed that the definition of unique policy requirements at the European level implies converging patterns and structures of domestic regulation (cf. Harcourt 1999; Schneider 2000), the empirical findings presented here suggest a much more differentiated picture. Convergence effects are generally identified and measured by decreasing variation in the relevant indicators (cf. Martin and Simmons 1998: 753), which in our case refer to the changes in policy instruments, administrative structures, and patterns of administrative interest intermediation. Although there is no doubt that European policymaking leaves its mark on domestic policies, administrative structures, and patterns of interest intermediation, the European impact is highly different across policies and countries. Instead of leading to uniform patterns and structures of domestic policymaking, European policy means different things in different domestic constellations. In other words, the domestic impact of Europe is highly dependent upon the specific policy practice and political constellations at the national level.

The same European policy may trigger fundamental reforms in one country, while having no consequences in others. Depending on the nature of its requirements, European legislation may either strengthen or weaken the strategic position of different actors in different member states. Moreover, even when having a similar effect on actors who are in a similar position, given the domestic policy dynamics, the way in which these actors adjust to the new opportunities and constraints provided by Europe may yield highly varying results in terms of domestic patterns of regulatory adjustment. As we have shown, both the scope and direction of domestic regulatory changes in the context of European policymaking are dependent upon the distinctive constellation of regulatory, ideological, and institutional factors at the national level.

There are two factors that account for the highly distinctive impact of European legislation across policies and countries. The first lies in the nature of the European policies being examined. In the case of road haulage, European policy demands basically are confined to restricting domestic policy options, namely the opportunities to protect domestic markets by limiting the market access of nonresident operators. Apart from these restrictions, which are emerging from the liberalization of cabotage, member states are free to regulate their domestic haulage markets. In other words, European legislation does not prescribe an institutional model for domestic adaptation. A contrast between market-correcting and market-making policies is generally assumed: while market-correcting policies, such as EU environmental policy, positively prescribe distinctive regulatory requirements to be complied with at the national level, market-making policies, such as road haulage policy, tend to exclude certain options from the range of national policy choices (Knill and Lehmkuhl 1999). In this context, however, it must be emphasized that market-making policies might vary a great deal in the extent to which they prescribe institutional models for domestic compliance. While this positive impact is rather limited for the policies investigated in this book, it is much more pronounced, for instance, in European policies for liberalizing the energy sector or in the proposals currently discussed for further specifying the conditions for accessing and operating in the European railways sector.

In the case of European railways policy, as a result of the relatively broad and positive prescriptions for domestic compliance, domestic requirements are similarly restricted. Due to the strong resistance—at the member-state level—to any EC attempt to intervene in domestic railways policies, the 1991 directive does not pose a serious challenge to the well-established railway policies of the member states at the domestic level. The directive is of a partially noncompulsory nature and its text is sufficiently ambiguous to allow domestic implementers far-reaching flexibility and discretion as to how they comply with its modest requirements. The most demanding requirement of the directive is that member states take the necessary measures to ensure that the accounts for business relating to the provision of the infrastructure and for business relating to the provision of transport activities are kept separate. That is, the directive only requires a change in the national accounting systems, not organizational or institutional adaptations (Knill and Lehmkuhl 2000).

In both policy areas, the domestic impact of European legislation is vague, prescribing only limited requirements for domestic adjustment. The European impact is basically confined to altering institutional opportunities and constrains for domestic actor coalitions, and with that, the distribution of power and resources between domestic actors. In this context, changes in domestic opportunity structures are not only concerned with providing domestic actors with new access or extending exit options from the political process; European policies may also strengthen or weaken the strategic position of domestic actors by providing cognitive resources, such as political legitimacy, policy ideas, and solutions to domestic policy problems. In the case of road haulage, for instance, transport users were provided with new exit options—that is, the opportunity to rely on foreign hauliers—while the opportunities of domestic hauliers to protect their market by access restrictions for nonresident competitors were significantly reduced. In European railways policy, by contrast, domestic opportunity structures were primarily affected through the support extended to domestic reformers in the form of expertise, political legitimacy, and the proposition of European solution to domestic problems (such as the financial crisis of the domestic railway systems).

Against this backdrop, the second factor accounting for the highly varying impact of European legislation at the domestic level is the marked variance in the domestic constellations. European policies had a diverging impact on the distinctive institutional opportunities and constraints shaping the strategic interaction of domestic actors. As discussed above, these differences in domestic constellations can be captured by three factors: the specific stage of liberalization (pre-liberalization versus liberalization) at which a country confronts the corresponding European policies; the sectoral capacity for regulatory reform (which includes not only the number of institutional veto points, but also the capacity to achieve political consensus); and the dominant belief system that affects the direction of potential domestic reforms.

## The Limited Explanatory Relevance of "Goodness of Fit"

It follows from these considerations that a static perspective that merely analyzes the "goodness of fit" of European policy requirements and existing domestic arrangements is hardly sufficient to explain the domestic impact of Europe. As our research makes clear, approaches emphasizing the congruence or incongruence of European and national arrangements might only constitute a first step in accounting for the national impact of Europe. They can neither fully account for the varying degrees nor the directions of domestic adjustment patterns.

Regarding the degree of change, our empirical cases reveal that there is no simple causal relationship between the level of incongruence and domestic adaptation. In contrast with the findings of other recent studies (Héritier, Knill, and Mingers 1996; Knill 1998; Börzel 1999; Caporaso, Cowles and Risse 2000), our cases reveal that incongruence—and the corresponding existence of European adaptation pressure—does not constitute a necessary condition for domestic change. The French case of road haulage shows that European policies can lead to national reforms, although the existing regulatory regime was fully in line with EU liberalization policy in this sector. In other words, change took place in the absence of European adaptation pressure. In Italy, by contrast, we observe the persistence of an interventionist policy, notwithstanding the fact that this interventionist approach is highly incompatible with the European policy. We find persistence despite policy incongruence. The same explanatory deficits are to be found when attempting to account for the direction of domestic changes. As we have demonstrated above, the extent to which national policy responses converge or diverge from European objectives and principles is not only a function of policy congruence or incongruence; it depends on the impact that European policies have on opportunity structures and the beliefs of domestic actors.

We have shown that the explanatory deficits associated with the "goodness of fit" perspective can be effectively addressed by applying a more dynamic approach that conceives of European policies basically as input into the domestic political process, which might be exploited by national actors in order to enhance their opportunities for achieving their objectives. In this context, the degree and direction of domestic change depends on the distinctive constellation of three factors: namely, the stage of the national policy process (pre-reform, reform, post-reform), the level of the sectoral reform capacity, as well as the prevailing belief system. The particular constellation of these factors not only affects which domestic actors are strengthened or weakened by EU legislation, but also whether those actors benefiting from European influence are actually able to effectively exploit their new opportunities, putting through regulatory reforms consistent with their interests. In order to account for the direction of potential reforms, we must analyze prevailing belief systems and ideological orientations that are closely linked with a specific stage of national regulatory reform. In contrast, with approaches relying primarily on the compatibility of European and domestic policies, we analyze policy congruence as one explanatory factor (albeit not the exclusive one) whose influence on the scope and direction of domestic change is contingent upon the dynamic interaction with two further variables: the level of sectoral reform capacity and prevailing beliefs and ideological orientations.

In advocating a more dynamic approach, our contribution resonates well with other studies emphasizing the limited explanatory relevance of the congruence/ incongruence perspective in order to account for the domestic impact of Europe. Knill and Lehmkuhl (1999), for instance, argue that the compatibility perspective can only be assumed to have explanatory power as long as European policies positively prescribe or impose a concrete model for domestic compliance (cf. Kohler-Koch 1999: 26). The perspective is of limited use, however, when the impact of European policies basically relies on changing domestic opportunity structures and/or belief systems. As emphasized above, this holds true in particular for many market-making policies of the EU (negative integration). These policies basically exclude certain options from the range of national policy choices, rather than positively prescribing distinctive institutional models to be enacted at the national level. Hence, domestic change (or persistence in the first place) is not a matter of adaptation pressure—which can be generally considered to be low, given the considerable degree of discretion for domestic compliance—but must be explained by analyzing the extent to which European policies have altered the strategic position and beliefs of domestic actors (cf. Eising 1999: 209; Kohler-Koch 1999).

Moreover, several studies have demonstrated the weakness of this static approach in constellations where the domestic institutional context is rather fragile as a result of endogenous transformation processes or performance crises. In these cases, existing domestic arrangements have a very limited influence in shaping policy responses to European requirements. Rather, European influence constitutes a crucial component in enforcing and shaping ongoing domestic reforms (Morlino 1999; Knill and Lenschow 2000).

## Addressing the Problem of Causality in Europeanization/ Internationalization Research

Against this backdrop, a dynamic framework, which explicitly takes into account the institutional, regulatory, strategic, and ideological context at the national level, not only provides a more promising starting point to explain the effects of Europeanization. It might also provide a useful approach in order to cope with a long-standing problem characterizing the research on Europeanization and internationalization, namely, the difficulty of establishing clear causal linkages between domestic changes and European or international developments. The explanatory emphasis placed on the domestic constellations helps to weigh the impact of Europe against other factors and developments that might influence the outcome of domestic reforms. As shown by Goetz (2000) in his analysis on the effect of Europeanization on the ministerial bureaucracy, there are serious doubts as to whether the EU can be conceptualized as a major independent variable amid the changing administrations across Europe. Rather than conceiving of Europeanization as a potential source of change and looking at its impact dichotomously, political scientists should account for its relative importance alongside other variables. On the basis of our dynamic explanatory approach, which explicitly takes account of the dynamic interaction of European policy provisions with the particular domestic context conditions, we are able to provide a more differentiated account of the causal relationship that Europeanization exerts on domestic change.

## Ideal-Type Patterns for European Influence

The comparative analysis of the various domestic responses to European policies allows us to distinguish between three ideal-type patterns for European influence. Depending on the preexisting policies, and distinctive regulatory, institutional, and ideological constellations at the national level, the domestic impact of European policies can be characterized as one of three sorts: a "positive" resource, which strengthens the strategic position of domestic-factor coalitions, which, for their part, promote domestic reforms in line with European policy objectives; a "negative" resource, which strengthens the strategic position of domestic actor coalitions opposing European policy objectives and which in turn promote a distinctive domestic approach; or neutral, implying no particular changes with respect to the strategic opportunities and constraints of the domestic actors.

The first pattern, with European policies serving as a positive resource for domestic reformers, is particularly evident in Germany and the Netherlands. In both countries, European policies reinforced domestic reforms that were concurrent with European policy objectives. The most striking case in this respect concerns the impact of European haulage liberalization in Germany, where European requirements served as an important resource for overcoming the veto position of those actor coalitions in favor of the existing interventionist approach. In the case of the German privatization of the railways, European constraints on domestic participants who had veto rights were also important in strengthening the position of the reformers. The fact that the reform model of the federal government was given a progressive "aura" by virtue of being congruent with the future European railway policies significantly constrained the potential opponents of the reform. Given the foreseeable developments, the question for potential vetoers—especially the Länder, the parliamentary opposition, and the railway union—was not how to block general developments, but how to best influence the shape of a reform that would almost inevitably occur (Teutsch in this volume; Knill and Lehmkuhl 2000). In the Netherlands, emerging European legislation, together with ideas, concepts, and models present in the European sphere, played a key role in shaping domestic haulage and rail policies. Domestic reformers used Europe as a resource to advance their economic and political interests, while developing domestic policies compatible with European objectives.

While the European influence strengthened and amplified domestic regulatory reforms that were concurrent with European policy objectives in Germany and the Netherlands, in France there was an inverse pattern regarding the domestic impact of European policies. With respect to the developments in both road haulage and railways policy, European influence paradoxically strengthened the strategic position of those actors promoting reform proposals that were divergent from, or even in opposition to, European policy objectives. In the case of road haulage, where France had already liberalized, European liberalization strengthened the political influence of actors in favor of reregulation rather than the pro-liberalization coalition. In other words, domestic actors were able to increase their political influence by arguing against European reforms. A similar pattern can be observed in the case of the railways. Instead of using concurrent European policies as a resource to promote the national railways reform in view of the prevailing interventionist tradition, the pro-liberalization coalition (consisting of the government and parts of the railways management) tried to disconnect its proposals from European initiatives in order to strengthen its position at the national level. By opposing European reforms it sought to win political support for a limited reform, hence using Europe as a "decompression chamber."

The third pattern, namely, of a rather neutral impact of European policies on domestic opportunity structures, becomes apparent when considering the influence of European policies on British road haulage and railways policy. Whereas in the other countries examined, domestic policies in these areas can no longer be explained without some reference to European developments, in Britain there is little connection and interdependence between national and European developments. In both road haulage and rail, fundamental domestic reforms took place that, albeit concurrent with European policies, were the result of separate, purely national developments.

In contrast to the four countries considered so far, the developments in Italy can hardly be linked to an ideal-type pattern of European influence. Instead, the impact of European policy in both road haulage and rail suggests that it is a hybrid version, including the three patterns distinguished above. In view of the highly fragmented political system, weak political leadership, and restricted time horizons of frequently changing executives, together with poor implementation, domestic actors tend to rely on ad hoc strategies rather than consistent and long-term concepts in order to advance their interests. Italy did not develop a clear and consistent responsive approach to sectoral problems in the context of European policymaking, either in road haulage or in the railways. Hence, the concrete way that European legislation was used as a resource in the political process is highly dependent on the particular, but unstable, strategic constellation. In the absence of clear domestic ideas and concepts, domestic actors were hardly capable of using Europe as a consequential resource, either positively or negatively. Moreover, as revealed by the attempts to reform the railways during the 1980s, domestic reform initiatives also emerged in complete independence from European developments.

Regardless of the different patterns of European influence to be observed in these five countries, we must stress that European policies cannot be considered to be the single and decisive factor bringing about domestic regulatory change in any of the cases examined. This is particularly obvious in the case of Britain, where domestic reforms occurred independently of European influence; but it also applies to the other member states, where we observe a complex picture of European policies reinforcing or weakening reform developments that originate from within the domestic context (Héritier 2000). The national impact of Europe merely amplifies and modifies ongoing domestic reforms. Rather than constituting an independent source of domestic change, the direction and scope of the European influence are dependent upon domestic developments.

## The Impact of Reform Capacity

Our case studies suggest that the extent to which Europe makes a difference for national policymaking is more pronounced in countries where the sectoral reform capacity can be characterized as medium-level, as in France, Germany, and the Netherlands. In view of such constellations, where successful reforms generally imply considerable effort in consensus building, it is highly likely that the impact of European policies on domestic opportunity structures will make a significant difference to national reform capacity, given that there are actor coalitions in favor of regulatory change that are able to able to exploit the resources emerging from European policies. The impact of Europe on the veto positions of domestic actors, together with access and exit options to the political process, may play a decisive role in facilitating national reforms that might not otherwise occur.

This scenario is particularly pronounced in the German haulage reform, where European influence proved crucial in tipping the scales in favor of the pro-liberalization coalition. This can also be observed, however, in the German railway reform, where European legislation reinforced domestic reform attempts. The same holds true for the two other countries characterized by a medium-level sectoral reform capacity, namely France and the Netherlands. In the case of French road haulage, Europe provided an important stimulus for domestic reregulation activities that might not have otherwise occurred in such a comprehensive way. Moreover, Europe constituted an important resource for the promotion and legitimization of the, albeit limited, domestic railway reform (see Douillet and Lehmkuhl in this volume). European road haulage and rail policy also significantly strengthened the potential for integrated leadership in the Netherlands (see Lehmkuhl in this volume).

By contrast, the case studies carried out for Britain and Italy reveal that the impact of Europe hardly makes a difference in countries where the sectoral capacity for regulatory reform is either very high or very low (see Knill and Kerwer, respectively, in this volume). In Britain, new opportunities and constraints emanating from European policies are of minor relevance within a domestic institutional constellation characterized by a low number of veto points and, correspondingly, a very high capacity for integrated leadership. In view of the "luxury" position of political leaders who can put through fundamental reforms against strong opposition, integrated leadership does not depend on the support of Brussels. In much the same way, the use of Europe as a resource by actors in the opposition in order to block governmental reform activities would hardly reflect a substitute for the lack of an institutional veto position. In short, in these cases Europe makes no difference for existing domestic opportunities to enact or block fundamental regulatory changes.

The same holds true for Italy, but for inverse reasons. In view of the numerous institutional veto points and the absence of integrated leadership capacities, the domestic impact of Europe may be considered to be too weak to improve the low capacity for sectoral reform. In both road haulage and rail policy the impact of Europe on national opportunity structures was not sufficient to overcome the existing institutional veto points. Pressure from Brussels is no substitute for missing leadership capacities at the national level.

The extent to which European politics exerts an influence on domestic politics and the national reform capacities seems to depend on several conditions. First, European reform objectives and national reform initiatives must—at least at a very general level—point in compatible or similar directions, regarding such issues, for instance, as privatization, deregulation, and liberalization, which reflect common focal points for both European and domestic policy objectives in our cases. Given this, the European influence on British transport policy could have been expected to be much higher, if national and European policies had been characterized by contradictory objectives.

Second, European policy requirements must leave a broad leeway for domestic adjustment. In other words, irrespective of differences in national reform capacity, the similarity of domestic responses and hence the similarity of European influence can be expected to increase in connection with the degree to which European policies prescribe detailed requirements for domestic compliance, as is found, for instance, in environmental matters. Notwithstanding the fact that some member states may implement European policies more effectively than others, the detailed and uniform prescriptions inherent in such policies define precise and concrete requirements for domestic adjustment that can hardly be ignored in the long run, either in countries with very high reform capacity or those with very low reform capacity.

Finally, variance in domestic reform capacities is expected to make less difference with respect to the domestic impact of Europe in cases of history making constitutional reforms, such as the formation of the European Monetary Union. Given the high political salience and visibility associated with such reforms, there is much greater potential even in countries with low reform capacities for sufficient leadership capacities to be mobilized in order to achieve a consensus on corresponding domestic adjustments.

# References

Aberle, G. 1996. *Transportwirtschaft*. Munich: Oldenbourg.

Aberle, G., and A. Brenner. 1994. "Trassenpreissystem der Deutsche Bahn AG—eine erste kartellrechtliche und ökonomische Beurteilung." *Internationales Verkehrswesen* 46, 704–12.

Adam Smith Institute. 1993. *The Omega Report: Transport Policy*. London: Adam Smith Institute.

*Agence Europe* 1991a. *Transport Council: Fist Step towards Free Competition between Railway Companies, and a Partial End to Monopolies*, 28 March, 7–8.

——. 11 April 1991b. No title, 10.

——. 1991c. No title, 22 June, 5.

——. 1995. *Parliament Takes a Stand for True Liberalisation of Rail Infrastructure by Amending Council's Common Position that It Considers Too Restrictive*, 22 March, 13.

Amati, A. 1991. "Ente FS e Stato: Il contratto di programma." *Ingeneria Ferroviaria* 46 (4): 231–41.

Andeweg, R. B., and G. A. Irwin. 1993. *Dutch Government and Politics*. London: Macmillan.

Anderson, S., and T. Burns. 1996. "The European Union and the Erosion of Parliamentary Democracy: A Study of Post-Parliamentary Governance." In *The European Union: How Democratic Is It?* ed. S. Anderson and K. A. Eliassen. London: Sage.

Aspinwall, M. 1999. "Planes, Trains and Automobiles: Transport Governance in the European Union." In *The Transformation of Governance in the European Union*, ed. B. Kohler-Koch and R. Eising London: Routledge

Aspinwall, M., and J. Greenwood, eds. 1998. *Collective Action in the European Union: Interests and the New Politics of Assicoalibility*. London: Routledge.

Assemblée nationale. 1994a. Commission d'enquête sur la situation de la SNCF, *Une nouvelle donne pour la SNCF*. Vol. 1, rapport, June, and Vol. 2, auditions, June.

——. 1994b. Délégation pour l'Union européenne, *Les transports de marchandises en Europe: Sortir de l'impasse*. Document d'information, no. 1068, April.

295

———. 1994c. Délégation pour l'Union européenne, *Les transports ferroviaires et l'Europe*. Document d'information, no. 1484, July.

———. 1994d. Délégation pour l'Union européenne, *Les Chemins de fer en Europe: une libéralisation à petite vitesse*. Document d'information, no. 1835, December.

———. 1995. Délégation pour l'Union européenne, *Faut-il défendre le service public?* Document d'information, no. 2260, October.

———. 1996a. Délégation pour l'Union européenne, *Hors de la voir libérale, y a-t-il pour le rail des chances de salut en Europe?* Rapport d'information, no. 3228, December.

———. 1996b. Délégation pour l'Union européenne, *Les Chemins de fer: à la recherche du temps perdu*. Document d'information, no. 2566.

Badie, B., and P. Birnbaum. 1983. *The Sociology of the State*. Chicago: Chicago University Press.

BAG (Die Bundesanstalt für den Güterfernverkehr). 1991. Cologne: BAG.

Baier, V. E., J. G. March, and H. Saetren. 1988. "Implementation and Ambiguity." In *Decisions and Organizations*, ed. J. G. March, 150–64. Oxford: Blackwell.

Barbati, S. 1992. "Pianeta Società Sinport: Pubblico e privato in consorzio, un accordo originale," *FER-MERCI* 13 (3): 21–23.

Bardi, L., F. M. Bindi, and M. Tarchi. 1993. "Italy: The Dominance of Domestic Politics." In *National Public and Private EC Lobbying,* ed. M. P. C. M. van Schendelen, 93–112. Aldershot: Dartmouth.

Bartolini, S. 1997. "Exit Options, Boundary Building, Political Restructuring." Paper presented at the Departmental Seminar, European University Institute, Florence, October, p. 27 (unpublished).

Basedow, J. 1989. *Wettbewerb auf den Verkehrsmärkten: Eine rechtsvergleichende Untersuchung zur Verkehrspolitik*. Heidelberg: C. F. Müller.

Bastmeijer, K. 1997. "The Covenant as an Instrument of Environmental Policy: A Case Study from the Netherlands," *Public Management Occasional Papers,* no. 18, Cooperative Approaches to Regulation. Paris: OECD.

Bauby, P. 1997. *Le service public: Un exposé pour comprendre, un essai pour réfléchir*. Flammarion: Dominos.

Bauer, M. 2000. "The Transformation of the European Commission: A Study of Supranational Management Capacity in EU Structural Funds Implementation in Germany." Ph.D. thesis manuscript, Florence.

Baumgartner, J. P. 1993. "Switzerland." In *Privatisation of Railways,* European Conference of Ministers of Transport (ECMT), 25–50. Paris: OECD.

Baumol, W. J., J. C. Panzar, and R. D. Willig. 1982. *Contestable Markets and the Theory of Industry Structure*. New York: Harcourt Brace Jovanovich.

Bayliss, B. T. 1987. "Die Deregulierung des Straßengüterverkehrs in Großbritannien." *Internationales Verkehrswesen* 39 (1): 9–12.

BDF (Bundesverband des Deutschen Güterfernverkehrs). 1994. *Jahresbericht 1993/94*. Frankfurt a.M.: BDF.

———. 1995a. *Jahresbericht 1994/95*. Frankfurt a.M.: BDF.

———. 1995b. *Verkehrswirtschaftliche Zahlen (VWZ) 1995*. Frankfurt a.M.: BDF.

———. 1995c. *Flexible Kapazitätssteuerung im Straßengüterverkehr. Konturen eines Steuerungsmodells*. Frankfurt a.M.: BDF.

BDI (Bundesverband der Deutschen Industrie). 1987. *Industrie und Deutsche Bundesbahn: Partner in einem europäischen Verkehrsmarkt*. Cologne: BDI.

——. 1989. *Die Bahn der Zukunft—Politik in der Pflicht*. Cologne: BDI.

Beesley, M. and S. Littlechild. 1983. "Privatisation: Principles, Problems, Priorities." *Lloyds Bank Review* 149: 1–20.

Befahy, F. 1995. "Thoughts on Privatisation and Access to Networks." In *Why Do We Need Railways?* ed. European Conference of Ministers of Transport (ECMT), 11–34. Paris: OECD.

Bellamy, C. W., and G. D. Child. 1993. *Common Market Law of Competition*. London: Sweet & Maxwell.

Beltrami, G. 1995. "Come ristrutturare le ferrovie: Vale la logica di mercato." *FER-MERCI* 16 (3): 9–11.

Benz, A. 1998. "Ansatzpunkte für ein europafähiges Demokratiekonzept." In *Regieren in entgrenzten Räumen*, ed. B. Kohler-Koch, PVS-Sonderheft 29 345–68. Opladen: West-deutscher Verlag.

Benz, A. and K. H. Goetz. 1996a. *A New German Public Sector? Reform, Adaptation and Stability*. Aldershot: Dartmouth Press.

——. 1996b. "The German Public Sector: National Priorities and the International Re-form Agenda." In *A New German Public Sector? Reform, Adaptation and Stability*, ed. A. Benz, and K. H. Goetz, 1–26. Aldershot: Dartmouth Press.

Bernadet, M. 1991. "France." In *Deregulation of Freight Transport: Report of the Eighty-Fourth Round Table on Transport Economics,* ed. European Conference of Ministers of Transport (ECMT), February 1990. Paris Cedex: OECD Publications Service.

——. 1997. *Le transport routier de marchandises, fonctionnement et dysfonctionnement.* Paris: Economica.

Bianco, L. 1996. "La ricerca nei trasporti." In *30 anni di trasporti in Italia,* ed. Ministero dei Trasporti. Rome: Istituto Poligrafico e Zecca dello Stato.

Bilancia, F. 1992. "La struttura divisionale." *L'Amministrazione Ferroviaria* 19 (6): 4–5.

Bilotta, B. 1983. "La burocrazia italiana tra tre culture: un'ipotesi sullo sviluppo della 'meridionalizzazione' della pubblica amministrazione." *Rivista Trimestrale di Scienza della Amministrazione* 3: 85–101.

Birginshaw, D. 1994. "BR break-up begins." *International Railway Journal* (April).

Blüthmann, H. 1997. *Unternehmen Kahlschlag.* In Die Zeit no. 12, 14 March 1997, vol. 52, 41.

BMV (Bundesminister für Verkehr) 1994. *Maßnahmen zur Stärkung der Wettbewerbsstel-lung des deutschen Güterkraftverkehrs und der Spedition (Stand 12.1.1995).* Bonn: BMV.

——. 1995a. *Maßnahmen zur Stärkung der Wettbewerbsstellung des deutschen Güterkraftverkehrs und der Spedition: Arbeitsprogramm 1995 (1. Sachstandsbericht, 28 Dec. 1995).* Bonn: BMV.

——. 1995b. "Strukturreform der Eisenbahnen." Bonn: unpublished.

BMV (Bundesminister für Verkehr), ed. 1996. *Verkehr in Zahlen.* Berlin: DIW.

Boes, M. F. 1997. "Die meisten haben den Selbsteintritt bereits abgebaut." *Deutsche Verkehrszeitung* (23 January 1997): 3.

Bordogna, L. 1991. "Relazioni sindacali e frammentazione della rappresentanza nelle Fer-rovie: dalla nascita del Coordinamento macchinisti al suo riconoscimento come soggetto contrattuale." In *Le relazioni sindacali in Italia, 1989–1990,* ed. CESOS Rome: Edizione Lavoro.

——. 1992. "Ristrutturazione e relazioni sindacali nelle ferrovie. Le difficoltà di un processo di risanamento aziendale nel settore pubblico." In *Nuove relazioni industriali per l'Italia in Europa: Quinto Rapporto CER–IRS sull'industria e la politica industriale in Italia,* ed. C. Dell'Arringa, and T. Treu. Bologna: Il Mulino.

Börzel, T. A. 1999a. *The Domestic Impact of Europe: Institutional Adaptation in Germany and Spain,* Ph.D. thesis, European University Institute, Florence.

———. 1999b. "Towards convergence in Europe? Institutional adaption to Europeanization in Germany and Spain." *Journal of Common Market Studies* 39 (4): 573–96.

Bradshaw, W. P. 1995. "Why British Rail is being privatised." *Rail International* 26: 15–21.

Brandborn, J., and L. Hellsvik. 1990. "Die neue Eisenbahnpolitik in Schweden." *Internationales Verkehrswesen* 42 (6): 342–48.

Brandt, E., M. Haack, and B. Törkel. 1994. *Verkehrskollaps: Diagnose und Therapie.* Frankfurt a.M.: Fischer.

Brenac, E. 1994. "De l'Etat producteur à l'Etat régulateur, des cheminements nationaux différenciés: l'exemple des communications." In *Le tournant néo-libéral en Europe: Idées et recettes dans les pratiques gouvernementales,* ed. B. Jobert. Paris: L'Harmattan.

BSL (Bundesverband Spedition und Lagerei). 1994. *Jahresbericht 1993/94.* Bonn: BSL.

———. 1995. *Jahresbericht 1994/95.* Bonn: BSL.

*Bulletin Quotidien: Europe.* 1992a. No title, 23 December, 7.

———. 1992b. No title, 24 February, 9.

———. 1992c. No title, 27 March, 8-9.

———. 1997a. No title, 30 May.

———. 1997b. No title, 19 June.

Bundestag. 1993. Plenary Debate 12/149 of 25 March 1993, Official Protocol, Bonn.

Burnham, J., S. Glaister, and T. Travers. 1994. *Transport Policy-making in Britain, with Special Reference to Roads.* London: LSE.

Burns, T. R., and H. Flam. 1986. *The Shaping of Social Organizations.* London: Sage.

Button, K. J. 1974. "Transport Policy in the United Kingdom, 1968–1974." *Three Banks Review* 103: 26–48.

———. 1991. "Regulatory Reform." In *Transport Deregulation: An International Movement,* ed. K. J. Button and D. Pitfield, 1–23. Basingstoke: Macmillan Academic & Professional.

———. 1993a. "Freight Transport." In *Transport in a Unified Europe: Politics and Challenges,* ed. D. Banister and J. Berechman, 143–70. Amsterdam: Elsevier Science Publishers.

———. 1993b. *Transport Economics.* Cambridge: Edward Elgar Publishing Ltd.

———. 1994. *Transport Policy: Ways into Europe's Future.* Gütersloh: Bertelsmann Foundation.

Button, K. J., and G. Chow. 1983. "Road Haulage Regulation: A Comparison of the Canadian, British and American Approaches." *Transport Reviews* 3 (3): 237–64.

Button, K. J., and A. D. Pearman. 1982. "Regulation of Road Haulage in the United Kingdom: A Critical Review," *Transportation Research Record* 851: 16–23.

Button, K. J. and D. Pitfield, eds. 1991. *Transport Deregulation: An International Movement.* Basingstoke: Macmillan Academic & Professional.

CAFI (Collegio Amministrativo Ferroviario Italiano). 1996. *La nuova struttura ferroviaria: Organizzazione, missione e responsabilità della FS Spa.* Rome: CAFI.

Campbell, J. L., and L. N. Lindberg. 1991. "The Evolution of Governance Regimes." In *Governance of the American Economy*, ed. J. L. Campbell, J. Rogers Hollingsworth, and L. N. Lindberg. Cambridge: Cambridge University Press.

Caporaso, J. A., M. Green Cowles, and T. Risse, eds. 2001. *Europeanization and Domestic Change*. Ithaca: Cornell University Press.

Cassese, S. 1995. *La nuova costituzione economica*. Bari: Laterza.

Cath, I. G. F., D. F. Eden, H. Hulsmann, and K. Seving. 1994. "Competition Law Implications of Deregulation and Privatisation in the Netherlands." SEW *Tijdschrift voor Europees en economisch recht* 42 (5): 353–84.

CEC (Commission of the European Communities). 1985 *Completing the Internal Market, White Paper from the Commission to the European Council*, COM (85) 310 final.

——. 1992. *The Future Development of the Common Transport Policy (White Paper)*, COM (92) 494 final, EC Bull., Suppl. 3/93. Luxembourg: Office for Official Publications of the European Communities.

——. 1994. *European Commission Statistics, Road Freight Transport in the Single Market*, Brussels, DG XII.

——. 1995a. *Droit de la concurrence dans les Communautés européennes. Volume IIA, Règles applicables aux aides d'États: Situation au 31 décembre 1994*. Luxembourg: Office for Official Publications of the European Communities.

——. 1995b. *Towards Fair and Efficient Pricing in Transport: Policy Options for Internalising the External Costs of Transport in the European Union (Green Paper)*. COM (95) 691, EU Bull., Suppl. 2/96. Luxembourg: Office for Official Publications of the European Communities.

——. 1995c. *Green Paper: The Citizens' Network: Fulfilling the Potential of Public Passenger Transport in Europe*. COM (95) 601 final. Luxembourg: Office for Official Publications of the European Communities.

——. 1996. *A Strategy for Revitalising the Community's Railways*. white paper, COM (96) 421 final. Luxembourg: Office for Official Publications of the European Communities.

——. 1996a. *Towards Fair and Efficient Pricing in Transport: Policy Options for Internalising the External Costs of Transport in the European Union*, Brussels.

——. 1996b. *White Paper: A Strategy for Revitalizing the Community's Railways*. Luxembourg: Office for Official Publications of the European Communities.

——. 1997. *Communication from the Commission to the Council, the European Parliament, the Economic and Social Committee and the Committee of the Regions, Transeuropean Rail Freight Freeways*. COM (97) 242 final.

——. 1998. *Communication from the Council to the Parliament on Directive 91/440/CEE Regarding the Development of the Community Railway Systems and on the Access Rights for Rail and Freight Transport*, COM (98) 202 final.

CER (Community of European Railways) 1996. *Response to the European Commission's White Paper "A Strategy for Revitalising the Community's Railways*," Brussels.

Centrum voor energiebesparing en schone technologie. 1996. *The Incorporation of the Environmental Dimension in the Freight Transport Policy*. Delft: Centrum voor energiebesparing en schone technologie.

Christopher, M. 1976. "Freight Transportation in the United Kingdom: The Regulative and Competitive Environment." In *Regulation, Competition and the Public Interest*, ed. K.

Ruppenthal, and W. Stanbury, The Centre for Transportation Studies, University of British Columbia.

CIT (Chartered Institute of Transport). 1994. "Charging for roads." *Transport* (January/February): 11–14.

Claudiani, C. 1996. *Ferrovie: La riforma e fallita? Convegno Nazionale Roma, Hotel Parco dei Principi, 6 dicembre 1996.* Rome: CISL.

CNEL (Consiglio nazionale dell'economia e del lavoro). 1994. *La riforma del ministero dei trasporti.* Rome: CNEL.

Cobb, R. W., and C. D. Elder. 1983. *Participation in American Politics: The Dynamics of Agenda Building.* Baltimore and London: Johns Hopkins University Press.

Coen, D. 1998. "European Business Interest and the Nation State: Large Firm Lobbying in the European Union." *Journal of Public Policy* 18 (1): 75–100.

Cohen, E. 1992. "Dirigisme, politique industrielle et rhétorique industrialiste." *Revue française de science politique* 42 (2) (April).

———. 1996. "Europe between Market and Power: Industrial Policies, Specialization, Technology, Competition and Foreign Trade." In *Adjusting to Europe: The Impact of the European Union on National Institutions and Policies,* ed. Y. Mény, P. Muller and J.-L. Quermonne. London: Routledge.

Colacito, M. 1989. "Ferrovieri." In *Enciclopedia Giuridica Treccani*, vol. 14, 1–9. Rome: Istituto Poligrafico e Zecca dello Stato.

Coletti, G. 1985. *Storia di una riforma: L'Ente "Ferrovie dello Stato,"* Rome: Collegio Amministrativo Ferroviario Italiano.

Commissariat Général du Plan. 1983. *Rapport du groupe de travail Politique des transports, préparation du IX plan 1984–1988.* Paris: Documentation française.

———. 1993. *La situation économique et sociale du transport routier de marchandises,* rapport du groupe présidé par G. Dobias, Paris.

———. 1994. *Contrat de progrès pour le transport routier de marchandises,* rapport du groupe présidé par G. Dobias, Paris.

———. 1995. *Transport: le prix d'une stratégie.* Vol. 2, l'avenir des entreprises publiques. Paris: Documentation française, June.

Committee of Enquiry. 1994. *Road Freight Transport in the Single European Market.* Brussels: Commission of the European Communities.

Communauté des Chemins de Fer Européenes. 1995. *Manuel à l'usage des entreprises ferroviaires à propos de leur accès aux infrastructures ferroviares dans l'Union Européenne, en Norvège et en Suisse. Récapitulatif des règles et principes en vigueur,* Brussels.

Conant, L. 2001. "Europeanization and the Courts: Variable Patterns of Adaptation among National Judiciaries." In *Transforming Europe: Europeanization and Domestic Change,* ed. M. Green Cowles, J. Caporaso, and T. Risse. Ithaca, NY: Cornell University Press.

Conferenza di Varese. 1985. *I problemi del trasporto e della spedizione delle merci.* Varese: Centro Congressi Ville Ponti.

Confetra. 1996. *Il libro bianco dei servizi logistici e di trasporto merci.* Rome: Confetra.

Cooper, J. 1990. "Freight Needs and Transport Policy." Rees Jeffreys Road Fund: Discussion Paper No. 15.

———. 1991. "Lessons for Europe from freight deregulation in Australia, the United Kingdom and the United States of America." *Transport Reviews* 11 (1): 85–104.

Correale, G. 1989. "Ferrovie dello Stato." In *Enciclopedia Giuridica Treccani*, vol. 14, 1–8. Rome: Istituto Poligrafico e Zecca dello Stato.

Corte dei Conti. 1996. *Relazione sul risultato del controllo eseguito sulla gestione finanziaria delle Ferrovie dello Stato Milan Società di trasporti e servizi per azioni per gli esercizi dal 1991 al 1994.* Rome: Corte dei Conti.

Costa, R. 1994. *Una politica del trasporto nel quadro comunitario: Linee di azione del governo in materia di trasporti e navigazione.* Rome: Presidenza del consiglio dei ministri, dipartimento per l'informazione e l'editoria.

Cozzi, T., and C.Govoni. 1989. *Le tariffe e gli accordi collettivi nazionali per il trasporto delle merci su strada.* Rimini: Maggioli.

Cowles, M. Green. 2001. "The TABD and Domestic Business-Government Relations: Challenge and Opportunity." In *Transforming Europe: Europeanization and Domestic Change*, ed. M. Green Cowles, J. Caporaso, and T. Risse. Ithaca, NY: Cornell University Press.

Crespi, G. 1986. *Camionisti: La ristrutturazione del trasporto merci in Italia.* Milan: Franco Angeli.

Czada, R. 1993. "Konfliktbewältigung und politische Reform in vernetzten Entscheidungsstrukturen." In *Verhandlungsdemokratie, Interessenvermittlung, Regierbarkeit. Festschrift für Gerhard Lehmbruch*, ed. R. Czada and M. G. Schmidt. Opladen: Westdeutscher Verlag.

Daalder, H. 1996. "The Netherlands: Opposition in a Segmented Society." In *Political Opposition in Western Democracies*, ed. R. A. Dahl, New Haven, Conn.: Yale University Press.

Dani, A., G. Conte, and G. Giacomini. 1994. *Memoria a sensi dell'art 20 del protocollo sullo statuto della Corte di Giustizia CEE presentata da 'La Spedizione Marittima del Golfo S.r.l.' nella causa n. C–96/94*, Genoa.

Daubertshäuser, K. 1997. "Regionalisierung im Nahverkehr: Eine erste Bilanz aus Sicht der Deutschen Bahn AG." Paper given at the conference Standortbestimmung der Bahnreform organised by DVWG and Deutsches Verkehrsforum, Bonn, September.

DBB (Deutscher Beamtenbund), GDBA (Gewerkschaft Deutscher Bundesbahnbeamten, Arbeiter und Angestellten), GDL (Gewerkschaft Deutscher Lokomotivführer und Anwärter). 1992. *Vorschlag zur Zukunft der Bahn—ein Modell zur Strukturreform.* Bonn: DBB.

de Bandt, J. 1994. "Policy Mix and Industrial Strategies." In *Europe's Economic Challenge: Analyses of Industrial Strategy and Agenda for the 1990s*, ed. P. Bianchi, K. Cowling and R. Sudgen. London and New York: Routledge.

degli Abbati, C. 1987. *Transport and European Integration.* Luxembourg: Office for Official Publications of the European Communities.

Deregulierungskommission, Unabhängige Expertenkommission zum Abbau marktwidriger Regulierungen. 1991. *Marktöffnung und Wettbewerb.* Stuttgart: C.E. Poeschel.

Derthick, M., and P. J. Quirk. 1985. *The Politics of Deregulation.* Washington, D.C.: Brookings.

Deutsche Bahn. 1994. *The Railway Reform.* Frankfurt a.M.: Deutsche Bahn AG.

———. 1996. *Stellungnahme zum Weißbuch der EU-Kommission "Eine Strategie zur Revitalisierung der Eisenbahn in der Gemeinschaft."* Frankfurt a.M.: Deutsche Bahn AG.

Di Miceli, G. B. 1985. "Considerazioni sulla tariffazione da parte del nuovo ente Ferrovie dello Stato." *Economia Pubblica* 15 (7–8): 357–62.

———. 1989. "Il ruolo delle ferrovie nel settore dei servizi pubblici." *Ferrovia & Trasporti* 11: 5–23.

———. 1990. "I nodi delle ferrovie alla vigilia dell'instaurazione del mercato interno." *Economia Pubblica* 20 (7–8): 353–59.

DIHT (Deutscher Industrie- und Handelstag). 1991. *Verkehrspolitik in Deutschland. Zukunftsaufgaben.* Bonn: DIHT.

———. 1992. "Stellungnahme zum Entwurf eines 'Gesetzes zur Neuordnung des Eisenbahnwesens' im Überblick." Bonn: unpublished.

DiMaggio, P. J. and W. W. Powell. 1991. "The Iron Cage Revisited: Institutionalised Isomorphism and Collective Rationality in Organizational Fields." In *The New Institutionalism in Organizational Analysis*, ed. W. W. Powell and P. J. DiMaggio, 63–82. Chicago: Chicago University Press.

DIW (Deutsches Institut für Wirtschaftsforschung). 1994. *Verminderung der Luft- und Lärmbelastungen im Güterverkehr 2010.* Berlin: DIW.

———. 1997. "Trassenpreise der Deutschen Bahn AG—diskriminierungsfrei und kostendeckend?" *DIW-Wochenbericht* 26/97: 457–62.

Dobbin, F. 1993. "What Do Markets Have in Common? Toward a Fast Train Policy for the EC," In *Making Policy in Europe: The Europeification of National Policy-Making*, ed. S. S. Andersen and K. A. Eliassen. London: Sage.

———. 1994. *Forging Industrial Policy: The United States, Britain, and France in the Railway Age.* Cambridge: Cambridge University Press.

Dodgson, J. 1993. "Railway Privatisation and Network Access in Britain," In *Privatisation of Railways*, ed. ECMT, 35–58. Paris: OECD.

———. 1994. "Railway Privatization." In *Privatization and Economic Performance*, ed. M. Bishop, J. Kay, and C. Mayer. Oxford: Oxford University Press.

Domberger, S. 1989. "Economic Regulation through Franchise Contracts." In *Privatisation and Regulation: The UK Experience*, ed. J. Kay, C. Mayer, and D. Thompson. Oxford: Clarendon Press.

DoT (Department of Transports). 1994.

Dowding, K. 1993. "Government at the Centre." In *Developments in British Politics*, ed. P. Dunleavy, A. Gamble, I. Holliday, and G. Peele. London: Macmillan.

Dunleavy, P. 1993. "Introduction: Stability, Crisis or Decline?" In *Developments in British Politics*, ed. P. Dunleavy, A. Gamble, I. Holliday, and G. Peele. London: Macmillan.

Dürr, H. 1994. "Die Strukturreform der Bahn." In *Verkehrswegerecht im Wandel*, ed. W. Blümel. Berlin: Duncker & Humblot.

DVZ. 1997a. "BDF fordert Korrekturen an GüKG-Novelle." *Deutsche Verkehrszeitung* 51 (1 March 1997): 7.

———. 1997b. "Neues Recht für den Güterkraftverkehr." *Deutsche Verkehrszeitung* 51 (11 March 1997): 1.

Dyson, K. 1980. *The State Tradition in Western Europe: A Study of an Idea and an Institution.* Oxford: Robertson.

———, ed. 1992. *The Politics of German Regulation.* Aldershot: Dartmouth.

Dyson, K., and K. Featherstone. 1996. "Italy and EMU as a '*Vincolo Esterno*': Empowering the Technocrats, Transforming the State." *South European Society & Politics* 1 (2): 272–99.

EBA. 1995. *Das Eisenbahn—Bundesamt stellt sich vor.* Bonn: EBA.

Ebeling, K. 1994. "Die Fortentwicklung des Europäischen Eisenbahnsystems: 'Interoperabilität' auch auf sprachlicher Ebene." *Rail International (Schienen der Welt)* 8/9: 17–23.

*Les Echos.* 1979a. No title, 14 May.

———. 1979b. No title, 15 October.

———. 1996. No title, 1 April, 17.

———. 1997. No title, 1 October, 22.

ECMT (European Conference of Ministers of Transport), ed. 1985. *Improvements in International Railway Transport Services.* Paris: OECD.

———. 1987. *Regulatory Reforms in the Transport Sector.* Paris: OECD.

———. 1994. *Internalising the Social Cost of Transport.* Paris: OECD.

Efficiency Unit. 1988. *Improving Management in Government: The Next Steps.* London: HMSO.

Eising, R. 1999. "Reshuffling Power: The Liberalisation of the EU Electricity Markets and Its Impact on the German Governance Regime." In *The Transformation of Governance in the European Union*, ed. B. Kohler-Koch and R. Eising, 208-227. London: Routledge.

Emerson, R. M. 1962. "Power-Dependence Relations." *American Sociological Review* 27: 31–41.

Enquete-Kommission "Schutz der Erdatmosphäre" des Deutschen Bundestages. 1994. *Mobilität und Klima: Wege zu einer klimaverträglichen Verkehrspolitik.* Bonn: Economica.

Erdmenger, J. 1981. *EG unterwegs: Wege zur gemeinsamen Verkehrspolitik.* Baden-Baden: Nomos.

———. 1983. *The European Community Transport Policy: Towards a Common Transport Policy.* Aldershot: Gower.

———. 1991. "Verkehrspolitik." In *Jahrbuch der Europäischen Integration*, ed. W. Weidenfeld and W. Wessels, 185–90. Bonn: Europa Union.

———. 1996. "Verkehr." In *Handbuch des Europäischen Rechts*, ed. H. von der Groeben, J. Thiesing, and C.-D. Ehlermann. Baden-Baden: Nomos.

Eurolog, SPA. 1996. *Relazione del V. Presidente all'assemblea Eurolog.* Rome: Mimeo.

European Centre for Infrastructure Studies. 1996. *The State of the European Infrastructure.* Rotterdam: European Centre for Infrastructure Studies.

Evans, Peter B. 1993. "Building an Integrative Approach to International and Domestic Politics: Reflections and Projections." In *Double-Edged Diplomacy: International Bargaining and Domestic Politics*, ed. Peter B. Evans, Harold K. Kaufman, and Robert D. Putnam. Berkeley: University of California Press.

Ferner, A. and R. Hyman. 1992. "Italy: Between Political Exchange and Micro-Corporatism." In *Industrial Relations in the New Europe,* ed. A. Ferner and R. Hyman, 524–600. Oxford: Blackwell.

Ferretti, M. 1996. "Il trasporto intermodale." In *30 anni di trasporti in Italia*, ed. Ministero dei trasporti, 369–76. Rome: Istituto Poligrafico e Zecca dello Stato.

Ferrovie dello stato. 1993. *Nuovo modello organizzativo delle Ferrovie dello Stato: Società di Trasporti e Servizi per azioni. Supplemento "linea news."* Rome.

———. 1996a. "Il gruppo ferrovie dello stato verso il nuovo piano di impresa." *L'Amministrazione Ferroviaria* 23 (6): 13–48.

———. 1996b. *Ordine di servizio n. 5 del 4 Marzo 1996 di modificazione dell'assetto di vertice e di istituzione di nuove strutture organizzative.* Rome: CAFI.

———. 1996c. "Il contratto di programma 1994–2000." *L'Amministrazione Ferroviaria* 23 (5): 9–24.

*Le Figaro.* 1989. No title.

*Financial Times.* 1998. No title, 24 June, 1.

Fiorentino, L. N.d. "La Riforma delle FF. SS. Legislazione e documentazione." *Rivista Giuridica della Circolazione e dei Trasporti,* quaderno no. 10.

FNTR. 1996. *Transports et logistique* 21.

Fontanella, G. 1974. *Il sistema dei trasporti in Italia: Lineamenti generali.* Padua: CEDAM.

———. 1993. "L'attività pianificatoria nel settore dei trasporti." *Uomini e Trasporti* 12 (93): 20–21.

Fragolino, V., and G. Rossi. 1987. "La nuova organizzazione strutturale dell'Ente FS." *L'Amministrazione Ferroviaria* 14 (1): 3–9.

Franchini, C. 1993. *Amministrazione italiana e amministrazione comunitaria. La coamministrazione nei settori di interesse communitario.* 2d ed. Padua: CEDAM.

Frieden, J. A., and R. Rogowski. 1996. "The Impact of the International Economy on National Policies: An Analytical Overview." In *Internationalization and Domestic Politics,* ed. R. O. Keohane and H. V. Milner. Cambridge, Mass.: Cambridge University Press.

Gamble, A. 1988. *The Free Economy and the Strong State: The Politics of Thatcherism.* London: Macmillan.

Garlichs, D., and E. Müller. 1977. "Eine neue Organisation für das Bundesverkehrsministerium." *Die Verwaltung* 3: 343–62.

GdED (Gewerkschaft der Eisenbahner Deutschlands). 1996. *Die Bahnreform: Herausforderung für die Eisenbahner.* Frankfurt a.M.: GdED.

Gelosi, G. 1995. "Quando la notte si accorcia: l'offerta merci cerca di adeguarsi, non senza difficoltà, alla sensibile espansione della domanda ferroviaria." *FER-MERCI* 16 (2): 22–25.

Genschel, P., and T. Plümper. 1996. *Wenn Reden Silber und Handeln Gold ist: Kommunikation und Kooperation in der internationalen Bankenregulierung.* Discussion Paper 96/4. Cologne: Max Planck Institut für Gesellschaftsforschung.

Gibb, R., T. Lowndes, and C. Charlton. 1996. "The privatisation of British Rail." *Applied Geography* 16 (1): 35–51.

Gibbs, W. W. 1997. "Transportation's Perennial Problems." *Scientific America,* special issue: *The Future of Transportation* 227: 4–7.

Girnau, G. 1997. "Beitrag zur Podiumsdiskussion." Paper given at the conference Standortbestimmung der Bahnreform, organized by DVWG and Deutsches Verkehrsforum, Bonn, September 1997.

Giuliani, M. 1992. "Il processo decisionale italiano e le politiche comunitarie." *Polis* 6 (2): 307–42.

Goetz, K. H. 1995. "National Governance and European Integration: Inter-Governmental Relations in Germany." *Journal of Common Market Studies.* 33 (1): 91–116.

———. 2000. Europeanizing the National Executive? Western and Eastern Style. Paper prepared for the UACES 30th annual conference, Budapest, 6-8 April 2000.

Gourevitch, P. 1986. *Politics in Hard Times: Comparative Responses to International Economic Crises.* Ithaca: Cornell University Press.

Gourvish, T. R. 1990. "British Rail's 'Business-led' Organization, 1977–1990: Government-Industry Relations in Britain's Public Sector." *Business History Review.* 64 (Spring), 109–49.

Grande, E. 1996. "Das Paradox der Schwäche: Forschungspolitik und die Einflußlogik europäischer Politikverflechtung." In *Europäische Integration*, ed. M. Jachtenfuchs and B. Kohler-Koch. Opladen: Leske & Budrich.

———. 1997. "Vom produzierenden zum regulierenden Staat: Möglichkeiten und Grenzen von Regulierung und Privatisierung." In *Privatisierung und staatliche Regulierung*, ed. K. König and A. Benz. Baden-Baden: Nomos.

Grassart, P., and C. Recoura. 1996. *Cheminots en lutte.* Paris: L'Harmattan.

Grin, J., and H. van de Graaf. 1996. "Implementation as Communicative Action: An Interpretive Understanding of Interactions between Policy Actors and Target Groups." *Policy Sciences* 29 (3): 291–319.

Gritten, A. 1988. *Reviving the Railways: A Victorian Future?* London: Centre for Policy Studies.

Gronemeyer, N. 1994. "Die Entwicklung des EU-Kabotage-Rechts bis zur neuen Kabotage-Verordnung (EWG) Nr. 3118/93." *Transportrecht* 17 (7/8): 267–71.

Guillaumat (Commission d'études sur l'avenir des transports terrestres). 1978. *Orientations pour les transport terrestres: Rapport pour M. le Premier Ministre.* Paris: Documentation française.

Gwilliam, K. M. 1979. "Institutions and Objectives in Transport Policy." *Journal of Transport Economics and Policy* 1: 11–27.

———. 1991. "A European Perspective: Long-term Transport Research Needs in the Netherlands." In *Longer-term Issues in Transport: Proceedings of Research Conference sponsored by the Department of Transport*, ed. J. H. Rickard and F. Larkinson. Aldershot: Avebury.

Gwilliam, K. M. and P. J. Mackie. 1980. *Economics and Transport Policy.* London: Allen & Unwin.

Haas, Ernst B. 1964. *Beyond the Nation-State: Functionalism and International Organization.* Stanford, Calif.: Stanford University Press.

Haas, P. 1992. "Epistemic Communities and International Policy Co-ordination." *International Organization* 46 (1): 1–35.

Hall, P. A. 1986. *Governing the Economy: The Politics of State Intervention in Britain and France.* Cambridge: Polity Press.

———. 1992. "The Movement from Keynesianism to Monetarism: Institutional Analysis and British Economic Policy in the 1970s." In *Structuring Politics: Historical Institutionalism in Comparative Analysis*, ed. S. Steinmo, K. Thelen, and F. Longstreth, 90–113. Cambridge: Cambridge University Press.

———. 1993. "Policy Paradigms, Social Learning, and the State: The Case of Cconomic Policy-making in Britain." *Comparative Politics* 26: 275–96.

Hallstein, W. 1974. *Die Europäische Gemeinschaft.* Düsseldorf: Econ.

Hamm, W. 1989. *Deregulierung im Verkehr als politische Aufgabe.* Munich: Minerva.

Hansson, L., and J.-E. Nilsson. 1991. "Neue Bahnpolitik in Schweden: Trennung von Fahrweg und Betrieb." *Schienen der Welt* 22 (6–7): 177–83.

Harcourt, A. J. 1999. Engineering Europeanisation: The Role of the European Institutions in Shaping National Media Regulation. Unpublished manuscript. presented at the Max Planck Institute seminar series, Bonn, November.

————. 2000. "European Institutions and the Media Industry: European Regulatory Politics between Pressure and Pluralism." Ph.D. thesis, Department of Government, University of Manchester.

Harcourt, A. J., and C. Radaelli. 1999. "Limits to EU Technocratic Regulation?" *European Journal of Political Research* 35 (1): 107–22.

Harman, R., G. Sanderson, G. Ferguson, and B. Atkin. 1995. *Investing in Britain's Railways*. Greenmore: Atkin Research & Development Ltd.

Harstrick, C. 1994. "Verkehrspolitische Entscheidungsprozesse und ihre Hintergründe in der Zukunftsplanung der niederländischen Eisenbahnen—eine Fallstudie." Diplom thesis, University of Hannover, Institute for Political Science.

Haverland, M. 2000. "National Adaptation to European Integration: The Importance of Institutional Veto Points." *Journal of Public Policy* 20 (1): 83–103.

Hemerijck, A. 1995. "Corporatist Immobility in the Netherlands." In *Organized Industrial Relations in Europe: What Future?* ed. C. Crouch and F. Traxler. Aldershot: Avebury.

Henke, H. J. 1997. "Wettbewerbsfähig durch 'open access.'" *Deutsche Verkehrszeitung* (68) (7 June): 31–21.

Herber, R. 1992. "Sind die deutschen Tarife im Straßen- und Binnenschiffsverkehr ungültig?" *Transportrecht* 15: 241–56.

Héritier, A. 1993. "Policy-Analyse: Elemente der Kritik und Perspektiven der Neuorientierung." In *Policy-Analyse: Kritik und Neuorientierung*, ed. A. Héritier. PVS special issue 24, 9–38. Opladen: Westdeutscher Verlag.

————. 1996. "The Accomodation of Diversity in European Policy-Making and Its Outcomes: Regulatory Patchwork." *Journal of European Public Policy* 3 (2): 149–76.

————. 1997a. "Market-Making Policy in Europe: Its Impact on Member State Policies: The Case of Road Haulage in Britain, the Netherlands, Germany and Italy." *Journal of European Public Policy* 4 (4): 539–55.

————. 1997b. "Policy-Making by Subterfuge: Interest Accommodation, Innovation and Substitute Democratic Legitimation in Europe—Perspectives from Distinctive Policy Areas." *Journal of European Public Policy* 4 (2): 171–89.

————. 1999. *Policy-Making and Diversity in Europe: Escape from Deadlock*. Cambridge: Cambridge University Press.

————. 2001. "Differential Europe: National Administrative Responses to Community Policy." In *Europeanization and Domestic Change*, ed. J. Caporaso, M. Green Cowles, and T. Risse. Ithaca: Cornell University Press.

Héritier, A., C. Knill, and S. Mingers. 1996. *Ringing the Changes in Europe—Regulatory Competition and the Transformation of the State: Britain, France and Germany*. Berlin: de Gruyter.

Héritier, A., C. Knill, S. Mingers, and M. Becka. 1994. *Die Veränderung von Staatlichkeit in Europa—Ein regulativer Wettbewerb: Deutschland, Grossbritannien und Frankreich in der Europäischen Union*. Opladen: Leske & Budrich.

Héritier, A., and S. Schmidt. 1999. After Liberalization: Public-Interest Services and Employment in the Utilities." In *Globalization and the Welfare State*, ed. Fritz W. Scharpf and Vivien Schmidt. Oxford: University Press.

Herr, C., and D. Lehmkuhl. 1997. "Was zu erwarten war und ist: Aktuelle und zukünftige Probleme des öffentlichen Personennahverkehrs." *Die Verwaltung* 30: 396–419.

Hesse, M. 1993. *Verkehrswende: Ökologisch-ökonomische Perspektiven für Stadt und Region*. Marburg: Metropolis.

Hirst, P., and G. Thompson. 1996. *Globalization in Question: The International Economy and the Possibilities of Governance.* Cambridge: Polity Press.

Holzapfel, H., and K. O. Schallaböck. 1992. "Weiterer Integrationsbedarf für das integrierte europäische Verkehrskonzept." In *Europäische Verkehrspolitik—Wege in die Zukunft, Strategie und Optionen für die Zukunft Europas: Grundlagen*, ed. K. Button. Gütersloh: Bertelsmann.

Hood, C. 1991. "A Public Management for All Seasons?" *Public Administration* 69: 3–19.

Hooghe, L., ed. 1996. *Cohesion Policy and European Integration Building Multi-Level Governance.* Oxford: Clarendon Press.

Hooghe, L., and M. Keating. 1994. "The Politics of EU Regional Policy." *Journal of European Public Policy* 1: 53–79.

Hulsink, W. 1996. *Do Nations Matter in Globalizing Industry? The Restructuring of Telecommunications Governance Regimes in France, the Netherlands and the United Kingdom (1980–1994).* Delft: Eburon.

Husmann, R. 1989. *Das Straßengütertransportgewerbe in den Niederlanden.* Bonn: DIHT.

Hylen, B. 1997. "Sweden." In *The Separation of Operations from Infrastructure in the Provision of Railway Services*, ed. European Conference of Ministers of Transport (ECMT), 91–129. Paris: OECD.

*The Independent.* 1993. No title, 29 August.

———. 1995. No title, 20 December.

Irvine, K. 1987. *The Right Lines.* London: Adam Smith Institute.

Jachtenfuchs, M. 1995. "Theoretical Perspectives on European Governance." *European Law Journal* 1 (2): 115–33.

Jachtenfuchs, M., T. Dietz, and S. Sung. 1999. "Which Europe? Conflicting Models of a Legitimate European Political Order." *European Journal of Political Research* 4 (4): 409–45.

Jacobs, A. T. J. M., and E. J. M. Herk. 1995. "Sociale aspecten van de Europese liberalisering van het beroepsgoederenvervoer over de weg." *Tijdschrift voor Europees en economisch recht* 43 (3): 155–70.

JB. 1996. "Regionalisierte Nebenbahnen im Aufwind." *Internationales Verkehrswesen* (special issue ÖPNV) 48: 15–20.

Jobert, B., ed. 1994. *Le tournant neo-liberal en Europe: idees et recettes dans les pratiques gouvernementales.* Paris: L'Harmattan.

Jobert, B., and B. Théret. 1994. "France: La consécration républicaine du néo-libéralisme." In *Le tournant néo-libéral en Europe: Idées et recettes dans les pratiques gouvernementales*, ed. B. Jobert, 21–86. Paris: L'Harmattan.

Jones, J. 1984. *The Politics of Transport in 20th Century France.* Kingston: McGill-Queens' University Press.

Jones, P. M. 1993. "Transport." In *Contemporary Britain: An Annual Review 1993*, ed. P. Catterall and V. Pretston. Oxford: Basil Blackwell.

Jordan, G., and J. Richardson. 1982. "The British Policy Style or the Logic of Negotiation." In *Policy Styles in Western Europe*, ed. J. Richardson. London: Allen & Unwin.

Kassim, H. 1994. "Policy Networks, Networks and European Union Policy Making: A Sceptical View." *West European Politics* 17 (4): 15–27.

Kassim, H., and A. Menon. 1996. "The European Union and State Autonomy." In *The European Union and National Industrial Policy*, ed. H. Kassim and A. Menon. London: Routledge.

Katzenstein, P. 1985. *Small States in World Markets: Industrial Policy in Europe*. Ithaca: Cornell University Press.

——. 1987. *Policy and Politics in West-Germany: The Growth of an Semi-Sovereign State*. Philadelphia: Temple University Press.

Kay, J., and D. Thompson. 1991. "Regulatory Reform in Transport in the United Kingdom: Priniciples and Application." In *Transport in a Free Market Economy*, ed. D. Banister and K. Button. London: Macmillan.

Kerwer, D. 2000. "Reforming Transport in Italy: A Case Study in Europeanisation." Ph.D. thesis, European University Institute, Florence.

Keus, L. A. D., and R. J. M. Tweel. 1991. "De nieuwe wet goederenvervoer over de weg." *Tijdschrift voor Europees en economisch recht* 39 (10): 622–35.

Kickert, W. J. M. 1993. *Verandering in management en organisatie bij de rijksoverheid.* Alphen aan den Rijn: Samsom H.D. Tjeenk Willink.

Kingdon, J. W. 1984. *Agendas, Alternatives, and Public Policies*. Boston: Little, Brown and Co.

Kiriazidis, T. 1994. *European Transport: Problems and Policies*. Aldershot: Avebury.

Klenke, D. 1995. "Freier Stau für freie Bürger." In *Die Geschichte der bundesdeutschen Verkehrspolitik*. Darmstadt: Wissenschaftliche Buchgesellschaft.

Knight, J. 1992. *Institutions and Social Conflict*. Cambridge: Cambridge University Press.

Knill, C. 1995. *Staatlichkeit im Wandel: Großbritannien im Spannungsfeld nationaler Reformen und europäischer Integration.* Opladen: Deutscher Universitätsverlag.

——. 1998. "European Policies: The Impact of National Administrative Traditions." *Journal of Public Policy* 18 (1): 1–28.

——. 1999. *The Transformation of National Administrations in Europe: Patterns of Change and Persistence*. Habilitationsschrift: FernUniversität Hagen.

Knill, C., and D. Lehmkuhl. 1999. "How Europe Matters: Different Mechanisms of Europeanization." *European Integration online Papers (EIoP)*. Vol. 3 (1999), no. 7 (http://www.eiop.or.at/eiop/texte/1999-007a.htm) [accessed **date**].

——. 2000. "An Alternative Route of European Integration." *West European Politics* 23 (1): 65–88.

Knill, C., and A. Lenschow. 1998. "Coping with Europe: The Impact of British and German Administrations on the Implementation of EU Environmental Policy." *Journal of European Public Policy* 5 (4): 595–614.

——. 2000a. *Implementing EU Environmental Policy: New Directions and Old Problems.* Manchester: Manchester University Press.

——. 2000b. "'New' Environmental Policy Instruments as a Panacea? Their Limitations in Theory and Practice." In *Environmental Policy in a European Community of Variable Geometry. The Challenge of the Next Enlargement*, ed. K. Holzinger and P. Knoepfel. Basel: Helbing & Lichtenhahn.

Kohler-Koch, B. 1996a. "Die Gestaltungsmacht organisierter Interessen." In *Europäische Integration*, ed. M. Jachtenfuchs and B. Kohler-Koch. Opladen: Leske & Budrich.

——. 1996b. "The Strength of Weakness: The Transformation of Governance in the EU." In *The Future of the Nation State: Essays on Cultural Pluralism and Political Integration*, ed. S. Gustavsson and L. Lewin. Stockholm: Nerenstoa and Santeruss.

——. 1996c. "Catching Up with Change: The Transformation of Governance in the European Union." *Journal of European Public Policy* 3 (3), 359–80.

———. 1999. "The Evolution and Transformation of European Governance." In *The Transformation of Governance in the European Union*, ed. B. Kohler-Koch and R. Eising. London: Routledge, 14-36.

Kohler-Koch, B., and J. Edler. 1998. "Ideendiskurs und Vergemeinschaftung: Entschließung transnationaler Räume durch europäisches Regieren." In *Regieren in entgrenzten Räumen*, ed. B. Kohler-Koch. Opladen: Westdeutscher Verlag.

König, H.-J. 1993. "Läuft die Bahn voll aus dem Ruder?" *Internationales Verkehrswesen* 45: 424–28.

Krasner, S. D. 1988. "Sovereignty: An Institutional Perspective." *Comparative Political Studies* 21 (1): 66–94.

Laaser, C.-F. 1991. *Wettbewerb im Verkehrswesen: Chancen für eine Deregulierung in der Bundesrepublik*. Tübingen: J.C.B. Mohr.

———. 1994. *Die Bahnstrukturreform: Richtige Weichenstellung oder Fahrt aufs Abstellgleis?* Kiel: Institut für Weltwirtschaft.

Labbé, D., and M. Croizat. 1992. *La fin des syndicats?* Paris: L'Harmattan.

Labour Party. 1996. *Consensus for Change: Labour's Transport Strategy for the 21st Century*. London: British Labour Party.

Ladrech, R. 1994. "Europeanization of Domestic Politics and Institutions: The Case of France." *Journal of Common Market Studies* 32: 69–88.

Lammich, K. 1991. "Die Vereinbarkeit der Preisbildung im Güterkraftverkehr und in der Binnenschiffahrt mit EG-Wettbewerbsrecht." *Recht der internationalen Wirtschaft* 37: 538–42.

LaPalombara, J. G. 1964. *Interest Groups in Italian Politics*. Princeton: Princeton University Press.

Larsson, S., and A. Ekström. 1993. "Sweden." In *Privatisation of Railways*, ed. ECMT. ECMT Roundtable 90. Paris Cedex: OECD Publications Service.

Laumann, E. O., et al. 1978. "Community Structure as Interorganizational Linkages." *Annual Review of Sociology* 4: 455–84.

Lehmbruch, G. 1987. "Administrative Interessenvermittlung." In *Verwaltung und ihre Umwelt: Festschrift für Thomas Ellwein*, ed. A. Windhoff-Héritier. Opladen: Westdeutscher Verlag.

———. 1991. "The Organization of Society, Administrative Strategies and Policy Networks." In *Political Choice, Institutions, Rules and the Limits of Rationality*, ed. P. Czada and A. Windhoff-Héritier, 121–55. Frankfurt a.M: Campus.

———. 1992. "Bedingungen und Grenzen politischer Steuerung im Verkehrssektor." In *Politik und Technik in der Verantwortung*, ed. Verband Deutscher Elektroingenieure (VDE), Frankfurt a.M.: VDE.

Lehmkuhl, D. 1996. "Privatizing to Keep It Public? The Reorganization of German Railways." In *A New German Public Sector? Reform, Adaptation and Stability*, ed. A. Benz and K. H. Goetz. Aldershot: Dartmouth Press.

———. 1999. *The Importance of Small Differences—The Impact of European Integration on the Associations in the German and Dutch Road Haulage Industry*. Amsterdam: Thela thesis.

Lehmkuhl, D., and C. Herr. 1994. "Reform im Spannungsfeld von Dezentralisierung und Entstaatlichung: Die Neuordnung des Eisenbahnwesens in Deutschland." *Politische Vierteljahresschrift* 35: 631–57.

Leibfried, S., and P. Pierson, eds. 1995. *European Social Policy: Between Fragmentation and Integration*. Washington D.C.: Brookings Institution.

Lepore, M. C. 1993. "La circolazione delle merci su strada." *Rivista Giuridica della Circolazione e dei Trasporti* 47 (2): 239–81.

Lequesne, C. 1996. "French Central Government and the European Political System: Change and Adaptation since the Single Act." In *Adjusting to Europe: The Impact of the European Union on National Institutions and Policies*, ed. Y. Mény, P. Muller, and J.-L. Quermonne. London: Routledge.

Liefferink, D. 1997. "The Netherlands: A Net Exporter of Environmental Policy Concepts." In *European Environmental Policies: The Pioneers*, ed. M. S. Andersen and D. Liefferink. Manchester: Manchester University Press.

Lindberg, L. N., and S. A. Scheingold. 1970. *Europe's Would-Be Polity: Patterns of Change in the European Community*. Englewood Cliffs: Prentice-Hall.

Linden, W. 1952. "Der Reichs-Kraftwagen-Betriebsverband (RKB)." *Zeitschrift für Verkehrswissenschaft* 23: 1–24.

Loraschi, G. C. 1984. *L'impresa pubblica: Il caso delle ferrovie dello stato*. Milan: Giuffrè.

Luhmann, N. 1991. "Soziologie des politischen Systems." In *Soziologische Aufklärung 1. Aufsätze zur Theorie sozialer Systeme*, N. Luhmann (6th edition), 154–77. Opladen: Westdeutscher Verlag.

Mair, P. 1999. "The Europeanization of Domestic Politics: The Limited Case of National Party Systems." Paper presented at Multi-Party Systems: Europeanization and the Reshaping of National Political Representation, European University Institute, Florence, December.

Majone, G., ed. 1990. *Deregulation or Re-regulation: Regulatory Reform in Europe and the United States*. New York: St. Martin's.

Majone, G. 1994. "The Rise of the Regulatory State in Europe." *West European Politics* 17 (3): 77–101.

———. 1996. *Regulating Europe*. London: Routledge.

March, J. G., and J. P. Olsen. 1989. *Rediscovering Institutions: The Organizational Basis of Politics*. New York: Free Press.

Marks, G. 1996. "Exploring and Explaining Variation in EU Cohesion Policy." In *Cohesion Policy and European Integration: Building Multi-Level Governance*, ed. L. Hooghe, 388–422. Oxford: Clarendon Press.

Martin, L., and B. Simmons. 1998. "Theories and Empirical Studies of International Institutions." *International Organization* 52 (4): 729–57.

Martinand, C. 1996. *Débat national sur lavenir du transport ferroviaire*. Rapport introductif du groupe de travail présidé par Claude Martinand, 25 February.

Massey, A. 1992. "Managing Change: Politicians and Experts in the Age of Privatization." *Government and Opposition* 27: 486–501.

Mayntz, R. 1993. "Policy-Netzwerke und die Logik von Verhandlungssystemen." In *Policy-Analyse: Kritik und Neuorientierung*, ed. A. Héritier. PVS special issue 24, 39–56. Opladen: Westdeutscher Verlag.

Mayntz, R., and F. W. Scharpf. 1995. "Steuerung und Selbstorganisation in staatsnahen Sektoren." In ed. R. Mayntz and F. W. Scharpf, *Gesellschaftliche Selbstregelung und politische Steuerung,* 9–38. Frankfurt a.M: Campus.

Mazey, S. and J. Richardson, eds. 1993. *Lobbying in the European Community.* Oxford: Oxford University Press.

Mény, Y., P. Muller, and J-L. Quermonne. 1996. "Introduction." In *Adjusting to Europe: The Impact of the European Union on National Institutions and Policies*, ed. Y. Mény, P. Muller, and J-L. Quermonne, 1–21. London: Routledge.

Merlini, S. 1994. "Il governo." In *Manuale di diritto pubblico,* ed. G. Amato and A. Barbera, 419–61. Bologna: Il Mulino.

Meyer, J. W. and B, Rowan. 1991. "Institutionalized Organizations: Formal Structure as Myth and Ceremony." In *The New Institutionalism in Organizational Analysis*, ed. W. W. Powell and P. J. DiMaggio, 41–62, Chicago: University of Chicago.

Ministerie van Verkeer en Waterstaat (VenW). 1990. *Verkeer en Waterstaat en het Europa zonder grenzen.* The Hague: Ministerie van Verkeer en Waterstaat.

———. 1991. *DGV: Van ambtelijke dienst naar ambtelijk berdrijf.* The Hague: Ministerie van Verkeer en Waterstaat.

———. 1997. Beleidskader toelating tot het spoorvervoer (brief aan de voozitter van de Tweede Kamer der Staten-Generaal, 11 February, kenmerk GDV/CPV/PVV-S/V 721483).

Ministero dei Trasporti. 1977. *Libro Bianco: I Trasporti in Italia.* Rome: Istituto Poligrafico e Zecca dello Stato.

———. 1992. *Il Mercato dei Trasporti con l'estero.* Rome: Istituto Poligrafico e Zecca dello Stato.

———. 1994. *Le ferrovie in concessione e in gestione governativa.* Rome: Istituto Poligrafico e Zecca dello Stato.

———. 1996. *30 anni di trasporti in Italia.* Rome: Istituto Poligrafico e Zecca dello Stato.

———. N.d.a. *I trasporti in Italia: Efficacia, efficienza e produttività per superare la crisi.* Rome: Ministero dei Trasporti.

———. N.d.b. *L'autotrasporto merci: Analisi, Problemi, Prospettive.* Rome: Ministero dei Trasporti.

*Le Monde.* 1985. No title, 13–14 October.

———. 1986. No title, 12–13 October.

———. 1995a. No title, 8 September.

———. 1995b. No title, 1 December.

———. 1996a. No title, 27 August.

———. 1996b. No title, 4 October.

*Le Monde Emploi.* 1997. No title, 26 February.

*Mondo Economico.* 1996a. *Il treno viaggia senza controllore: Cosa nasconde il bilancio delle Ferrovie dello Stato*, 29 April, 86–88.

———. 1996b. *Vagoni di denaro*, pp. 10–15.

Moravcsik, A. 1993. "Preferences and Power in the European Community: A Liberal Intergovernmental Approach." *Journal of Common Market Studies* 31 (4): 473–524.

———. 1998. *The Choice for Europe: Social Purpose and State Power from Messina to Maastricht.* Ithaca: Cornell University Press.

Morlino, L. 1999. *Europeanization and Representation in Two Europes: Local Institutions and National Parties.* Paper given to the conference on multi-party systems: Europeanization and the Reshaping of National Political Representation, European University Institute, Florence, 16–18 December.

Mückenhausen, P. 1994. "Die Harmonisierung der Abgaben auf den Straßengüterverkehr in der Europäischen Gemeinschaft." *Europäische Zeitschrift für Wirtschaftsrecht* 5: 519–23.

Mulder, G. 1992. "Uitgerangeerd?" *Intermediair* (16–17 April): 11–15.

Muller, P. 1990. *Les politiques publiques.* Paris: PUF.

Munari, F. 1994. "'La segnalazione dell'Autorità Garante della Concorrenza e del Mercato in materia di servizi di autotrasporto di merci." *Diritto dei Trasporti* 7 (3): 903–18.

Nash, C. 1993. "Developments in Transport Policy: Rail Privatisation in Britain." *Journal of Transport Economics and Policy* 27 (3): 317–22.

Nash, C. A. 1997. "United Kindgom." In *The Separation of Operations from Infrastructure in the Provision of Railway Services,* ed. European Conference of Ministers of Transport (ECMT). Paris: OECD.

Nash, C. A., and J. Preston. 1991. "Appraisal of Rail Investment Projects: Recent British Experience." *Transport Reviews* 11 (4): 295–309.

Nash, C. A., and J. Preston. 1993. "The Policy Debate in Great Britain." In *Privatisation of the Railways,* ed. European Conference of Ministers of Transports (ECMT), 81–119. Paris: OECD.

Natalicchi, G. 1996. "Telecommunications Policy and Integration Processes in the European Union." Ph.D. thesis manuscript, City University of New York, New York.

*La Nazione.* 1996. "Autotrasportatori: Nuovo Consorzio," 25 April, 5.

Necci, A. L. 1992. "Per una politica di alleanze." *FER-MERCI* 13 (3): 4–5.

———. 1994. "Il futuro delle ferrovie: L'armonizzazione delle condizioni di concorrenza. Intervento del presidente dell'Union de Chemin de Fer alla conferenza paneuropea dei trasporti." *L'Amministrazione Ferroviaria* 21 (4): 4–7.

Necci, A. L., and R. Normann. 1994. *Reinventare l'Italia.* Milan: Mondadori.

Nederland Distributieland. 1993. *Nederland Distributieland: Sector, Concept, en Organisatie 1987-1990-1995: Terugblik en Toekomstvisie.* The Hague: Nederland Distributieland.

*Nieuwsblad Transport.* 1997. No title, 12 June.

Noël, È. 1988. "Italia-Cee. Vizi e virtù di un membro fondatore." *Relazioni Internazionali* (10 June): 94–99.

Nora, S. (Group de travail du comité interministériel des entreprises publiques). 1968. *Rapport sur les entreprises publiques.* Paris: Documentation française.

*NRC Handelsblad.* 1997a. No title, 12 February, 1.

———. 1997b. No title, 24 June, 7.

———. 1997c. No title, 6 March, 3.

———. 1997d. No title, 3 September, 1.

———. 1998. No title, 24 June, 17–21.

Oberti, P. 1995. "Riforma della disciplina in materia di autotrasporto delle merci ed istituzione dell'Agenzia nazionale autotrasporto per conto terzi." In *XII Legislatura, Disegni di Legge e relazioni N. 3215, 4.10.1995.* Camera dei Deputati.

Observatoire Economique et Statistique des Transports (OEST). 1995. *Bilan social annuel du transport routier de marchandises,* Secrétariat d'Etat aux transports, October.

Ocqueteau, F. 1997. *Sécurité dans le transport routier de marchandises: Contexte économique et régulations locales.* Report for the ENM and DISR, March.

Ocqueteau, F., and J.-C. Thoenig. 1997. "Mouvements sociaux et action publique: Le transport routier de marchandises." *Sociologie du travail* 4: 397–423.

OECD. (Organization for Economic Co-operation and Development). 1990. *Competition Policy and the Deregulation of Road Transport*. Paris: OECD.

——. 1995. *OECD Environmental Performance Reviews: Netherlands*. Paris: OECD.

*L'Officiel Des Trasporteurs* (OT). 1996a. No title, 1–8 Feburary.

——. 1996b. No title, 19–26 October.

——. 1997a. No title, 1–8 March.

——. 1997b. No title, 12 July, 21–23.

Olsen, J. P. 1995. "European Challenges to the Nation State." ARENA Working Paper No. 14/95. Oslo: ARENA.

——. 1996. "Europeanization and Nation-State Dynamics." In *The Future of the Nation-State*, ed. S. Gustavsson and L. Lewin, 245–85. London: Routledge.

Olsen, J. P., and B. Guy Peters. 1994. "Lessons from Experience: Experiential Learning in Administrative Reforms in Eight Democracies." ARENA Working Papers No. 3, University of Oslo, Advanced Research on the Europeanization of the Nation-State.

Olson, M. 1965. *The Logic of Collective Action*. Cambridge, Mass.: Harvard University Press.

OPRAF. 1996. *Passenger Rail Industry Overview*. London: Office of Passenger Rail Franchising.

Ostrowski, R. 1993. "Neue Wege der Infrastrukturfinanzierung." *Zeitschrift für Verkehrswissenschaft* 64 (2): 49–66.

Owens, S. 1995. "From 'Predict and Provide' to 'Predict and Prevent'? Pricing and Planning in Transport Policy." *Transport Policy* 2 (1): 43–49.

Page, Sir Edward, and N. Robinson. 1995. "Future Generations, Ethics and Transport Policy." Working Paper No. 122, University of Warwick, Department of Politics and International Studies.

Page, E. C., and L. Wouters. 1995. "The Europeanization of National Bureaucracies? In *Bureaucracy in the Modern State: An Introduction to Comparative Public Administration*, ed. J. Pierre. Edward Elgar: Aldershot, 185-204.

Parsons, C. 2000. "Domestic Interests, Ideas and Integration: The French Case." *Journal of Common Market Studies* 38 (1): 45–70.

Pendleton, A. 1993. "Railways." In *Public Enterprise in Transition—Industrial Relations in State and Privatized Corporations*, eds. A. Pendleton and J. Winterton. London: Routledge.

Pezzoli, A. 1995. "Privatizzazione e riorganizzazione dei servizi di pubblica utilità: Il trasporto ferroviario." *Rivista di Politica Economica* 85 (12): 221–44.

Pezzoli, A., and A. Venanzetti. 1996. *I trasporti e la concorrenza: Una rassegna dei principali problemi a partire dagli interventi dell'Autorità Garante della Concorrenza e del Mercato. Convegno del Libero Istituto Universitario Carlo Cattaneo: Liberalizzazione e Regolazione nei Trasporti*. Castellanza (Va): Mimeo.

Pinna, G. 1997. "Intermodalità: Svolta cruciale." *Lo Spedizioniere Doganale* 3: 3–8.

Pollitt, C. 1993. *Managerialism and the Public Services*. Oxford: Blackwell.

Ponti, M. 1992. "Il caso delle ferrovie dello stato." In *I trasporti e l'industria: Quinto rapporto CER/IRS sull'industria e la politica industriale italiana*, ed. M. Ponti. Bologna: Il Mulino.

——. 1996a. *Struttura del settore e politiche in atto. Convegno del Libero Istituto Universitario Carlo Cattaneo: Liberalizzazione e Regolazione nei Trasporti*. Castellanza (Va): Mimeo.

——. 1996b. "70mila miliardi in libera uscita." *Mondo Economico* (September): 18–20.

Port of Rotterdam. 1996. *Port Statistics.* Rotterdam: Port of Rotterdam.

Press Release C/99/134 1999. 2191st Council Meeting Transport. Luxembourg, 17 June.

Preston, J. 1996. "The Economics of British Rail Privatisation: An Assessment." *Transport Reviews*, 16 (1): 1–21.

Pryke, R. 1981. *The Nationalised Industries: Policies and Performance since 1968.* Oxford: Martin Robertson.

Putnam, R. D. 1988. "Diplomacy and Domestic Politics: The Logic of Two-Level Games." *International Organization* 42 (3): 427–60.

Radaelli, C. M. 1997a. "How Does Europeanization Produce Policy Change? Corporate Tax Policy in Italy and the UK." *Comparative Political Studies.* 30 (5): 553–75.

——. 1997b. *The Politics of Corporate Taxation in the European Union: Knowledge and International Policy Agendas.* London: Routledge.

——. 2000. "Whither Europeanization? Concept Stretching and Substantive Change." Paper given at the conference Europeanization: Concept and Reality, organized by the Bradford University, Bradford, Mai.

Railtrack. 1996. *Network Management Statement 1995/96: Developing a Network for Britain's Needs.* London: Railtrack.

*Railway Gazette International.* 1994. "NS Reaps the Benefit of Business Management." *Railway Gazette International* 34 (1): 663–66.

Ranke, P. M. 1996. "Access to the Dutch Rail Network." Informal document. The Hague: Railned.

RCEP (Royal Commission on Environmental Pollution). 1994. *Eighteenth Report: Transport and the Environment.* London: HMSO.

Regierungskommission. 1991. *Regierungskommission Bundesbahn Bericht.* Bonn: Unpublished report.

Regonini, G., and M. Giuliani. 1994. "Italie: Au-delà d'une démocracie consensuelle?" In *Le tournant néo-libéral en Europe: Idées et recettes dans les pratiques gouvernementales*, ed. B. Jobert, 123–99. Paris: L'Harmattan.

Reid, Sir Robert. 1990. "On Track for the 1990s." *Transport* (Jan./Feb): 15–17.

*La Repubblica: Affari & Finanza.* 1996a. "Cimoli e le Ferrovie dello status quo" (18 September): 4

——. 1996b. "FS, il grande 'Progetto' finito negli scambi: Una gestione che ha rivoluzionato la vecchia struttura, nel bene e nel male, cercando sempre il consenso in ogni modo possibile" (23 September): 1–5.

Reviglio, F. 1994. *Meno stato, più mercato: Come ridurre lo stato per risanare il paese.* Milan: Mondadori.

Reynolds, P., and D. Coates. 1996. "Conclusion." In *Industrial Policy in Britain*, ed. D. Coates. Houndmills: Macmillan.

Rhodes, M. 1995. "A Regulatory Conundrum: Industrial Relations and the Social Dimension." In *European Social Policy: Between Fragmentation and Integration,* ed. S. Leibfried and P. Pierson, 78–122. Washington D.C.: The Brookings Institution.

Rhodes, R. A. W. 1996. "The New European Agencies: Agencies in British Government: Revolution or Evolution?" EUI Working Papers RSC No. 96/51, European University Institute, Florence.

Ribeill, G. 1992. "Les cheminots français: Un statut toujours en débat. Genèse, avatars et représentations." In *Transports 93, professions en devenir.* ed. P. Hamelin, G. Ribeill, and C. Vauclare. Paris: Presse nationale des Ponts et chaussées.

———. 1994. "SNCF: Du malaise social à la cassure corporative." *Travail* 31, (spring-winter): 37–62.

Richardson, J. 1996. "Actor-Based Models of National and EU Policy-Making: Policy Communities, Issue Networks and Epistemic Communities." In *The European Community and National Institutional Policy*, eds. H. Kassim and A. Menon, London: Routledge.

Rometsch, D., and W. Wessels. 1996. *The European Union and the Member States: Towards Institutional Fusion?* Manchester: Manchester University Press.

Rommerskirchen, S. 1985. "Gestaltung und Kostenbedeutung der Abgabensysteme für Lastkraftfahrzeuge in ausgewählten ECMT-Ländern." *Zeitschrift für Verkehrswissenschaft* 56 (3): 216–36.

Rosanvallon, P. 1989. "The Development of Keynesianism in France." In *The Political Power of Economic Ideas: Kenesianism across Nations*, ed. P. A. Hall. Princeton: Princeton University Press.

Ross, J. F. 1994. "High-Speed Rail: Catalyst for European Integration?" *Journal of Common Market Studies* 32 (2): 191–214.

Rouban, L. 1993. *Les cadres de la fonction publique et la politique de modernisation administrative, recherche pour le Commissariat Général du Plan et la Direction Générale de la fonction publique.* Paris: FNSP.

RPR (Rassemblement pour la Republique). 1986. "Une nouvelle politique des transports." February.

Ruggie, J. G. 1998. *Constructing the World Polity: Essays on International Institutionalization.* London: Routledge.

Russo Frattasi, G. G., and A. Russo Frattasi. 1984. *Note di Economia e di pianificazione dei trasporti.* Turin: CLUT.

RVI (Rijksverkeerinspectie). 1995. *Jaarbericht.* The Hague: RVI.

Sabatier, P. A. 1993. "Advocacy-Koalitionen, Policy-Wandel und Policy-Lernen: Eine Alternative zur Phasenheuristik." In *Policy-Analyse: Kritik und Neuorientierung*, ed. A. Héritier. PVS Special Issue 24, 116–48. Opladen: Westdeutscher Verlag.

Sabatier, P. A. 1998. "The Advocacy Coalition Framework: Revisions and Relevance for Europe." *Journal of European Public Policy* 5 (1): 98–130.

SACTRA. 1994. *Trunk Roads and the Generation of Traffic.* London: HMSO.

Sandhäger, H. 1987. "Das deutsche Interesse in der gemeinsamen Verkehrspolitik." *Zeitschrift für Verkehrswissenschaft* 58: 14–26.

Santoro, F. 1974. *La politica dei trasporti della Comunità Economica Europea.* Turin: UTET.

Sanviti, G. 1992. *Il Ministero dei Trasporti.* Rome: La Nuova Italia Scientifica.

Scazzocchio, B. 1995. "Tre questioni di vitale importanza: La parola ai vertici di UNATRAS." *Uomini e Trasporti* 14 (105): 4–5.

Scharpf, F. W. 1988. "The Joint-Decision Trap—Lessons from German Federalism and European Integration. *Public Administration* 66: 239–78.

———. 1994. *Optionen des Föderalismus in Deutschland und Europa.* Frankfurt a.M: Campus.

————. 1996. "Negative and Positive Integration in the Political Economy of European Welfare States." In *Governance in the European Union,* ed. G. Marks, F. W. Scharpf, P. C. Schmitter, and W. Streeck, 15–39. London: Sage.

————. 1997a. *Games Real Actors Play: Actor-Centered Institutionalism in Policy-Research.* Boulder, Colo.: Westview Press.

————. 1997b. "Introduction: The Problem-Solving Capacity of Multi-Level Governance." *Journal of European Public Policy* 4 (4): 520–38.

————. 1999. *Governing in Europe: Effective and Democratic?* Oxford: Oxford University Press.

Schmidt, S. K. 1997. "Die wettbewerbsrechtliche Handlungsfähigkeit der Europäischen Kommission in staatsnahen Sektoren." Ph.D. thesis, University of Hamburg.

————. 1998. *Liberalisierung in Europa: Die Rolle der Europäischen Kommission.* New York: Campus.

Schmidt, V. A. 1997. "Discourse and (Dis)integration in Europe: The Cases of France, Germany, and Great Britain." *Daedalus* 126 (3): 167–97.

————. 2000. "Discourse and the Legitimation of Economic and Social Policy Change." In *Globalization and the European Political Economy,* ed. S. Weber. New York: Columbia University Press.

Schmitt, V. 1988. "Entwicklung und Perspektiven der EG-Tarife für den Strassengütersverkehr." *Zeitschrift für Verkehrswissenschaft* 59 (4): 229–52.

————. 1993. "Die Harmonisierung der Wettbewerbsbedingungen in der EG-Binnenverkehrspolitik: Eine Bilanz der technischen, sozialen und steuerlichen Rechtsetzung." *EuZW* 4: 305–11.

Schmitter, P. C., and G. Lehmbruch, eds. 1979. *Trends toward Corporatist Intermediation.* Beverly Hills: Sage.

Schmuck, H. 1992. "Die Eisenbahnen in der Gemeinsamen Verkehrspolitik der EG." *Transportrecht* 15 (2): 41–53.

Schneider, V. 2001. "Europeanization and the Re-dimensionalization of the Public Sector: Telecommunications in Germany, France and Italy." In *Transforming Europe: Europeanization and Domestic Change,* ed. M. Green Cowles, J. Caporaso, and T. Risse Ithaca: Cornell University Press.

Schneider, V., G. Dang-Nguyen, and R. Werle. 1994. "Corporate Actor Networks in European Policy-Making: Harmonising Telecommunications Policy." *Journal of Common Market Studies* 32: 473–98.

Sénat. 1993. "Rapport de la commission d'enquête chargée d'examiner l'évolution de la situation financière de la SNCF, les conditions dans lesquelles cette société remplit ses missions de service public, les relations qu'elle entretient avec les collectivités locales et son rôle en matière d'aménagement du territoire," June.

————. 1996a. "Annexe au procès-verbal de la séance du 12 juin 1996, rapport fait au nom de la Commission des affaires économiques et du plan sur la proposition de résolution présentée en application de l'article 73bis du règlement par M. Nicolas sur la communication de la Commission sur le développement des chemins de fer communautaires."

————. 1996b. Délégation du Sénat pour l'Union européenne. *Les chemins de fer en Europe: L'heure de la vérité et du courage.* Rapport d'information, November.

————. 1996c. Délégation du Sénat pour l'Union européenne. *L'Europe, une chance pour la SNCF?* Rapport d'information.

SES (Service Economique et Statistique). 1996. *Bilan social annuel du transport routier de marchandises.* Secrétariat d'Etat aux transports.

Singer, O. 1993. "Policy Communities und Diskurs-Koalitionen: Experten und Expertise in der Wirtschaftspolitik." In *Policy-Analyse: Kritik und Neuorientierung,* ed. A. Héritier, 149–74. Opladen: Westdeutscher Verlag.

Sinnecker, E. 1997. "Wir wollen auch im Ausland anbieten." Interview with the DB-Güterverkehrs-Chef Sinnecker. *Deutsche Verkehrszeitung,* 12 April, 3.

Siwek-Pouydesseau, J. 1993. *Les syndicats des grands services publics et l'Europe.* Paris: L'Harmattan.

Skocpol, T. 1985. "Bringing the State Back In: Strategies of Analysis in Current Research." In *Bringing the State Back In,* eds. P. B. Evans, D. Rueschemeyer, and T. Skocpol, 3–37. Cambridge: Cambridge University Press.

Sleuwaegen, L., with F. Pot and S. Lashtek. 1993. "Road Haulage." In *Market Services and European Integration. The Challenges for the 1990s, European Economy,* ed. P. Buigues, F. Ilzkovitz, J.-F. Lebrun, and A. Sapir. Social Europe. Reports and Studies. Brussels: Commission of the European Communities.

*Il Sole 24 Ore.* 1 May 1992. *Fs, una Spa per linee in nero: Necci ha approvato e inviato al Cipe il progetto di trasformazione dell'Ente in società azione,* 22.

——. 17 May 1992. *Bernini dà luce verde alle Fs formato Spa: Inviato al Cipe con molte riserve il piano Necci,* 15.

——. 12 May 1995. *Per le authority alla Camera commino ancora accidentato,* 25.

——. 13 May 1995. *Si accende la polemica sull'Authority-trasporti,* 18.

——. 24 August 1995. *Trasporto merci, gli uffici doganali lasciano i porti,* 1.

——. 31 August 1995. *Confetra guida la crociata sulle dogane: Chiesto il rinvio della riforma,* 17.

——. 14 December 1995. *Autotrasporto: Lotta continua,* 13.

——. 17 December 1995. *Autotrasporto: per l'accordo il "buco" è di 177 miliardi,* 5.

——. 8 January 1996. *Il Fisco preme sull'acceleratore: Sono più salati il bollo sulla patente, la tassa di proprietà, la benzina verde e, anche, i pedaggi autostradali,* 3.

——. 20 February 1996. *Gli sconti agli autotrasportatori "dimezzano" bollo e pedaggi: Approvato dall'ultimo Consiglio dei ministri un decreto legge da 206 miliardi,* 18.

——. 1 May 1996. *Per l'autotrasporto aiuti nel mirino UE: Ultimatum di due settimane al governo,* 9.

——. 11 June 1996. *Computer selvaggio,* 14.

——. 3 September 1996. *Burlando, entro la fine del mese un altro vertice sulle tariffe,* 13.

——. 29 September 1996. *Comincia per le Fs la lotta agli sprechi,* 2.

——. 1 February 1997. *Prodi vara lo spezzatino ferroviario e "mette a dieta" costi e personale,* 13.

——. 5 February 1997. *Una società unica per gestire i servizi: Il ministro Burlando conferma la disponibilità a modificare il progetto (ma non la TAV) e media sull'attuazione della derettiva Prodi,* 10.

——. 13 February 1997. *Bloccato il treno della riforma: Le condizioni poste dai sindacati rischiano di frenare il risanamento,* 3.

——. 20 February 1997. *Fs, al via la nuova struttura, Conti e Forlenza alla direzione,* 9.

——. 15 March 1997. *Cimoli: "Certezze dal governo." Senza indicazioni dell'azionista c'è il rischio di uno slittamento dei tempi del piano di impresa*, 9.

——. 3 December 1997. *Ferrovie, c'è intesa sui tagli: azienda e sindacati firmano il protocollo sulla gestione degli esuberi*, 21.

——. 5 December 1997. *Ferrovieri, il no di Ciampi: Il ministro ha manifestato critiche e perplessità sulla gestione degli esuberi nel settore*, 2.

——. 19 December 1997. *Fs, deficit da 5mila miliardi. Prodi ribadisce la fiducia a Cimoli mentre viene rinviata ancora la decisione sugli aumenti tariffari*, 11.

Spirito, P. 1996a. *Le ferrovie europee verso la liberalizzazione*. Rome: Mimeo.

——. 1996b. "La riforma del trasporto pubblico locale tra regionalizzazione ed incentivi alla efficienza gestionale." *L'Amministrazione Ferroviaria* 23 (5): 4–8.

Staniland, M. 1993. "What to Do about the Railways? The Politics and Problems of E.C. Rail Policy," October, University of Pittsburgh (unpublished paper).

Stocchi, L., and A. De Angelis. 1992. *Relazioni industriali nell'ente FS e regolamentazione dell'esercizio del diritto di sciopero nei servizi pubblici essenziali*. Rome: Edizione Collegio amministrativo ferroviario italiano (EDICAFI).

Stoffaës, C., J.-C. Bertold, and M. Feve. 1995. *L'Europe, avenir du ferroviaire*. Rapport au Ministre des transports, 1 December.

Stone Sweet, Alec. 2000. *Governing with Judges: Constitutional Politics in Europe*. Oxford: Oxford University Press.

Stornelli, R., and G. Battistoni. 1994. *Autotrasporto merci: Guida a leggi, decreti, e circolari*. Milan: FAG.

Strati, F., M. Franci, and M. Ferroni. 1996. *The Incorporation of the Environmental Dimension in Freight Transport: The Italian Case Study. Final Report*. Florence: Studio Ricerche Sociali.

Streeck, W. 1995a. "From Market-Making to State-Building? Reflections on the Political Economy of European Social Policy." In *European Social Policy: Between Fragmentation and Integration*, ed. S. Leibfried and P. Pierson, 389–431. Washington, D.C.: Brookings Institution.

——. 1995b. "Neo-Voluntarism: A New European Social Policy Regime?" *European Law Journal* 1: 31–59.

Streeck, W., and P. C. Schmitter. 1991. "From National Corporatism to Transnational Pluralism: Organized Interests in the Single European Market." *Politics and Society* 19 (2): 133–64.

——. 1985. *Private Interest Government: Beyond Market and State*. London: Sage.

Strohl, M. P. C. 1993. *Europe's High-Speed Trains: A Study in Geo-Economics*. Westport: Praeger.

*Süddeutsche Zeitung* 1997a. "Bundesbahn stellt die Weichen Richtung Straße." vol. 53, (12 March): 4.

——. 1997b. "Deutsche Bahn will international mitfahren." vol. 53, (18 September): 27.

Suleiman, E. N. 1974. *Politics, Power and Bureaucracy in France: The Administrative Elite*. Princeton: Princeton University Press.

——. 1990. "The Politics of Privatisation in Britain and France." In *The Political Economy of Public Sector Reform and Privatization*, ed. E. N. Suleiman and J. Waterbury. Boulder: Westview Press.

Sylos-Labini, P. 1995. *La crisi italiana*. Rome: Laterza.

Taylor, S. M. 1994. "Article 30 and Telecommunications Monopolies." *European Common Market Law Review* 31 (6): 322–34.

Teasdale, A. L. 1993. "The Life and Death of the Luxembourg Compromise." *Journal of Common Market Studies* 31: 567–79.

Thatcher, M. 1995. "Regulatory Reform and Internationalization in Telecommunications." In *Industrial Enterprise and European Integration*, ed. J. Hayward. Oxford: Oxford University Press.

Thoenig, J.-C. 1983. "La réglementation des transports en France: comportements réels et effets de système." In *Les transports et la puissance publique*, ed. E. Quinet. Paris: Presses de l'Ecole nationale des Ponts et chaussées.

*The Times*. 1989. No title, 17 October.

Toonen, Th. A. J. 1987. "The Netherlands: A Decentralised Unitary State in a Welfare Society." *West European Politics* 10: 108–29.

Transport DoT (Department of Transport). 1994. *Britain's Railways: A New Era*. London: HMSO.

Transport en Logistiek Nederland (TLN). 1996. *Transport in Cijfers. Editie 96*. Zoetermeer: TLN.

*La tribune des fossés*. 1997. No title, 4 February.

Truelove, P. 1992. *Decision Making in Transport Planning*. Burnt Mill: Longman.

Tsebelis, G. 1995. "Decision-Making in Political Systems." *British Journal of Political Science* 25 (3): 289–325.

*Tuttotrasporti*. 1988. "Blocco delle autorizzazioni: Ogni decisione rinviata." No. 92, Dec.

van der Burgh, Y. 1994. "Convenanten als beleidsinstrument: De case sociale vernieuwing." In *Beleidsinstrumenten bestuurskundig beschouwd*, ed. J.T.H.A. Bressers, P. de Jong, P.-J. Klok, and A.F.A. Korsten. Assen: Van Gorcum.

van Empel, F. 1997. "De tijdige bekering van een monopolist." *NRC Handelsblad* (18 February).

van Kolk, H. L., F. C. Kuik, and R. Onverzaagt. 1991. *De relatie overheid—NS in Europees perspectief*. The Hague: Instistuut voor Onderzoek van Overheidsuitgaven.

van Schendelen, M. 1984. "Consociationalism, pillarization and conflict management in the Low Countries." *Acta Politica* special issue, January.

van Suntum, U. 1986. *Verkehrspolitik*. Munich: Vahlen.

van Waarden, F. 1992. "The Historical Institutionalization of Typical National Patterns in Policy Networks between State and Industry: A Comparison of the USA and the Netherlands." *European Journal of Political Research* 21: 131–62.

———. 1995. "National Regulatory Styles: A Conceptual Scheme and the Institutional Foundations of Styles." In *Convergence or Diversity? Internationalization and Economic Policy Response*, ed. B. Unger and F. van Waarden. Aldershot: Avebury.

Vickers, J., and G. Yarrow. 1989. "Telecommunications: Liberalisation and the Privatisation of British Telecom." In *Privatisation and Regulation: The UK Experience*, ed. J. Kay, C. Mayer, and D. Thompson. Oxford: Clarendon Press.

Visser, J., and A. Hemerijck. 1997. *The Dutch Miracle*. Amsterdam: Amsterdam University Press.

VKS (Vereinigung Deutscher Kraftwagenspediteure). 1995. *Jahresbericht 1994/95*. Bonn: VKS.

Voilland, M. 1985. "Le déréglemetation des transports routiers de marchandises: L'expérience française." Laboratoire d'économie des transports, Ph.D. thesis, University of Lyon II.

Wallace, H. 2000. "Analysing and Explaining Policies." In *Policy-Making in the European Union*. 4th ed., ed. H. Wallace and W. Wallace. Oxford: Oxford University Press.

Wallace, H., and W. Wallace, eds. 2000. *Policy-Making in the European Union*. 4th ed., Oxford: Oxford University Press.

Weiler, J. H. H. 1991. "The Transformation of Europe." *Yale Law Journal* 100: 2403–83.

Weinstock, U. 1980. "Einige Gedanken zur gemeinsamen Verkehrspolitik—Vom Legalismus zum Pragmatismus." *Zeitschrift für Verkehrswissenschaft* 51: 200–22.

White, P. 1995. *Public Transport: Its Planning, Management, and Operation*. London: UCL Press.

Whitelegg, J. 1988. *Transport Policy in the EEC*. London: Routledge.

Wijffels, H. H. F., R. J. Veld, and J. F. A. de Soet. 1992. "Sporen voor Straks; Advies over de toekoemstige relatie tussen overheid en Nederlandse Spoorwegen." Unpublished manuscript.

Willeke, R. 1995. "40 Jahre Verkehrswissenschaft und Verkehrspolitik." *Zeitschrift für Verkehrswissenschaft* 66: 167–86.

Williamson, O. E. 1975. *Markets and Hierarchies: Analysis and Antitrust Implications*. New York: Free Press.

Willis, F. R. 1971. *Italy Chooses Europe*, New York: Oxford University Press.

Willke, H. 1995. "The Proactive State: The Role of National Enabling Policies in Global Socio-Economic Transformations." In *Benevolent Conspiracies: The Role of Enabling Technologies in the Welfare of Nations: The Cases of SDI, SEMATECH, and EUREKA*, ed. H. Willke, C. P. Krück, and C. Thorn. Berlin: de Gruyter.

Windhoff-Héritier, A. 1989. "Institutionelle Interessenvermittlung im Sozialsektor: Strukturmuster verbandlicher Beteiligung und deren Folgen." *Leviathan* 17 (1): 108–26.

———. 1991. "Institutions, Interests and Political Choice." In *Political Choice: Institutions, Rules, and the Limits of Rationality*, ed. R. M Czada and A. Windhoff-Héritier, 27–52. Frankfurt a.M.: Campus.

Wissenbach, K. 1994. "Die verschleppte Bahnreform: Eine Dokumentation der vergangenen viereinhalb Jahrzehnte." *Schienen der Welt* 25: 32–41.

Wissmann, M. 1994. "Verkehrspolitik und Verkehrsrecht in Europa." *Deutsches Autorecht* 63: 428–32.

———. 1997. 'Verkehrspolitik für Wachstum und Beschäftigung." *Zeitschrift für Verkehrswissenschaft* 68: 3–11.

Witte, B. 1932. *Eisenbahn und Staat: Ein Vergleich der europäischen und nordamerikanischen Eisenbahnorganisationen in ihrem Verhältnis zum Staat*." Jena: Gustav Fischer.

Woolcock, S. 1996. "Competition among Rules in the Single European Market." In *International Regulatory Competition and Coordination*, ed. W. Bratton, J. McCahery, S. Picciotto, and C. Scott, 289–321. Oxford: Clarendon.

Young, A.R. 2000. The Adaptation of European Foreign Economic Policy. *Journal of Common Market Studies* 38 (1): 93–116.

Zahariadis, N. 1996. "Selling British Rail: An Idea Whose Time Has Come?" *Comparative Political Studies* 29 (4): 400–422.

Zijderveld, A. C. 1989. "Een spoor door de verzorgingsstaat: De sociale en culturele betekenis van de NS na de Tweede Weredoorlog." In *Het Spoor—150 jaar spoorwegen in Nederland*, ed. Nederlandse Spoorwegen. Utrecht and Amsterdam: Nederlandse Spoorwegen / Meulenhoff Informatief.

# Appendix

## ACTORS INTERVIEWED

**European Union**

Commission, DG VII, 16 April 1996.
Commission, DG VII, 20 March 1997. *Rees*.
Commission, DG VII, 24 March 1997. *Wilson*.
Community of European Railways, 17 April 1996.
ex-DG VII, 22 May 1996.

**Britain**

BRB, British Railways Board; February 1997.
BRF, British Road Federation; May 1995.
British Steel; February 1997.
CBI, Confederation of British Industry; November 1994, 1995.
CEC, Commission of the European Communities, DG XII; April 1996.
CIT, Chartered Institute of Transport; January 1996.
DoT, Department of Transport; November 1995, January 1996, November 1996
    February 1997, November 1997.
Freightliner; November 1996.
FTA, Freight Transport Association; November 1995, April 1996.
Labour Party; November 1995.
OPRAF, Office of Passenger Rail Franchising; November 1996, November
    1997.
ORR, Office of the Rail Regulator, November 1996, November 1997.

Railtrack; November 1996, November 1997.
RCEP, Royal Commission on Environmental Pollution; November 1994.
RHA, Road Haulage Association; November 1995.
RIA, Railway Industry Association; February 1997.
Save Our Railways; February 1997.
Traffic Commissioner; January 1996.

### France

CFDT1, 27.3.1997, secretary general and deputy secretary general of the road department of FGTE-CFDT (Fédération Générale des Transports et de l'Equipement-Confédération Française Démocratique du Travail).

CFDT2, 4.6.1997, workers' representative in the SNCF board of directors (Confédération Française Démocratique du Travail).

CGT, 28.5.97, workers' representative in the SNCF board of directors (Confédération Générale du Travail).

CLTI, 2.4.1997, secretary general.

DTT1, 1996, Department of Land Transport, Ministry of Transport (1983–1993).

DTT3, 1996, Department of Land Transport, Ministry of Transport (1982–1985, 1989–1994).

DTT4, 1996, Department of Land Transport, Ministry of Transport (1987–1994).

DTT5, 5.6.1997, Department of Land Transport, Ministry of Transport.

FNTR2, 18.12.1997, former president of the Fédération Nationale du Transport Routier.

FO, 12.6.1997, national secretary of the railwaymen trade union for communication and transport policy (*Force Ouvrière*).

MELTT1, 24.3.1997, member of Charles Fiterman's cabinet (1982–1984), director of international and economic affairs in the Ministry of Public Works, Housing, Tourism and Transport (1989–1997); president of RFF since May 1997.

MELTT2, 25.5.1996, member of Bernard Bosson's cabinet and now working at SCETA, a SNCF road haulage subsidiary.

RFF, 27.6.1997, RFF administrator, former civil servant at the Ministry of Transport.

RP, 10.4.1997, adviser for transport.

RPR, Rassemblement Pour la République.

SNCF1, 13.6.1997, SNCF representative in Brussels.

SNCF2, 27.6.1997, Department of Infrastructure.

SNCF3, 7.7.1997, Department of International Development.

UDF, Union Démocratique Française.

UNICOOPTRANS, 1996, president of UNICOOPTRANS (Fédération nationale des coopératives et groupements du transport).

UNOSTRA, 1996, national secretary of UNOSTRA.

## Germany

BAG, 20 February 1996.
BDF, 26 January 1995, 19 April 1996.
BDI, 12 July 1995.
BDN, 21 February 1996.
BGA, 31 January 1996.
BMV, 30 January 1996, 25 November 1996.
BMV, Advisory Council, 29 January 1996.
BMWi, 26 January 1995.
BSL, 31 January 1996.
BWV, 30 January 1996.
MP/CSU, 31 January 1996.
DB, 13 February 1997.
Deutsches Verkehrsforum, 17 February 1997.
DG VII, 22 May 1996.
DIHT, 21 November 1995.
EBA, The Federal Railway Agency, 14 February 1997.
Ex-DG VII, 22 May 1996.
GdED, Gewerkschaft der Eisenbahner Deutschlands, 12 February 1997.
MP/CDU, 11 May 1995.
MP/CSU, 11 May 1995.
MP/SPD, 22 June 1995.
Regierungskommission, 29 January 1996.
VKS, 30 January 1996.

## Italy

ANITA (Associazione Nazionale Imprese Trasporti Automobilistici), 1 March 1996.
Camera dei Deputati, 27 February 1997.
Camera dei Deputati, April 1996.
CISL, 28 February 1997.
Confcooperative (Confederazione Cooperative Italiane), 16 February 1996.
Confetra (Confederazione generale italiana del traffico e dei trasporti), 16 April 1996.
Confetra (Confederazione generale italiana del traffico e dei trasporti), 4 December 1995.
Confindustria (Confederazione Generale dell'Industria Italiana), 3 May 1996.
Ferrovie dello Stato (FS), 6 March 1997.
Ferrovie dello Stato (FS), Area rete, 28 February 1997.
Ferrovie dello Stato (FS), ASA rete, 28 February 1997.
FISAFS (Federazione Italiana Sindacati Autonomi Ferrovieri Stato)/CISAL, 6 March 1997.

FIT (Federazione Italiana Trasporti)/CISL, 28 February 1997.
F& L (Freight Leaders Club/European Freight and Logistics Leaders Club), 18 March 1997.
FTA (Freight Transport Association), 17 April 1996.
Italcontainer, 6 March 1997.
Ministero dei Trasporti, 11 May 1995.
Ministero dei Trasporti, 2 May 1996.
Ministero dei Trasporti, 25 November 1996.
Ministero dei Trasporti, 3 January 1996, No. 2.
Ministero dei Trasporti, 30 January 1996, No. 1.
Ministero dei Trasporti, 30 January 1996, No. 2.
Ministero dei Trasporti, 9 May 1995.
Sticco-sped (freight forwarder Naples, 12 May 1995.
Unatras (Unione Nazionale delle Associazioni dell'autotrasporto di merci), 16 February 1996.

## The Netherlands

Centrum voor energiebesparing en schone technologie (Centre for Energy Conservation and Environmental Technology), Delft, 1 November 1994.
EVO, Algemene Verladers- en Eigenvervoer Organisatie (Ondernemers Organisatie voor Logistiek en Transport, Employers Organisation for Logistics and Transport); Rijskwijk; 12 December 1995.
FNV, Vervoersbond, Utrecht, February 1997, June 1997.
FSV, Federatie Spoorweg Vakvereniging, Utrecht, February 1997, June 1997.
Ministerie VenW, Ministerie van Verkeer en Waterstaat (Ministry for Transport and Public Works); The Hague; 1 November 1994; 27 November 1995; December 1995; 19 February 1997; 20 February 1997, two interviews.
Ministerie van Volkshuisvesting, Ruimtelijke Ordening en Milieubeheer, The Hague, 1 November 1994.
NDL, Nederland Distributieland (Holland International Distribution Council), The Hague, 29 November 1995.
NS, Nederlandse Spoorwegen, International Affairs, February 1997.
Raad voor het Vervoer, June 1997.
Railned, February 1997.
RVI, Rijksverkeersinspectie (State Traffic Inspectorate), The Hague, 27 November 1995.
TLN, Transport en Logistiek Nederland (Dutch Transport Operators Association); Zoetermeer; 29 November 1995; 30 June 1997.
Vereniging Nederlands Vervoeroverleg; Kamer van Koophandel en Fabrieken voor Rotterdam en de Beneden-Maas (General Transport Association; Chamber of Commerce of Rotterdam), Rotterdam, 12 December 1995.

# DOCUMENTATION

## EC Legislation

*Regulations*

Council Regulation 1191/69/EEC on action by member states concerning the obligations inherent in the concept of a public service in transport by rail, road and inland waterway, OJ 1969 L 156/1.

Council Regulation 1192/69/EEC on common rules for the normalisation of the accounts of railway undertakings, OJ 1969 L 156/8.

Council Regulation 1107/70/EEC on the granting of aids for transport by rail, road and inland waterway, OJ 1970 L 130/1.

Council Regulation 2831/77/EEC on the fixing of rates for the carriage of goods by road between member states, OJ 1977 L 334/22.

Council Regulation 3820/85/EEC on the harmonization of certain social legislation relating to road transport, OJ 1986 L 206/36.

Council Regulation 1841/88/EEC amending Regulation 3164/76 on access to the market in the international carriage of goods by road, OJ 1988 L 163/1.

Council Regulation 4058/89/EEC on the fixing of rates for the carriage of goods by road between member states, OJ 1989 L 390/1.

Council Regulation 4059/89/EEC, OJ 1989 L 390/3 replaced by Council Regulation 3118 93 EEC OJ 1993 L 279/1.

Council Regulation 1893/91/EEC amending Regulation 1191/69/EEC on action by member states concerning the obligations inherent in the concept of a public service in transport by rail, road and inland waterway, OJ 1969 L 156/1.

Council Regulation 881/92/EEC on access to the market in the carriage of goods by road within the community or from the territory of a member state passing across the territory of one or more member states, OJ 1992 L 95/1.

Council Regulation 3118/93/EEC laying down the conditions under which non-resident carriers may operate national road haulage services within a member state, OJ 1993 L 279/1.

*Directives*

Council Directive 91/440/EEC on the development of the community's railways, OJ 1991 L 237/25.

Council Directive 92/82/EEC on the approximation of the rates of excise duties on mineral oils, OJ 1992 L 316/19.

Council Directive 92/106/EEC on the establishment of common rules for certain types of combined transport of goods between member states, OJ 1992 L 368/38.

Council Directive 93/89/EEC on the application by member states of taxes on certain vehicles used for the carriage of goods by road and tolls and charges for the use of certain infrastructures, OJ 1993 L 279/32.

Council Directive 95/18/EC on the licensing of railway undertakings, OJ 1995 L
143/70.
Council Directive 95/19/EC on the allocation of railway infrastructure capacity
and the charging of infrastructure fees, OJ 1995 L 143/75.
Council Directive 96/48/EC on the interoperability of the trans-European high-
speed rail system, OJ 1996 L 262/18.
Council Directive 98/76/EC amending Directive 96/26/EC on admission to the
occupation of road haulage operator and road passenger transport operator and
mutual recognition of diplomas, certificates and other evidence of formal qualifications intended to facilitate for these operators the right to freedom of establishment in national and international transport operations, OJ 1998
L277/17.

*Commission Documents*

CEC, Commission of the European Communities (1993) Decision of 9 June 1993
concerning state aid procedure, OJ 1993 L 233/10.
CEC, Commission of the European Communities (1995) *Commission Report to
the Council and European Parliament COM (95) 285 Final.*
CEC, Commission of the European Communities (1995) *Communication from
the Commission on the Development of the Community's Railways (Application of Directive 91/440/EEC) COM (95) 337 Final.*
CEC, Commission of the European Communities (1996) Communication, OJ
1996 C-3/2.
CEC, Commission of the European Communities (1996) Proposal for a Council
Directive on the Charging of Heavy Goods Vehicles for the Use of Certain In-
frastructures COM (96) 331 Final.
CEC, Commission of the European Communities (1997) Amended Proposal for
a Council Directive Amending Directive 91/440/EEC on the Development of
the Community's Railways COM (97) 34 Final.
Communication on a community railway policy COM (89) 564 final.
EC Bull. 6-1985, 1. 2. 5.
EC Bull. 11-1985, 2. 1. 161, *Announcement by the Council of Ministers*. 1985.

*Table of Cases*

13/83 *European Parliament* v. *Council of the European Communities* [1985] ECR
1513.
C-195/90 *Commission of the European Communities* v. *Federal Republic of Ger-
many* [1992] ECR I-3141.
C-185/91 *Bundesanstalt für den Güterfernverkehr* v. *Gebrüder Reiff GmbH &
Co. KG.* [1993] ECR I-5801.
C-153/93 *Bundesrepublik Deutschland* v. *Delta Schiffahrts- und Speditionsge-
sellschaft mbH* [1994] ECR I-2517.

C-96/94 *Centro Servizi Spediporto Srl* v. *Spedizioni Marittima del Golfo Srl.* [1995] ECR I-2883.

C-280/95 *Commission of the European Communities* v. *Italian Republic* [1998] ECR I-259.

## British Legal Acts

1933 Road and Rail Traffic Act.
1968 Transport Act.
1985 Transport Act.
1991 Citizen's Charter.
1993 Railways Act.

## French Legal Acts

1982 Law on Inland Transport, *Loi d'Orientation sur les Transports Intérieurs* (LOTI).
1995 Law on National and Regional Development.

## German Legal Acts

Allgemeines Eisenbahngesetz (AEG).
Bundesbahngesetz, The State Railway Act.
Deutsche Bahn Gründungsgesetz.
Eisenbahnneuordnungsgesetz, BGBl. I, 30.12.1993, p. 2378ff.
Geschäftsordnung der Bundesregierung.
Gesetz über die Eisenbahnverwaltung des Bundes.
Gesetz zur Änderung des Grundgesetzes vom 20. Dezember 1993, BGBI. I, 22.12.1993, p. 2089f.
Grundgesetz (GG), The German Basic Law.
Regionalisierungsgesetz.
Schienenwegeausbaugesetz.
Tarifaufhebungsgesetz 13.8.1993, BGBI. I, p. 1, 489.

## Italian Legal Acts

Decreto of 19 October 1990 (G.U. n. 246, 20 October 1990, Ministero dei Trasporti.
Decreto of 15 February 1991 (G.U. n. 42, 19 February 1991, Ministero dei Trasporti.
Decreto-legge 29 marzo 1993, n. 82 in G. U. n. 73 del 29.03.1993.
Decreto-legge 20 febbraio 1996, n. 67 in G. U. n. 42 del 20.02.1996.
Legge 6 giugno 1974, n. 298 in G. U. n. 200 del 31.07.1974.
Legge 27 novembre 1980, n. 815.
Legge 30 luglio 1985, n. 404 in G. U. n. 189 del 30.07.1985.

Legge 5 febbraio 1992, n. 68 in G. U. n 35 del 12.02.1992.

Legge 27 maggio 1993, n. 162 in G.U. (Gazzetta Ufficiale della Repubblic Italiana) n. 123 del 28.05.1993.

Legge 5 gennaio 1996, n. 11 in G. U. n. 9 del 12.01.1996.

*Dutch Legal Acts*

Wet Autovervoer Goederen (WAG), The Vehicle Freight Act 1951.

Wet goederenvervoer over de weg (Wgw), The Road Freight Act 1992.

Wet Milieubeheer, The Environmental Control Act 1993.

# Index

331

# About the Contributors

**Adrienne Héritier** is a professor of political science and codirector of the Max Planck Project Group "Common Goods: Law, Politics, and Economics." Her research focuses on policy research, European policy, and the comparative analysis of member-state policymaking under the impact of European policies.

**Christoph Knill** is a professor of European studies at the University of Jena and senior research fellow at the Max Planck Project Group "Common Goods: Law, Politics, and Economics" at Bonn. He has been research assistant at the European University Institute (1995–1998) and received his postdoctoral degree (habilitation) from Hagen University in 1999. His research interests include governance in multilevel systems, European integration, comparative politics, public administration, and environmental politics.

**Michael Teutsch** is a research assistant at the Institute for Sociology of the University of Heidelberg and has completed a study on institutional evolvement in the field of European Union cohesion policy. He studied political science and public law at the universities of Hamburg and Urbino.

**Dieter Kerwer** is a senior research fellow at the Max Planck Project Group "Common Goods: Law, Politics, and Economics" at Bonn and a former researcher at the European University Institute in Florence. His current interests include governance and organization theory, European integration, and financial markets.

**Dirk Lehmkuhl** is a senior research fellow at the Max Planck Project Group "Common Goods: Law, Politics, and Economics." He has been research assistant at the universities of Konstanz, Bielefeld, and at the European University Institute in Florence. His research interests include patterns of public–private interaction, transnational commercial arbitration, European integration, and comparative politics.

**Anne-Cécile Douillet** is a graduate of the Institute of Political Studies of Paris (Sciences Pô) and studied social sciences at the University of Paris-Sorbonne and the "Ecole Normale Supérieure de Cachan." Currently, she is a Ph.D. student under the supervision of Jean-Claude Thoenig, from the Analysis Group on Public Policies (GAPP). Her research, carried out at the Cemagref in Grenoble (agricultural and environmental engineering research center), deals with local development policies and changes in local government in France.